# Educational Policy Making
# and the Courts

# EDUCATIONAL POLICY MAKING AND THE COURTS

*An Empirical Study of Judicial Activism*

Michael A. Rebell
and
Arthur R. Block

THE UNIVERSITY OF CHICAGO PRESS

CHICAGO AND LONDON

MICHAEL A. REBELL and ARTHUR R. BLOCK are partners in the firm
of Rebell & Krieger, Attorneys-at-Law. Rebell, author (with
Robert S. Jordan and Caroline Ifeka) of *Government and Power
in West Africa*, is Adjunct Professor of political theory
and law at the State University of New York, Purchase.
Block is Lecturer in Law, Columbia Law School, and Adjunct
Assistant Professor of Law, Cardozo School of Law, Yeshiva University.

THE UNIVERSITY OF CHICAGO PRESS, CHICAGO 60637
THE UNIVERSITY OF CHICAGO PRESS, LTD., LONDON

*The research reported herein was performed pursuant to contract numbers
400-77-0011 and 400-79-0040 of the National Institute of Education
U.S. Department of Health, Education and Welfare (NIE).
Contractors undertaking such projects under government sponsorship are
encouraged to express their professional judgment freely in the conduct
of the project. Points of view or opinions stated here do not, therefore,
necessarily represent official NIE position or policy. Similarly, the opinions
expressed by the authors are not necessarily shared by the consultants
and colleagues whose helpful comments are acknowledged herein.
Copyright is claimed under current registration until 1989 and is
renewable thereafter by permission of the U.S. Department of Education.*

LIBRARY OF CONGRESS CATALOGING IN PUBLICATION DATA

Rebell, Michael A.
   Educational policy making and the courts.

   Includes bibliographical references and index.
   1. Educational law and legislation—United States.
2. Judicial process—United States.   I. Block, Arthur R.
II. Title.
KF4119.R4        344.73′07        81–16225
ISBN 0–226–70598–6   347.3047   AACR2

To our parents
SYLVIA and HARRY REBELL
LORETTA and HAROLD BLOCK
who gave us the education that enabled us
to write this book

———◆———

# Contents

———◆———

# List of Tables

————◆————

# Preface

This book describes and analyzes the role of the courts in educational policy making. Using the results of a detailed empirical study, we attempt to answer some of the central questions raised by both scholars and the press concerning the court's capacity to resolve social policy issues and the "legitimacy"—in a democratic political system—of the judiciary's intervention into the public policy-making process.

Part I presents a summary overview of the major issues concerning judicial involvement in social policy matters and provides a framework for our empirical investigation of these issues. Part II sets forth the findings and conclusions drawn from our study of a representative sample of 65 federal court litigations decided between 1970 and 1977. The implications of these findings are explored further in Part III through two detailed qualitative studies set in New York and Colorado. These provide a comparative analysis of how, in each state, a federal court and a state legislature simultaneously approached a similar major educational policy problem. Finally, in Part IV, we reconsider the legitimacy and capacity issues of the judicial activism debate from the perspective of our empirical investigations.

Our general conclusion is that the courts are able to make a unique contribution to public policy making without violating fundamental principles of separation of powers. We found that in public litigations the courts operate more politically than is contemplated by the traditional adjudication model, but less politically and more "analytically" than legislative bodies. This comparative perspective indicates that the judiciary has a substantial capability for policy-oriented fact-finding and remedial action and that the critical question is when the courts should be engaged in such activity. The legitimacy of the court's exercise of these capabilities depends upon the degree to

which "principle" rather than "policy" arguments are relied upon in
the particular intervention decision. If intervention is proper, then
the judicious use of a variety of fact-finding and remedial processes to
counteract the effects of unlawful policies would appear to be appropriate.

When we began this project five years ago, our primary concern, as
researchers, was the gap between theoretical debates about judicial
activism and empirical research into actual trial court behavior. At the
same time, as legal practitioners who had invoked the jurisdiction of
the courts in litigating several major education cases, we were, of
course, receptive to some of the arguments supporting judicial activism. But we were also troubled by the results of some court inter-
ventions and by the absence of clear criteria for evaluating the legitimate scope of judicial activity. Our research data, by and large, have
borne out our sense that several of the key arguments against judicial
activism were not empirically valid. Our ultimate concerns about
legitimacy, however, have not been laid to rest but redefined. In particular, the difficulties we encountered in distinguishing between
"principle" and "policy" point to the need for a more comprehensive
approach to a complex mixture of conceptual and factual issues.

No researchers, of course, can be sure that their initial perspectives
did not influence the interpretation of the data. In this case we did,
however, attempt to subject ourselves to a rigorous methodological
discipline, to create a more extensive empirical data base than had
ever before been applied to these issues, and, finally, to report our
findings in a manner permitting critics to challenge our assumptions
and reinterpret our data. Thus, while our conclusions certainly will
not stand as the last word on the subject of judicial activism, we hope
that our attempt to bring theoretical and empirical analysis closer
together will stimulate discussion and help to set the future research
agenda in this field.

Our empirical investigation of 65 judicial "caselets" (a term borrowed from Professor Abram Chayes) and four major judicial/
legislative case studies took over two years to complete. The Project
Director, Arthur Block, supervised and coordinated the efforts of
three research associates, Valerie Wolk, Ludwig Adams, and Martin
Eakes, who performed the arduous task of compiling and analyzing
an avalanche of legal documents and background information with
dedication and perceptive insight. Additional research functions were
ably performed by Roland Betts and Deborah Fogel. Fieldwork for

the New York and Colorado judicial case studies as well as interviewing for the New York legislative case study were conducted by Arthur Block. Fieldwork for the Colorado legislative case study and documentation of the New York legislative case study were carried out by Michael Rebell. We jointly devised the study's conceptual framework and methodology and collaborated on both the final data analysis and the writing of this book.

We wish to express our gratitude to Professor Abram Chayes of the Harvard Law School, whose own research provided much of the original inspiration for this study, for his many helpful comments. We also wish to thank Professor Mark Yudof of the University of Texas School of Law; Professor David Kirp of the Center for Public Policy, University of California at Berkeley; Professor J. Roland Pennock, Swarthmore College; Professor Robert Nagel, University of Colorado Law School; Leonard Rubenstein; and Dr. Gregory Jackson. Their insightful comments, criticisms, and suggestions were of great value, as was the assistance on methodological problems provided by Professor Maurice Rosenberg of Columbia Law School, Professor Stanton Wheeler of the Yale Law School, and Dr. Carlyle Maw of the National Institute of Education.

The complexity of collecting data for a study of this scope and nature made us dependent on the support and courtesies of many persons. We would like to express our appreciation to the dozens of attorneys, legislators, representatives of various educational organizations, and expert witnesses who contributed their time and interest in interviews that added an important dimension to this study and who, in many instances, gave their comments on the manuscript as well. Helpful logistical arrangements were effected through the office of Caryle Imlay, General Counsel to the Administrative Office of the United States Courts. Our survey methodology also profited from the assistance of Mr. James McCafferty, Chief, Statistical Analysis and Reports Division, Administrative Office of the United States Courts, and from the cooperation of Mead Data Central, Inc. The National Organization for Legal Problems in Education provided help by mailing an information request for us to its broad membership.

A central figure, whose ingenuity and persistence solved innumerable logistical problems, was our Program Officer at the National Institute of Education—Ronald Anson. We owe Mr. Anson a special debt of gratitude, not only for these administrative efforts but also for his unflagging interest and commitment to this project.

Finally, our thanks to Caren Stolbach, Sherry Teitelbaum, Diane

Cipollone, Sharyn Davis, and Jeanne Hall, our typists over the past three years, and to Irena Klepfisz and Meryl Macklin, our manuscript and proof editors. They surely will not believe that the "final draft" of this work has been completed until they see it in print.

Michael A. Rebell

Arthur R. Block

May, 1981

# Suggestions for Readers

It may suit the needs of some readers to find shortcuts through this extensive research report. The organization of the book follows the logical development of our work—literature review, research framework, findings, and conclusions—a comprehensive format exposing every important element of our methodology and reasoning to detailed scrutiny. Those of our readers, however, who are educators, social scientists, practicing attorneys, or judges, may find it useful to focus immediately on portions of the book most closely related to their professional experience and interests.

We have tried to help readers who wish to focus on specific interests by setting forth summaries of our findings, at the end of chapters 2–9, which contain our data analysis. After noting the summaries, some readers may find it helpful to skip from the introductory chapter directly to the conclusions and then return to the heart of the book. Finally, we would note that many readers, particularly educators, have been drawn to the *Otero* case study with its story of conflict and misunderstanding in a local school system and its depiction of a courtroom contest between nationally known educational experts; lawyers, in particular, have been intrigued by the complex remedial process in *Chance;* and political scientists have expressed special interest in the comparative institutional approach carried forward in chapters 6–9.

# PART I

## Introduction

# 1

# The Judicial Activism Debate

———◆———

In 1973 the Supreme Court explained its conclusion that education was not a "fundamental interest" under the United States Constitution by observing, "Education, perhaps even more than welfare assistance, presents a myriad of 'intractable economic, social, and even philosophical problems . . .' [citation omitted]. In such circumstances, the judiciary is well advised to refrain from imposing on the States inflexible constitutional restraints that could circumscribe or handicap the continued research and experimentation so vital to finding even partial solutions to educational problems and to keeping abreast of ever-changing conditions" (*San Antonio Independent School District* v. *Rodriguez*).[1]

Despite this pronouncement, the Supreme Court in subsequent years has seen fit to issue rulings that limited the discretion of school districts to handle disciplinary problems among students,[2] to establish leave-of-absence policies for teachers,[3] and to determine curricula offerings for non-English-speaking students.[4] By denying petitions for review, the Court has also indirectly sanctioned such far-reaching remedial decrees ordered by lower federal courts as the placing of a public high school under the control of a receiver directly accountable to the court.[5] In short, despite the Supreme Court's admonition in *Rodriguez*, judicial activism in this area remains substantial.[6]

The Supreme Court majority under Chief Justice Burger is undoubtedly more conservative in many areas than was its predecessor Court under Chief Justice Warren.[7] Nevertheless, the Burger Court has continued to develop innovative legal paths opened up by the Warren Court precedents, and has itself opened new areas for judicial involvement in educational affairs. The lower courts also have continued to innovate broadly.[8] Recent federal statutes establishing broad educational rights provide a further impetus for judicial involvement in the enforcement, if not in the creation, of basic rights.[9] At the same time many state courts have become more daring in defining new educational entitlements based on long-standing state constitutional provisions.[10]

Judicial involvement in educational policy matters is, of course, not an isolated phenomenon. The courts have also been increasingly active in state mental health systems,[11] state prison systems,[12] and in local regulation of land use.[13] The causes for this acceleration of judicial activism are frequently attributed to the expansion of government activities in the welfare state era. Over the years this expansion has simultaneously led to an increase in regulations with concomitant judicial review, and to an easing of traditional limitation of court jurisdiction (e.g., standing rules and doctrines of justiciability). In "The Role of the Judge in Public Law Litigation,"[14] Abram Chayes describes some of the new trends. He discusses the traditional role of the courts as "umpire" for private disputes and the new pressures created by the advent of social and economic regulatory legislation over the course of the past century. According to Chayes the traditional lawsuit is "bipolar" (i.e., a contest between two individuals or entities with diametically opposed interests), "retrospective" (i.e., concerning already completed events), or involving an "interdependence between right and remedy" (i.e., the impact of the court's judgment is confined to the immediate parties). In contrast, the "new model" public law litigation is multipolar (involving numerous parties and points of view), forward looking, or involving broad remedial decrees (which often are negotiated by the parties), and the court's decree often has important consequences for many persons, including absentees. In short, "[t]he subject matter of the lawsuit is often not a dispute between private individuals about private rights, but a grievance about the operation of public policy."[15]

The advent of the "new model" public law litigation has, not unexpectedly, occasioned fierce debate between those who seek to limit or reverse this trend, and those who welcome the new direction (or at least accept its inevitability). The issues in the controversy fall into two basic categories: "legitimacy" (i.e., is the "new model" in keeping with the court's proper role in the American political system?) and "capacity" (i.e., legitimacy aside, can the judiciary capably handle the new responsibilities it has apparently assumed?).

## I. LEGITIMACY

### The Court's Proper Role

Separation of Powers

As every American schoolchild learns, the framers of the Constitution established a tripartite system which divided the responsibilities of government among the legislative, executive, and judicial branches. According to the eighteenth-century ideal of the separation of powers on which our Constitution is based, the legislature was responsible for making the laws, the executive branch for enforcing them, and the judiciary for interpreting them.

This separation of powers, however, has never been perceived in a rigid, mechanistic manner. In fact, the framers of the Constitution foresaw the necessity of "blending" powers in many areas of government activities and drafted provisions to reflect this view. Thus, the presidential veto power granted "legislative" authority to the chief executive; the Senate's ratification of presidential appointments and treaties and Congress's power to impeach the president and to try high government officers granted "executive" and "judicial" authority to the legislature.[16]

Recognizing that some degree of blending was specifically written into the Constitution, critics of judicial activism nevertheless claim that the courts today have far exceeded any legitimate interpretation of the original intent and are in violation of the principle of separation of powers. Arguing from this historical perspective, Raoul Berger states: "[J]udicial review was conceived in narrow terms—as a means of policing the constitutional boundaries, the 'limits' of a given power.... In fact, judicial participation in legislative policy making was unmistakably excluded.... [The Court today] has violated the injunction of the separation of powers, made explicit in the 1780 Massachusetts Constitution, that 'the judiciary shall never exercise the legislative power.'"[17] But since it is difficult to determine the precise boundaries set by the founding fathers for the judicial branch (it was "[l]egislative not judicial despotism, [that] worried the founders"),[18] most contemporary critics of judicial activism, unlike Berger, focus on the basic philosophy they see as underlying the Constitution: the principle of majoritarian democracy or "popular sovereignty."

Popular sovereignty, for its original expositor, Rousseau, meant that all rightful governmental authority originates with the people and that all "magistrates" are directly answerable and subject to recall by them. Under the contemporary version of this theory, the expres-

sion of the people's will on policy issues is through elected legislators
and executive branch officials, and any attempt by the unelected judicial branch to make pronouncements concerning basic political matters is illegitimate and in violation of the terms of the basic social
contract.[19]

Contemporary critics accuse the courts of assuming an elitist posture that violates popular sovereignty and "reach[es] into the lives of
people, against the will of the people, deeper than they ever have in
American history."[20] This elitism is variously portrayed as a class bias
(e.g., upper-middle-class judges and lawyers imposing their values on
middle- and working-class constituencies), or as an academic or professional bias (e.g., court-appointed university experts supplanting
the practical administrative philosophies of prison wardens, school
superintendents, or hospital managers).[21] Furthermore, the critics in-
sist that judicial activism is dangerous to democratic government because it tends to atrophy the sense of responsibility of citizens and
elected representatives alike in making fundamental political decisions. It also is argued that the judicial branch has a limited supply of
"capital" that it draws upon each time it nullifies policies supported by
political majorities; consequently, the judiciary threatens its own institutional power base through interventionism.[22]

Defenders of the "new model" judicial activism try to counter these
arguments by emphasizing the central role of the Constitution as a
body of "fundamental law" which was established for the specific purpose of insuring that basic individual rights and liberties would not be
compromised by the "tyranny of the majority" operating through the
legislature.[23] Independent courts, they add, are the best expositors of
such fundamental law and, indeed, are now established as the final
interpreters of the principles of individual liberty. As government
institutions assume a greater role in citizens' lives, it becomes the duty
of the courts to maintain a proper balance between governmental
powers and individual rights.[24]

Defenders of judicial activism maintain that the courts have accepted this duty reluctantly and only to fill a void created because the
other branches of government do not take responsibility for resolving
disputes affecting basic rights; judges respond to "a need for a final
decision-making authority."[25] Judge Skelly Wright has explained his
reluctance—and activism—in these terms: "It would be far better indeed for these great social and political problems to be resolved in the
political arena by other branches of government. But these are social
and political problems which seem at times to defy resolution. In such

situations, under our system, the judiciary must bear a hand and accept its responsibility to assist in the solution where constitutional rights hang in the balance."[26]

From this perspective, judicial activism is seen not as being anti-democratic, but rather as providing an important element of popular sovereignty in ensuring that the rights of the people are effectively enforced. Along these lines, former Attorney General Edward Levi has observed that in the American system "[n]o branch could correctly claim to be the sole representative of the people. Representation was to be by each of them, according to the functions they performed."[27] Aside from these theoretical perspectives, defenders of judicial activism claim that the "popular sovereignty" objections to judicial activism are overstated and unrealistic. First, our political system provides specific methods to assure judicial accountability to the popular will—constitutional amendments to nullify rulings based on statutory interpretation; and popular reaction that may lead courts to reconsider and modify earlier decisions. Second, as Professor Chayes has pointed out, the target of judicial activism "is generally administrative rather than legislative action."[28] Administrative actions are derivative rather than direct expressions of the popular will.[29]

Finally, the comparative frame of reference used by the popular sovereignty critics is said to be fundamentally flawed. Professor Tribe, after indicating the wide variety of political inputs into the judicial process which are largely responsive to majoritarian concerns,[30] states: "The result then is an imperfectly anti-democratic judicial process and an imperfectly democratic political process; the conclusion which this results suggests is that, *contra* the critics, it cannot be consent which is the sole touchstone of legitimacy."[31]

Principle/Policy

The political theory debate on separation-of-powers notions has been paralleled in the legal literature by a discussion articulated in terms of "principle/policy" issues. The question raised there is whether courts should be limited to deciding cases on the basis of strict "principles" or should be free to engage in broader "policy" deliberations. A strict "principle" approach coincides with the views of those who favor a limited judicial role within the separation-of-powers scheme; a broader "policy" approach would be consistent with the view of those who accept more substantial judicial "intrusions" into the policy-making domains of the other branches.

The link between the principle/policy distinction and separation-of-powers theory resulted from a dramatic shift in jurisprudential thinking at the beginning of the twentieth century. Formalism, the dominant theory of law in the nineteenth century, had viewed the law as a closed logical system. The judge was expected to locate the relevant legal premises in both written and "natural" law and to apply these to the facts at hand. Since no exercise of discretion was involved, court decisions could not impinge on the separate prerogatives of legislators and executives.[32]

"Legal realism," which became the dominant jurisprudential approach[33] by the 1930s, maintained that law is a matter not primarily of logic but of fact.[34] Realists saw substantive law as being nothing more than the actual decisions of authoritative institutions. While the law tends to be in tune with prevalent notions of morality and natural rights, it is conceptually distinct from morality and takes precedence over it.[35] Recognizing that existing legal rules could not possibly dispose of all the concrete disputes that might come before a court, realists allow the judge to act as a lawmaker and to exercise discretion to fill "gaps" in the law. Thus realists believe that, in the "hard" cases,[36] the court may render decisions to further what they believe to be desirable social purposes. In other words, for the realists legal reasoning at times becomes instrumental.

The legal realists' openness to a judicial role in the making of law and policy[37] and their receptivity to the use of social science evidence by the courts[38] sparked much of the concern and debate about the legitimacy of these activities and the need for establishing limits on judicial discretion. The most notable reaction to the realists' position was Herbert Wechsler's famous lecture, "Towards Neutral Principles of Constitutional Law."[39] Here Wechsler maintained that court decisions should be explicitly based on neutral, general principles that transcend a particular result. This principled judicial approach was contrasted with the legislator's policy prerogative to consider the desirability and consequences of various arguments affecting the overall social welfare. Wechsler's critics have argued, however, that there are no clear standards for determining what is or is not a neutral principle.[40] Furthermore, they claim that even in cases where a decision based on neutral principles is possible, there may be compelling policy reasons for sacrificing Wechsler's method.[41]

Mindful of the difficulties encountered by Wechsler's attempt to establish a consistent principle/policy distinction, Ronald Dworkin has tried anew to deal with this problem.[42] Like Wechsler, Dworkin insists that judicial decisions be based on neutral principles of law. But he takes a different view of what is encompassed by "law." He argues that legal rights may be based not only on a discrete set of applicable precedents and statutes, but also on justifying principles derived from institutional structures and morality, and political theories integrating the two. These sources, Dworkin maintains, are sufficiently rich to provide a single right answer to every "hard case," thereby eliminating the realists' troublesome "gaps" and the problems of judicial discretion.

In relation to judicial action Dworkin believes that judges should not decide "policy" issues, because these are the proper concern only of legislative agencies; court rulings based on "principles," however, are proper even if such rulings have substantial social or political implications. His approach therefore claims to fit much of contemporary judicial activism into a "principled" mold.[43] According to some, however, Dworkin's intricate distinctions between principles and policies are so ephemeral that they serve simply as a shield protecting "activist judges from the charge of usurpation."[44]

### Interest Representation

Related to the foregoing legitimacy arguments is the question whether the parties for whom lawyers speak are sufficiently representative of all those interests likely to be affected by a court order. Traditionally, the legislature has been viewed as the prime arena for articulating public policy issues, presumably because all affected views and interests are represented during its policy deliberations. To the extent that courts today engage in such policy deliberations, the legitimacy of their actions is clearly undermined if (as under the traditional bipolar model) a limited number of litigants speak only for their particular interests and the courts receive no direct input concerning the perspectives or needs of the majority of citizens who might be affected by a wide-ranging decree.

It is generally acknowledged that the primary constituency of the federal courts in constitutional cases is "discrete and insular minorities,"[45] whose rights may need protection from majoritarian biases. Recognizing the need to protect minority interests in a proper case,[46] critics of judicial action nonetheless caution against generalized remedies that extensively impinge on the interests of groups not represented in the litigation. A graphic illustration of lack of broad representation in court cases appears in Horowitz's discussion of litigation arising out of New York City's 1958 Fair Housing Ordinance. During a particular three-year period, 685 complaints were brought to enforce the anti-discrimination provisions of the ordinance. Eighty-one percent of these were by blacks, although Puerto Ricans and others were also experiencing housing discrimination. Even more significant was the fact that the black complainants were disproportionately young and middle class. On the basis of these figures, Horowitz concluded: "It goes without saying that general solutions devised on the basis of the particular cases brought, while they might be quite appropriate for handling the problems of upwardly mobile blacks who wished to move from one white residential area to another, might be wholly misguided and inapt for the problems of the black working class in search of decent housing."[47]

Nathan Glazer develops this line of reasoning further by alleging that the social interests pressed on the courts are artificial and perhaps ephemeral. He points to the expansion in recent years of public interest advocacy centers funded by foundation or government grants. Financial independence enables their directors and staff often to pursue their own "ideological exercises" unrelated to the concrete grievances of actual clients. The public interest cases, Glazer claims, "lead a life of their own" with lawyers arguing for "ghostly plaintiffs who never appear and, for all one knows, may not exist."[48] Related to this position, is Derek Bell's claim that civil rights attorneys in class action cases often overlook or ignore the specific subgroups within a plaintiff class, or even the majority of class members in a particular locality, when their interests differ from the overall litigation strategy of a national organization like the NAACP.[49]

Kenneth Clark has dealt with some of these criticisms by arguing that when courts protect the basic constitutional rights of minorities they strengthen "American democracy for the benefit of all human beings."[50] Thus, although minority groups, like any plaintiffs, address the courts initially from their own parochial perspective, the issues they raise tend to have broad social implications. Furthermore, when other institutions are unwilling to deal with important social issues, it is the courts that must consider them.

In a more specific rejoinder, Chayes challenges the contention that the judiciary is ill-equipped for canvassing diverse policy perspectives, and instead asserts that "multipolar" participation by a broad range of groups is one of the hallmarks of contemporary public law litigation. Although Chayes admits that some interests may be unrepresented or underrepresented in the judicial process, a comparative perspective reveals that these interests may be better represented in the courts than in the legislative and administrative forums.[51]

## II. CAPACITY

In addition to the legitimacy questions, the current debate on the courts' proper role in public law has also focused on judicial "capacity." Capacity here means the *comparative* ability of the courts to deal effectively and efficiently with social problems that traditionally were handled exclusively by the legislative and administrative branches.[52] In this regard, the key concerns are the courts' ability to obtain and comprehend complex factual information ("fact-finding"); and to devise and implement appropriate remedies for the social problems under consideration ("remedies").

### Fact-finding

One of the articles of faith in Anglo-American legal education and scholarship has been the superiority of the adversary process over any other fact-finding procedure.[53] For example, in an oft-quoted statement, Wigmore asserted that "cross-examination is the greatest legal engine ever invented for the discovery of truth."[54] Critics of judicial activism say, however, that these axioms do not apply to public law litigation. They argue, first, that courts usually are incapable of obtaining adequate social science data and, second, that judges generally are unable fully to understand and digest the data which is obtained. Typically, these conclusions are presented in a framework comparing the adversary process to legislative or administrative fact-finding capabilities.

With regard to data gathering, the critics argue that the common law system emphasizes a piecemeal approach to data gathering in which attorneys for the competing parties are responsible for providing information to the court. Their sources of information are normally based on the personal knowledge and experience of their immediate clients. The critics argue, however, that when the legality and effects of a public policy are being assessed, the personal knowledge and experiences of the individuals who decide to bring a lawsuit may be highly limited.[55] Instead, the most valuable evidence is probably contained in books, articles, and reports that may be excluded from the case under traditional rules of evidence, such as the "hearsay" rule.[56] Further, in an adversary proceeding, there is an inherent motivation to present the facts in a partisan fashion. No participant, the judge included, is responsible for building an evidentiary record containing a broad overview of all relevant information.[57] When courts try to stretch the rules of evidence to compensate for these limitations the results may be haphazard. For example, critics say that when judges on their own initiative delve into social science literature or explore information outside the record under the guise of "judicial notice," the resulting information flow is unsystematic, amateurish, and possibly unfair to one or more of the parties since the courts' sources are neither identified nor subjected to refutation or explanation.[58]

"Social fact-finding" poses problems not only for gathering data, but also for analyzing it. Assertions about the judiciary's inability to deal effectively with data in social policy cases are largely based on a distinction between the "historical" or "adjudicative" fact-finding process traditionally used by courts and the "legislative" or "social" fact-finding process used by the legislature.[59] Under the historical model, fact-finding is focused on specific ascertainable facts, i.e., whether or not a certain event took place or whether a specific statement was made on a particular occasion. Such traditional judicial techniques as cross-examination are appropriate for this mode, since they can ascertain the truth of these types of assertions. Social fact-finding, however, is concerned with understanding recurrent patterns of behavior upon which policy decisions must be based. It raises questions for which there may be no single correct answer, or for which there may be several. Thus, although traditional trial fact-finding techniques are generally effective in determining whether an alleged sexual deviant molested a particular child (historical fact-finding), they are not well adapted to determining whether prohibiting sales of pornographic materials will decrease the incidence of such assaults (social fact-finding). Though the critics would recognize that the appellate courts long have made judgments of the latter type (e.g., in determining the extent of First Amendment protection to accord sellers of sexually suggestive materials), they argue that there has been a quantum leap in the frequency and intensity of presentation of such issues, particularly in the trial court forums where concrete policy choices are made.[60]

Finally, analyzing social facts may require specialized training and experience. But, since judges have "generalist" backgrounds and are expected to act in an impartial rather than an investigatory mode, "a real possibility exists that substantial misinterpretation and overstatement will accompany the increasing use of social science evidence in the courts."[61]

Defenders of judicial activism take the position not only that many of the traditional strengths of the adversary process carry over to the new public policy cases, but also that a process of institutional change and experimentation is occurring in contemporary new model cases—consistent with the developmental tradition of the common law—through which promising new fact-finding approaches are evolving. The adversary system, they say, is a disciplined and highly effective mechanism for maximizing information flow to the judge as decision maker.[62] Relating this point to procedural developments in public litigation and class actions, Chayes argues that when the party structure is broadly representative (which procedural rules now make possible) a considerable range of relevant information can be presented to the court—information that may be more substantive, and in more manageable form, than comparative information presented to a legislature. Opposing parties, after all, have the strongest possible incentive to produce relevant information.[63] Unlike the administrative and legislative forums, the adversary process also provides a built-in corrective to distortions or one-sided presentations. Once the raw information is assembled, a judge can supervise the discovery process and pretrial conferences and therefore induce the parties to focus on the major issues, to identify all factual issues not in dispute, and to limit the actual fact-finding process to specific critical issues.[64]

Defenders further allege that the courts' "generalism" and inexperience with social science data is overstated. The courts, they say, have always delved into complex economic and social facts,[65] and the processes of judicial appointment (or election) assure that judges are "likely to have some experience of the political process and acquaintance with a fairly broad range of policy problems."[66] Besides, judges may find ways to stay within their range of competencies. Commentators have challenged the assumption that courts often rely strongly on social science evidence; they believe that courts tend to avoid relying on the most disputed form of social science information—causal hypotheses—and instead use social science research in framing issues and supplying relatively objective and noncontroversial reporting data (e.g., surveys and census reports).[67]

Finally, the importance of a meaningful frame of reference for assessing institutional fact-finding capabilities is stressed. The generally accepted presumption of legislative superiority in this area may be illusory. Judge Cardozo once pointed out that both judge and legislator obtained their information from the same basic source: "experience and study and reflection; in brief, from life itself."[68] Along these lines Professor Wellington has maintained that the legislature's ability to hold hearings and investigations is not necessarily an important advantage: "On many issues more than enough factual information is generated without hearings; legislative facts abound and for every expert there is his equal and opposite number. Each has published widely; each researched extensively. Judges, then, often have as many useful facts as do legislators."[69] Furthermore, students of the legislative process have noted that staff limitations, lack of expertise on the part of the legislators themselves, and time pressures that demand quick analyses render legislators neither effective nor efficient users of social science data.

### Remedies

The culmination of the new public law litigation model as described by Chayes is the remedial decree.[70] Unlike the final decrees of a traditional litigation which require the defendant to simply pay a stated amount or take a specific action, the remedial decree provides for a "complex, on-going regime of performance." Frequently, this involves the court in prolonged supervision of the implementation of new policies and practices designed to overcome the problems exposed by the case.

The basic criticism of remedial decrees is that they involve courts in administrative or legislative processes which they are incapable of adequately handling. Unlike the legislative and executive branches, courts are said to lack a "vast array of techniques for implementing and monitoring a policy,"[71] i.e., sanctions, incentives, and subsidies. The courts' sole implementation weapon is "coercive orders: injunctions that direct parties to do or refrain from doing something."[72]

In addition to these institutional shortcomings of the judicial branch, the legal process is said to be inherently unsuited for complex social policy implementation because it proceeds on a "piecemeal" basis rather than on a "comprehensive" one.[73] Issues are presented in a case-by-case format, and judges have little occasion to make a broad policy review or to consider the overall implications and consequences of the specific orders. This means that at times court decrees may "produce deleterious consequences."[74] For example, judges are not in a position to consider whether increased expenditures mandated to correct a particular social ill may result in decreased funds for other vital areas.[75] Moreover, the judiciary lacks the mechanism by which remedies, once set in motion, can be modified. Howard Kalodner, summarizing the findings contained in eight detailed case studies of the implementation of recent desegregation decrees, concluded that the courts have evidenced limited capacity to enforce their decrees. Settlements or cooperative undertakings by the parties have been rare, court-appointed masters have not proved effective, and, perhaps most important, the degree of public acceptance necessary for smooth implementation of major changes in controversial areas has not been forthcoming.[76]

Defenders of judicial remedial capacity hold that the courts' lack of established organization and resources permits a flexible response, tailored to the needs of a particular situation. The court "does not work through a rigid, multilayered hierarchy of numerous officials, but through a smaller, representative task force, assembled ad hoc, and easily dismantled when the problem is finally resolved."[77] Thus, the courts can modify their decrees to cope with unexpected problems,[78] and once the remedy is completed no "sunset law" is needed to protect against the senseless perpetuation of bureaucratic structures.

Still, few defenders would deny that in some areas the courts' remedial record is poor. They attribute the failures, however, to generic problems in designing and implementing public policy.[79] From this point of view, the lack of public acceptance which Kalodner and Fishman identified as being at the core of the implementation problems in the desegregation case studies (as well as fundamental problems of ambiguity in basic policy goals)[80] would also plague reform efforts undertaken by other agencies.[81] In fact, it is argued, in comparison to loosely organized legislative bodies and overly rigid executive structures, the court presents a more effective combination of command and flexibility.[82]

### III. EDUCATIONAL POLICY MAKING AND THE COURTS: THE EPAC STUDY

Despite the importance of the judicial activism controversy there has been little research which systematically investigates actual judicial practices and integrates relevant theory with such empirical findings. By and large, the existing literature has been either strictly theoretical or based on atheoretical empirical case studies. Thus, elaborate theoretical models are constructed on educated impressions that are substantiated only by citations to illustrative court opinions, or individual cases are examined in detail without proof of their representativeness or their theoretical significance.[83] Another limitation of most theoretical work has been its preoccupation with the impact of Supreme Court decisions rather than with the process of implementing public rights at the local level where most of the policy-related fact-findings and remedy formulation take place.[84]

In our research, therefore, we sought to apply a comprehensive theoretical framework to a systematic survey of a large number of representative cases with the focus on local trial-court proceedings. Our survey involved 65 small-scale studies ("caselets") of education policy litigations randomly selected from all such cases decided during the period 1970–77. Having selected our sample cases, we devised an analytic survey instrument that would allow us to test empirically the validity of many of the propositions put forward by the competing sides in the legitimacy-capacity debate.[85] We considered such issues as the extent of "policy" or "principle" claims in the litigations, the range of group interests represented in judicial proceedings, and the degree of compliance with court orders.

In designing our quantitative survey, we decided that we would not spread our sample thinly over several social policy areas (as, e.g., by selecting 9 or 10 cases from each of seven fields), but would concentrate on the single area where judicial activism has had the most direct, visible, and controversial impact on Americans—public education. Then, since a disproportionate amount of attention on the judicial activism debate has been highly focused on controversial desegregation disputes, we excluded pupil desegregation from our caselet sample and concentrated our resources on rounding out the picture of public education litigation with studies of cases involving special education reform, intradistrict finance cases, student speech and dress, censorship of student publications, discrimination against minority educators, etc. Our findings could then be compared to those of existing desegregation studies.

Our survey data, based on a systematic analysis of a large number of representative cases, is capable of providing quantitative insights concerning important general trends. There are a number of limitations inherent in such an undertaking, however. One is the degree to which the different theoretical issues posed in the judicial activism debate could be reduced to measurable criteria. Those lending themselves to objective statistic analysis (e.g., prevalence of minority plaintiffs or representation by public interest lawyers) could be compiled relatively easily. Others, such as "principle" versus "policy" claims, required some degree of independent judgment by the investigators. In order to minimize subjectivity, the analytic criteria utilized were carefully articulated and uniformly applied; we realize, however, that some of our assumptions may not be accepted by all.

Another limitation is that the survey approach necessarily treats cases as equal, homogenous, and independent units. Therefore, a major litigation such as the *PARC* case (Pennsylvania Association for

Retarded Children), which directed fundamental reform of all special education services throughout the Commonwealth of Pennsylvania for a period of years, and which became a precedent that influenced subsequent cases in the sample, is given the same weight in our tabulations as a challenge to a newspaper censorship policy of a small suburban school board. Finally, our survey research might not turn up some factors in the judicial process that were not reflected in public documents or known to the attorneys we interviewed, e.g., the omission from a hearing of important, relevant social science research findings.

In order to overcome partially some of these limitations we decided to undertake a small number of in-depth case studies, utilizing the same theoretical framework that had been applied to the larger caselet sample. Accordingly, we examined in detail two major education litigations, one in which the court became actively involved in institutional reform, and one in which it did not. The former is *Chance* v. *Board of Examiners,* a case in which the court invalidated the examination system used to select New York City principals and other supervisors and had a new system created under its auspices. The latter is *Otero* v. *Mesa County School District,* a case in which bilingual-bicultural education issues in rural Colorado were at issue.

Our study has one other important aspect. Much of the current judicial activism debate presumes the superior capabilites of the legislative process; yet we were unable to find any systematic empirical comparisons of educational policy in judicial and legislative forums. We therefore undertook to study the New York legislature's handling of the employment discrimination issues considered by the court in *Chance,* and the Colorado Legislature's handling of the identical bilingual-bicultural issues in *Otero.**

*Our legislative comparison is with state legislatures rather than with the U.S. Congress, since the type of educational issues with which we are concerned are, in the legislative arena, primarily state matters. We do not, of course, claim that all (or any) of our conclusions based on a study of two state legislatures would necessarily be applicable to the U.S. Congress—or indeed to the legislatures of any of the other 48 states. Our goal was to provide an additional dimension for consideration of the basic empirical data that was obtained from our caselet sample. Similarly, our findings concerning the conduct of the federal courts in educational policy matters do not necessarily hold true for the workings of the state courts, where case loads appear to consist of very different types of issues. However, because the state courts are generally subject to the same social and institutional pressures as federal courts, we believe that our findings and conclusions would be relevant to any evaluation of these bodies.

A brief survey of the reported trial court decisions of the New York State courts indicated that, for the years 1970–77, 96 cases met our sampling criteria for educational

In short, our study of educational policy making and the courts attempts to relate significant empirical data to the critical issues raised in the judicial activism debate by subjecting to a common theoretical framework a broad survey of representative cases, two in-depth judicial case studies, and two comparative legislative case studies. We will be taking a look first at the forest (survey data, chs. 2–5), then at the trees (case study analyses, chs. 6–9), before finally returning to a reconsideration of the basic legitimacy and capacity questions from both these perspectives in our concluding comments (ch. 10).

---

policy disputes; thus, the courts in just one state handled approximately 50% of the number of cases handled by the federal district courts in all states, as indicated in our *Federal Supplement* review (see appendix B). Although these findings need to be analyzed in greater detail and extended to other state court systems, they do support the hypothesis that, consistent with the larger role of state governments in education, state courts probably handle the bulk of education reform cases. (Whether these constitute typical "new model cases" could not be revealed by our brief survey.) In the state court sample, however, subject matter appears to differ substantially from the federal court pattern. The New York courts concentrated heavily in the areas of professional staff, labor relations, and electoral process, which constituted 63% of the state sample as compared with 29% of the federal sample. Conversely, while 51% of the federal cases were in the area of regulation of student speech, conduct, and appearance, only 6% of the state cases fell into these categories. See National Center for State Courts, *Student Litigation: A Compilation and Analysis of Civil Cases Involving Students 1977–81* (1981), for additional statistics on certain education law cases handled by state courts.

# PART II

Analysis of Caselet Data

# Introduction

———◆———

The empirical survey component of our research consists of a systematic analysis of 65 federal trial court proceedings decided between 1970 and 1977. The results of this analysis are organized around the four main issues in the judicial activism debate identified in chapter 1. Specifically, those findings relating most directly to the legitimacy of judicial involvement in educational policy making are discussed in "Principle/Policy Issues" (ch. 2) and "Interest Representation Issues" (ch. 3). Findings relating to the capacity of the courts to resolve policy disputes effectively are discussed in "Fact-finding Capability Issues" (ch. 4) and "Remedial Capability Issues" (ch. 5). The data on which the findings are based appear in tables either in the text or in appendix C.

The methodology utilized to select the sample of federal cases studied is discussed in appendix B. The subject matter of the cases was as shown below. In a majority of the cases (62%) plaintiffs succeeded in winning at least partial judgments.

| POLICY AREA | % SAMPLE[a] |
|---|---|
| Regulation of student appearance, speech, and conduct | 42 |
| Personnel policies and practices of school authorities | 28 |
| Curriculum | 9 |
| School finance | 9 |
| Special education | 6 |
| Electoral process | 5 |
| Labor relations | 2 |

[a]Total percentages add up to 101% due to rounding off.

21

For each of the cases selected, we obtained from district courts copies of the docket sheet, the complaint, and other important papers in the cases. These documents, and additional information obtained from telephone interviews of attorneys involved in each case, were then analyzed in terms of a detailed survey instrument, which broke down the main issues in the judicial activism debate into specific analytic categories (see appendix B). The research findings were recorded in 65 standardized reports—the "caselet studies"—which were then correlated and analyzed by the authors. The information revealed by these caselets became the basis for the specific findings reported in the chapters which follow.

# 2

## Caselet Analysis
### *Principle/Policy Issues*

───◆───

The most useful approach for considering separation of powers-
legitimacy issues is to analyze judicial decisions in terms of a
principle/policy perspective. To the extent that courts decide issues in
terms of "principles," they are acting within the proper sphere of
judicial decision making; to the extent that they decide issues in terms
of "policies," they are, according to the critics, intruding into the
legislative or executive domain. In order to test the "legitimacy" of the
65 judicial decisions in our sample, then, we attempted to determine
the degree to which parties justified their claims and defenses—and
courts explained their decisions—on the basis of "principle" or of
"policy."

As critics of Wechsler and Dworkin have indicated, the line between
"principle" and "policy" is difficult to establish (at least in "hard
cases"),[1] and the characterization of a particular claim can be controversial. Nevertheless, we agree with Dworkin that "the direction to
these judges to decide cases on grounds of principle cannot have the
same effect that the direction to decide on grounds of policy would
have."[2] In other words, how judges perceive their role and formally
justify their decisions and the manner in which the parties present
their claims, although not providing incontrovertible principle/policy
distinctions, constitute important behavioral data.[3]

In classifying and analyzing the cases in our sample, we utilized the
following definitions:[4]

*Principle:* A statement establishing a right of an individual against
the state or against another individual (or, less frequently, the right of
an institution to maintain the integrity of its legally defined prerogatives). A principle is expressed as a general rule that should be enforced whenever applicable, regardless of social welfare consequences, except when it is outweighed by a countervailing principle.

23

*Policy:* A statement concerning collective goals. Policy arguments consider the relative importance or desirability of particular social goals, and/or the relative efficiency and desirability of particular methods for achieving such goals. A policy statement is normally expressed in more specific terms than is a principle, and in a particular context it may be subordinated to competing policy claims that are determined to be better able to serve collective goals more effectively.

An initial attempt to clarify all the cases in our sample under these bipolar headings was to some degree frustrated. We realized that many claims encompassed assertions of principle which simultaneously involved policy consequences or considerations. Student free speech claims, for example, are based on the principle that students have a right to express their views in school *except* when regulation is necessary to avoid substantial disruption of the educational program.[5] Such a claim is not based entirely on principle because the basic free speech right can, in the school context, be subordinated to a competing consideration (disruption) that is not a countervailing principle. In other words, some amount of instrumental judgment inevitably enters into the determination as to whether, given the facts of the particular case, the need to maintain effective order outweighs the individual right of free expression. On the other hand, to label this claim as policy would also be misleading. Under clearly established judicial precedents, the students' free speech claim is not simply a desirable goal to be balanced with other social goals; rather, the constitutional rule permits only certain specific policies to be balanced against the right.[6]

The key characteristic of these hybrid cases of "qualified principle" is that their primary principle cannot be applied in individual disputes without substantive consideration of certain limited policy arguments. Consequently, we established a category of "principle/policy balancing," and formulated the following working definition:

*Principle/policy balancing:* A statement based on a general principle that may be enforced only after consideration is given to a *limited* number of specific policy factors, relevant under defined circumstances; it precludes consideration of a broad range of other policy factors which are not relevant to these circumstances.[7]

## I. Categorization of Basic Issues

In 64 out of the 65 cases in our sample (a listing of which appears in appendix A[8]) the complaints contained at least one claim based on alleged constitutional rights.[9] This almost unanimous inclination by the plaintiffs to frame their claims in terms of fundamental principles does not, however, reflect the type of judicial decision-making process that was actually being triggered by initiation of a lawsuit. Some claims, framed in the form of principle, lacked any principled substance, while others were set forth as mere window dressing.[10] Thus, the thrust of the basic claims[11] had to be analyzed not only in terms of the texts of complaints, but also in terms of the nature of the disputes they described and the weight of relevant current legal authority.[12]

On this basis, we determined that in 12 cases (18%) the predominant claim was based on principle, and in only 2 cases (3%) were policy arguments at the heart of the claim. Fifty-two or 80% (by far the largest number) of cases fell within the hybrid category of principle/ policy balancing. The specific breakdown of the cases is contained in table 1.

The most striking aspect of these findings is that so few of the cases (3%) appeared in the strict "policy" classification. Defenders of judicial activism might interpret these results as an indication that courts are limiting themselves to principled claims and that lawyers, aware of this fact, are avoiding cases that primarily involve policy issues. Critics, however, might view these statistics as indicative of the unreasonable breadth of current "principled" concepts and of lawyers' efforts to shape arguments to fit within these contours. Our data neither supports nor refutes either of these positions, but the significance of these (and other) findings will be assessed from a broader perspective in chapter 10.

The predominance (80%) of the principle/policy balancing cases in our sample is striking and unexpected. The prevalence of these cases may explain the extreme divergence of positions in the judicial activism debate. If four-fifths of the cases involve principle/policy balancing, then critics focusing only on "policy" aspects can find substantial evidence to support their allegations in the very same cases in which defenders can find illustrations of the "principled" basis of most court rulings. Thus, at the least, our findings call for a clarification and a reconsideration of the terminology and assumptions behind much of the current controversy. A brief discussion of examples of the types of cases which fit into each of the three categories listed in table 1 seems, therefore, appropriate at this point.

### Principle (table 1, col. 1)

The 12 principle cases included eight "strict-scrutiny" equal protection claims. In six of these, racial discrimination was alleged, and of the two remaining strict-scrutiny equal protection claims, one in-

Table 1
Principle/Policy Nature of Claim[a]

| PRINCIPLE (1) | PRINCIPLE/POLICY BALANCING[b] (2) | | POLICY (3) |
|---|---|---|---|
| Race: | Speech: 6-P | Special Education: | 8-D 65-D |
| 3-P  37-P | 10-D  20-P  46-D | 23-P  45-P | |
| 4-P  64-P | 12-D  24-P  54-P | 41-P  52-P | |
| 9[a] | 14-D  31-P | | |
| 15-P | | Ed. Finance: | |
| | Grooming: | 39-D  49-P | |
| Alienage: | 2-P  17-P  55-D | 48-P | |
| 33-P | 13-D  21-P  57-D | | |
| | 16-P  50-P  61-P | Corporal Punishment: | |
| Voting: | | 58-D  59-D | |
| 18-P | Student Procedural | | |
| 62-P | Due Process: | Race/balancing: | |
| | 5-D[c]  28-P  53-D | 11-D  32-D | |
| Religion: | 27-P  43-P  63-D | 25-P  40-D | |
| 5-P[c] | | | |
| 35-D | Equal Protection | Other: | |
| 60-P | (non-strict-scrutiny review): | 34-D | |
| | 1[a]  26-P | | |
| | 7-D  29-P | | |
| | 19-P  30-P | | |
| | 22-P  36-D | | |
| | 38-P | | |
| | 51-P | | |
| | | | |
| | Other: | | |
| | 44-P  56-P | | |
| | 47-D  42-D | | |
| N = 12 18% | N = 52 80% | | N = 2 3%[a] |
| P win = 10[a] (91%) | P win = 30/51[a] (59%) | | P win = 0 |

[a]"P" and "D" after a column entry indicate whether the plaintiff or the defendant prevailed. Tabulations of "plaintiff win" rates are listed at the bottom of each column. (Because Cs. 1 and 9 could not be considered a "win" for either party, these caselets are not computed in the "plaintiff win" calculations.)

[b]In 12 instances it was found that a plaintiff presented both a substantial principle claim and a substantial principle/policy balancing claim. These 12 cases were placed in col. 2, which represented the more policy-oriented of the two applicable categories, but were grouped separately in the right-hand subcolumn to provide a reference point for later analysis.

[c]C. 5 is listed in two separate columns because it was in essence a double case involving substantial challenges both to a flag salute regulation and to the school's general disciplinary practices.

volved both a denial of a fundamental right and discrimination based on alienage (C. 33),[13] and the other was a straightforward application of the one person-one vote principle (C. 18).

Three First Amendment religion claims were classified under the principle heading. Two of them involved balancing two First Amendment principles, i.e., prohibitions against establishment of religion and the guarantee of free exercise of religion (Cs. 35 and 60). The third was a flag salute case requiring application of the free exercise doctrine prohibiting compulsory expressions of belief contrary to one's religious tenets (C. 5)[14]

### *Principle/Policy Balancing (table 1, col. 2)*

Challenges to school hair and dress codes gave rise to a substantial volume of litigation during the first four years covered by our sample (1970–73). According to attorneys in the cases, the suits received considerable media coverage and were sometimes the subject of tense school board meetings and of petition campaigns. In many instances, the disputes were proxy wars reflecting views on the Vietnam conflict and on the youth counterculture. Plaintiffs asserted that the codes denied their individual rights to personal liberty, privacy, and free expression. Defendant school officials argued that the codes were necessary to ensure the orderly operation of the schools; that they promoted the legitimate goal of inculcating conformity to social customs of dress and grooming; and (in few cases) that enforcing rules, *per se*, taught respect for authority.

The trial judges in the nine grooming cases viewed plaintiffs' claims in a variety of ways. Some saw them as based on strong principle, others as based on principle subject to policy balancing, while still others as based on pure policy. In order to classify these factually similar cases consistently, we accepted the predominant trend among the eleven United States Courts of Appeals,[15] which treated them as principle/policy balancing.[16]

The basic question in challenges to student discipline procedures was whether suspension from school ever amounted to a "deprivation of liberty" sufficient to trigger due process procedural protections. If such a deprivation was found, then it was necessary to decide what process was due. This called for substantial principle/policy balancing. To determine when a student should be granted a pre- or postsuspension hearing and what procedural rights were applicable (e.g., right to confront witnesses, or to be represented by counsel), a court had to balance the interests of the students against those of the school system (e.g., maintaining order, preserving the nonadversary "counseling" mode of discipline procedures, and avoiding undue expense and administrative burdens).

The four special education cases, like the other cases listed in the right subcolumn of column 2, combined substantial principle claims with substantial balancing claims.[17] The complaints filed in *PARC* (C. 52) and *Mills* (C. 45) alleged as their central proposition the principle that totally excluding handicapped children from public education was a denial of a fundamental right which could not be justified by any competing social purpose. Even after the Supreme Court in *Rodriguez* precluded the assertion that education *per se* is a fundamental right,[18] an alternative theory was available—i.e., the claim that when the state undertakes to provide free public education, each child is entitled to receive "minimally adequate" instructional services. Such claims, based on questions of "adequacy," obviously involved substantial balancing issues. The concepts of "appropriate education" was also carried forward from constitutional decisions into the texts of state and federal special education statutes.[19] Consequently, principle/policy balancing usually was a major element of special education litigation both statutory and constitutional.

### Policy (table 1, col. 3)

*Zoll* (C. 65) was an offspring of the New York City fiscal crisis. The city's central board of education had entered into an agreement with the teachers' union to avoid layoffs or other economy moves by shortening the school day by 45 minutes, twice a week. Community school board representatives, parents, and some professionals protested the agreement through a variety of political actions, and in some instances resisted enforcement. They also instituted *Zoll*. The arguments in the lawsuit were essentially the same policy arguments that had been expressed politically—that children were being denied a full education; that the same economies could be effected throught actions less detrimental to the children; that early dismissal was burden on working parents, etc. These issues called for the weighing of competing social goals and for assessing the efficiency of the means chosen to achieve given ends. As such they clearly fit under our definition of policy claims.[20]

## II. Subsidiary Policy Arguments

The preceding discussion indicates that in almost all 65 cases the claims involved application of principles, or limited policy review within a "principled" framework. In only 2 cases did the plaintiffs' claim essentially ask the court to order educational reform on the basis of straightforward judicial policy judgments. These approaches, however, do not exhaust the ways in which policy arguments can be introduced into litigation. Having pleaded legal claims and defenses based on principle or principle/policy balancing, the plaintiffs and defendants may try to bolster their position by advancing additional arguments and evidence about the political, fiscal, and educational implications of the controversy and of possible court actions with respect to it.

The type of policy arguments referred to here are not matters that would be germane to the legally cognizable policy issues incorporated under the principle/policy balancing mode discussed above—hence, we have labeled them "subsidiary policy arguments." Specifically, a *subsidiary policy argument* is a policy statement (as defined at p. 24 *supra*) which is outside the scope of considerations encompassed by a principle/policy balancing rule (as defined at p. 24 *supra*) applicable to the particular situation.

To illustrate these distinctions, consider an action involving allegations of censorship of an article in a student newspaper. A claim that suppression of an article was justified by a likelihood of serious disruption to school operations would be properly considered as a principle/policy balancing application of the *Tinker* rule (see p. 24, note 5 *supra*). However, a defense based on an allegation that the article has no educational merit or expresses an "unpatriotic" political idea would fall outside the scope of the *Tinker* rule and, therefore, would be an improper issue for a court to consider.

The extent to which such subsidiary policy arguments were raised by the parties provides some objective measure of the degree to which policies that are, by definition, legally extraneous are introduced into the judicial process. Our analysis indicated that subsidiary policy arguments were made in 37 of the 63 principle and principle/policy balancing cases or 59% of the time.[21] (Included in the total of 37 cases are 13 instances in which both parties advanced subsidiary policy arguments.) In 23 cases (37%) plaintiffs raised such arguments, as compared to 27 cases (43%) for defendants (see appendix C, col. 1).

Most frequently, subsidiary policy statements were predictions about the potential consequences of a court decision. For example, in *PARC* (C. 52) the plaintiffs argued that educating mentally retarded children now would avoid the need for their institutionalization later, and would thus result in a substantial long-term fiscal savings for the public.[22]

Other subsidiary policy arguments were sometimes simply excuses by defendants for their admitted noncompliance with legal requirements. In *Natonabah* (C. 48), e.g., the defendants said it was politically impossible to equalize construction spending between Indian and Anglo facilities because the voters would approve only those bond referendums that authorized funds for facilities primarily benefiting Anglo neighborhoods. A third genre of subsidiary policy arguments spoke to the achievement of noneducational social goals. In mandatory leave cases, for example, a school board sometimes asserted that keeping a woman at home for several months after childbirth would improve mother-child relationships.

The substantial extent to which subsidiary policy issues were raised has significance for basic legitimacy questions. The large number of plaintiffs bringing subsidiary policy arguments to the courts supports the criticism that reformers attempt to use courts for "improper" policy purposes.[23] That these policy issues are usually presented together with basic principle claims may lessen the force of such a conclusion. It is interesting that defendants tended to raise subsidiary policy arguments as frequently as did plaintiffs. If plaintiffs' attempts to involve courts in school board policy decisions is said to be illegitimate, then the boards' own apparent eagerness to ask the court to consider policy is noteworthy.[24]

To obtain at least a partial explanation for the use of subsidiary policy arguments in certain cases, we tested the hypothesis that they are presented more often in "novel" cases, i.e., cases raising new issues for which applicable standards had not been established by the appellate courts. Examples of novel claims would be mandatory maternity leave prior to the Supreme Court's decision in *La Fleur* or applications of equal protection doctrine to the exclusion of handicapped children. If our hypothesis was true, then we could conclude that these policy matters were raised because the boundaries of the applicable principles were unclear. The corollary of this hypothesis would be an assumption that once clear standards are established, there would be a decrease of requests for courts to delve into subsidiary policy matters.

In our analysis, we classified the main claims as either "novel," "relatively novel," or "not novel." Approximately one-quarter of our sample was classified as novel, over one-half as "not novel," with the balance in between (see appendix C, col. 2).

We further cross-tabulated "novelty" with the presence of subsidiary policy arguments and found that in 75% of the novel cases, one or more parties advanced subsidiary policy arguments. This rate was substantially greater than in the not-novel cases, where one or more parties advanced subsidiary policy arguments in only 39% of the cases. Even more striking was the finding that in the novel cases, two or more adverse parties (i.e., plaintiff, defendant, intervenor, or *amicus*) offered subsidiary policy arguments 44% of the time, whereas with not-novel cases, the corresponding figure was 6%. Obviously, the degree of novelty of a case provides a substantial explanation for the introduction of subsidiary policy arguments.

In examining how judges reacted to the various claims and arguments, we found that, although they often expressed concern about the collateral impact of their rulings, they generally tried to restrict the stated bases of their decisions to matters relevant to principled analysis.

Comparing the courts' statements concerning the legal basis of plaintiffs' claims with our tripartite classifications, we found that the court decisions characterized the thrust of the plaintiffs' claims in a manner consistent with our own classifications. Most of the small divergence in ratings stemmed from a group of five cases which the courts described as policy disputes, but which we believed contained some elements of principle.[25]

Defendant school boards won 100% of seven[26] cases which courts characterized as based on policy; thus, determination that the claims were policy-based inevitably led to a defendant victory. Whether these results indicate that judges consider intervention seriously only when *actual* principle issues are raised, or that they *frame* cases in policy terms when they are inclined to defer to school authorities, it seems clear that judges are highly conscious of the principle/policy distinctions and, therefore, that these perceptions cause some amount of institutional restraint on their judgments.[27]

Consistent with these findings, we noted that in 23 cases (35%), judges specifically articulated concerns about legitimacy and separation-of-powers issues.[28] These judges seemed aware of the judicial activism debate and were concerned with rendering "legitimate" decisions. Plaintiffs won 12 of these cases, or 52%, as compared to winning 66% of the remaining 42 cases in which these concerns were not articulated. Though awareness of legitimacy issues, therefore, may have inclined judges in some cases to refuse to intervene, still, in a majority of cases in which the legitimacy issue was directly addressed, the court did find for plaintiffs. Presumably, these claims had a proper principled basis.

### III. Impact of Rodriguez

The final principle/policy issue tested in our analysis was the impact of the U.S. Supreme Court's decision in *San Antonio School District* v. *Rodriguez*.[29] Given the Supreme Court's holding there that education is not a fundamental interest under the U.S. Constitution, one would expect the lower courts to show reluctance to grant relief in cases raising educational policy issues. Our data, however, did not support such a hypothesis.

Thirty-two of the liability decisions in our sample were decided prior to *Rodriguez*, 33 afterward. Before *Rodriguez*, plaintiffs won 18 out of 32 cases, or 56%; after *Rodriguez*, plaintiffs' success rate increased to 21 out of 33 cases, or 64%. Hence, neither in absolute numbers nor in terms of relative success was there any decrease in plaintiffs' judicial activity. In fact, a slightly larger number of educational policy cases were decided during the later period, and plaintiffs were winning them more frequently.[30]

The apparent lack of impact of *Rodriguez* indicates that even if education itself is not *per se* a fundamental interest, numerous other principled claims for judicial intervention in the education arena (e.g., students' right to free speech, equal treatment, and procedural due process) continue to be applicable.[31] Furthermore, the advent of comprehensive statutory schemes defining educational equity in special education, sex discrimination, bilingual education, etc., has provided courts with statutory alternatives to constitutional innovations as a basis for continued involvement in educational matters.[32] Probably the *Rodriguez* hypothesis would have been correct if stated inversely; if the Supreme Court had held education to be a fundamental interest, a broad new principle category would have been created and the number of education cases (and plaintiff successes) probably would have increased substantially.

### IV. Summary of Findings

1. The polar concepts of "neutral principles" and "policy" were inadequate for classifying litigations involving educational issues. A workable definitional scheme could be made, however, using these three concepts: principle; principle/policy balancing; policy. In 18% of the cases the predominant claim was based on principle; in 80% the claims involved principle/policy balancing; in only 3% were policy assertions unrelated to authoritative principles.

2. Policy arguments that were not legally relevant to basic principle or principle/policy balancing claims were categorized as "subsidiary policy arguments." Plaintiffs and defendants showed an almost equal propensity to raise such arguments in support of their principled claims. Overall, one or more of the parties presented subsidiary policy arguments in 59% of the cases. Subsidiary policy arguments were made most often in "novel" cases, presumably because the parties considered judges more concerned with consequences of decisions when legal principles were in a formative stage. Judges did not, however, appear to base their decisions on these subsidiary policy arguments.

3. Judges generally were aware of the issues in the judicial activism debate and rejected claims which they considered to be based strictly on policy considerations. Judges specifically articulated separation-of-powers concerns in 35% of the cases. In 72% they expressed concern about the consequences of their intervening into school district affairs. Nevertheless, in the majority of these cases they issued decisions favorable to plaintiffs, thereby indicating their belief that plaintiffs' claims of individual rights were substantial enough to outweigh considerations of institutional restraint.

4. The Supreme Court's decision in *Rodriguez* has not resulted in a decline in judicial involvement in educational policy cases. Apparently, even if education *per se* is not to be considered a fundamental interest, other principled bases for constitutional involvement in the educational arena, as well as newly created statutory rights, provide a basis for continued activism.

# 3

## Caselet Analysis
### *Interest Representation Issues*

━━━◆━━━

The legitimacy issues concerning interest representation surveyed in chapter 1 centered on whether all those having a substantial interest in a controverted issue were being represented in the court proceedings. We attempted to answer this question empirically by trying to determine the following: (1) Are most social policy lawsuits in the federal courts filed, as is commonly assumed, by minority plaintiffs, and, if so, what are the implications of this phenomenon? (2) To what extent are class action procedures used to argue *depth* of representation? (3) To what extent does the party structure follow the broad *breadth* of representation implied in Professor Chayes's model of multipolarity? (4) Are there any indications that a significant number of cases litigated by public law advocacy centers remain unresponsive to the concrete interests of the groups they purport to represent?

### I. MINORITY PLAINTIFFS

Both critics and defenders of judicial activism generally agree on the premise that most plaintiffs in public law litigations are members of minority groups. Critics use this premise to assure that, as a result, the issues presented to courts are relatively narrow and do not provide a broad basis for policy-oriented activity. Defenders, on the other hand, emphasize the vital function of the courts in defending the rights of disadvantaged groups who lack adequate access to majoritarian legislative and administrative processes; and they assert that, at least from a comparative perspective, sufficient broad facts and implications of the issues are brought to the courts' attention.

To test the basic assumption that most cases are brought by minority plaintiffs, we categorized the identity of the plaintiffs in our 65

# Table 2
## Characteristics of Plaintiffs[a]

| Suspect Classes (1) | | | Semisuspect Classes (2) | | | | Nonconformists (Political, Religious, Social) (3) | Other (4) |
|---|---|---|---|---|---|---|---|---|
| Black | Hispanic, Indian | Aliens | Female | Handicapped | Poor | Elderly | | |
| 3 | 31[b] | 33 | 19 | 29 | 27 | 44 | 1 | 7 |
| 4 | 47 | | 22 | 23 | 39 | | 2 | 8 |
| 9 | 48 | | 26 | 41 | 49 | | 5 | 36 |
| 11 | (15) | | 30 | 45 | (9) | | 13 | 18 |
| 15 | (40) | | 34 | 52 | (53) | | 20 | 6 |
| 16 | | | 38 | | | | 21 | 10 |
| 25 | | | 51 | | | | 17 | 12 |
| 32 | | | (3) | | | | 50 | 14 |
| 37 | | | | | | | 55 | 24 |
| 40 | | | | | | | 57 | 28 |
| 43[c] | | | | | | | 61 | 35 |
| 53 | | | | | | | 54 | 42 |
| 59 | | | | | | | (3) | 46 |
| 62 | | | | | | | | 56 |
| 63 | | | | | | | | 58 |
| 64 | | | | | | | | 60 |
| | | | | | | | | 65 |
| N = 16 25% | N = 3 5% | N = 1 2% | N = 7 11% | N = 5 8% | N = 3 5% | N = 1 2% | N = 12 18% | N = 17 26% |
| N = 20 31% | | | N = 16 25% | | | | | |
| N = 48 74% | | | | | | | | |

[a]Cases are listed in columns 1, 2, and 3 only if the case was brought by a minority group member alleging or implying discrimination against his or her minority status; e.g., a woman plaintiff is not listed in column 2 if sex discrimination was not alleged. There are multiple listings of cases in which the plaintiffs qualify under several headings, e.g., a suit by a black unwed mother. Only the first listing is counted in the column total. Subsequent listings are set off by parentheses, and are not counted in the totals. In three cases, public officials were the plaintiffs. They are listed in column 4 (Cs. 7, 36, 56) because their impact would have primarily benefited minority groups.

[b]This case involved a challenge to school censorship of publications by a Hispanic organization (ethnic issue implicit).

[c]Race discrimination was an implicit issue in this suit brought by black plaintiffs during a period of racial conflict in the schools.

cases. In doing so, we classified plaintiffs under four main headings: "suspect classes"; "semi-suspect classes"; "nonconformists";[1] and "other." "Suspect classes" is a term established by the Supreme Court in equal protection cases to refer to historically disadvantaged minority groups whose claims require the most searching judicial scrutiny. The suspect classes participating as plaintiffs in our sample were blacks, Hispanics, American Indians, and aliens. "Semi-suspect classes" is our own term devised to include other disadvantaged groups treated more recently by statutes and court decisions as disadvantaged minorities in need of special protection, even though the Supreme Court has not explicitly identified them as suspect classes. This category includes plaintiffs who are female, handicapped, poor, or elderly (and are alleging discrimination against them because of their minority status).

The category of "nonconformists" encompasses cases brought by persons who are challenging governmental actions that they claim are directed against unconventional political, religious, or cultural beliefs or practices. Most of these (8 out of 12) were brought on behalf of students suspended from school for wearing prohibited hairstyles or clothing. Also included here are two actions brought by advocates of socialist and anti-establishment ideas, one by a male who wanted to be granted child-care leave, and the other by a member of a religious minority conscientiously opposed to patriotic activities.[2]

The findings indicate that 56% of the cases were brought by suspect and semi-suspect class minority plaintiffs, alleging status discrimination. When "minority" is defined to include "nonconformists," the figure grows to 74%. The specific breakdowns of these figures are contained in table 2. Minority plaintiffs succeeded in convincing judges to order changes in school policies in 71% of their cases, whereas "other" plaintiffs won only 35% of theirs.

Not unexpectedly, these figures indicate that minority groups do disproportionately bring their grievances before the courts. That minorities prevailed in almost three-quarters of these cases suggests minorities may not have access to substantial consideration of their justifiable grievances in the legislative and administrative forums. Another explanation would be that minorities seek relief in the courts precisely because of an awareness that special judicial solicitude for their rights promises a greater likelihood of success, even though they may actually have relatively fair access to the legislative process.

## II. CLASS ACTION STATUS

Because systemwide injunction cases affect many persons and interests beyond the individual plaintiffs, it is critical to determine whether the individual plaintiffs speak only for their limited individualistic concerns or for the broader group interests of all persons who have a direct stake in the outcome of the suit. The only way of fully answering this question would be to survey all potentially affected interests and determine their knowledge of and involvement in the suit; such a task was far beyond the scope of our resources. We determined, however, that the depth of representativeness could be ascertained to some degree by determining the extent to which the cases were filed as "class actions," i.e., cases in which individual plaintiffs purported to speak not only for themselves, but also for members of the broader group "similarly situated."

Plaintiffs seek class actions for a variety of reasons, including broadening the scope of information subject to discovery procedures; precluding dismissal if the problem of the immediate individual plaintiff is resolved; and broadening the scope of the remedial order if the suit is successful.[3] Within the context of representativeness, however, class action status is significant since it can serve as a barometer of the plaintiffs' intentions to speak for a broad group of individuals interested in policy reform. Furthermore, if the court grants the plaintiffs' request for class action "certification," there is some objective indication that, following the requirements of Federal Rule of Civil Procedure 23, the plaintiffs have proven their claims to be typical of the interests of the members of a class, that they will provide fair and capable representation for these broader interests, and that all members of the class can be notified of developments in the suit and given an opportunity to present any objections to these developments.

Forty-six of the complaints in our sample, or 71%, contained class action allegations. However, in only about half of these cases (45%) did the court specifically grant class action certification, while in virtually all of the remaining cases (53% of the total) the court either rejected or ignored the certification requests (see appendix C, col. 3). Thus, the Rule 23 requirement that certification decisions be made "by order" and "as soon as practicable" was apparently not being taken very seriously. (Even where the court issued specific certification rulings, these decisions often were not made until after trial.) Nor did plaintiffs or defendants seem greatly concerned about class certification. Plaintiffs sometimes filed motions for certification as protective motions (to avoid a denial of class action status because of untimeliness), and usually there were no objections by any parties if the courts postponed deciding these motions.

The most frequently cited reason for denial of certification (occurring in 19% of cases styled as class actions) was failure to meet the Rule 23 requirement that a class "too numerous" for all affected individuals to appear directly in the case actually exists. There was only one explicit denial of certification on grounds of unrepresentativeness, C. 59, in which the judge held that the individual plaintiff was not a proper representative of the purported class of all students who might be subjected to corporal punishment, since no corporal punishment had been administered to her.

The implications of these findings would appear to be as follows. Plaintiffs in a large majority of the cases purport to speak for a broad group interest. The courts do not generally dispute these claims, since class action status was explicitly denied in only 19% of the instances, and in almost none of these was representativeness an issue. In 34% of the cases, the courts ignored the claims. They, thereby, *ipso facto* failed to provide the protective mechanisms of Rule 23 which hold plaintiffs' attorneys responsible for explaining what groups they represent and how they propose to represent the broader interests. The general lack of controversy about class certification in these cases may be interpreted as indicating an acceptance by the parties and the courts of the general adequacy of plaintiffs' representation, but the courts' general failure to invoke available mechanisms makes us reluctant to accept such a conclusion at this time. In short, our findings indicate that although class certification procedures potentially can provide substantial assurance of representativeness, they are not presently being utilized in a manner that actually could do so.

### III. Multipolarity

In addition to analyzing information on class action status in order to assess the depth of plaintiffs' representation of the interests for which they claim to speak, we examined party structures in order to determine the extent to which a broad range of different interests were represented. In this survey we used Professor Chayes's model which assumes that a "multipolarity" of interests will appear in public law litigations, as contrasted with the "bipolarity" of representation in traditional private litigation.

We first sought to ascertain the degree of "multipolarity" as indicated by the presence of parties other than a single plaintiff or defendant. We found that 11 cases were initiated by multiple plaintiffs, and 20 were initiated against multiple defendants. After filings, motions for joinder of additional parties were granted in 12 cases, and motions by outside groups to intervene were granted in 12 others; moreover, other groups and individuals were given permission to file *amicus curiae*[4] briefs in 11 cases. Because in many instances additional parties may have come into a case through one or more procedural mechanisms, the 60 instances of party expansion actually occurred in 38 cases, indicating that 58% of the cases in the sample were "multipolar," when multipolarity is defined by the physical presence of more than two parties or *amicae*. The breakdown of these figures is contained in table 3.

Our analysis also uncovered interesting information concerning the courts' receptivity to representation of additional interests. As indicated in table 3, the courts granted 12 out of 14 motions for joinder, or 86%. Requests for intervention were granted in 12 instances and denied in 6 instances[5] (although two of these were granted *amicus* rights). All 13 applications for *amicus* status were granted. Hence, fully 88% of the applicants for intervention were allowed some formal participation in litigation, either as a party or as an *amicus*.

Although the courts were extremely receptive to requests for interest representation, there is little indication that judges actively encouraged nonparties to become involved in the litigation, as might be expected under Professor Chayes's multipolarity model.[6] In at least a few of the cases, it was apparent that certain groups which had a clear interest did not actually participate.[7]

In the great majority of cases where multiple parties were present, distinct perspectives were not clearly articulated to the court. Only in 6[8] of the 38 multipolarity cases (16%) were more than two substantially different basic positions on the issues presented at the liability stage. At the remedial stage (when the broad implications of most policy issues emerged), "issue" multipolarity occurred in 8 out of 25 multipolarity cases[9] (32%) which reached this stage. In short, in contradiction to the apparent assumptions of Chayes's model, additional parties tended to support, with variations, the arguments of the main participants, rather than to set out distinct, independent perspectives.

The significance of these findings for the issues raised in the judicial activism debate is not clear. The courts appear to be open to broad involvement of all interested groups, but not all potentially affected

## Table 3
## Party Polarity[a]

| MULTIPLE Ps (1) | MULTIPLE Ds (2) | JOINDER GRANTED (3) | INTERVENTION GRANTED (4) | AMICUS STATUS GRANTED (5) |
|---|---|---|---|---|
| 4 | 6 | 6 | 22 | 3 |
| 5[b] | 7 | 15[c] | 23 | 6 |
| 15 | 15 | 22 | 36 | 18[d] |
| 25 | 18 | 25 | 40 | 23 |
| 32 | 22 | 27 | 42 | 24 |
| 37 | 23 | 36 | 46 | 29[e] |
| 42 | 26 | 40 | 49 | 32 |
| 47 | 33 | 41 | 51 | 39[e] |
| 49 | 35 | 43 | 52 | 43 |
| 52 | 36 | 45 | 53 | 45 |
| 64 | 39 | 48 | 56 | 46 |
| | 40 | 60 | 63 | 48 |
| | 41 | | | 52 |
| | 45 | (Joinder | (Intervention | |
| | 47 | Denied): | Denied): | |
| | 48 | | | |
| | 51[b] | 9[f] | 6[g] | |
| | 52 | 48 | 7 | |
| | 58[b] | | 23[g] | |
| | 60 | | 49 | |
| | 65[h] | | 52[i] | |
| | | | 58 | |
| N = 11 | N = 21 | N = 12 | N = 12 | N = 13 |

| Running Total of Separate Cases Involving Multiple Parties | | | | |
|---|---|---|---|---|
| N = 11 17% | N = 29 45% | N = 31 48% | N = 35 54% | N = 38 58% |

[a]In these listings, a distinct "party group" was deemed a single plaintiff or defendant. Thus, several individual plaintiffs with a single integrated set of claims were considered a single entity. Any organizational entity which joined the individual plaintiffs was treated separately, even if the individuals were members of the organization (e.g., a suit by five teachers as individuals and their professional education organization constituted two plaintiffs). Among defendants, education officials at the same political level were treated as a single entity (e.g,. a principal, local superintendent, and local school board were considered one defendant). Since *denials* of motions for joinder and intervention did not expand the party structure, they are not included in the column totals. However, they are set out for comparative purposes in parentheses, in columns 3 and 4, so that those cases with multiple motions, whether granted or denied, can be identified.

[b]Three separate cases are consolidated. Plaintiffs in each were students suing as individuals. Plaintiffs sued a class of local school boards.

groups seek to participate, and even these groups who do participate do not present a broad spectrum of strongly diverse perspectives to the courts. It may be that the real issues in education litigations are essentially bipolar[10] and that all interests are generally being adequately represented; or, one might conclude that the inherently bipolar orientation of the adversarial judicial process discourages a broad, multipolar approach. Given these possibilities, a comparative frame of reference that looks to the legislative process and considers whether a greater extent of multipolarity emerges in that forum would seem especially important. Such a comparative perspective, at least in an illustrative sense, will be attempted in chapters 7 and 9.

## IV. Public Law Advocacy Centers

The final issue concerning the adequacy of interest representation is the allegation that a substantial number of new model cases are litigated by "public interest" attorneys[11] who pursue their own abstract philosophical preferences rather than the concrete grievances of actual clients.

Our statistical analysis confirmed the supposition that a substantial number of cases are brought by "public interest" attorneys. In the 65 cases, 33 of the plaintiff groups were represented by public interest legal organizations and 27 by the private bar. In the 5 remaining cases, plaintiffs were represented by government or union lawyers. (see appendix C, col. 4.)

The subject matter breakdown of the cases is illuminating. Private counsel brought 7 out of the 8 student appearance cases and each of the 3 election cases. By way of contrast, public interest attorneys brought all 6 student procedural due process cases[12] and all 4 special education cases. Two-thirds (6 out of 9) of the First Amendment

---

[c]A group of residents affected by the court order brought a separate action which was later consolidated with this case.

[d]Although not formally designated an *amicus curiae*, a mayor acted in that role in this case.

[e]*Amicae* become involved on appeal.

[f]An intervention motion was denied without prejudice to a renewed application in the remedial phase of the case, should there be one.

[g]Intervention motion(s) denied by applicant(s) given *amicus* status.

[h]The local community school board defendant was considered separate from the citywide defendants.

[i]This denial of intervention occurred early in the liability phase; intervention of the teachers' union was permitted years later in the remedial phase by another judge.

speech plaintiffs had private lawyers, but two-thirds (4 out of 6) of the plaintiffs in school finance cases were represented by public interest lawyers.

These results seemed to indicate that the larger, more complex cases, involving a greater degree of substantive reform of educational practices, were brought by the public interest attorneys. To test this hypothesis further, we correlated the type of representation with the 15 cases involving broad reform decrees, set forth in chapter 5, table 7. We found that 33% of the public interest attorney cases resulted in broad reform decrees, as compared with only 15% of the private attorney cases. Thus, cases brought by public interest attorneys clearly did result in more substantial intrusions into the educational process.

A further correlation of the type of representation with degree of novelty of the claims (appendix C, col. 2) indicated that public interest attorneys tend disproportionately to press innovative legal theories. Fifty-two percent[13] of the cases brought by public interest attorneys fell into our categories of "novel" and "relatively novel" cases, whereas only 33% of the cases brought by the private bar fit under these headings.

Taken together, these findings appear to corroborate the critics' assertion that public interest attorneys are involved in most public law cases and tend to raise issues which are the most novel and result in the most substantial intrusions into administrative areas. Whether, as critics assert, the issues raised by these attorneys reflect their own philosophical preferences rather than concrete grievances of actual clients is more difficult to test objectively, but the more strict adherence of public interest attorneys to class action procedures implies that they may be better group representatives than private attorneys.[14]

## Summary of Findings

1. Minority group interests, broadly defined, initiate most educational litigations. Fifty-six percent of the cases in our sample were brought by "suspect" and "semi-suspect" class minority plaintiffs, and when "minority" is defined to include "nonconformists" the rate rises to 74%. Minority plaintiffs tended to prevail in 71% of the cases they brought, whereas "other" plaintiffs won in only 35%.

2. Plaintiffs requested class action certification in 71% of the cases in our sample. Such certification was granted in 45% of these situations, denied in 19% (mainly for technical reasons not related to rep-

resentativeness), and essentially ignored or neglected in 36%. Thus, although plaintiffs purport to speak for broad classes, available judicial mechanisms for verifying claims of representativeness are not applied with regularity.

3. Multiple participants, beyond a single plaintiff or defendant individual or group, participated in 57% of the cases, and the courts granted motions for joinder, intervention, and *amicus* status at exceptionally high rates (86%–88%). However, judges do not appear actively to encourage additional interests to seek participation, and our data raised questions as to whether, in a comparative framework, a significant number of potential additional interest groups or potential additional perspectives failed to become represented in the judicial process.

4. A substantial number of educational litigations (57%) are brought by public interest attorneys. Furthermore, these attorneys tend disproportionately to be involved in the cases resulting in the major reform decrees (33% vs. 15% for private attorneys) and in cases raising "novel" and "relatively novel" legal issues (52% vs. 30% for private attorneys).

# 4

## Caselet Analysis
### *Fact-finding Capability Issues*

———————◆———————

The issues surrounding the judiciary's fact-finding capability focused on two basic questions: First, how well are the courts able to obtain necessary information? Second, how effectively do the judges deal with and comprehend the social science data that is presented to them? In order to provide some answers to the first question, we analyzed the discovery process and the social science submissions of the parties. In regard to the second question, we considered the types of evidentiary issues presented to the courts and the specific analytical devices judges used in deciding (or more often in avoiding the necessity to decide) social fact issues.[1]

## I. INFORMATION-GATHERING CAPACITY

### *Discovery*

"Discovery" is a generic term used to describe a variety of devices available to litigants for ascertaining the amount and the type of information which the opposing party possesses. Such knowledge allows a party both to be aware of potential evidence which the adversary may introduce and to obtain data which may be helpful in presenting his own case.[2] Specific discovery rules permit a party to pose "interrogatories" (questions) which enable the litigant to find out which documents may be available and to subpoena documents in the adversary's possession. If the parties cooperate with each other in the discovery process there may be little need for active involvement by the court. However, if a party believes that the adversary is either withholding available data, or, conversely, unreasonably demanding irrelevant, unavailable, or highly confidential information, motions may be made to the court either to compel disclosure or to "protect" a party from having to comply with such unreasonable discovery demands.

In 38 of the 65 caselets formal discovery requests were made.[3] Roughly speaking, there was extensive discovery in 11 cases, moderate discovery in 13 cases, and small amounts of discovery in 14 cases. (See appendix C, col. 5.)

One indication of the effectiveness of this process is the amount of motion practice arising out of discovery disputes. If the parties are able to obtain most of the information they seek without adversarial resistance, one can assume that the information flow will be maximized. In 15 of the 38 cases involving discovery in our sample, there was at least one discovery motion entered on the docket sheet. In 5 of these 15 cases more than one motion was filed. Court action was needed to resolve a dispute in 9 cases, but at least 2 of the 9 instances involved minor, technical disagreements. Therefore, in only 7 cases, 11% of the sample, was the court forced to determine whether a party was using discovery procedures fairly. In the others, a solution was worked out or the dispute was rendered moot, e.g., by a dismissal of the complaint. (See appendix C, col. 6.)

*Brown* (C. 9) is a good example of how utilization of the liberal federal discovery rules can efficiently build a comprehensive factual record and focus the major areas of agreement and disagreement. In order to establish their claim that the Chicago school system allocated lower per pupil funding levels for children living in poor neighborhoods than for those living in wealthier ares, the plaintiffs needed to obtain massive records from the Board of Education concerning expenditure patterns, staffing policies, and other practices. The school district turned over five cartons of documents to the plaintiffs.[4] As a result, the defendants' data became the basis of the plaintiffs' case. The defendants in this case also made use of discovery, but for a different purpose. They obtained the interpretative reports prepared by the plaintiffs' experts, and prepared counteranalyses for presentation at trial. During this extensive process only one discovery motion was filed, and it later was resolved by a consent order. Finally, as in many of the other case studies, mutual discovery led to agreement on a number of previously disputed factual issues.[5]

The picture that emerges from the quantitative data, from qualitative analysis (of cases like *Brown*), and from attorney interviews[6] indicates that the information exchange breakdowns so frequent in antitrust cases and other commercial litigation situations rarely took place in educational policy cases. Although our data cannot definitively establish that in formulating their discovery requests the parties were aware of all the arguably relevant information,[7] the relative efficiency of the process and the magnitude of the information actually obtained substantiate the veiw that the adversary system is a highly effective data-gathering mechanism in social policy litigations.

The effectiveness of the discovery process in our sample partially stemmed from a felt obligation on the part of the public agency defendants (who in any event may have been required to provide most relevant information under federal and state freedom-of-information acts) to divulge broad-based information to adversaries who were raising issues of wide public concern. Another incentive for a public defendant to cooperate in discovery was that in "multipolar"[8] cases involving shifting alliances, its interests and those of the plaintiffs sometimes were not fully adversary. This phenomenon is exemplified by a comparison of the positions of the Commonwealth of Pennsylvania and of the School District of Philadelphia in *Nicholson* (C. 49) and in *Frederick L.* (C. 23). In *Nicholson,* the state apparently saw merit in the plaintiffs' charges of misuse of Title I funds by Philadelphia, and despite its status as a party defendant, it gave plaintiffs' attorneys broad access to its files. According to plaintiffs' counsel, however, access to city files was more difficult. In *Frederick L.,* on the other hand, the city and the plaintiffs had the same programmatic goals and differed primarily over the legal implications of allegedly inadequate state funding. As a result of cooperative discovery practices, the plaintiffs and the district stipulated to the accuracy of many important facts, and even to a remedial plan (premised on adequate state funding).[9]

### Adversary System Distortions

Critics of judicial capacity contend that the adversary system tends to distort the information flow to the court. According to this view, since the parties are motivated to present only one side of an issue, the court's decision may be based on a biased, one-sided view of the true facts if the adversary does not provide adequate countervailing information on a particular issue. The dangers of judicial error may be especially acute when biased social fact conclusions, packaged in a scientific format, are undetected by a generalist judge.

We hypothesized that if serious adversarial distortion of social fact information was widespread in educational policy cases, then our 65 caselets would reveal a substantial number of instances in which there was a one-sided presentation of social fact evidence, and within this subgroup of cases there would be a disproportionate number of victories by the party introducing such evidence.[10] In fact, our analysis showed 20 instances of such one-sided data presentations (11 plaintiffs, 9 defendants); in 14 out of 20 cases, however, the sole party introducing social fact evidence was the loser. (Findings are set forth in table 4.) Surprisingly, then, the relationship between submitting such data unopposed and winning the case was strongly negative.

Table 4
Balance in Social Fact[a] Presentations
(Total N = 41)

| SOCIAL FACT EVIDENCE SUBMITTED ONLY BY PLAINTIFFS (1) | | SOCIAL FACT EVIDENCE SUBMITTED ONLY BY DEFENDANTS (2) | | SOCIAL FACT EVIDENCE SUBMITTED BY PLAINTIFFS AND DEFENDANTS (3) | |
|---|---|---|---|---|---|
| Pl. Win (1A) | Def. Win (1B) | Pl. Win (2A) | Def. Win (2B) | Pl. Win (3A) | Def. Win (3B) |
| 25 | 11 | 5 | 57 | 3 | 8 |
| 27 | 32 | 17 | | 4 | 39[b] |
| 33 | 34 | 21 | | 9 | 40 |
| 37 | 36 | 26 | | 15 | [44][c] |
| 49 | 46 | 31 | | 16 | 58 |
| | 47 | 38 | | 18 | 59 |
| | | 44[c] | | 22 | |
| | | 61 | | 23 | |
| | | | | 29 | |
| | | | | 30 | |
| | | | | 41 | |
| | | | | 43 | |
| | | | | 45 | |
| | | | | 48 | |
| | | | | 51 | |
| | | | | 52 | |
| N = 5 | N = 6 | N = 8 | N = 1 | N = 16 | N = 5 |

[a]This table analyzes 41 of the 42 cases listed as "social fact" in table 5, col. 2, *infra*. C. 2 is omitted because it cannot be fairly characterized as a "win" for either side.

[b]The plaintiff and the local defendant both introduced social fact evidence to show the educational harm suffered by students who did not have textbooks. The state defendant did not concede this point, although it did not introduce opposing evidence. The court considered the social fact evidence to be irrelevant.

[c]Both sides submitted substantially similar statistics. The defendant prevailed on the issue of whether there was a systemwide practice of age discrimination. Only the defendant, however, presented expert testimony regarding the rationality of using remaining years of service as a criterion for promotion decisions, and plaintiffs prevailed on this issue. Overall, the most accurate listing of this case was under column 2A, although it also is entered in brackets (but not counted for tabulation purposes) in column 3B.

The figures in table 4 suggest that the courts were able to compensate for one-sided evidentiary presentations. In the 14 cases in which the party presenting social fact evidence lost, there were two main types of compensation: (a) courts found that the asserted facts, even if true, were not legally significant;[11] or (b) the judges rejected "expert" testimony because they did not accept either the proposed policy objectives or the means chosen to achieve them.[12] In 4 other cases the court analyzed the evidence submitted and either decided that it actually supported the other side's claim[13] or counterposed its own knowledge and views to that of the expert witness.[14]

Of the 6 cases in which the party presenting evidence prevailed, 3 were such that there was almost no possibility of mounting a convincing social fact defense.[15] Only in the remaining 3 cases did substantial possibilities of adversarial distortion exist.[16]

In short, then, while it is not clear why, in many cases, a party did not seek to rebut its adversary's social fact evidence, our caselet analysis reveals no substantial pattern of adversarial distortions and indicates that in most instances, judges were able to compensate for one-sided presentations.

## II. Information Assessment Capacity

### *Nature of Social Fact Disputes Presented*

From a perusal of the literature on judicial activism, one might anticipate that judges would be required to grapple with complex social science issues in almost all educational policy cases. Our study, however, supports Judge Doyle's assertion that "social science data . . . are less important in judicial decision-making in the field of constitutional law than most people think."[17]

Although every case in our sample challenged the systemwide application of an educational policy, in relatively few cases was the resolution of conflicting social fact evidence central to the court's decision. Social fact evidence was actually introduced in 42 of the 65 cases in our sample.[18] However, although the social fact submissions were disputed by the parties in 86% of these cases, for the most part they were relatively straightforward and could readily be decided by a generalist judge "on the basis of common experience or the usual modicum of expert testimony."[19] Specifically, we determined that only 11 out of the 42 cases involved "complex" evidence which could not be validated on the basis of common-sense analysis (findings are set forth in table 5).

The importance of social fact evidence in a case appeared to be

# Table 5
## Introduction of Historical/Social Fact Evidence[a]

| ONLY HISTORICAL FACT EVIDENCE INTRODUCED (1) | | SOCIAL FACT EVIDENCE INTRODUCED (2) | | |
|---|---|---|---|---|
| Undisputed (1A) | Disputed (1B) | Undisputed (2A) | Disputed (2B) | |
| 6 | 1 | 26 | 2[b] | 34 |
| 7 | 12 | 27 | 3 | 37 |
| 10 | 13 | 33 | 4* | 38 |
| 14 | 19 | 36 | 5 | 39 |
| 20 | 24 | 46 | 8 | 40* |
| 42 | 28 | 49 | 9* | 41* |
| 56 | 33 | | 11 | 43 |
| 60 | 35 | | 15 | 44 |
| 62 | 50 | | 16 | 45* |
| | 53 | | 17 | 47 |
| | 54 | | 18 | 48 |
| | 55 | | 21 | 51 |
| | 63 | | 22 | 52* |
| | 64 | | 23* | 57 |
| | 65[c] | | 25* | 58* |
| | | | 29* | 59* |
| | | | 30 | 61 |
| | | | 31 | [65][c] |
| | | | 32 | |
| N = 9 | N = 14 | N = 6 | N = 36 | |
| N = 23 35% | | N = 42 65% | | |

[a]An asterisk (*) denotes a case in which "complex" social fact evidence was introduced; "complex" evidence requires the fact-finder to rely on expert opinions which cannot easily be validated by common-sense scrutiny. Examples are technical, statistical data or reviews of the majority "consensus" in the literature of a particular scientific discipline. The concept of "complexity" is more subjective than the other classifications used for quantitative analysis in this study. However, because we have used a very inclusive definition of social fact evidence, it is important to attempt to distinguish between cases with rather straightforward social fact materials and those that more closely resemble the model of public law/policy fact-finding described in the literature on judical capacity.

[b]Defendants' social fact "evidence" was introduced through a stipulation indicating how defendants' proposed witness "would testify." The court entered a temporary injunction without commenting on the social fact issues, and then abstained from a decision on the merits. There were no subsequent liability decisions in state or federal court.

[c]In C. 65 the court denied plaintiffs' motion for a preliminary injunction. Later, the defendants introduced some social fact evidence (and the plaintiffs sought, without success, additional social fact information through discovery), but the court issued no further decision on the merits. Since the social fact evidence was submitted too late to be considered, C. 65 is listed for statistical purposes in column 1 and is entered in brackets in column 2.

related to the subject matter areas of the litigations. Thus, social fact evidence was presented in all of the special education, intradistrict school finance, and corporal punishment cases, and in at least half of the cases involving grooming and dress codes, student discipline, and mandatory leave policies.[20] Historical fact issues predominated in the 11 First Amendment cases (speech, association, religion).

In certain subject areas, the novelty of the claim also appeared related to the use of social fact evidence.[21] Corporal punishment, for example, is a policy over which reputable education experts fundamentally disagree. Both cases in this area involved complex social fact evidence.[22] In the maternity cases, by way of contrast, social fact presentations were commonly made prior to the Supreme Court's decision in *Cleveland Board of Education* v. *La Fleur,* but their use subsequently declined.[23]

### *Judicial Methods for Resolving Social Fact Disputes*
#### Avoidance Devices

In analyzing how judges actually deal with contested social fact issues, we found that in most instances they utilized various "avoidance devices" which allowed for the disposal of plaintiff's claims on the merits without close scrutiny of the parties' competing social fact arguments. Four types of judicial rulings or actions amounting to avoidance devices were identified: irrelevance, burden of proof, maximizing areas of agreement, and social fact precedent. (See table 6 for a breakdown of the cases.)

*a) Irrelevance.* The first basic "avoidance device" in table 6 is "irrelevance," which refers to decisions that rejected a party's evidence on the grounds that it was outside of the scope of the legal rule being applied. In most cases such evidence was related to "subsidiary policy arguments."[24]

A prime illustration of such irrelevance was presented in *Banks* (C. 5) where the plaintiffs challenged a school rule requiring all students to stand respectfully during flag salute ceremonies. Expert witnesses for the defendants testified that this rule promoted students' respect for their country and the rights of others. The courts held, however, that the only respect that mattered—legally—was respect for the rights of religious minorities who considered it a violation of their faith to take part in any way with the flag salute ceremony.

*b) Burden of proof.* On any given issue, the applicable law places on one party a burden of persuasion. In the present context, failure to meet a burden of proof means that even though judges either find or assume (for argument's sake) that a party's social fact evidence is valid,

Table 6
Judicial Methods for Resolving
Disputed Social Fact Issues[a]

| AVOIDANCE DEVICES (1) | | | | FACT-FINDING (2) | |
|---|---|---|---|---|---|
| Irrelevance (1A) | Burden of Proof (1B) | Maximizing Areas of Agreement (1C) | Social Fact "Precedent" (1D) | One Party Only Submits Social Fact Evidence (2A) | Both Parties Submit Social Fact Evidence (2B) |
| 5 | 3 | 9* | 17 | 11 | 4* |
| 39 | 16 | (23)* | (23)* | 15 | 8 |
| 40* | 18[a] | (41)*[b] | (41)* | 25* | 22 |
| 47 | 21 | 43 | 51 | 31[c] | (23)* |
| | 58* | (52)*[d] | | 32 | 29* |
| | 59* | | | 34[c] | 30 |
| | 61 | | | 37 | 44 |
| | | | | 38 | 45*[b] |
| | | | | 57* | 48 |
| | | | | | (52)*[e] |
| N = 4 | N = 7 | N = 5 | N = 4 | N = 19 | |

[a]This table breaks down 35 of the 36 "social fact" cases listed in appendix C, column 7 (omitted is C. 2; see table 4, note a). Three cases (indicated by parentheses) are listed in more than one column because separate social fact issues were treated in different ways. These cases *are* included in the column totals, which add up to 39, although only 35 cases are involved. The breakdown of column 2 into subcolumns A and B, is based on the distinction (used previously in table 4) between single party and multiple party evidentiary submissions. An asterisk (*) denotes a case in which "complex" social fact evidence was introduced (see table 5, note a).

[b]This method was used in relief proceedings. Note also that in C. 45 the court relied on the expertise of a master it appointed, rather than on a party's witness, for its findings.

[c]In Cs. 31 and 34 the court rejected the expert testimony introduced by one party.

[d]This method was used in both liability and relief proceedings.

[e]This listing refers to a dispute between plaintiffs and settling defendants, on the one side, and the intervenor defendants, on the other, regarding due process procedures.

they nevertheless conclude that the weight of the evidence was insufficient to decide the issue in that party's favor. For example, in *Dostert* (C. 21), the court struck down a school dress code basing its decision on the legal premise that the code must be shown to be a "compelling part of the public education mission." Though the court did not deny the defendants' experts' claims that permitting long-haired students to play in the marching band or on the basketball team had some negative impact on music and sports competitions, it found that the degree of negative impact alleged was insubstantial.

A variation of this avoidance device is sometimes found when a holding uses either the traditional "rational relationship" test of equal protection or the newer, middle-ground equal protection standard the requires proof of "substantial rationality." Under the former standard, the court refused to second-guess the judgment of public officials if they set forth any plausible justification for a disputed action. When plaintiffs satisfy the prerequisites for application of substantial rationality, however, the officials have the burden of showing that their policies have a substantial factual basis. The shifts in burden between these two tests become crucial when social fact evidence is inconclusive—i.e., when there is no consensus among experts and in professional literature. Hence, in Cs. 58 and 59 the courts applied the traditional test and determined that the debate on the educational value of corporal punishment was far from settled; they therefore upheld the school boards' practices as meeting minimum rationality under the circumstances. By way of contrast, the defendants in *Andrews* (C. 3) failed to meet their burden—under the substantial rationality test—because conflicting testimony about the alleged role-model effect on students of a teacher who was an unwed parent was found to be inconclusive.

*c) Maximizing areas of agreement.* Courts sometimes resolved social fact issues by basing their decisions on areas of agreement between the parties, thus avoiding any need for independent judicial fact-finding. The clearest instance of such reliance is, of course, court approval of a settlement between the parties by entry of a consent order. In *PARC* (C. 52), a class action, e.g., plaintiffs' key factual contention was that all retarded children could benefit from educational training. If this social fact premise were upheld, the legal conclusion would follow that depriving them of such services was discriminatory. At trial, plaintiffs submitted extensive expert testimony and detailed exhibits containing social science data and analyses on this issue. Rather than refute this presentation, the state defendant negotiated a settlement which accepted the premise that retarded children are educable and entitled to appropriate public educational service.

In *Frederick L.* (C. 23), a special-education class action, each side presented one nationally known expert in the field of learning disabilities ("LD") and a number of other lesser known, but qualified administrative, psychological, and pedagogical experts who disagreed on basic definitions and statistics. Nevertheless, the court based some of its major social fact findings upon isolated areas of agreement among the parties and their experts. For example, although the experts testified that there were wide differences of opinion among researchers and policy makers concerning the precise definition of "learning disability," and the percentage of children who suffered from that handicap, the parties stipulated for the purposes of the case that there were about 8,000 "LD" children enrolled in Philadelphia public schools. Starting with the parties' agreement on this point, the court pieced together a number of facts and figures in the record which had not been systematically organized by any of the parties. It then reached the conclusion that the defendants' information concerning the remedial services already available—though not specifically designed for LD children—combined with their admission about the number of LD students, did not support their assertion that virtually all LD children, including those not individually identified, were receiving appropriate instruction. The court supplemented its analysis with a memorandum, written by a Pennsylvania Department of Education official, which stated that services for LDs in Philadelphia did not meet state standards.[25]

Tacit, as well as explicit, admissions of agreement were utilized by the courts. For instance, in *Brown* (C. 9) the parties' experts disagreed as to whether disparities in per pupil expenditures for educational staff would detrimentally affect educational quality. The court accepted the plaintiffs' harm thesis on the grounds that the school board's voluntary decision to take some corrective measures to equalize staffing allocations was "an admission" showing the board's own belief that these expenditures must have some educational importance.[26]

*d) Social fact "precedent."* On occasion a judge will "follow" the fact-finding conclusions of another governmental body regarding social fact questions similar to those presented in the pending litigation. The "precedent" used may be found in a statute, administrative decision, or another court's opinion.

A prime example of this method is *Paxman* (C. 51), a mandatory maternity leave case in which evidence was presented prior to the Supreme Court's decision in *La Fleur*, but in which the decision was issued subsequent to that major precedent. The trial court opinion ignored specific testimony of defendants' experts and instead stated that in light of the *La Fleur* holding, the defendants' purported justifications were insubstantial *per se.*

The courts ruled in Cs. 23 and 41 that they did not have to consider, *de novo*, questions as to whether individual screening of all suspected LD children was a necessary element of legally mandated "appropriate education" or whether regular school programs could provide appropriate education in some instances for LD children. Relying on applicable state statutes, they concluded that the legislature(s) had already decided that individualized identification and use of specialized programs were mandatory.

Approaches to Fact-finding

Out of the 65 cases in our sample, in only 19 did the courts scrutinize social fact evidence in order to reach their conclusions. In 9 of these cases (listed in table 6, col. 2A), only one party submitted social fact evidence. In the remaining 10, where both parties submitted social fact evidence, only 5 involved "complex" issues.[27] Thus, the cases resulting in close judicial scrutiny of contested complex social fact questions constituted only 8% of the overall sample.

The fact that in practice judges tend not to base their rulings directly on complex social science fact-finding does not, however, answer the ultimate question about the courts' capacity to comprehend and to decide these issues when they attempt such an undertaking (or the normative question of how often such attempts should be made). Qualitative assessments of this sort are inherently resistant to quantitative statistical sampling techniques;[28] a thoroughgoing analysis of judicial fact-finding capacity must, therefore, await the detailed case studies presented in chapters 6 and 8. Nevertheless, some useful general insights can be obtained from a brief discussion of certain patterns that emerged from those caselets in which judges did scrutinize disputed social fact issues.

In the cases involving relatively noncomplex factual issues, the courts utilized standard judicial techniques of assessing the relative credibility of competing experts and evaluating the weight and significance of the documentary evidence. For example, in *Fabian* (C. 22) and in *Heath* (C. 30) the judges believed plaintiffs' medical testimony that women usually can fully perform their teaching duties during the second trimester of pregnancy and probably well into the third trimester, and rejected the statements of defendants' psychologists that extended mandatory maternity leave was necessary for the emotional well-being of mother and child. In Cs. 44 and 48 both sides submitted substantially similar statistical data, but differed on the inferences to be drawn. The court in each case found one party's inferences to be "more closely reasoned." In C. 8, the court believed the defendants' experts (an education professor and school officials) who testified that mandatory student cafeteria service as practiced in Hawaii served a valid educational purpose, and rejected the contradictory opinion of plaintiffs' expert (a high school teacher).

Judicial fact-finding in the more complex cases was also largely based upon standard judicial techniques rather than upon independent analysis of asserted causal hypotheses or controversial data.[29] In these cases, however, assessments required the mastering of specialized concepts and technical language in order to grasp the arguments. The judges apparently did not have major difficulties in obtaining at least a working familiarity with those concepts that they used to assess the credibility of key witnesses, in lieu of undertaking a full independent analysis of the data.

This interesting pattern is illustrated by *Armstead* (C. 4), a suit brought to challenge a policy enacted by the Starkville School District during the transition period from a segregated to a unitary school system, a period of enrollment decline and faculty retrenchment. The board's new policy stated that a teacher would not be reemployed unless he or she either held a master's degree or achieved a minimum cutoff score on the Graduate Record Examination (GRE). The plaintiffs charged that the application of these criteria resulted in a disproportionately large layoff of black teachers. Without much difficulty, the court found that plaintiffs' statistics supported this allegation and ruled that the defendants had to justify the validity of hiring requirements that resulted in such a disproportionate pattern. After considering testimony on behalf of each party by experts in the field of testing, the court concluded that the defendants had failed to prove compellingly the job-relatedness of the employment requirements in terms of accepted psychometric practices. To reach this conclusion the court relied mainly on the strong credibility of plaintiffs' expert, a representative of the Educational Testing Service, which had created the GRE. This witness stated that the exam was designed to assess ability to pursue graduate studies, not to teach elementary and secondary schoolchildren.[30]

Courts sometimes resolved disagreements between qualified experts by believing the witness who appeared to have concrete experience with the immediate problem or came from the immediate geographical area. In *Frederick L.* (C. 23), e.g., the judge credited the opinions of a local Philadelphia witness over the views of an out-of-town witness who was unfamiliar with specific local conditions.

A similar process occurred in *Gurmankin* (C. 29), a case in which defendants argued that a blind teacher could not recognize students, maintain discipline, administer tests, or stay abreast of scholarship. The plaintiffs relied heavily on the testimony of an expert witness, Dr. Edward Huntington, who had studied the performance of blind persons teaching in a number of locations throughout the country.

Though the court noted that Dr. Huntington's generalizations were not based on the study of any large urban school districts,[31] his credibility still compared favorably with that of the two school district officials who had administered plaintiff's oral examination and had "had no prior contact with blind teachers or blind applicants for teaching positions." The court found that the final grade was "based, at least in part, on misconceptions and stereotypes about the blind, and on assumptions that the blind simply cannot perform."[32]

*Mills* (C. 45) shows how a court may engage in complex fact-finding only after a long and fruitless effort to resolve major issues by avoidance techniques. In 1972, the court found the defendants liable for denying educational opportunities to handicapped and "problem" children. Without trial, the court granted summary judgment to plaintiffs based on areas of "agreement." During the next two and a half years and over the plaintiffs' objections, the court relied primarily on the defendants to devise and implement a comprehensive remedy plan and repeatedly encouraged the parties to negotiate compromise solutions to their disagreements. In 1975, this phase ended abruptly. A hearing was held at which plaintiffs submitted extensive, essentially unrebutted evidence about the inadequacies of the defendants' programs and plans. The defendants submitted statistics and other materials to show that they were making reasonable progress in implementation, considering budgetary constraints. At this stage, the judge finally reviewed and analyzed the history of defendants' actions and concluded that they could have provided adequate education to many more children than they had actually served.[33]

### III. SUMMARY OF FINDINGS

1. Formal discovery procedures were utilized in 38 out of the 65 cases, with extensive discovery taking place in 11. Overall, the discovery process appeared to be an effective means for obtaining and organizing extensive information, since no adversarial resistance occurred in most of these situations and courts were required to decide disputed submission of discovery information in only 7 cases (11%).

2. Of 41 cases that were decided after submission of social fact evidence, approximately half (20) involved one-sided data presentations by only the plaintiff or only the defendant. However, in 70% of the one-sided evidentiary submission cases, the opposing side prevailed in the actual decision. Analysis of the factual issues revealed no readily recognizable pattern of adversarial distortions caused by evidentiary imbalance.

3. In most educational policy litigations, judges did not actually decide complex social fact issues. Social fact evidence was introduced in 42 out of the 65 cases. In about half of these, the courts utilized "avoidance devices," thereby resolving the legal issues without directly scrutinizing the conflicting social fact evidence.

4. In 19 cases (31%) judges actually engaged in social fact-finding. In 9 of these instances, evidence was submitted by only one party. Only 5 of the 10 remaining cases—in which both parties submitted social fact evidence—involved "complex" facts. Thus, detailed scrutiny of complex social fact materials submitted by adversaries occurred in only 8% of the sample cases.

5. Generally speaking, judges were averse to basing (or at least acknowledging that they were basing) their decisions on causal social fact hypotheses. Instead, fact-finding primarily relied on traditional judicial techniques such as assessing witness credibility, or on reportorial social fact data and "interpretative judgments." In these cases, judges appeared to have reasonable working knowledge of social science concepts and terminology.

# 5

## Caselet Analysis
### *Remedial Capability Issues*

———◆———

The remedial decree is the core of the new public law litigation model. It is the most significant factor in judicial policy making and, therefore, the stage of litigation that brings to the forefront issues of judicial intrusiveness into traditional administrative and legislative domains. Plaintiffs prevailed in 41 of our 65 cases, and remedial orders were issued in virtually all of them. In studying the remedial process in these cases, we analyzed both the extent of judicial intrusion into traditional legislative and executive domains (as measured by the content of the decrees, party participation in their formulation, and the use of monitoring mechanisms) and some indications of the effectiveness of such judicial remedial intervention in terms of compliance, modification of decrees, and adaptability in responding to implementation problems.

## I. EXTENT OF JUDICIAL INTRUSION

### *Content of Decrees*

Chayes's public law litigation model contemplates a broad remedial decree establishing the boundaries within which systematic policy changes are to be implemented. We term this type of remedy a "reform decree." The key characteristics of a reform decree are that it creates or restructures basic institutional arrangements and that it involves a continuing relationship between the parties and the court.[1]

Although plaintiffs in our sample cases generally would request reform decrees, judges frequently ordered less intrusive remedies in cases where plaintiffs prevailed. The main alternative form of such relief we have termed "a self-executing judgment." A self-executing judgment directs the defendant merely to refrain from a discrete action or course of conduct or to restore a readily attainable *status quo*[2] and does not normally demand further court involvement. Injunctions requiring school districts to rescind censorship regulations or to expunge the disciplinary records of children suspended without hearings are an example. Also included in this category are declaratory judgments, which clarify the legal rights of the parties (and presumably set the controversy to rest) without issuance of any coercive order by the court.[3]

In order to measure the extent of judicial intrusion into local policy-making processes, we classified all of the 41 caselets in which plaintiffs prevailed into the categories of "reform decree" and "self-executing judgments." Reform decrees, which included not only systemwide institutional restructuring, but also complex, continuing judicial oversight mechanisms, were obviously highly intrusive. Self-executing judgments did not call for such continued judicial supervision; but those that resulted in systemwide institutional reforms would be more intrusive than those that involved only changes affecting a single individual (e.g., expunging the disciplinary record of a particular student). Therefore, within the broad category of self-executing judgments, we also distinguished between "systemwide self-executing injunctions," "systemwide declaratory judgments," and "individual self-executing injunctions." Roughly speaking, therefore, remedial orders were classified on a continuum of intrusiveness ranging from reform decrees on one extreme to systemwide self-executing injunctions, systemwide declaratory judgments, and individualized self-executing injunctions on the other.

Specifically, our analysis indicated that reform decrees, the most intrusive approach, were entered in 15 cases, systemwide self-executing injunctions in 17 cases, systemwide declaratory judgments in 3, and individual self-executing injunctions in 6. If all cases involving systemwide institutional reforms are considered intrusive, then 85% of all cases in which plaintiffs prevailed or 54% of the entire sample resulted in such intrusion. If judicial intrusion is considered substantial only when policy changes are brought about through continuing judicial involvement in or supervision of compliance (i.e., pursuant to reform decrees), then 37% of the cases in which plaintiffs prevailed or 23% of the entire sample would be intrusive (see table 7).

Why were reform decrees—the form of relief generally requested by plaintiffs—not used in most of the cases in which plaintiffs prevailed? Two interrelated factors appear to provide an explanation. First, judges, consistent with traditional canons of judicial caution,

Table 7

Intrusiveness of Relief[a]

| REFORM DECREE (1) | SELF-EXECUTING JUDGMENTS | | | RELIEF DENIED (5) |
| | Systemwide Self-executing Injunction (2) | Systemwide Declaratory Judgment (3) | Individualized Self-executing Injunction (4) | |
|---|---|---|---|---|
| 4    48 | 3    51 | 21[b] | 2[c] | 1    39 |
| 6    49 | 5    54 | 22[d] | 19 | 7    40 |
| 15    52 | 16    60 | 56 | 26 | 8    42 |
| 18 | 17    61 | | 29 | 9    46 |
| 23 | 20    62 | | 50 | 10    47 |
| 27 | 24 | | 64 | 11    53 |
| 28 | 25 | | | 12    55 |
| 30 | 31 | | | 13    57 |
| 33 | 34[e] | | | 14    58 |
| 37 | 38 | | | 32    59 |
| 41 | 43 | | | 35    63 |
| 45 | 44 | | | 36    65 |
| N = 15 23% | N = 17 26% | N = 3 5% | N = 6 9% | N = 24 37% |

[a]The classifications in this table are based on district court orders, without regard to possible modifications or reversals by appellate courts.

[b]In addition to the declaratory judgment, the court issued an individualized injunction.

[c]The injunction in this case was not a final order but a temporary restraining order (TRO). The court abstained on the merits, continuing the TRO in effect, and there was no order closing out the case.

[d]Note that although coercive relief was denied, in this case, substantial policy changes were made prior to issuance of the liability decision.

[e]The injunction provided very minor relief. Overall, defendants prevailed on the merits in this case.

generally attempted to impose the least intrusive method of vindication of a plaintiff's rights. Second, in many types of cases, effective relief was feasible without resort to reform decrees.[4]

In some areas the subject matter of the case seemed to be related to the court's decision to enter a reform decree. Reform decrees were consistently absent in cases dealing with student appearance, First Amendment speech and religion matters, [5] and maternity leave. On the other hand, they were regularly employed after liability findings in the areas of special education, elections, and intradistrict finance.[6]

*Party Participation in Decree Formulation*

We measured "intrusiveness" not only by considering the basic structure of the remedial order, but also by examining the extent to which the policy changes that were ordered were formulated by the defendant institution itself, as opposed to outside agents (including the judge, a master, the plaintiff, or other parties or *amici*). Obviously, the greater the extent of substantive policy formulation by the judge or other outside agents, the greater the "intrusion" into school board affairs.

In analyzing the 15 reform decree cases, we found three main kinds of input from defendant public officials: incorporation of legislative and administrative policy standards which had been enacted outside the context of the litigation; primary drafting of the remedial plan; and negotiating of the details of the remedy with the plaintiffs.[7] Explicit categorization of the cases according to mode of participation proved to be unworkable because in most of the cases more than one type of participation was operative. We consider it significant, however, that in 13 out of the 15 reform decree cases, one of the three modes of participation played a significant role in shaping the remedy. A brief narrative description of these modes will illustrate the basic trends in these cases.

## Incorporation of Legislative/Administrative Standards

In 8 of the 15 reform decree cases there were legislative or executive enactments which provided authoritative policy frameworks for at least some aspects of court-ordered relief. For example, in *Baughman* (C. 6) the state education authority enacted "student involvement" guidelines that were incorporated by reference into the settlement of that student free speech case. In *Graham* (C. 28), a student discipline case, the Nebraska legislature passed a due process law with stricter procedures than the court had ordered; the decree was thereafter amended to include the stricter statutory procedures.[8] Federal standards in the Education of the Handicapped Act entered into the remedy formulation process in all of the special education cases in our sample (Cs. 23, 41, 45, 52).[9] Similarly, federal Title I standards were important in Cs. 48 and 49.[10]

## Primary Drafting of Remedial Plan

In five cases, the court indicated that it would prefer a remedial decree based on a plan drafted by the defendants. This approach was exemplified by *Dameron* (C. 18), a reapportionment case in which the defendants sought to delay all remedial action until after the results of the next regularly scheduled decennial census would become available. The court ordered the defendants to submit an interim reapportionment plan, and this plan was approved. When the next census became available, the defendant submitted four alternative permanent plans, and the plaintiff submitted one. The court selected one of the defendant's plans as the basis for its final remedial plan. In *Givens* and *Graham* (Cs. 27 and 28), the courts basically approved the school board's newly adopted student discipline due process regulations, although in *Graham* the plaintiffs obtained some amendments to defendants' standards.

A more complex but less successful defendant plan drafting occurred in *Mills* (C. 45). There, the initial reform order allowed the school board to draft a comprehensive plan. In the years that followed, however, the terms and implementation of the plan repeatedly proved inadequate. Ultimately, the court transferred much of the planning responsibility to a master.[11]

## Negotiated Relief

The parties negotiated agreements about important elements of relief in at least 8 of the 15 reform decree cases. In *PARC* (C. 52) there was a consent judgment (no liability determination) and very detailed remedial planning. In *Nicholson* (C. 49) and *Baughman* (C. 6), declaratory judgments were combined with consent remedial orders. Similarly, there were major settlements with regard to some—but not all—issues and parties in *Armstead* (C. 4), *Natonabah* (C. 48), *Kruse* (C. 41), and *Frederick L.* (C. 23).

A hybrid process of decree formulation is found in *Coalition* (C. 15), a case involving school board election irregularities. A court-appointed panel of experts participated in an intensive series of negotiations between the parties. Although the defendants ultimately consented to the election plan drawn up through this process, they considered the process itself to be an improper intrusion into the domain of the regularly appointed election commissioners.

The judges' role as actual draftsmen of reform decrees usually was surprisingly limited. We identified only one reform decree which clearly was drafted by a judge *sua sponte*.[12] This does not mean, however, that the judges were altogether passive. On the contrary, they played important roles as catalysts, mediators, and supervisors of the policy formulation process. For example, in *Natonabah* (C. 48) the court rejected an initial plan submitted by the federal defendant but kept negotiations going until enough progress was made that it became necessary, in the court's opinion, to enter an injunction against that defendant.

## Monitoring Mechanisms

Institutional reform can rarely be accomplished in a single act. After the entry of a reform decree, it normally will take some time to determine whether an order is fully effective or needs to be modified. Consequently, courts often consider it necessary to establish information feedback systems to keep track of the progress and problems of implementation. For the purposes of our analysis we identified, in ascending order of "intrusiveness," three specific monitoring modes—retention of jurisdiction; reporting requirements; and remedial discovery.

*Retention of jurisdiction* means that, after the final judgment, the court remains readily accessible to any party that is encountering implementation problems. *Reporting requirements* are directives to the defendant to compile specific information and to file it with opposing parties, and/or with the court. Finally, *remedial discovery* occurs when a court grants discretionary authority or specific rights to obtain certain information to either plaintiffs' counsel, a master or independent expert, or a task force (typically consisting of party representatives, experts, officials, and perhaps representatives of affected interests). In some instances, task force groups are given a mandate to investigate facts actively and to recommend solutions to particular implementation problems.

Consistent with our findings on decree content and defendant participation, the extent of judicial intrusion in terms of monitoring devices was oriented in the direction of minimal intrusion. The great majority of reform decrees provided for continuing jurisdiction[13] and reporting requirements.[14] By way of contrast, remedial discovery was authorized in less than half of the reform decrees.[15] These results are summarized in table 8.

Special education cases were disproportionately represented in more intrusive monitoring categories. In *Frederick L.* (C. 23), *Mills* (C. 45), and *PARC* (C. 52), the court relied on masters and sometimes other experts armed with investigatory authority to monitor implementation and to determine whether defendants were proceeding expeditiously. Similarly, in *Nicholson* (C. 49) expertise was needed to help the court determine what progress it could reasonably expect of

Table 8
Monitoring Devices used in
the 15 "Reform Decree" Cases

| JURISDICTION RETAINED[a] (1) | REPORTING REQUIREMENTS (2) | REMEDIAL DISCOVERY (3) |
|---|---|---|
| 4 | 4 | 4 |
| 15 | 15 | 15 |
| 18 | 18 | 23 |
| 23 | 23 | 45 |
| 27 | 27 | 49 |
| 28 | 37 | 52 |
| 33 | 41 | |
| 37 | 45 | |
| 41 | 48 | |
| 45 | 49 | |
| 47 | 52 | |
| 52 | | |
| 12 | 11 | 6 |

[a]Unfortunately, judgments and orders are frequently ambiguous about the length of jurisdiction. Ordinarily, if the order does not provide otherwise, the clerk of the court will terminate a case if it appears that "all contemplated judicial action has been taken" and the case has been "dormant" for one year. (Memorandum to Chief Judges of District Courts from R. Kirks, Director, Administrative Office of the United States Courts, p. 1 [June 15, 1973]). In a certain sense, however, jurisdiction continues indefinitely with a permanent injunction and the case can be reopened upon a plausible assertion that it is being violated. Among the reform decree cases, one (C. 6) had a record that was too ambiguous to provide a basis for classification. Among the non-reform decree cases (which are not listed in this table), remedial discovery was ordered in C. 29, and reporting requirements were used in C. 51. Jurisdiction was retained in Cs. 2, 3, 22, 29, 44, and 51. The records in Cs. 16, 38, 43, 60, and 63 were ambiguous with respect to retention of jurisdiction.

the state and local school district in changing programming to remedy past violations of Title I. The court sought to avoid the severe statutory sanction of withholding all Title I funding, but, at the same time, it relied on a panel of three independent experts to make certain that reforms were being instituted with all possible speed.

In assessing the intrusiveness of these remedial monitoring mechanisms, it is also important to consider the attitudes of the parties concerning these procedures. In three cases, the parties agreed to the appointment of a master or panel and jointly selected the persons to fill these positions: *Frederick L.* (C. 23); *PARC* (C. 52); *Nicholson* (C. 49). In *Armstead* (C. 4) the broadening of remedial discovery was part of a straightforward *quid pro quo*. The court granted defendants' request for a one-year extension of the original deadline for restoration of a specified racial balance in their teaching staff, but, simultaneously, expanded the plaintiffs' rights to investigate the district's employment practices to determine if there were insufficient minority applicants as the board claimed. Only in two cases, *Mills* (C. 45) and *Coalition* (C. 15), did the defendants object to the use of masters/experts for monitoring and planning.

## II. Effectiveness of Judicial Intervention

### Compliance

The most straightforward measure of the effectiveness of a judicial order is compliance, i.e., whether the court's directives are carried out. Our sample revealed that basic compliance with court orders by school officials predominated overwhelmingly over instances of either intentional or unintentional noncompliance. The most direct indicator of this pattern was the rarity of the filing of contempt motions by plaintiffs in order to compel enforcement against recalcitrant defendants.[16] On the docket sheets of the 41 cases in which some measure of relief was granted, we found only 4 filings of contempt motions against allegedly recalcitrant defendants. Only 2 of these motions were resolved by formal court action, and in only 1, *Mills* (C. 45), was the defendant actually held in contempt.[17]

Another indicator of compliance was a strong consensus among attorneys interviewed that compliance had been effected. Relying primarily on interview response data, we classified the 41 cases according to the decree of compliance under four headings: "complete," "partial," "token," and "none." We found that there was complete compliance in 32 cases (78%) involving remedial orders. Moreover, no cases were rated "token" or "none." This left a balance of 9 cases with some compliance problems (see appendix C, col. 8).

Four of the 9 partial compliance cases involved major difficulties in implementing reform decrees (Cs. 4, 45, 49, 52). For example, in *Nicholson* (C. 49) there were substantial problems in bringing Title I program services up to the articulated legal standards, and in *Armstead* (C. 4) the defendants failed to restore the minority teaching representation to 30%, as the court had ordered. In each of these cases, eventual compliance was achieved, sometimes after modification of the initial decree. The other cases listed as "partial compliance" involved reports of retaliatory actions against the individual plaintiffs

(Cs. 2, 21) or questions as to whether compliance was adequate (Cs. 37, 48, 64).

## Modification of Decrees

A second measure of the effectiveness of judicial action is the extent to which an original remedial decree needs to be modified in the course of its implementation. On the one hand, the need for such modifications may indicate an inability of the judicial process to foresee potential problems and to engage in comprehensive policy making. On the other hand, the judiciary's ability to respond to developing problems may be a reflection of its adaptability to implement comprehensive reforms over an extended period of time.

Our analysis of the 41 remedial decree cases indicated that very substantial modifications were made by the district courts in 3 cases, substantial modifications in 4 cases and minor modifications in 4 others. Overall, then, substantial modifications or very substantial modifications were made in 17% of the cases. Of the subset of 15 cases, substantial or very substantial modifications occurred in 6 cases and minor modifications in 1. Thus, as might be expected, modifications occurred disproportionately in the reform decree cases where judical intrusiveness and ongoing supervision were greatest; in almost half of these the original decree proved to be inadequate, at least to some extent (see appendix C, col. 9).

The need for modification appeared to be prompted by three main types of difficulties: (a) unforeseen developments; (b) cost factors; and/or (c) "complexity" obstacles. A brief discussion of cases exhibiting each of these kinds of difficulties will serve to indicate the type of problems encountered by courts in implementing educational policy changes and the mechanisms utilized to deal with them.

### Unforeseen Developments

In *Armstead* (C. 4), the court found that the use of the Graduate Record Examination scores for the selection of teachers was racially discriminatory. In addition to enjoining further use of the test and ordering compensation for individual plaintiffs who had suffered injury from its use, the court directed that all new teaching positions be filled with qualified black teachers until the previous proportion of blacks on the teaching staff (30%) was achieved. Because this specific figure proved impossible to achieve, despite apparent good-faith efforts by the defendants, the court granted three waivers of original compliance dates (at least two with the consent of the plaintiffs). Thus, it seemed that the court's original target figure was too ambitious. Yet, the court's inclusion in the original decree of waiver procedures based on good-faith attempts may be viewed as an indication that the court was not purporting to establish a precise quota figure, but was attempting to apply maximum pressure on the defendants to proceed in good faith.

Other examples of unforeseen developments are provided by *Frederick L.* (C. 23), where teacher strikes and a fiscal crisis prevented the district administration from meeting the directives in the relief orders, and *PARC* (C. 52), where substantial problems arose in finding sufficient numbers of qualified teachers and psychologists to fill new special education positions.

Cost Factors

When reform decrees involve substantial new costs, a school district must either obtain new appropriations or shift funds from other programs. Either approach may meet resistance from officials, taxpayers, or persons served by the other programs. The implementation of the *PARC* decree (C. 52), e.g., was initiated by an infusion of new state money, but as remedial proceedings continued years later, the parties and the court, attuned to political pressures, tacitly accepted the concept that the proportion of the state budget earmarked for special education should constitute a firm limit on state resources available for these programs. Cost factors were not dealt with as amicably in *Mills* (C. 45), where the defendants' main defense to the plaintiffs' liability claim was insufficient resources. The court ruled that the lack of funds could not lawfully be borne disproportionately by handicapped children. In the remedial stage, funding problems again were cited by defendants as a reason for noncompliance. The court gradually escalated the coerciveness of its response, ultimately appointing a special master to oversee implementation.

In dealing with the funding problem, courts have a narrower range of options than legislative and executive decision makers. They cannot directly order changes in taxation and appropriations to pay for improved services for the victims of discrimination. But they can make clear that they will order equalization of program efforts among different categories of school children. Thus, in *Hosier* (C. 33) the judge conceded that admitting alien children to public schools would cause overcrowding—absent new appropriations—but insisted that an equalization of services (even if it meant leveling down) was constitutionally required.

But, like "political" decision makers, the courts could approve—in the short run, at least—compromise program goals to remedy violations. Such pragmatism was evident, for example, in the equalization process in the Title I cases (Cs. 48 and 49) and in the first remedial phase of *Kruse* (C. 41). Unlike the political process, however, in judicial remediation there was a liability finding which served as a standard of accountability that had to be satisfied in the long run. The possible tension between short-term flexibility and ultimate accountability is exemplified by *PARC* (C. 52), where the elusiveness of the legally required goals have perpetuated protracted relief proceedings carried out in the form of interparty negotiations (see below).

"Complexity" Obstacles

The third pattern in decree modifications involved a generalized breakdown in implementing far-reaching policy reform, a failure which cannot be attributed primarily to unforeseen developments or cost factors. The pattern is exemplified by *Nicholson* (C. 49) and by the later stages of *PARC* (C. 52).

In 1972 the court in *Nicholson* found that the state's supervision of Title I fund applications and programs in the School District of the City of Philadelphia was unsatisfactory. In 1973, the state defendants and the plaintiffs stipulated to a relief order which, among other things, empowered a committee to direct changes in current Title I programming and in applications for future funding. In carrying out its functions, the committee evaluated numerous programs and made recommendations in relation to them. Often these were strongly criticized by parent groups and by city school district officials. The state and the plaintiffs blamed the school district for the slim record of accomplishment in the case. Until then, however, the district had not been a party in the case because, at the urging of the state and plaintiffs, the court had denied its motion to intervene. But now the local district and the teachers union were allowed to intervene, and subsequent negotiations involving these new parties resulted in 1975 in a new consent decree. In marked contrast to previous events, there apparently was substantial compliance with the final 1975 consent decree to which the school district and the union—in addition to the plaintiffs and state education authority—had pledged their support.

In *PARC*, after a five-year period in which considerable progress had been made in implementing the basic consent decree,[18] the plaintiffs moved for contempt because many other substantial court-

ordered reforms allegedly were still overdue. Judge Becker dramatically changed the climate of this situation from confrontation to
cooperation by instituting a process best described as "Task Force"
negotiations. At monthly sessions all the policy and administrative
issues relevant to a "comprehensive" approach to the policy changes
mandated by the reform decree were considered.

A typical meeting of the PARC task force in April 1978[19] was attended by approximately 15 state and local education officials and
representatives from the PARC organization and from the city
teachers' union. Counsel for the parties were seated around a large
conference table that had been set up in the center of the courtroom.
Judge Becker arrived (wearing a business suit rather than a robe) and
announced the agenda. He then explained for the benefit of the
dozen or so spectators that the last part of the conference would be a
"gripe session" at which time they could discuss specific problems.
The minutes of the last conference were read, and persons who had
reporting or negotiating tasks presented their reports. The main issues discussed were: (a) the district's progress in creating Individual
Educational Plans and completing "staffing" for each retarded child;
(b) the hiring of sufficient numbers of physical therapists; and (c) the
qualifications of special education teachers.

To maintain the atmosphere of a working task force Judge Becker
sidetracked comments which he called "strident" or "rhetorical" and
tried to keep the focus on specific factual assertions. What is the
problem? Is more information needed? What is a realistic plan? Who
will be in charge of implementing it and reporting back to the conference group?

Not every issue was tackled head on, however. One of the delicate
aspects of Judge Becker's role was to decide which problems should
be ruled out of the scope of the group's function. For example, at the
April meeting he declined to take on the following issues: (a) the
merits of a legislative bill establishing a residency requirement for
Philadelphia teachers; (b) a dispute about whether clinical instruction
must be part of inservice training for teachers of the severely retarded; and (c) a dispute about the closing of a particular school.[20]

This detailed judicial involvement in *PARC* was an exception to our
general finding that courts in educational policy cases do not tend to
become fully involved in the myriad day-to-day administrative and
policy ramifications of their orders. It is interesting to note that in
contrast to analogous desegregation cases, Judge Becker's intervention was tolerated, and perhaps even welcomed, by all the parties

concerned. Clearly, this acceptance or receptivity enhanced his efforts
We shall return to a consideration of these comparative issues in the
concluding chapter.

### III. Summary of Findings

1. Remedial orders were entered in 41 of the 65 cases in our sample. Reform decrees were issued in 15 out of the 41 cases, systemwide self-executing injunctions in 17, systemwide declaratory judgments in 3, and individual self-executing injunctions in 6. The subject matter of the case appeared to be related to the issuance of a reform decree.

2. In 13 of 15 "reform-decree" cases, defendants or related public agencies substantially participated in the formulation of the policy content of the decree. This participation took the forms of incorporation of statutory or regulatory standards, basic drafting of orders by defendants, or negotiation of details of the remedy with the plaintiffs. Only one clear example of a judge acting as sole drafter of an extensive reform decree was identified.

3. In terms of three basic mechanisms for monitoring compliance with judicial decrees (retention of jurisdiction, reporting requirements, remedial discovery), the courts tended to emphasize the least intrusive devices. Thus, retention of jurisdiction occurred in 13 of 15 reform decree cases and reporting requirements in 11 of 15, whereas remedial discovery was provided in 6 cases.

4. Compliance was achieved without use of the court's ultimate sanctioning authority. Only 4 contempt motions were filed in the 41 remedial stage cases, and only 1 of these resulted in a judicial contempt finding. Data based on attorney interviews indicated full compliance with court orders in 32 cases, partial compliance in 9, and no cases with "token" or "novel" compliance.

5. Modifications of remedial orders in response to implementation problems occurred in 11 of the 41 cases, or 27% (7 being "substantial" or "very substantial"). These modifications were primarily related to general implementation problems—unforeseen difficulties, cost, and "complexity"—rather than to inherent deficiencies of the judicial process.

# PART III

Judicial-Legislative
Case Studies

# Introduction

———◆———

Our analysis of 65 representative cases in Part II reveals a number of findings on the legitimacy and capability of judicial involvement in social policy making. In order both to illustrate in greater detail these quantitatively based findings and to expand upon them, with more qualitative analysis, we have undertaken comprehensive studies of two complex federal court cases, and, for purposes of comparison, of two closely related instances of state legislation.

The cases, *Chance* v. *Board of Examiners* and *Otero* v. *Mesa County Valley School District No. 51,* presented highly diverse characteristics. The first took place in the nation's largest urban area, New York City, the second in rural Colorado; the first challenged job selection and retention procedures affecting school supervisors, the second raised broad questions about learning. In *Chance,* plaintiffs prevailed and obtained substantial long-term relief. In *Otero,* plaintiffs were denied relief. But perhaps most significant, when viewed from the fourfold analytic perspective utilized in Part II, these two cases reveal the very trends and characteristics delineated in the areas of principle/policy, interest representation, fact-finding, and remedies.

Donald Horowitz has warned researchers to be "chary of drawing inferences about the courts without an institutionally comparative frame of reference."* Such a comparative frame of reference is possible in *Chance* and *Otero,* where several of the key educational issues addressed in the courts were being considered, almost simultaneously, by the state legislatures having jurisdiction over the school district defendants. In Colorado, where Chicano groups sought bilingual bicultural programs, the court denied relief and the legislature "granted" it. In New York, where blacks and Hispanics sought an

*D. Horowitz, The Courts and Social Policy 18 (1977).

73

affirmative action employment remedy, the court granted it and the legislature "denied" it. Thus, those parallels provide a rare opportunity for comparison of a public law litigation with the process of legislation.

Our four case studies are based on official documents and records, as well as personal interviews with key participants. (Persons interviewed are listed in appendix D). For the court cases, we reviewed voluminous files (pleadings, briefs, submissions, and transcripts of trials and hearings) as well as background reports, newspaper accounts, and other documents; we interviewed expert witnesses, representatives of affected interests, and one of the judges. In studying legislation, we reviewed official committee records and heard all significant hearings and debates, either through personal attendance or by listening to available tapes,* and interviewed key legislators, staff assistants, lobbyists, and advocates.

In order to provide a comparative framework integrating the caselet and the detailed case study findings, we have focused in these four chapters on the facts and issues most relevant to principle/policy, interest representation, fact-finding and remedies. At the end of each case study there appears a "summary perspective," which analyzes the study from this fourfold point of view.

---

*In Colorado, all committee hearings and debates were available through complete recordings stored in the State Archives. In New York, Michael Rebell attended all relevant meetings and debates in his capacity as Special Counsel for the Assembly Education Committee. To maximize objectivity, Arthur Block conducted interviews with the New York legislators.

# 6

## New York Judicial Case Study
### *Chance* v. *Board of Examiners*

———————◆———————

In September 1970, a complaint was filed on behalf of a class of black and Puerto Rican educators alleging that the traditional examination system used to license principals and other supervisors in the New York City public school system was racially discriminatory. During the next eight years, this employment discrimination claim mushroomed into a litigation that confronted such complex educational policy issues as validation of standardized tests, definition of the qualities of professional competency and leadership, parental involvement in the hiring and evaluation of professional personnel, and affirmative action requirements for staff layoffs. In short, virtually every aspect of the employment of supervisory personnel in New York City came under the direct and indirect supervision of the United States District Court. Thus, *Chance,* in which plaintiffs sought to change public policies affecting millions of New Yorkers, provides a classical example of the "new model" litigation pattern.

The *Chance* case study is organized as follows: Section I describes the historical background of the lawsuit. Section II summarizes the entire federal litigation—introducing the parties and judges and reviewing the main court proceedings and out-of-court negotiations. Section III analyzes the treatment of policy-related issues in the courtroom. Since most important remedial decisions were made outside the courtroom, Section IV focuses on the negotiation process in the Task Force (a group composed of representatives of the plaintiffs and of the Board of Examiners) and also examines the role of the Chancellor's Advisory Council, a representative body of affected interest groups, which helped to formulate procedures for selecting supervisors.

## I. Historical Background

To understand the central issues in *Chance,* we must first go back to 1898, the year when the New York State Legislature established a Board of Examiners for the New York City school system. The creation of this body was one of the accomplishments of a reform movement that aimed to rid the school system of corrupt, clubhouse appointments and assure the application of "merit and fitness" principles in the selection of teachers and supervisors in New York City.[1]

Though dependent on the Board of Education for its funding, the newly created Board of Examiners was given considerable power and autonomy. One of its major functions, the one over which there would be significant debate in the *Chance* lawsuit, was to design and administer tests for the purpose of evaluating the qualifications of applicants for supervisory positions.[2] From that time on, all appointments to supervisory positions in New York City were made through "competitive" examinations which it conducted. This meant that the Examiners promulgated "eligible lists" which ranked candidates who had passed the examination according to their test scores. When a vacancy became available, it was filled by the selection of one of the first three persons on the current list. No new tests could be administered until the list was exhausted or had expired at the end of four years.

The implementation of the Decentralization Law in 1970, however, had an important effect on these long-standing procedures. Under the new law (N.Y. Ed. Law Art. 51–A) 31 community school boards were created that had primary jurisdiction over the operations of the New York City elementary and junior high schools. These community boards were now empowered to appoint supervisory personnel. Their appointments were still limited to those persons on the Examiners' "eligible" list, but under the liberalized law "eligibility" was redefined. Ranking restrictions were eliminated, and the community school boards could now select any person who had passed the examination regardless of his or her score.

In September 1970, Boston Chance, a black, and Louis Mercado, a Puerto Rican, were serving as "acting principals" in two New York City elementary schools. Both had been assigned to their positions by their respective community school boards, and both possessed all the credentials and experience required for state certification as a principal. Neither, however, had the city license necessary for a permanent appointment. Chance had failed the Examiners' written test, and

Mercado had refused to take it on the grounds that it was discriminatory in nature. Because they had been appointed during the interval
which sometimes occurred between the exhaustion of an old list and
promulgation of a new one, their boards would have to dismiss them
as principals as soon as the Examiners certified a new list. Chance and
Mercado, therefore, sought the help of the NAACP Legal Defense
Fund to challenge the allegedly discriminatory licensing tests and to
seek an injunction against the issuing of a new eligible list.

In 1970, 55% of the students in the New York City's public schools
were black or Hispanic, but only 1% of the permanent principals in
the city's schools were members of these minority groups.[3] Bare
statistical comparison between students and supervisors does not
prove discrimination in licensing, since supervisors are not drawn
from the student population, but from a labor pool of educators.
Nevertheless, the figures were striking, particularly when compared
with those from other urban areas which had far greater numbers of
minority supervisors, and no selection agency like the Board of
Examiners.[4]

But the race discrimination question had also become intertwined
with policy issues that went beyond the immediate individual interests
of minority candidates denied access to advancement. With the implementation of decentralization in 1970, many community school
board members, particularly in black and Hispanic areas, became
increasingly dissatisfied with the pool of licensed persons from which
they could select supervisors for their schools. They believed that
many of the minority candidates who had failed the licensing examinations were uniquely qualified to deal with motivations and learning
needs of minority youngsters, were especially committed to the school
community, and were able to serve as crucial "role models" for the
minority children.[5] Hence, the testing system was seen as an anach-
ronism in a decentralized governance system and as a basic deterrent
to the advancement of qualified candidates.

Apart from the allegations of racial bias, the Examiners had been
criticized over the years by investigators who concluded that existing
procedures failed to identify the best candidates and actually screened
out many who were not only competent, but in fact superior.[6] But
despite the many critical reports and intense local political opposition
to the examination system, no fundamental reforms were enacted by
the state legislature. A token recognition of the testing problem occurred in 1967 when an amendment to N.Y. Ed. Law §2569 was
enacted requiring the examiners to "periodically review the validity

and reliability of examinations as well as examination procedures."
But two years later, during the legislative battles concerning school
decentralization,[7] advocates of more sweeping reform were defeated.
The Board of Education had introduced legislation that would have
abolished the Examiners. It was supported by established New York
City civic groups such as the Public Education Association and the
United Parents Association. These initiatives ran into solid opposition
not only from the Examiners but from groups such as the supervisors'
and teachers' unions.

The Examiners and their supporters viewed this extensive criticism
as a confirmation that their procedures were effective in protecting
the civil service system from obvious pressures to relax standards and
foster an environment of patronage and favoritism.[8] Many New York
City educators also saw the Examiners as the bastion of defense for a
merit system which was under siege. Increased discretion for community boards was viewed by some as synonymous with nepotism,
patronage, corruption, and the parceling out of leadership roles in
the public school system to unqualified individuals.[9] Maintaining a
passing grade on a written test was, therefore, seen as the minimal
possible assurance of a person's ability to supervise or administer
public school programs, and the extensive safeguards against partiality in test grading were considered proof of objectivity.[10] In a broader
framework, the Examiners' testing procedure was seen as reflective of
the American work ethic and of the ideal of upward mobility through
fair competition.[11]

Though both the critics and defenders of the Examiners agreed on
the importance of selecting supervisors on the basis of "merit and
fitness," they disagreed on the critical question of defining these
terms. The Examiners' tests emphasized general knowledge, mastery
of New York City administrative practices and regulations, ability to
analyze educational issues, and articulation of refined English grammar. The critics, however, wanted assessment to be based on evaluation of actual performance, use of techniques such as simulation tests,
and measurement of personal qualities such as leadership ability and
empathy for minority children. Complicating this basic disagreement
over the qualifications of a "good" supervisor were difficult state-of-
the-art questions about psychometrics. What validity standards should
the Examiners' present testing techniques be required to meet? Are
there feasible techniques for objectively and impartially assessing the
supervisory qualities that the Examiners' critics said were essential?

In short, then, the criticisms of the examination system that were about to be brought before the court were not novel. They had been the subject of earlier reports and investigations; they had been a focal point of the legislative debate concerning school decentralization; and they were contemporaneously under investigation by the city's Human Rights Commission.[12] But in none of these forums had there been a clear resolution of these issues. Because they believed the time had come to obtain a firm decision, Chance, Mercado, and their supporters decided to seek their day in court.

## II. Eight Years of Litigation: A Summary

### The Parties

*Chance* v. *Board of Examiners*[13] was filed by Boston Chance and Louis Mercado against the Board of Examiners of the City School District of the City of New York, the Chancellor of the City School District of the City of New York, and the Board of Education of the City School District of the City of New York. The plaintiffs, Chance and Mercado, were both interim principals who were automatically to lose their jobs when the Examiners posted a new eligible list for their positions. They sued on behalf of themselves and on behalf of all black and Hispanic educators who might be subject to discrimination because of racial and ethnic bias in the Examiners' testing procedures for licensing supervisors and administrators. The broad class action allegations were reflective of the plaintiffs' objective to bring about systemwide structural reforms. Representing them in this effort was the NAACP Legal Defense Fund, a public interest law firm obviously experienced in the use of race discrimination litigation aimed at institutional reforms. Elizabeth Bartholet DuBois was lead counsel.[14] Also supporting the suit (and acting as lead counsel on layoff issues) were lawyers from the Public Education Association (the "PEA"), a civic organization founded in the nineteenth century to help monitor and improve the quality of education in New York City.

From the moment suit was filed, the three defendants adopted mutually antagonistic positions. Harvey Scribner, the chancellor (who was the chief operating officer of the city school district), all but joined the plaintiffs in condemning the Examiners' testing and licensing procedures. The Examiners, on the other hand, headed by Dr. Murray Rockowitz, a staunch defender of the Examiners' basic testing procedures, strongly contested the plaintiffs' charges of bias in testing. The Board of Education (which had previously supported proposed legislation to curtail the powers of the Examiners) failed to reach a consensus among its members on a response to the lawsuit and, consequently, did not even file a formal answer admitting or denying plaintiffs' allegations.

Leonard Bernikow, Assistant Corporation Counsel of the City of New York,[15] represented the chancellor and the Board of Education (hereinafter referred to as the "Board"). The equivocal positions of his clients often left Bernikow without firm instructions about how to proceed. The Examiners, in the meantime, exercised their option to retain outside counsel[16] and retained Saul Cohen, a senior partner of the prestigious firm of Kaye, Scholer, Fierman, Hays and Handler.

Besides those named in the complaint, other groups and individuals tried to intervene as parties at various stages, most notably, the Council of Supervisors and Administrators, AFL-CIO (the "CSA"), the collective bargaining representatives of school supervisors and administrators in New York City. The suit was less than two weeks old before the CSA applied—unsuccessfully—to intervene as a party defendant. They renewed their intervention efforts three times during the life of the case. Twice they were granted limited intervention rights to contest particular issues.[17] Shortly after federal court jurisdiction terminated in June 1978, the CSA filed its own action in state court challenging the Board's continuation in modified form of some of the procedures originally adopted in *Chance*.

Another putative intervenor was the New York City School Boards Association whose membership consisted of most of the local community school boards in the city. On all of the licensing and testing issues the plaintiffs were generally perceived as vigorously promoting community board interests, but when the issue of affirmative action arose, the community boards sought direct representation. Although the court denied it party status, the association successfully argued to the court as an *amicus curiae* on this issue for certain positions, which, in fact, were different from those asserted by any of the parties.[18]

### The Judges

*Chance* passed through the hands of three different trial court judges. Originally presiding over the case was Walter R. Mansfield, who was later elevated to sit on the Second Circuit Court of Appeals. The importance Judge Mansfield and his brethren attached to *Chance* is reflected in the unusual manner of his withdrawal from the case. After assuming his appellate duties, he continued by special appointment to preside over *Chance* for 2½ years. He relinquished this role after the Judicial Council for the Southern District of New York agreed to designate a specific successor, Harold Tyler, Jr., rather than have the case reassigned, in the usual manner, by the luck of the draw. Judge Tyler presided over the case from January 1974 until April 1975, when he left the bench to accept President Ford's appointment as Deputy United States Attorney General. At this point, Milton Pollack became the third and last trial judge in the case, presiding from April 1975 until termination of federal jurisdiction in June 1978.

During the course of the litigation, there were numerous appeals to the Second Circuit Court of Appeals. The Second Circuit reviewed the issues in the case in depth on four occasions.[19] These appellate decisions were rendered by three-judge panels with rotating memberships. All appeals from the Second Circuit to the United States Supreme Court were dismissed without comment.

### Court Proceedings

The plaintiffs' immediate goal was to preserve the positions of Chance, Mercado, and other minority persons holding temporary supervisory appointments pending a trial to determine the complex questions of alleged discrimination in the existing licensing and appointment system. Plaintiffs quickly obtained emergency relief in the form of a temporary restraining order in which Judge Mansfield enjoined the Examiners from issuing any new eligible lists for supervisory appointments.[20] The Examiners were allowed, however, to continue to conduct examinations.

The plaintiffs' next step was to obtain a preliminary injunction extending the temporary injunction up until the trial date (and, if possible, expanding the scope of the temporary order to prohibit further examinations). Because Judge Mansfield insisted on a thoroughgoing investigation of the racial impact on the tests, the preliminary injunction proceedings lasted ten months, and included surveys, expert analysis of statistics and test validity, and court hearings. Judge Mansfield granted the motion and issued a detailed opinion which found preliminarily that the present examination system caused adverse racial and ethnic impacts that had not been justified. He ordered a continuation of the freeze on issuance of new eligible lists, barred the permanent appointment of supervisors, and prohibited the Examiners from administering any tests. The Examiners appealed.

The preliminary injunction created a vacuum. (Ordinarily, such an order is a simple prohibition temporarily preserving the *status quo,* pending a full trial on the issues.[21] In this case, however, the preliminary injunction brought a large and dynamic personnel system to a sudden halt and made inevitable the adoption of major procedural reforms on an interim basis. Since permanent appointments were barred, an enormous number of "acting" appointments had to be made so that the school system could function. The court, alone, was ill-equipped to deal with the numerous legal and educational details involved in establishing a system for selecting such acting personnel and supervising their work. Fortunately, it was spared this task because Chancellor Scribner and the Board of Education moved quickly (in consultation with interested persons and groups) to draft "interim" procedures which were generally perceived to be fair. The Board adopted these procedures and established a permanent consultative group of nine members appointed by the chancellor, known as the Chancellor's Advisory Council. Over its five-year lifetime, the council formulated extensive revisions to the original procedures (officially promulgated as Circular 30: 1972–1973); advised community school boards about methods for selecting supervisory personnel; heard grievances about violations of the selection procedures; and kept abreast of the *Chance* negotiations dealing with establishing new licensing and appointment procedures.

In April 1972, the Second Circuit dismissed the Examiners' appeal from the preliminary injunction. At that time, three of the four permanent members of the Board of Examiners either had retired or were about to retire.[22] Rockowitz, the only examiner in active service, proposed modified examination procedures that, he believed, would satisfy any reasonable concerns about testing bias and would be a basis for resolving the litigation. If Judge Mansfield did not approve his proposal, he was ready to press ahead for a full trial of the liability issues so that the Examiners could be vindicated and the injunction against examinations lifted.

Judge Mansfield tried to steer clear of the Rockowitz proposal and to move toward a broader-based settlement. His approach received crucial support when the Board of Education announced in June that two vacancies on the Board of Examiners would be filled by Sylvester King, a black, and Nathan Quinones, a Puerto Rican. Both King and Quinones had been critical of the Examiners' previous practices and had openly advocated a settlement of the case. The Examiners' attorney, therefore, agreed to return to the bargaining table. In September 1972, the group ultimately known as the "Task Force" was created; its ten members consisted of parties, attorneys, and testing experts.

Eight months later, in May 1973, there was agreement among Task

Force members on an operational plan for interim licensing and a skeleton plan for a future permanent licensing system. Both plans accepted a concept of on-the-job performance evaluation: Under the interim procedures, individuals with proper course credits and experience could be appointed to supervisory positions (usually by community school boards); after five months they were to be subject to a performance evaluation on the job. The permanent plan required applicants to pass a battery of modern, validated tests administered by the Examiners (the procedures and content were still to be worked out) before being eligible for initial appointment, to be followed by a final on-the-job evaluation.

Several pressures had dictated that temporary licensing procedures be instituted while the Task Force was still negotiating the terms of a permanent system. Plaintiffs wanted to alleviate the serious morale problems of acting supervisors, many of whom were black and Hispanic; these stemmed from the fact that they were performing the duties of permanent administrators with inappropriate pay and very little job security. The Examiners and their staff also had morale problems. Having no tests to design or administer, they suspected that an extended period of inactivity might erode traditional perceptions of their indispensability. Thus, both parties' interests were served by a joint proposal to Judge Mansfield for the partial lifting of his injunction.[23] This proposal became the July 1973 Final Judgment.

Judge Tyler took over Judge Mansfield's role in the midst of a number of skirmishes about the interpretation and administration of the new interim procedures. The CSA had been granted intervention on the question of whether the injunction nullified transfer rights set forth in their collective bargaining agreement. Plaintiffs were demanding a voting role for community board representatives who sat on the performance evaluation panels (and some community board officials were asserting this position outside the courtroom through protests and obstruction). The Examiners were being criticized for failing to start actual performance testing. And, despite Judge Tyler's imposition in March 1974 of a May deadline for completion of Task Force negotiations, the parties reported at that time that they still had failed to resolve important differences about entry level testing. Judge Tyler dealt swiftly and decisively with these issues, ruling against the plaintiffs on the community board representation issue and resolving the major problems delaying final agreement on the testing issues. These rulings led to a March 1975 order adopting the Permanent Plan.

One reason the issues about the Permanent Plan went unresolved for so long is that the parties and the court became sidetracked by difficult and controversial questions about affirmative action. In their original papers and arguments, the *Chance* plaintiffs had not sought an affirmative action hiring remedy (e.g., a specific minority percentage of new appointments), probably because they were confident that the community school boards would hire minority applicants in substantial numbers once the licensing procedures had been reformed.[24] In 1974, however, a significant number of supervisors were expected to be laid off throughout the school system because of New York City's financial crisis. Without court intervention, the traditional "last hired, first fired" (or reassigned) concept was expected to cause a disproportionate laying off of recently hired blacks and Hispanics. To protect recent gains in minority representation, the plaintiffs asked for an affirmative action remedy. Judge Tyler eventually issued an order which provided such a remedy, an order which was substantially modified by the Second Circuit on appeal.

Judge Pollack took over the case in April 1975, soon after Judge Tyler's affirmative action order and ruling establishing the procedures for developing a permanent examination system. Less than a year later, however, the Examiners grew suspicious about the Board's failure to approve and officially release the job analysis report of a consulting firm it had hired; this report was to provide the basic data for the Examiners to commence test construction under the Permanent Plan. To force an explanation from the Board, the Examiners made a motion to implement the Permanent Plan in accordance with the consent judgment. The Board's response was a motion to modify the Permanent Plan in a way that would eliminate any major role for the Examiners in the future licensing system. Step 1 eliminated the use of instruments such as written tests, simulation tests, and optional performance tests of candidates in present jobs; instead the entry level screening was to be a verification of the applicants' credentials and a simple writing exercise. At Step 2, responsibility for administering the on-the-job performance test was to shift from the Examiners to the community school boards. The Examiners were outraged and accused the plaintiffs, who actively supported the Board's motion, of reneging on the bargains struck in 1973 and 1975.

Judge Pollack, however, adopted most of the Board's proposal and ordered a Modified Permanent Plan. In Step 1 tests were replaced by an "unassembled examination" which was essentially a credentials check. But Judge Pollack refused to reallocate the function of administering on-the-job performance tests to the community school boards. He stated that the Examiners' control over such evaluations was necessary for compliance with state statutes.

Within only ten weeks of entry of Judge Pollack's order, the Second Circuit reviewed it and vacated it. The thrust of the appellate opinion was that after eight years of litigation, *Chance* had narrowed itself to a jurisdictional battle between two local agencies. Because both the 1975 Permanent Plan and the 1976 Modified Permanent Plan satisfied all federal law requirements, the remaining issues had to be determined under state law. So, to the chagrin of all the parties, the Second Circuit gave no definitive answer to the question of how to set up the permanent examination system; instead, it told Judge Pollack that he had an absolute deadline of June 1978 for ending jurisdiction in the case. It also informed the parties that they were free at any time to take their dispute to state court. After the federal court terminated its jurisdiction in 1978, the dispute between the parties on the structure of the Permanent Plan continued unabated, and further state court proceedings were initiated.[25]

### III. POLICY ISSUES INSIDE THE COURTROOM

The litigation summary presented in the preceding section provides a sketch of the extraordinarily complex panorama of technical legal issues and substantive principle and policy concerns that occupied the attention of the parties and the court over an eight-year period. Although it is beyond the scope of this chapter to recount the detailed development of each of these issues, an understanding of the manner in which the federal court handled this landmark "new model" educational litigation can be conveyed by focusing on several of the major policy-oriented issues which came before each of the three district court judges who sat on the case. To begin this analysis we have set forth in table 9 a chronology of the litigation.

### *Judge Mansfield*
Discovery: "A Heavy Investigation"[26]

After plaintiffs moved for a preliminary injunction, Judge Mansfield called a hearing at which he castigated the plaintiffs for presenting little substantive evidence of racial discrimination in their voluminous affidavits and exhibits. He said, "[Y]ou seem to think that by putting speculation in, by having somebody say that, well, he was told by somebody that somebody else had a belief or opinion that some examination tended to discourage Blacks from even applying to take

# Table 9
## *Chance* at a Glance:
## Chronology of the Litigation

| DATE | EVENT |
|---|---|
| **1970:** | |
| September 24 | Complaint and preliminary injunction motion filed |
| November 4 | TEMPORARY RESTRAINING ORDER |
| **1971:** | |
| February 17 | National Opinion Research Center appointed to undertake racial survey |
| September 20 | PRELIMINARY INJUNCTION ORDER |
| **1972:** | |
| February | Chancellor's Advisory Council convenes |
| April 5 | Court of Appeals AFFIRMS preliminary injunction |
| June | Board of Education announces that it will appoint King and Quinones as acting members of the Board of Examiners |
| September | Task Force created |
| **1973:** | |
| July 10 | Consent order APPROVED; interventions DENIED |
| July 12 | FINAL JUDGMENT binding plaintiffs, Board of Examiners, and chancellor MODIFIED PRELIMINARY INJUNCTION ENTERED AGAINST BOARD OF EDUCATION |
| **1974:** | |
| January | Case reassigned to Judge Tyler |
| April 6 | ORDER ruling in favor of Examiners on "in conjunction with" issue |
| May 24 | Parties present court with disagreements about Permanent Plan |
| July | CSA granted limited intervention; Community School Board Association granted *amicus* status |
| July 30 | EXCESSING ORDER #1 |
| November 8 | EXCESSING ORDER #2 |
| **1975:** | |
| February 7 | EXCESSING ORDER #3 |
| March 25 | ORDER adopting Permanent Plan, resolving disputes about consultants, and reporting requirements |
| April 17 | Case reassigned to Judge Pollack |

| 1976: | |
|---|---|
| January 19 | ORDER by Second Circuit Court of Appeals REVERSING Tyler Excessing Order #3 (on May 17, Second Circuit modifies its order to permit constructive seniority credits) |
| June 1 | ORDER modifying Permanent Plan |
| **1977:** | |
| August 11 | ORDER by Second Circuit Court of Appeals VACATING Judge Pollack's order modifying Permanent Plan, and directing termination of federal jurisdiction in June 1978 |
| **1978:** | |
| June 20 | ORDER terminating all constructive seniority |
| June 21 | Board of Education RESOLUTION adopting "permanent" plan and "transitory" plan for licensing supervisors |
| June 30 | Federal jurisdiction TERMINATED as to all issues |

| POSTSCRIPT |
|---|

| 1978 (cont.): | |
|---|---|
| October 12 | CSA files *Elsberg* in New York State Supreme Court, challenging "transitory plan" in Resolution promulgated by Board of Education on 6/21/78. |
| **1980:** | |
| February 15 | Judge Pollack reassumes jurisdiction only to the extent of entering CONSENT ORDER reinstating 1973 Final Judgment interim procedures through December 31, 1980. (*Elsberg* complaint withdrawn on this basis). |
| December | Results of first licensing exam by Examiners under "permanent" system show strong racial impact; chancellor calls for new test. |

the examinations, that somehow or other than is proof . . . You ought to offer what would be admissible in evidence. *This is a court of law, not a debating society.*"[27]

Yet, despite his initial impression that the exams were probably not discriminatory,[28] Judge Mansfield felt that plaintiffs' early shortcomings should not preclude a rigorous investigation of the allegation that the largest school district in the United States used discriminatory criteria to select its supervisory personnel. Intervening to an unusual degree, and acting on his own initiative, he discarded the usual formal step-by-step discovery procedures—which could have easily bogged down such a complex litigation—and ordered the parties to design a comprehensive plan for collecting the needed data. At the same time, he made himself available on a prompt and informal basis to act as an arbitrator of disputes in this undertaking.

Specifically, Judge Mansfield ordered the parties to agree on a procedure for undertaking a racial survey of persons who had taken (and passed or failed) Board of Examiners' tests during the previous three years. He predicted that this project would be relatively simple as compared to complex surveys carried out by courts in private class action lawsuits involving securities fraud.[29] However, when it became clear that such a survey required the coordinated participation of the Board of Examiners, the central Board of Education community school district superintendents, and a private consulting firm, Judge Mansfield became more, not less, insistent that the task be carried out as fully and promptly as possible.[30]

The racial survey conducted between November 1970 and May 1971 encompassed fifty previous examinations, most of which had been administered during the previous seven years. It entailed a search for the names and addresses of persons who had applied to take the fifty examinations and identification by supervisory personnel of the racial background of those still working in the school system. To learn the race of the balance of the persons on the list, a private polling firm, National Opinion Research Company, was appointed by the court in February 1971. By these methods, the race of 5,910 out of the 6,201 persons who took the supervisory examinations was determined.[31] The results provided the data for the parties and the court from which a statistical analysis could be made of the relationship between each candidate's race and his/her performance on the challenged examinations. In the long run, Judge Mansfield's insistence on detailed discovery appeared to have aided the plaintiffs, for this racial data became the touchstone of later relief.[32]

"Preliminary" Liability Findings

After completion of the racial survey, Judge Mansfield applied the two-step analysis established in private-sector employment discrimination litigation[33] to determine the liability of the defendants. The first step was to determine whether the examinations had an adverse impact on black and Hispanic applicants as measured by disproportionate failure rates. The establishment of such a statistical *prima facie* case would trigger the second step, forcing the defendants to prove that, despite the disproportionate number of failures by minority candidates, the examinations were fair and accurately measured abilities clearly related to successful performance on the job.

Despite the undisputed survey statistics which showed whites passing the exams at a 1.5 greater rate than blacks and Hispanics, Judge Mansfield's initial common-sense impression was that this did not prove discrimination.[34] But, the plaintiffs' statistician changed his mind. He selected from the large variety of license areas covered by the overall survey certain examinations that acted as critical control points for the entry of large numbers of educators into school-level leadership positions. The racial disparities on these tests far exceeded the overall differential of 1.5 to 1.0. Judge Mansfield apparently was impressed by the expert testimony that the probability that these racial differences were coincidental was "one in one billion"[35] and became convinced that a *prima facie* case had been established.[36]

Job-relatedness

The Examiners now had to carry the legal burden of proving that their tests were "job-related,"[37] i.e., that a high score on one of the challenged tests actually indicated that the candidate was qualified to run a New York City school.

The trial of the job-relatedness issue revolved around the three most dominant components of the various licensing tests—written short answer questions, written essay questions, and oral interviews. The short answer questions probed a candidate's knowledge in such areas as English vocabulary and grammar, current events, mathematics, and culture. Plaintiffs and their experts said that the actual questions were either so esoteric or so trivial as to bear no valid relationship to a person's supervisory abilities. They cited such questions as the following:

> 211. "I've Got A Little List" from *The Mikado,* is sung by (1) Nanki Poo (2) Pish Tush (3) Ko-Ko (4) Pooh-Bah"

> 218. Which of the following violin makers is NOT of the great triumvirate of Cremona? (1) Amati (2) Stradivarius (3) Guarnerius (4) Maggini

The Examiners retorted that those were unrepresentative examples and, moreover, that such multiple choice questions either had been eliminated or greatly improved.

A typical written essay question concerning educational administration was intended, according to the Examiners, to present the candidate with a serious problem-solving task. The plaintiffs argued, however, that even with the essays, successful examination performance merely measured the candidate's ability to memorize lists of pat answers.

The oral interviews were supposed to elicit problem-solving behaviors, as well as provide an occasion for the assessment of a candidate's grammar, clarity of expression, and poise. It was in this area that the plaintiffs claimed that racial discrimination was overt. It was undisputed that the oral examination teams had almost never had blacks or Hispanics in their ranks. Furthermore, plaintiffs' witnesses charged that minority group candidates had been penalized for their speech "Southernisms" and Hispanic accents.

Psychometric experts testified for both sides. The threshold technical question was whether the Examiners would have to establish the validity of their tests by using criterion referenced validation[38]—a technique recommended by the Equal Employment Opportunity Commission guidelines—which is both the most scientifically rigorous and the most expensive program to carry out. Since no such comprehensive studies of the challenged licensing tests had yet been done, the courts' acceptance of this technical argument would have assured plaintiffs' victory. But instead of dealing with this threshold question, the court undertook an analysis of whether the examinations met even the less rigorous validation standards that the Examiners admitted to be applicable. Consequently, the trial became an investigation of the job-relatedness of the tests as seen from the more flexible standards of "content validation." This approach to job-relatedness involved comparing the content of the items on the tests with the specific knowledge, behaviors, and traits needed to succeed on the job as described in a systematic, empirical analysis of the job's actual requirements. The Examiners' psychometricians testified that the Examiners' procedures were well designed to produce "content valid" examinations.

The court accepted the defendants' experts' testimony about the principles of content validation—as did experts on all sides—but it concluded that the Examiners had not implemented these principles in practice and that the licensing tests were not job related. Though this conclusion required a reasonable working knowledge of psychometric principles, it ultimately rested on traditional historical fact-finding. For example, defendants' psychometricians said that exam questions could be developed by panels of educational experts, and the Examiners cited an example of the use of such a panel. The plaintiffs, however, produced a witness who participated in one of these panels and reported that it had not been used in the way the Examiners claimed. In short, once the framework of issues was established, the court's conclusion reduced to the simple idea that the Examiners had not done what they themselves said needed to be done.

Undoubtedly, both the trial court and court of appeals felt strengthened in this conclusion because of other common-sense indicators of invalidity. Particularly significant were Chancellor Scribner's thinly veiled denunciation of the licensing procedures[39] and the persistent testimony by community school board members and superintendents that the procedures barred them from appointing qualified supervisors. Equally important was the courts' armchair judgment that the content of the examinations—"esoteric words, general cultural knowledge, expertise in current events and flawless English grammar"—did not fairly reflect the executive, managerial, and leadership qualities essential for a school supervisor.[40]


As indicated in the summary in the preceding section, Judge Mansfield's preliminary findings were never followed by full findings of fact issued after a full trial on the merits. He repeatedly advised the parties that they probably would all be better off with a negotiated plan for an examination system, rather than one imposed by the court. Even though the 1973 "Final Judgment" left the details of the permanent licensing plan still to be worked out, Judge Mansfield was willing to put the court's imprimatur on a partial settlement in order to keep up the momentum of negotiated relief. This approach, however, clearly promised to bring the court into a sort of partnership with the parties regarding future relief.

Since *Chance* never came to trial, and because the Final Judgment was a compromise document which contained no admission of liability, as disputes later arose about interpretation of the Final Judgment and other related remedial orders, Judges Tyler and Pollack had no firm reference points. Instead, they had to decide how much weight to give Judge Mansfield's "preliminary" liability findings, how much to give to the contractual aspects of the quasi-consent orders, and how much they would rely on their independent judgment about the soundness of policy arguments being asserted by the parties in the particular dispute.

*Judge Tyler*

Harold Tyler, Jr., the person whom Judge Mansfield selected to take over *Chance*, was a conscientious and tough-minded trial judge. Judge Tyler's comments on the bench, and during a retrospective interview, revealed a pursuit of two, sometimes difficult to reconcile goals—doing justice to the parties (and vindicating constitutional rights) while also keeping the court out of policy making. We will examine his attempts to resolve the tensions between these goals in the course of three disputes.

"In Conjunction With"

Under the Final Judgment's two-step interim licensing system, the community school boards that had operational control over elementary and junior high schools would appoint an acting supervisor pursuant to the Circular 30 selection procedures. After a supervisor had been on the job for five months, a three-person testing panel would visit his school and assess his actual performance. Instead of spelling out in detail the roles of the Examiners and the community school boards in this critical performance assessment process, the Final Judgment only stated generally that the Board of Examiners would carry out these evaluations *"in conjunction with"* the appointing authority and pursuant to criteria developed with the appointing authority.[41] The community school boards asserted that this language entitled them to place a voting member on each testing panel. The Examiners insisted, however, that the community board representative was to sit on a panel solely in an advisory capacity, without compensation, and that the Examiners' staff would make the final assessments. Because of this disagreement, some community superintendents refused to allow members of the testing panels to enter their schools. Thus, the interim system was stalled.

Judge Tyler, of course, had neither drafted nor approved the controversial language in the judgment. The plaintiffs urged him, nonetheless, to order the "best" solution to the dispute that would be consistent with the general purposes of the consent judgment. But Judge Tyler insisted on deciding the issue by a close reading of the disputed text. He therefore decided in favor of the Examiners. "While a substantial degree of input by the community boards surely was intended, the precise quantitative involvement by the Boards— necessarily and wisely, in my view—was left open. If the parties had intended equality of roles to a mathematically ascertainable percentage of the membership of the rating panels, the judgment as agreed upon would have so specified."[42]

According to Judge Tyler, giving the community school boards a greater role in the evaluations than was clearly set forth in the consent order would have violated the doctrine of separation of powers: "I am also concerned that you [plaintiffs] may be unwittingly asking this Court to make what I consider to be a political decision . . . [F]ederal Courts are not commissioned or empowered to make *political decisions* for the City of New York or for the community of the City of New York. I think that's a very dangerous idea."[43]

The Permanent Plan

Judge Tyler's preference for the traditional model of the trial judge's role again came under stress when the parties reported to him in March 1974 that they failed to agree fully on a joint permanent plan for a new examination system. In reply, the judge again asked the parties to try to reach a settlement, but he indicated that if they were unable to do so, he wanted the issues readied for trial. He was keenly aware that traditional trial court procedures did not lend themselves to dealing with the remedial issues in *Chance*. He said: "I am trying to point out we are not here as a legislative body, we are not an executive body, we are not an administrative agency, we are not an Appellate Court . . . [T]rial Court procedures are really counter-productive for this kind of a case, but greater minds than mine have said, 'Put it in the Trial Court.' That is where America puts all [its] problems."[44]

Plaintiffs' counsel objected to Judge Tyler's set of alternatives, stating that "the nature of the future examination system" could not be tried.[45] But Judge Tyler responded that, if negotiations failed, he would order the Examiners to submit a plan. The plaintiffs would submit objections, and any necessary hearings and arguments would be held to explore the contested issues. Further negotiations narrowed the differences between the parties, but after several months they were still at an impasse on two key issues. Thus, litigation was required on these points.

The first issue was whether the plaintiffs would have the right to participate in the selection of the two outside consulting firms which the parties had agreed would be hired to develop the job-analysis and testing instrument to be used in Step 1 of the new licensing system. The judge ruled that it would not be legitimate for the court to make

the plaintiffs "partners" with "approval" authority in test development along with the defendants.[46] Because of the important role of
the consultants in the implementation of the Permanent Plan, plaintiffs' advice should be sought, but they were not entitled to such direct
involvement in administrative matters.[47]

The second dispute concerned "reporting requirements." At issue
were (1) the kinds of records that defendants would be required to
maintain during the development of the new examination system and
in connection with administering the first generation of new tests;
(2) the information to be shared with the plaintiffs; and (3) the time
when this information would be available—before or after administering the tests. Here, Judge Tyler, though initially indicating that he
was disposed to limit drastically the role of the plaintiffs and of the
court in continued monitoring of defendants' practices, ultimately
ruled in plaintiffs' favor.[48] He ordered the defendants to prepare and
share with plaintiffs such records as would "ensure that no lengthy
and costly discovery will be necessary to aid in the determination of
whether the test meets Constitutional standards."[49] He felt that the
detailed reporting procedures were both desirable (in that they would
permit the plaintiffs to carry out an oversight role that otherwise
might be the court's initial responsibility) and necessary (in order to
allow expeditious court involvement if compliance problems should
arise).

Taken together, Judge Tyler's rulings on the "in conjunction with"
and the consultants issues might be said to show an unwillingness to
grant administrative or policy-making authority to plaintiffs unless
defendant public officials had agreed explicitly to share such authority. On the question of reporting requirements, by contrast, he
appeared to consider extensive disclosure of information to be an
important adjunct to the litigation process, even if defendants could
argue that these requirements also infringed on their administrative
policy prerogatives.

Excessing,[50] Layoffs, and Affirmative Action

Under the Circular 30 procedures for selecting acting supervisors
and the licensing procedures established by the Final Judgment, black
and Hispanic educators were assuming supervisory positions at a
greater rate than ever before. In 1974, however, these gains became
threatened by budget cutbacks growing out of the New York City
fiscal crisis. Under the seniority rules incorporated into state law[51] and

the CSA Collective Bargaining Agreement, the first persons to lose their jobs or to be reassigned would be those who had been the last hired. The latter group included many members of the plaintiff class, because the percentage of blacks and Hispanics hired after the preliminary injunction far exceeded the minority representation in the supervisory corps prior to the injunction. From the plaintiffs' perspective, the more senior persons who had been licensed and appointed under a discriminatory system were not entitled to job security preference over minority supervisors hired under the post-1971 constitutional procedures.

The Board initiated litigation on this issue by presenting Judge Tyler with proposed new administrative bylaws intended to harmonize with legal rights of preinjunction and postinjunction supervisors. The new rules involved the recomputation of seniority so that supervisors who were appointed originally as "actings" under the Final Judgment and who later passed on-the-job evaluation tests and received permanent appointments would now be given credit for the period of acting service. The plaintiffs objected to this plan. According to their projection of systemwide staffing cutbacks, the modified seniority rules would not prevent drastic layoffs of minority supervisors. They, therefore, asked Judge Tyler to suspend fully the contractual seniority rules.

Judge Tyler responded by asking the parties[52] for more facts concerning the likely impact of these rules when school opened in the fall. The Board predicted that approximately 25 supervisors would be excessed to other positions in 1974–75, that no supervisors would actually be laid off, and that therefore there was no basis for an injunction. The plaintiffs argued that the Board's figures were understated and renewed their request for sweeping relief.

The figures available in September,[53] however, showed that excessing and possible layoffs would be more extensive than the Board had predicted in July. Lifting the interim injunction would, it said, lead to the excessing of 63 supervisors, approximately 27% of whom were blacks or Hispanics, as compared with 15% minority supervisors in the entire system. The plaintiffs reiterated their objection, and Judge Tyler urged the parties to reach a compromise that would protect the federal orders in the case with the least interference in school administration and with the best accommodation to the equitable interests of white supervisors. Unsure that all these objectives could be achieved, he seemed to agree with the plaintiffs' general assertion that their class, as an entity, had a right in the context of the litigation to maintain substantially their present degree of representation in the supervisory force.

Despite the judge's urgings, however, the four active parties were unable to make visible progress, and Judge Tyler began to draft his own proposals. The first was a rather cumbersome procedure under which the loss of jobs would be rotated between lists of preinjunction and postinjunction supervisors. When this approach was criticized by all sides, he worked up another plan which prohibited any reduction in the overall percentage of blacks and Hispanics in the supervisory force. Judge Tyler said his plan was "designed to protect the basic orders in this case."[54] At the same time, however, he believed that he was entering an order " . . . which did not meddle unnecessarily or, if possible, at all in issues of state law, contract obligations and the community districts' or the central district's policy."[55]

The Board of Education strenuously opposed this second plan, contending that these rules simply were unnecessary for preventing layoffs and would increase racial segregation of the supervisory staff.[56] But while objecting to the plan's main concept, the Board urged that, if implemented, it should be carried out on a centralized rather than a community district basis, as urged by the Community School Boards Association. Judge Tyler agreed, on the grounds of "common sense."[57]

But only after the Board's procedural request was incorporated into Judge Tyler's first affirmative action order did the Board realize the magnitude of administrative problems in centralized control. Fully centralized processing would result in community districts flooding the central Board with voluminous data on abolished positions, seniority, race, and vacancies, and demands for reassignments based on constantly updated racial calculations, all of which would be much more easily calculated and implemented on a local basis. In December, at the Board's urging, the court changed the unmanageable centralized format by instituting a two-step procedure that would permit as many personnel changes as possible to be handled on an intradistrict basis by the local community districts, under central supervision.

Judge Tyler's handling of the affirmative action issue was the apex of judicial participation in the formulation of remedies in *Chance*. In the thirty-odd pages of text of the 1973 Final Judgment, the 1975 Permanent Plan, and the 1976 Modified Plan, there is scarcely a sentence drafted by Judge Mansfield, Judge Tyler, or Judge Pollack. But in the excessing/layoff controversy Judge Tyler, reluctantly,[58] drafted complex rules that were intended to balance the equities of all categories of incumbent supervisors. He felt compelled to undertake such a role despite the fact that his proposals were based on highly speculative figures concerning staffing cutbacks by the 31 community districts and the Central Board, the opening of new vacancies, and the likely "musical chairs" effects of interdistrict bumping.[59] The court also had to evaluate the anticipated administrative problems of the central and community boards, under various possible proposals, and at times it appeared that the court itself might be directly built into the administrative process.

Judge Tyler apparently believed that his active participation as a trial judge was necessary and appropriate in this particular dispute because it involved the difficult resolution of conflict between important principles. The plaintiffs' insistence on an equitable remedy for past discrimination against their class members (and the loss of their services to minority communities) had to be balanced against the defendants' refusal to penalize nonminority individuals who had neither caused nor benefited from the alleged discrimination (many of the recently appointed minority supervisors were too young to have been eligible to take the traditional exams prior to 1972). Judge Tyler's final order largely adopted the plaintiffs' perspective. Its apparent rationale was that when precise adjustment of competing equities is impossible, the court must emphasize protection for the victims of racial discrimination. The elusiveness of a conclusive resolution of the tension between these principles seemed ever present in Judge Tyler's mind, as when he remarked: "I am by no means satisfied that justice can truly be done in any of these matters . . . [W]e might end up penalizing people who have nothing to do with perpetuating or inducing discrimination. It's just an agonizing problem."[60]

The Court of Appeals, however, rejected the idea that the trial court could do "rough justice" when "perfect equity" was not achievable.[61] Even though this same court had previously approved the use of racial quotas in hiring situations,[62] it labeled as "reverse discrimination"[63] a system that would require experienced white employees to be excessed in favor of less experienced blacks or Puerto Ricans. The Court of Appeals, therefore, ordered a new remedy based on the concept of granting "constructive seniority" to minority supervisors who had actually failed a pre-*Chance* licensing exam or who could affirm that they had been "chilled" from taking such an exam.[64]

## Judge Pollack

A major shift in party alliances in *Chance* presented Judge Pollack with a difficult remedial issue in Spring 1976. The plaintiffs, who had developed the essentials of the permanent licensing plan in Task Force negotiations with the Board of Examiners, now backed the Board of Education's application to Judge Pollack for a major modification of the Permanent Plan. Sophisticated testing instruments would be eliminated from Step 1; and at Step 2, the responsibility for administering on-the-job performance tests would be shifted to the community school boards. The Examiners would essentially be left with a mere clerical function. The Examiners' cross-motion asked Judge Pollack to authorize them to complete the job analysis and test construction independently of the Board of Education and to implement the Permanent Plan as set forth in the 1975 order.

These cross-motions intertwined legal issues and policy arguments. There were three main legal questions: (1) did the modified licensing procedures set forth in the Board's new motion satisfy the merit and fitness standards of the New York State Constitution? (2) even if they did, were these procedures nevertheless in violation of New York State statutory law by denying the Examiners a role expressly devolved upon them by the legislature?[65] and (3)—the seemingly perennial question in *Chance*—what was the scope of the equitable powers of the court within the framework of the preliminary injunction motion findings, the consent 1973 Final Judgment, and the "hybrid"[66] 1975 Permanent Plan?

On the policy side, the Board argued that "the latest research" showed that job analyses and complicated structured exams for entry into executive/managerial positions were not reliable because "[O]ur experts have told us that the qualities that are necessary to make an effective supervisor—leadership qualities, creativity—are impossible to assess."[67] This opinion brought the case full circle. At one of the first *Chance* hearings, Judge Mansfield had expressed skepticism about the usefulness of a prestructured examination in testing qualities for this kind of position. When plaintiffs' counsel assured him that a valid examination could be developed and the Examiners' counsel stipulated to that fact, the judge relented.[68]

Another policy problem raised by the Board was that of the rapidly shifting student population at many schools. The changing educational needs of the students required corresponding changes in the qualifications of supervisors and a flexibility in the process which the Permanent Plan lacked. The Board foresaw problems in the future. If the Examiners simply prepared exams "in a vacuum," they said, a new *Chance* case might be instituted in another few years.[69]

The Board of Education also stressed its own fiscal problems. Budget cutbacks had already created an excess of licensed persons so that licensing new supervisors was unnecessary. Developing and administering examinations under the Permanent Plan was also needlessly expensive and should be replaced by a simpler, more flexible, and more economical procedure. Finally, the Board argued for taking performance testing out the hands of the Examiners because "the Board of Examiners in Step 2 performs no useful function."[70] Community school boards complained that examining panel members came into a school for two-day test observations with no substantial knowledge about the school and were not qualified to rate the supervisor's performance.

The Examiners countered these arguments in a number of ways. They attempted to finesse the Board of Education's policy arguments by maintaining that it was the court's role only to determine the constitutionality of the tests and not to compare their efficiency.[71] The Examiners also challenged the merits of the policy arguments by charging that the Board was manipulating the evaluations of the job analysis report it had received from its consultants, American Institutes for Research (the "AIR report"), in order to justify an essentially political decision.[72] The Examiners stated that the assessment center procedures, as outlined in Step 1 of the Permanent Plan, were viable procedures used effectively in the public and the private sector. And, although the Examiners were far from enthusiastic about AIR's job analysis, they did have confidence in the ability of their consulting firm, Development Dimensions Inc. ("DDI"), to perform the next stage of the examination development.

Judge Pollack decided to resolve these disputes without resorting to detailed hearings on the technical issues. His approach stemmed from his skepticism about the value of expert testimony in a case of this type. In one instance he characterized the assertion of a Board of Education expert witness as "the philosophical observation" of "a theorist."[73] In another, he reflected on the Examiners' expert witness by noting: "I have never known a good expert to fail to tout his own wares."[74] Although both of the boards covered themselves in cloaks of public responsibility, the judge suspected that theirs was "a dispute between petty kingdoms . . . as to who is going to conduct the affairs of the school system."[75]

In the end, the court treated policy questions as soft issues and legal

requirements of state law as hard issues. The judge granted the requested modification—but only insofar as it largely removed the
Examiners from Step 1 by eliminating the comprehensive entry level
test. In this compromise, the Modified Permanent Plan's procedures
closely resembled the interim job performance testing and licensing
procedures. Circular 30 procedures would be used to select interim
supervisors, whose on-the-job performance would be evaluated at
Step 2 by the Examiners (not by community boards). With this
change, the court concluded that the overall examination system
satisfied the merit and fitness requirements of the state constitution,
and that the Examiners had the kind of control over the design and
administration of the examinations contemplated by the legislature.

In rendering his decision, Judge Pollack was seemingly less
troubled than Judge Tyler had been about the court's exercise of
broad equitable powers in the context of the previous orders in the
case. Despite the largely consensual basis of the Permanent Plan, he
held that " . . . if its underlying objectives are capable of attainment by
simpler, more practical means, less susceptible of controversy and un-
witting perpetuation of past vices, the law allows the court in its discretion to order its modification."[76]

The Examiners appealed from Judge Pollack's order modifying the
Permanent Plan, and the Court of Appeals reversed. The appellate
opinion focused primarily on the role of the federal courts in open-
ended public policy litigation and left unanswered the main questions
about the nature of a future examination system.

The appellate court found that Judge Pollack had committed two
main errors. First, he failed to lay a proper factual foundation before
modifying the 1975 Plan. The court did not order Judge Pollack
actually to hold evidentiary hearings, however, because of the second
reason for its refusal—that Judge Pollack should not have decided
important but unsettled questions of state law. The key state law issue
was whether civil service requirements that appointments be based on
"examinations" to determine merit and fitness would be satisfied by
appointments based on a credentials review and on-the-job performance assessment, as the Board was now proposing. The appellate
court's view was that *Chance* had reduced itself to a jurisdictional
dispute between two state agencies, a dispute in which the federal
courts had no necessary or proper role to play: "At this stage of the
litigation with the parties presenting two inchoate plans, either of
which is federally acceptable, continuing supervision of this vital state
function seems inconsistent with principles of federalism."[77]

To implement its decision, the Court of Appeals ordered the district court to achieve a phased withdrawal of jurisdiction by no later than June 30, 1978. Until that date, Judge Pollack could exercise jurisdiction over remedial questions, but could not restrain any party from seeking relief in the state courts or from taking unilateral action it deemed necessary for implementing a new examination system.[78]


## IV. POLICY MAKING OUTSIDE THE COURTROOM: THE TASK FORCE AND THE CHANCELLOR'S ADVISORY COUNCIL

After Judge Mansfield entered his preliminary injunction order invalidating procedures for licensing supervisors and administrators, the New York school system operated for seven years under reasonably successful interim procedures, and the parties agreed on the essentials of a permanent new system, without the court becoming involved in administrative details or policy making. Relief from these potential administrative and planning burdens was accomplished through the activities of the Task Force and of the Chancellor's Advisory Council, whose origins and main accomplishments we described earlier. In this section, we will analyze the nature of deliberations in these bodies and try to isolate the factors responsible for their generally successful functioning.

### The Task Force

The deliberations of the ten Task Force negotiators, five representatives for each side,[79] quickly became centered on questions about the basic features of the new two-step system for permanent licensing. The two-step concept appealed to the plaintiffs, and their representatives set out to work on the details. Examiner Rockowitz opposed the concept at first because he did not want the Examiners to be in the difficult position of withholding licenses from those persons already serving in a postion with support of the local community board. The Examiners' counsel submitted memoranda arguing that under current New York State law, appointment of provisionally licensed school personnel on a regular basis would be unlawful, and plaintiffs' representatives submitted memoranda supporting the opposite position. Ultimately, these policy and legal objections were dropped, and on-the-job evaluation became the heart of the interim procedures under the Final Judgment, and one of the two major components of the Permanent Plan.

In working out the plan, the parties had to reach agreement in a number of areas, including a critical policy dispute concerning the actual role of the Board of Examiners.[80] The plaintiffs had argued that the Examiners should provide assessments which community school boards would use to determine whether the candidate was suited for the particular position to be filled. But the Examiners maintained that in issuing a license they were certifying that the recipient was qualified to fill positions throughout the city, not merely in specific community districts, and that they, therefore, had a responsibility to apply general, citywide standards of competence. Under the two-step compromise plan, the parties agreed relatively early on about those qualities that would be assessed by the examiners and reported to the community boards in the form of a "profile." But it took lengthy negotiations to agree finally on specific criteria of general competence that would be considered absolutely essential for Step 1 provisional licenses.[81]

### The Incentives for Settlement

The Task Force wrestled with a complex mixture of difficult psychometric and educational questions (how to prepare an adequate job analysis, what methods of validation are feasible, etc.) and thorny political controversies (the long-term role of the Board of Examiners, the degree of community involvement, etc.). Given these difficult issues, the extent of its deliberations and the degree of consensus ultimately reached (at least during the early stages of the litigation) are impressive.[82]

What factors were responsible for these achievements? The consistent emphasis by Judges Mansfield and Tyler on the desirability of a negotiated settlement was certainly significant. The Task Force originally came into existence because Judge Mansfield refused to rule on major issues raised by the Examiners without an attempt at intensive negotiations.[83]

But political and institutional factors external to the litigation played an important role as well. A prime impetus for stimulating serious negotiations in *Chance*, for example, was the appointment of provisional examiners King, a black, and Quinones, a Puerto Rican, in 1972, at a time when Rockowitz (then chairman of the Examiners) was apparently bent on continuing to fight the liability issue in a full trial. The Board of Education had let membership on the Board of Examiners dwindle, instead of promptly ordering civil service tests for regular appointments. It then appointed two men who played an important intermediary role because they wanted to reach an agreement with the plaintiffs on the creation of a new nondiscriminatory system that would give a greater role to community districts.[84]

Another important point is that negotiation had political advantages for both sides. If they stonewalled the case, the Examiners could count on support from only two quarters—the CSA and some Jewish community organizations. The Examiners had no guarantee that the politically appointed members of the Board of Education would continue appropriating funds for them at the levels to which they had become accustomed. The Examiners understood that to resist reformation of the examination system, with particular emphasis on increased community school board discretion in appointments, was to increase their isolation.

For the plaintiffs, a major incentive to negotiate was a commitment to educational policy objectives (particularly increased community school board control) which could not easily be presented to the court as an integral part of a remedy for a discriminatory examination system.[85] It seemed more effective to threaten the possibility of major court-ordered policy innovations in order to win less extreme concessions through immediate negotiations. Of course, the Examiners grasped the plaintiffs' strategy. They tended to stand firm on policy issues which they thought the court would consider outside its competence to resolve, so long as their position was not likely to cause a total breakdown of negotiations.

Time, however, gave the plaintiffs leverage and increased the Examiners' desire to make compromises to achieve a final agreement. When the interim procedures proved to be adequate, the Examiners were under pressure to revive their traditional testing role before too many people drew the conclusion that perhaps they really were not needed. Simultaneously, the plaintiffs' incentive for negotiating a permanent plan weakened as major features of their policy objectives became incorporated into the 1973 stipulation and the interim licensing arrangements.

In summary, the public policy context of *Chance* generated unique incentives for settlement that supplemented the traditional concerns about avoiding costly trials and avoiding exposure to the risk of an adverse judgment. The court reinforced these perceptions by emphasizing that its attempts to resolve open issues might please neither party, and might be ill-conceived because of the court's lack of expertise in testing and education. With these factors operating, the litigation served as a catalyst for productive negotiations without the court needing to become involved in the drafting of either the interim or the Permanent Plan.

### The Chancellor's Advisory Council

As explained earlier, Judge Mansfield's preliminary injunction had created a vacuum by barring the central and community boards from making permanent supervisory appointments. But in order for the system to continue functioning, an enormous number of "acting" appointments had to be made. The court was spared the task of attempting to resolve the numerous legal, administrative, and policy considerations involved in constructing such an interim system, because, to cope with this substantial administrative problem, the Board and the chancellor quickly moved to set up a process that was perceived as being fair by the plaintiffs. Built into the process was the Chancellor's Advisory Council, a group which was charged with responsibility to consult for the chancellor with interested groups about citywide standards, to devise model procedures, to recommend revised standards, to advise community school boards on local selection procedures, and to hear grievances.[86] The nine members of the council were appointed by the chancellor as individuals, but it was generally understood that they would represent the views of the educational interests and groups with which they were associated.[87]

In a remarkable chapter in the history of advisory committees to public agencies,[88] over a five-year period the council substantially performed each of its designated functions.[89] Its recommendations had as much impact as those of any decision maker in the litigation. Judged by the standards that can reasonably be applied to the diverse and politicized New York City school system, the council's interim system has worked smoothly. Though there were reports of improprieties, they were too few to allow any party to allege before the court rampant patronage, corruption, and incompetence. No party or intervenor ever suggested that the court should exercise ancillary jurisdiction over this area of administration and policy making.

The council began meeting semimonthly in February 1972. In the next five months, it elaborated on skeletal rules contained in the chancellor's original procedures by, first, defining the "vacancies" to which the rules applied (type of position, location, and reason for availability), and, second, by developing procedures for fair public notice of vacancies, and for the processing and screening of applicants. With the help of community districts and civic and education groups, citywide mandated requirements and optional local procedures were drafted. The council supplemented the optional procedures with descriptions of suggested techniques for advertising, recruiting, evaluating résumés, interviewing candidates, and evaluating on-the-job performance. These models were based on the practices that had proved successful in certain community districts. The council also served as a clearinghouse for information.

Not all community school districts, however, cooperated with the council. Under the original citywide procedures, each district was responsible, among other things, for adopting its local procedures at a public meeting and submitting them in writing for the council's review.[90] In May 1972, the council seriously considered recommending that sanctions be imposed against community boards that had not filed satisfactory procedures.[91] Instead, it proposed to the chancellor that a permanent monitoring staff be appointed to assist the council.

When the council's regulations and recommendations were formally promulgated in November as Circular 30,[92] activist parents treated it "like the Emancipation Proclamation." It gave a focus and legitimacy to their demands for specific roles in recruitment and screening of supervisors. According to the field staff of the United Parents Association,[93] most activist parents assumed that Circular 30 was Chancellor Scribner's effort to put the principles of the 1969 decentralization legislation into practice. They did not realize that the need for the regulations had been created by a court injunction. The *Chance* case thus precipitated a major event in the history of New York City school decentralization, yet for the most part the public did not at first even realize the connection.

After drafting Circular 30, the council worked on several projects related to selection of supervisors. It sponsored workshops to explain the new regulations and also to teach recruitment and performance evaluation. Beyond that, it also focused on strengthening the annual performance reviews of supervisors. It gathered information from the Board of Examiners, and the Advisory Council of Colleges and Universities in Teacher Education (ACCUTE), and briefed community school board representatives on assessment techniques. On the basis of this information, the council developed a new evaluation form to replace the outdated one in current use. Although he knew his decision would be unpopular among professional staff, Chancellor Anker (who replaced Chancellor Scribner in July 1973) put the council's form into use.[94]

Full compliance continued, at times, to be an intractable problem.

After the Bureau of Educational Staff Recruitment assumed the responsibility for seeing that all community districts filed their local procedures, formal compliance with that aspect of the regulation improved. But many grievances were instituted against the actual practices of community boards. From these reports and from their own knowledge, council members concluded that "real" hiring decisions were sometimes made during informal discussions or executive meetings of members of community boards and then merely ratified by formal votes at open meetings. Similarly, some of the candidate interviews conducted to comply with Circular 30 were *pro forma*,[95] though it was difficult in these subtle cases to prove discrimination[96] or favoritism. The Board of Education's Office of Community Affairs (created in 1973) was assigned the task of investigating complaints concerning unfair hiring actions. According to the UPA field staff, however, that office, though sometimes effective, was extremely slow in taking action and avoided serious investigation of highly politicized controversies. Council members requested a staff of professionals that would focus on compliance. This group would not only investigate specific complaints but travel around the city, sitting in on interviews, observing school board proceedings, and generally establishing a presence—a feeling of oversight—in the community districts. But the council's request never was granted.

The council, the Task Force, and the court were never formally linked.[97] But after 1974, the council's activities became more directly related to the court proceedings. The council's major project was to revise the Circular 30 procedures that had been incorporated into the *Chance* interim plan. In the revised document ("Circular 30R"), certain previously optional procedures were made mandatory; the entire circular was made applicable to all supervisory positions (not merely to actings); and there were additional clarifications and adjustments in the rules. The council submitted its draft Circular 30R to the chancellor in June 1975, but before taking formal action to ratify it, the Board of Education procrastinated and delayed for more than two and a half years.

The council's criticisms of the Board of Education's consultant, AIR,[98] and of AIR's work product, the prototype job analysis, was another area of significant council impact on pending court issues. From the outset, council members voiced doubts about AIR's qualifications to write a job analysis for a managerial position, since none of its previous work was of that nature. When the council eventually received a copy of the AIR report, it concluded that the report provided no adequate basis for constructing tests under the new examination system.[99] This conclusion was stated in a letter to the chancellor that became an exhibit in the Board's motion to modify the Permanent Plan.

The denouement of the council's involvement in *Chance*-related issues occurred between April and December 1977. At the council's April meeting, members seriously considered a group resignation as a way of protesting against the failure of the Board of Education to adopt Circular 30R (drafted by them about two years earlier) and against the Board's reluctance to investigate serious allegations of irregularities in the appointment of supervisors in the Staten Island district.[100] At the beginning of December, Chairperson Blanche Lewis tendered a letter of resignation to the chancellor. On December 8, the Board finally adopted Circular 30R. At the council's December 14 meeting, Ms. Lewis reported her resignation to the council, stressing the dire need for creating effective monitoring of the appointment system if Circular 30R was not to become simply "promotional" material. The council's future role, if any, was left unclear.[101]

What did remain clear, however, was that Circular 30R—a carefully worked-out set of procedures for reconciling parent participation, fairness to applicants, and maintenance of merit standards—was to be a lasting legacy of the council's work. When federal court jurisdiction terminated in June 1978, the Board of Education reenacted 30R as part of both its "transitory" and its permanent plans.[102]

Assessing the Council's Role

The council ably performed representation, fact-finding, policy analysis, rulemaking, and administrative functions which helped to resolve many of the problems arising out of court intervention. Over a five-year period, approximately 100 different people attended council meetings, among them school officials from the central and the community boards, members of the Board of Examiners, academicians, testing experts from private firms, and attorneys. Some persons who were invited to speak on one occasion stayed on as unofficial council members. Throughout, council deliberations had an open-minded, "academic" atmosphere with individual members representing, though not rigidly, the perspectives of their organizations. If the council had obtained actual, rather than advisory powers, or if it had been formally representational, composed along interest group lines, a more rigid atmosphere may have developed. Council Chairperson Blanche Lewis was repeatedly praised by council participants for her leadership.

Because of the frank and informed quality of council deliberations, its recommendations were perceived as serious proposals conceived in an effort to further the best interests of the school system; its statements were not the results of political bargaining, but of consensus.[103] Both Chancellor Scribner and Chancellor Anker (who quickly reaffirmed the council's charter when he took office) clearly valued the council as an important resource.[104] In retrospect, the council appeared to have made the *Chance* litigation more manageable for the court in the following respects:

1. It filled the vacuum left by the injunction by creating a basically fair and smooth-running system for acting appointments, and thus provided time for the parties in the case to develop a permanent examination system.

2. The council's acting appointment system became a laboratory for testing many of the policy arguments being deliberated in the Task Force negotiations and in the court proceedings, e.g., community participation in the selection of professionals; on-the-job performance testing; and the potential for patronage, nepotism, and racial discrimination if personnel selection was left largely in the hands of the community school boards.

3. Through its publications, workshops, and individual contacts by its members, the council explained the purpose and effect of court orders to interested persons throughout the school system.[105]

4. The council was a fact-finding group and a think tank for the hard-pressed bureaucracy of the defendant Board. of Education. Whatever disputes the council's advice and actions resolved or prevented from arising reduced the probability of such issues eventually being brought before the court for a decision.

5. The council was a forum for comprehensive consideration of the many broad adminstrative issues and policy goals that were intertwined with the more specific legal issues in *Chance*. The court's jurisdiction was basically limited to selection procedures and to personnel practices related to the invalidated traditional examination system. But the council was able to consider recruitment, selection, performance evaluation (including evaluation of both probationary and tenured supervisors), and grievance procedures, not to mention such miscellaneous topics as the appropriateness of union contract demands, sexism, and the educational expertise of candidates.

## V. SUMMARY PERSPECTIVES

### *Principle/Policy*

*Chance* v. *Board of Examiners* dramatically illustrates why the principled orientation of the judicial process often comes to be applied to complex social policy problems in contemporary society. For years, indeed for decades, the examinations given by the New York City Board of Examiners had been challenged by a wide variety of groups, and numerous study commissions and legislative committees had studied these issues. Because the controversy over the definition of "discrimination" and the meaning of "merit and fitness" was principled and profound, and the various interest groups supporting the existing system were politically entrenched, the result was a stalemate.

By 1970, the plaintiffs, as well as many school system representatives, had concluded that there was no avenue for change within the structure and that the deadlock could only be broken by resort to the federal court.[106] Frank Arricale, the Board's Executive Director of Personnel stated that the court was the best institution to resolve potentially explosive interracial and interethnic confrontations: "I think it is very convenient from the human-relations point of view for the court to do things, which, if we were to go through the legislative process, would create terrible kinds of human relations problems during the period of transition, during the change . . . Everyone accepts '*quo serpsit lex, scriptos est,*' what the law has written, it has written and so be it."[107]

The court's involvement, however, made it clear that policy and political considerations could not be divorced from the basic principle issues. Like most of the cases in our survey sample, the liability determinations were made primarily on a "principle/policy balancing" basis. In order to decide the basic constitutional issues concerning the fairness or rationality under Fourteenth Amendment equal protection standards of the New York City examination system, the court, in the preliminary injunction proceedings, had to consider the factual content of the examinations and their relation to the qualifications or duties of the job. The importance of factual and policy issues to the application of basic constitutional doctrines in a principle/policy balancing situation was graphically demonstrated by the fact that Judge Mansfield himself indicated that his initial reaction before analyzing the evidence in the case was to assume that the exam was probably fair and job-related. This impression was quickly set aside when he assessed the weight of the actual evidence produced in the case under the applicable fairness principles.

Although factual and policy issues inevitably entered into the judicial process, it is nevertheless clear that the court's principled orientation made its approach substantially different from that of the executive or legislative agencies. The policy factors were considered not in their own right, but only in relation to the basic legal principles. Note in this regard that the *Chance* plaintiffs, despite their broad policy objectives in bringing suit, basically framed their liability arguments within the limits of their principle and principle/policy claims. It was not inconsistent with this perspective, therefore, for the *Chance* plaintiffs to submit affidavits from community school board superintendents and board members saying that the examination system prevented them from providing their neighborhoods with persons qualified for local needs. Although these affidavits hinted at the broader decentralization issues that would be strongly developed at the remedial stage, they were offered in the context of the liability issues in support of the plaintiffs' basic assertions about the racial impact and the validity of the exams, and thus they cannot be considered examples of "subsidiary policy issues," as defined in chapter 2.[108] Unlike the majority (59%) of cases in our sample, the parties in *Chance* did not raise subsidiary policy issues at the liability stage. Even at the remedial stage, when policy issues inevitably come to the fore, the court tended to return to first principles (discrimination findings and original stipulations of the parties) as the context in which intricate implementation problems would be resolved.

Judge Tyler's affirmative action order illustrates the point that policy tends to become involved in court decisions to a greater extent when the basic issue presented is a "novel" question of law.[109] The difficult questions concerning an employer's affirmative action obligations during a period of staff retrenchment, were, in 1974, relatively unprecedented. In considering this novel issue, Judge Tyler apparently was influenced by plaintiffs' arguments concerning the importance of maintaining the proportional representation of minority supervisors in the various community districts. Since Judge Tyler repeatedly articulated his concern that a federal court avoid excessive involvement in policy issues, it is significant that the appellate court differed with him on this issue and held that the factors considered by Judge Tyler went beyond the scope of rights involved. The reversal of Judge Tyler's decision, therefore, exemplifies the difficulty in novel cases of sorting out precisely which policy-oriented questions will, by later judicial development, be considered legally relevant and which will be subsidiary. These uncertainties encourage litigants to present all arguable relevant policy considerations, and judges, even if generally chary of policy involvement, may find that these arguments about consequences help to clarify the basic rights and principles at stake.

Despite their repeatedly expressed reservations about judicial policy making, all three *Chance* judges intervened dramatically into traditional legislative and executive domains when they found that the plaintiffs had established a substantial principle claim. Ironically, Judge Tyler, who, of the three judges, expressed the greatest reluctance to become involved in policy-making matters, was the judge who, on the excessing issues, issued the most intrusive orders in the case. This contrast between separation-of-powers concerns and aggressive remediation of constitutional violations illustrates the pattern we found in the caselet sample.[110]

This judicial activism was accompanied, however, by the judges' self-doubts about their technical expertise for resolving disputes about statistics, psychometrics, and educational leadership. One obvious concern was that if they substituted their own judgment for that of the school officials, the court's decision might later be proved wrong. A school board has a limited "right to be wrong" because, like a legislature, it is given broad discretion to experiment (or reject experimentation) with the understanding that some new policies will not be successful. But a court is supposed to deal in questions of right and wrong and render "correct" decisions. Along these lines, Judge Tyler specifically articulated a concern that the public (and other courts) read too much into policy decisions based on particular circumstances. A judge is not, according to Judge Tyler, qualified to lay down general rules for school administration, and, therefore, a court ruling approving or disapproving procedures for appointing supervisors in New York City should not be cited as "precedent" in Chicago.

The judicial concern over adminstrative expertise and resources and the desire to forestall criticism were met in *Chance* by involvement of the parties (including, at any point in time, at least one of the defendants) in the formation of remedies. Judge Mansfield, e.g., was willing to establish a controversial interim system for permanent appointments over the objections of the Board of Education largely because the plan was supported by the Examiners and the chancellor. Judge Pollack partially modified the 1975 Permanent Plan at the request of the Board of Education, supported by the plaintiffs. In short, the judges found that some involvement in these areas was unavoidable and that many of the technical shortcomings of the judicial process could be ameliorated by harnessing the expertise and resources of the parties themselves.[111]

## Interest Representation Issues

### Minority plaintiffs

As in the majority of our caselets, the *Chance* complaint was filed on behalf of a class of minority group plaintiffs alleging discrimination. The suit was a last resort after politics had failed. Professional unions and their allies had consistently blocked efforts for major licensing reform in the legislature, even when these reform efforts had been backed by the mayor and the Board of Education.

Although the plaintiffs were specifically concerned about access for minorities, once the threshold finding of discriminatory impact was made, the court had to consider the general validity of the examinations as they applied to all candidates.[112] Consequently, the development of the lawsuit led to a comprehensive review of examination content and procedures and to the implementation of decisive reform measures which were negotiated by broadly representative bodies and which affected the employment of all supervisors throughout the city system.

### Class Action Status

Unlike the majority of cases in the caselet sample, class action certification was granted to the plaintiffs in *Chance*.[113] It was of critical importance at various stages of the suit, primarily because of the extensive duration of the "interim" remedies and because of the Court of Appeals' "constructive seniority" resolution of the excessing issue.

If the preliminary injunction in *Chance* had been quickly followed by implementation of a new permanent system, only the named plaintiffs would have been held temporarily in the positions, but all minority (and nonminority) supervisors would have quickly received the benefits of the new system. Since this did not occur, however, class action certification was important to ensure the rights and needs of all minority supervisors during the lengthy interim stages. Without class status, the court would not have had jurisdiction to enjoin the entire traditional testing mechanism and to supervise the acting appointments and interim licensing of the hundreds of affected supervisors.

*Chance* also was a case in which the attorneys for the class appeared to be fairly representative of the interests of the broad group for which they purported to speak. The litigation was widely publicized.

Prior to entering any major relief order, the court gave individual members of the class an opportunity to oppose agreements and positions accepted by the named plaintiffs. None ever did. Similarly, supervisors and other individuals had the opportunity to oppose positions taken by school officials on behalf of the "public." Broad participation of the members of the class (and others) was also accomplished through formal mechanisms such as the Task Force and the Chancellor's Advisory Council, and through informal mechanisms such as strategy sessions organized through the Public Education Association.

Multipolarity

*Chance* was a classic example of the "multipolar" new model litigation described by Professor Chayes. At the outset, diverse interests were represented, since the plaintiffs sued three separate entities, the Examiners, the Board of Education, and the chancellor, and each of these defendants brought different perspectives and different interests to the proceedings. In addition, a wide variety of educational, civic, and labor organizations, representing virtually all conceivable affected interests, managed to participate in the proceedings either as intervenors or as *amici*.

Party alliances were complicated and volatile, in contrast to the stable bipolar alignment of interests marked by two-sided adversary contests. Chancellor Scribner all but endorsed the complaint. The kaleidoscope of parties was given further twists in 1973—when Examiners and chancellor together with the plaintiffs agreed to a proposed Final Judgment which the Board of Education opposed—and in 1977—when the Board of Education joined the plaintiffs to propose changes in the Permanent Plan that would have eliminated any substantial role for the Examiners in rating and screening candidates. While the original parties advanced through the steps of this round-robin litigation contest, numerous other individuals and organizations such as the CSA and the Community School Boards Association[114] participated in particular phases of the case.

The court resisted granting full intervenor status to any groups beyond the original parties,[115] although the CSA and the Community School Boards Association were permitted to participate fully in particular issues that affected their interests.[116] The court's intervention decisions could be said to have made the remedial proceedings more manageable. By denying full party status to CSA and the community boards, the court avoided the reopening of the substantive liability issues or further appeals on these issues. At the same time, permitting these interested groups to participate as "limited intervenors" or "active *amici*" in the remedial hearings and negotiations guaranteed full input from the affected groups, input that proved important in fathoming and reconciling the complex policy and administrative issues. The extent of this input was so great that it would seem fair to conclude that substantial "issue multipolarity" as well as "party multipolarity"[117] was achieved.[118]

Public Law Advocacy Centers

The representation of the *Chance* plaintiffs was supported by foundation-funded advocacy organizations—NAACP Legal Defense Fund, Legal Action Center, Public Education Association—an illustration of our caselet finding that educational policy litigations involving major reform decrees tend to be brought by attorneys from public interest advocacy centers. In all phases of the case—but especially in the liability hearing and Task Force negotiations—it was apparent that the technical and financial resources of these groups were essential for vigorous prosecution of such an extensive reform case. So far as fairness of representation was concerned, there were no indications that abstract ideological positions of the attorneys were being pressed as part of the plaintiffs' case. On the contrary, the community control-decentralization issues that surfaced at various points during the litigation originated from the experiences and commitments of individual plaintiffs (such as Louis Mercado who had long been active in local community district affairs) and of community board members involved with them. The only reference in our interviews to a possible divergence between client and attorney interests was the PEA's long-standing public commitment to the retention of maximum classroom teacher presence as the top priority during the fiscal crisis which was inconsistent with the immediate need of the individual plaintiffs to maintain the maximum numbers of supervisory positions.[119] PEA, however, did not formally advocate supervisory layoffs in the litigation, and, in fact, largely as a result of its strong position on the excessing issues, Judge Tyler issued a quota-type remedy. Because the remedy was an anathema to the Board of Education and the CSA, ways were found to maintain supervisory positions in order to avoid layoffs that would trigger its implementation.

*Fact-finding Issues*

Information Gathering: Efficiency of Discovery

One of the most striking features of the *Chance* litigation was the virtual absence, on a docket sheet of over 400 entries, of the numerous discovery motions and counter motions one would normally expect to find in a litigation of this magnitude. The discovery process in *Chance* was impressively efficient. A prime example was the parties' cooperation in devising and implementing a survey procedure that brought before the court the precise evidentiary materials that were necessary for the initial preliminary injunction decision. Avoided were the numerous delays and interpretative complications which would have arisen if the plaintiffs had been compelled to try to recover documents and statistics on a piecemeal basis from defendants' files, or if the parties had presented separate survey results to the court and argued for the acceptance of their particular approaches. Discovery (and the broad independent resources of the parties and those affiliated with them) appears to have brought before the court a presentation of relevant facts and information.

The effectiveness of the discovery mechanism in *Chance* was at least partially due to Judge Mansfield's decision to fashion actively an efficient discovery mechanism—and to the parties' (especially the defendants') willingness to accept this novel approach. Judge Mansfield ordered the defendants to undertake their ambitious and potentially expensive information-gathering project, to which a private litigant might have successfully objected on the grounds of burdensomeness, because he believed it was the Examiners' and the Board of Education's public duty to investigate fully the basis for the claim against them.

The early success of judicial discovery techniques in the liability stage was not, however, fully matched later when it was necessary to gather statistical data on anticipated layoffs in connection with the excessing hearings. Basic statistical data presented by the defendant Board of Education was challenged by the plaintiffs, and was later substantially revised by the Board, without any clear explanation for the disparities. Perhaps Judge Tyler did not feel compelled to obtain hard, precise data at this stage, since from a constitutional point of view the magnitude of the impact of layoffs on members of the plaintiff class was irrelevant, so long as clear injury to some of the members of the class could be shown.[120]

Information Assessment

Despite the large body of social science and expert evidence presented in the preliminary proceedings, and the prospective and open-ended nature of the proposed remedies, the fundamental decisions in *Chance* exhibited little direct judicial resolution of basic social fact controversy. Numerous "complex" social fact issues were raised, but most of them were handled either through classical judicial fact-finding techniques or through the types of judicial "avoidance techniques" discussed in chapter 4.

Judge Mansfield's approach to the job-relatedness issue most clearly illustrated these approaches. Important parts of his analysis were based on "maxmizing the agreement" among the parties' experts on many technical concepts. But even when the experts disagreed, Judge Mansfield did not attempt independently to analyze the social science validity of the competing positions. Instead, he seized on certain specific "admissions" in the Examiners' papers to show that they had not put their own theories into practice. Specific "admissions" by other defendants, especially Chancellor Scribner's general condemnation of the examination system, also were important.

Judge Tyler felt somewhat disoriented by being presented with disputed issues that could not be decisively resolved by traditional evidentiary hearings and fact-finding techniques.[121] He approached the potentially complicated issues of community board participation in performance evaluations and plaintiff participation in the choice of consultants by relying on strict interpretations of the applicable text, and avoided all technical issues of evaluation or job description methodologies. Similarly, Judge Pollack's refusal to hold evidentiary hearings about the proposed modifications to the Permanent Plan indicated a reluctance to delve into social science fact-finding.[122]

*Remedy Issues*

Intrusiveness

*Chance* v. *Board of Examiners* resulted in an extensive "reform decree," and in this respect it was unlike the majority of cases in our caselet sample. The preliminary injunction halting the examination process was merely a prelude to a seven-year period during which a series of remedial decrees dramatically restructured the traditional system for selecting and assigning supervisory personnel in the New York City school system. Not only was the conventional written examination system—in effect since the turn of the century—radically reformed, but, in addition, existing union contract provisions concerning transfers and layoffs and the relative powers and roles of the Board of Education, the community school boards, and the Examiners were substantially revised.

Throughout, the court manifested a consciousness of the need to define carefully its role in the reform process to minimize the intrusiveness of its actions. This was evidenced by a consistent differentiation between principle and policy arguments, and a reliance on party participation in remedy formulation.

Three kinds of policy impact were at work in *Chance*. First, there were direct reform orders issuing from relatively traditional adjudicative processes, such as the preliminary injunction, which was based on detailed findings of fact and conclusions about violations of law. Second, there were court-ordered reform provisions which had been agreed upon by opposing parties. Some of these enacted policy choices which were not necessarily required to remedy the specific violations of law, but which were, nevertheless, generally related to the particular legal violations. (For example, the finding of discriminatory racial impact did not necessitate the replacement of a written examination system by a performance evaluation system, but the latter was clearly a remedy directly related to the legal violation.) Finally, the outermost range of impact included changes carried out administratively[123] as a result of the lawsuit, but which were not directly related to the liability findings and which were not specifically ordered by the courts. Foremost among these were the Circular 30 selection procedures developed by the Chancellor's Advisory Council and the collective bargaining agreement on excessing reached by the CSA and the Board of Education, which effectively obviated layoffs.

The effectiveness of the Task Force spared the court the responsibility of framing and implementing coercive reform orders. However, the remedial problems were inherently so complex and difficult that even within the context of generally productive negotiations, important disagreements concerning implementation arose on occasion. Consistent with its attempts to minimize its own intrusion into the educational process, the court, although willing to order extremely far-reaching and innovative policy reforms proposed jointly by the parties, generally acted conservatively when asked by one party to impose a policy concept on another.

This caution was most pronounced in critical remedial policy issues, such as the question of whether in a decentralized community school board district system the traditional role of the Board of Examiners should be maintained. As a corollary question, the role of the community school boards in any new examination system was continually raised in various forms by the plaintiffs, and by the Community School Boards Association itself when it intervened at a later stage in the procedures.[124] The district court judges in *Chance* resisted these continuing attempts to widen the policy implications of the court's involvements. Most directly illustrative of this trend was Judge Tyler's decision on the "in conjunction with" question, in which he specifically refused to consider the desirability of increased community school board participation in the examination process.[125] But, despite its fundamental caution on policy questions that were not integrally tied to the original liability claims, the court at times found itself drawn into the role of arbitrator. In 1975, for example, when a deadlock occurred, the court resolved the differences between the parties about consultants and reporting requirements.

In short, despite the broad policy impact of the *Chance* orders and the revolutionary changes they caused, the court's direct policy-making role was essentially nonintrusive. It consisted primarily of review and mediation on particular points in broad agreements largely negotiated by the parties. The court might be said to have served at the remedial stage more as a catalyst and mediator than as an adjudicator. And even in this role it is remarkable that in eight years no judge ever met with the Task Force, the Chancellor's Advisory Council, or any other working group or interest group. By comparison, judges in desegregation cases and in reform cases like *PARC* held extensive conferences with such groups. None of the Board officials interviewed believed that the court had become unduly involved in the day-to-day administration of the schools. Frederick Williams, who was Executive Director of Personnel in 1971–73, called it a "healthy intervention."

## Effectiveness

No definitive evaluation of the effectiveness of the court's involvement in New York City's supervisory selection system can be undertaken, especially since eight years after commencement of the lawsuit no permanent plan was in place and there was no indication of when, if ever, a final resolution of the complex issues set in motion by the case would be achieved. Despite this, it is clear that the court achieved a number of significant accomplishments. First, it overcame the historic stalemate and moved the system as a whole to undertake fundamental changes in an examination system that almost all agreed was in need of substantial reform. Second, it established workable "interim" mechanisms (by and large, faithfully implemented by the parties) which allowed the system to function efficiently throughout the many years that the final remedy was being negotiated. Third, the court gave impetus and sustained direction to a complex ongoing negotiating and implementation process through the Task Force and the Chancellor's Advisory Council. Given the complexity of scientific uncertainty about many of the test validation issues, as well as the intense pressures inherent in the situation, this somewhat open-ended process may, in fact, have been the best available means to attempt to resolve the licensing dispute. That is, the intractable nature of the controversies may have precluded the short-term possibility of formulating and implementing a job-related, nondiscriminatory, politically acceptable "Permanent Plan."

From this perspective, the charge that long-lasting judicial supervision of remedial reforms is a sign of judicial ineffectiveness seems inappropriate.[126] The necessity of reconciling competing political forces and of digesting major social (and technical) changes, in order to achieve implementation of meaningful reform is, at best, a time-consuming process.[127] Although it may be intolerable for the judicial system to play the role of supervisor of politically charged negotiations indefinitely, the impatience of the *Chance* judges to end their involvement may not have been appropriate. In particular, the timing of the Second Circuit order to terminate jurisdiction seems somewhat arbitrary when one considers that the federal court was playing a relatively nonintrusive role—acting as mediator and catalyst—and that all of the parties, even the defendant public agencies, wanted the federal court to resolve the outstanding disputes. The history of further delays, confrontations, and state court litigation developments in the case since the termination of federal court jurisdiction certainly does not indicate that alternative forums can deal with their problems more effectively.

The history of the lengthy remedial stage in *Chance* was, to a large extent, a story of repeated revisions and modifications of judicial orders and settlement agreements. In addition to calls for changes or interpretations, entirely new major questions such as transfer and excessing arose as the remedial process unfolded. As Judge Tyler succinctly put it, the lawsuit was "like a conflagration that one puts out in one department and then suddenly a new fire breaks out somewhere else."[128] But because virtually every affected interest participated in the detailed negotiations, and the calls for modifications were requests to revise the policies that the parties themselves had devised, it is difficult to attribute the lack of foresight or comprehensiveness of the original decrees to a failing of the court or the judicial process. In 1972 or 1973, no one could have foreseen the relevance of transfer and excessing issues. Indeed, the CSA, the group most immediately involved at a later point in the transfer issue, probably would not have initially been denied intervenor status if it could have predicted the future relevance of this issue. Similarly, the difficulties of preparing an effective job analysis under the 1975 Permanent Plan were not foreseen by the parties or the expert psychometric consultants who bid for this task. In short, it would seem that the lack of effective foresight and comprehensiveness in the remedial planning process stemmed from inherent limitations of any human attempt to deal with complex, ongoing social issues of this nature.

## Postscript

As this chapter was undergoing its final editing in December 1980, the Board of Examiners announced the results of its first administration in eleven years of a "permanent" examination procedure. The licensing test for the position of assistant principal, junior high school, yielded a failure rate for minority candidates, as far as could be determined, of approximately 90%—as compared to 50% for whites.[129] In response to these figures, Chancellor Macchiarola immediately pressed the Board of Examiners to suspend issuance of licenses based on this test, and civil rights groups began to consider possible legal action.

Events leading up to this announcement, between June 1978 and December 1980, indicated substantial difficulties in implementing the judicial withdrawal strategy that the Second Circuit Court of Appeals had imposed on Judge Pollack. In the 1977 appeal of Judge Pollack's order modifying the Permanent Plan, all of the parties asked the appellate court for a definitive ruling on the merits of the outstanding federal and state law issues. Instead, as indicated above, the Second Circuit insisted that the Permanent Plan be worked out through normal administrative and political processes, and, if necessary, state court litigation. The response of the Board of Education was the June 1978 Resolution setting forth "transitory" procedures—which did not allow for issuance of permanent licenses—together with a very sketchy "Permanent" Plan. In October 1978, the CSA filed a state court action challenging the transitory procedures. The action, *Elsberg* v. *Board of Education*,[130] asked the court to declare that persons holding licenses issued through the pre-*Chance* examination system could be permanently appointed to vacant positions. (These pre-*Chance* licenses had been declared invalid by Judge Mansfield in 1971, then revalidated as part of the interim system under the compromise 1973 Final Judgment, and again treated as invalid by the Board in the

June 1978 resolution.) *Elsberg* was settled with an agreement to rein-state the interim procedures from the *Chance* 1973 Final Judgment.

In order to immunize the *Elsberg* settlement from challenges on the ground that the interim procedures violated state merit and fitness standards, the parties went back to Judge Pollack asking him to re-open *Chance* for the limited purpose of entering an order reviving the 1973 Final Judgment. Judge Pollack accommodated this request, en-tering an order putting the interim procedures back into effect until December 31, 1980.[131] This consent order also directed the chancel-lor to: "call for new examinations for supervisory positions consistent with New York State and federal law and rules..." in cooperation with the Board of Examiners. Accordingly, the Examiners pressed forward with the development of test instruments intended to be used in accordance with the 1975 Permanent Plan. (Their consultant, De-velopment Dimensions, Inc. [DDI], preparing the junior high school principal examination as a prototypical test, and the Examiners' own staff developed two other principal examinations, neither of which had been administered by December 1980.)

The racially disproportionate impact of the junior high test has led the chancellor, the Board, the Examiners, DDI, and civil rights groups to reconsider their positions, and both the long-term and short-term prospects for the licensing system were left far from clear as Judge Pollack's order expired on December 31, 1980. The chan-cellor's immediate response has been to suggest the search for an alternative test procedure which would not yield a disparate racial impact.[132] However, the DDI test had already been represented as the best "state of the art" for evaluation of the relevant managerial abili-ties; thus the question Judge Mansfield asked a decade earlier—whether any paper and pencil test could fulfill this licensing function—was raised again.

The prospects for further federal judicial involvement are also un-certain. If the Board and the Examiners fail to agree on a new ap-proach early in 1981, uncertainty about the job status of newly as-signed supervisors will undoubtedly create pressure to seek another "temporary" extension of the *Chance* interim procedures from Judge Pollack. However, if any of the participants are inclined to press the federal court to resume an active supervisory role in the negotiation process, the 1977 appellate order will, of course, stand as a barrier—unless, perhaps, if new allegations of discriminations are lodged. Another important factor relative to judicial involvement will be the role of the Office for Civil Rights (OCR) of the Federal Department of

Education. Pursuant to a 1977 Memorandum of Understanding between OCR and the Board of Education, the Board is obligated to make all reasonable good-faith affirmative action efforts to insure that the "levels of minority participation in the teaching and supervisory service will be within a range representative of the racial and ethnic composition of the relevant qualified labor pool."[133] The Board's adoption of an examination system yielding disparate racial impact in test results might be held by OCR to be a violation of the Memorandum of Understanding, leading to administrative enforcement proceedings and eventual court review.[134]

## ADDENDUM TO POSTSCRIPT

On August 3, 1981, Chancellor Macchiarola and seven named individuals filed a new suit against the Board of Examiners in the United States District Court for the Southern District of New York (Docket No. 81 CIV 4798). The complaint sought to enjoin the Examiners from appointing any persons to the position of High School and Junior High School principal from eligible lists arising from the 1980 examinations and from promulgating any lists for licensing of supervisory personnel "until such time as Defendant can establish to the Court's satisfaction that the tests upon which such lists are based have no racially discriminatory impact or are substantially related to job performance . . ."

Although the plaintiffs' request for preliminary relief still was pending in December 1981, further permanent appointments of supervisors were halted by an administrative order from the Chancellor, which the CSA had not challenged. Instead, once again acting appointments were being made pursuant to the procedures in Circular 30R.

# 7

# New York Legislative Case Study
## *The Teacher Seniority-Layoff Bill*

———◆———

New York City's fiscal crisis, which precipitated extensive litigation in the *Chance* case about the "excessing" of supervisors, also caused wide-ranging reverberations in other areas of personnel policy within the school system. In 1975 and 1976, thousands of teacher positions were eliminated, with an especially hard impact on recently hired minority teachers. Because the court's jurisdiction in *Chance* was limited to supervisory personnel, Judge Tyler's order did not purport to deal with the even more extensive problem of teacher layoff. But, obviously, it was a problem that had to be faced.

The New York State Legislature addressed the teacher layoff issue early in 1976. Two basic factors explained why the affirmative action questions of the teachers' situation were addressed in the legislature, while analogous supervisory excessing problems were brought before the court. First, although a court challenge to the teacher examination system had been started in 1974,[1] no liability determination had been made by 1976,[2] so there was no legal basis for broad judicial intervention on behalf of minority teachers. That is, if a preliminary injunction had been issued, as in *Chance,* then there might have been a foundation for a claim that minority teachers should be granted special seniority consideration to make up for past illegal discrimination. In the absence of such a preliminary injunction, resort to the courts for relief on the immediate layoff problems, would have required either a major effort to speed preliminary stages in the pending teacher case, or the filing of a new action addressed specifically to this issue. In either event, quick, decisive action such as had been obtained from Judge Tyler in *Chance* was unlikely.[3]

Second, and perhaps more important, the legislature had made it clear that the impact of New York City's fiscal crisis on the school system would be one of its major priorities in the 1976 session.

Minority interests, therefore, felt compelled to participate in that forum. Although they were pessimistic about what could be achieved, they felt, at the least, that "harmful" retrogressions might be countered.[4]

Because these events placed the teacher excessing problem before the legislature shortly after the court had considered the excessing of supervisors, we are presented with a rare opportunity, to trace the almost simultaneous development of closely parallel issues in the judicial and legislative forums. The legislative case study which follows will be organized in five parts. After background discussions of the impact of the fiscal crisis on minority teachers, we describe the legislative setting in which these issues were considered. Then, after summarizing the broad spectrum of seniority-layoff issues (of which the affirmative action questions were only one part), we recount the unwinding of the legislative process. We conclude with summary perspectives on the legislative approach to the affirmative action issues, using the fourfold analytic framework developed in our caselet analysis and applied in *Chance*.

## I. Background Factors

### The Impact of the Teacher Layoffs

In the early 1970s, the representation of blacks and Puerto Ricans in professional staff positions in the New York City school system trailed far behind minority student enrollment. In *Chance*, the pattern was proven with respect to supervisors. Similar disparities also applied in regard to teachers. For example, in the 1971–72 school year, at a time when 64.4% of the student body in the New York City public schools were of minority group origin, only 11.4% of the teaching staff were from minority backgrounds.[5] Among major American cities having minority group student populations of 60%–70%, New York City had the lowest percentage of minority group teachers. The comparable figures for Chicago in 1971–72 showed that the system had a minority student population of 59.2% and a minority teaching staff of 39.6%. Los Angeles, with a minority student population of 52.7%, had a minority teaching staff of 22.5%.

New York City minority group representatives had long claimed that the Board of Examiners' licensing system discriminated against minority applicants, not only for supervisory positions (the subject matter of *Chance*), but for teaching positions as well. In response to these claims, the state legislature, as part of its 1969 school decentralization law, modified the role of the traditional Board of Examiners' system in minority communities by creating an alternative hiring procedure that was expected to open the door to greater numbers of minority teachers.[6] Therefore, schools that ranked in the lower 45% in the city on the basis of student reading scores were authorized to appoint (a) teachers from available eligible lists, regardless of their rank, or (b) teachers who had not taken the regular Board of Examiners' test, if they had achieved a certain minimal level on the National Teachers Examination (NTE). Between 1971 and 1975, approximately 40% of the teachers hired under this method (often called the "NTE alternative") were minority.[7]

Partially as a result of the new NTE approach, the overall percentage of minority teachers in the New York City school system began to increase in the early seventies. For example, between 1970 and 1974, the percentage of minority teachers rose from 9.4% to 12.9%. Many groups, however, found this increase inadequate. As indicated above, in 1974, attorneys for the New York Civil Liberties Union, the Puerto Rican Legal Defense and Education Fund, and the Public Education Association, among others, filed a class action lawsuit alleging that both the Board of Examiners' system and even the NTE alternative were racially discriminatory.

With the onset of the New York City fiscal crisis in 1975, however, civil rights groups began to shift their focus from hirings to layoffs. Minority representatives were now determined to prevent the limited progress in minority hirings from being erased by enforced layoffs. The most vulnerable licensed teachers were those serving as "regular substitute teachers." Twenty-seven percent of this group were minority, and they were the first casualties of the fiscal cutbacks: 7,600 regular substitutes who had taught in the 1974–75 school term were not rehired the following fall.[8] The next phase of budgetary cutbacks forced the layoff of regularly appointed teachers on a "last hired, first fired" basis. Since minority teachers had been hired in greater percentages in recent years than in earlier years, the percentage of minority persons within the group of laid-off teachers would be substantially higher than the systemwide percentage of minority teachers.[9]

The black and Puerto Rican leadership position on this issue was reflected in a telegram to the Assembly Education Committee from the superintendent of Community School District No. 13 in the Bedford Stuyvesant section of Brooklyn:

> The seniority system is unfair to minority employees and to the students of a district like 13. District 13 over the past five years has spent thousands of dollars recruiting qualified teachers from

Puerto Rican and black colleges in order to have a staff mix more closely related to our student population . . . The lay-off countered our effort towards affirmative action and widened the ethnic gap between our students, community and teachers. We need an affirmative retention program. Seniority only works when everything else is fair and equal.

## The Legislative Setting

When the legislative session of January 1976 began, it was clear that revision of the seniority and layoff statutes would be one of the two major education problems on the agenda. Earlier that fall, the Assembly Education Committee had conducted a number of hearings in New York City to assess the impact of the financial crisis upon the educational process. As a result, the chairman of the committee, Dr. Leonard Stavisky, had proposed a bill to limit the disproportionate cutbacks in educational services he had documented by guaranteeing the school system a percentage of total city revenues equal to the annual percentage of the city's budget expended on education over the previous three years. This bill was eventually enacted into law over the governor's veto.[10]

Even if expenditure reductions were slowed, however, it was apparent that additional staff layoffs could not be avoided in the near future. Already, almost 10,000 full-time staff positions had been eliminated in the New York City school system, and all affected groups (teachers, parents, boards of education) were dissatisfied with the seniority-layoff statutes that determined who would be laid off. Although these laws had been on the books for decades, such massive layoffs had never before been experienced. Everyone seemed to demand a reexamination of the mandatory seniority rules.

The focus of initial legislative consideration of this matter was in the Assembly Education Committee. Since the New York State Legislature, like most other legislative bodies, is organized around a basic committee structure, all bills must first be reviewed by an appropriate standing committee. Because of the plethora of bills considered in each session (approximately 11,000 were introduced in the Assembly in the 1976 session),[11] the amount of attention that can be given by the committee to each bill is, of course, limited. Major bills, such as the seniority-layoff bill, however, receive more substantial attention from the committees than do more routine or nonserious items, especially in terms of staff support. But, even though New York State is ranked first among all state legislatures in terms of information resources[12] and, unlike most states, has a regularly established staffing and research system for its committees, the resources available to the legislators are far from adequate. A typical assemblyman is provided with a small office and a $10,000 budget which will support a secretary-receptionist and possibly a part-time counsel.[13] Committee chairmen, especially chairmen of major committees such as education, receive more substantial staff appropriations which permit the hiring of an executive director, a general counsel, and one or more additional professionals, in addition to clerical staff.[14] Nevertheless, as will be shown in more detail in the pages which follow, legislative staff and resources do not appear sufficient to permit extensive original research or fact-finding, even on a major issue such as the seniority-layoff bill.

## II. THE BASIC ISSUES

The affirmative action concerns brought to the legislature by minority group representatives were not, and could not have been, considered in isolation from the broad range of issues raised by the massive layoff situation in New York City at the time. The strong demands for statutory changes being made by all groups affected by the layoffs forced the legislature to adopt an approach to the problem which was relatively "comprehensive." The affirmative action questions (like all other aspects of the situation) were subject to compromises and trade-offs involving a much broader range of concerns; and the amount of time and attention that could be expended on these particular concerns was inherently limited.

In order to understand the developments in the affirmative action arena, it is first necessary to describe briefly the other major seniority-layoff issues with which they were inextricably intertwined. The basic operative statute at the time was Education Law §2585.3 which provided that " ... whenever a board of education abolishes a position under this chapter, the services of the teacher having the least seniority in the system within the tenure of the position abolished shall be discontinued." This straightforward four-line statutory provision raised at least five major problems for all affected parties: definition of tenure areas, reversion rights, computation of seniority, recertification, and reappointment rights.

### Definition of Tenure Areas

The statutory requirement that layoffs be effected in seniority order "within the tenure of the position abolished" had recently been interpreted by the Court of Appeals to mean that layoffs must be effected in accordance with seniority within such traditionally defined broad areas as elementary school teaching or secondary school teaching, rather than within such specific subject areas as English, and mathematics.[15] This led to the anomalous result that abolition of a French position could lead to the layoff of a mathematics teacher and the transfer of a French teacher to a mathematics department, if all French teachers had greater seniority than the mathematics teacher with the lowest seniority.

The legislature, therefore, was asked to consider narrowing the definition of "tenure areas" to correspond to the "license areas" or "certification areas," both of which were generally synonymous with specific subject area teaching. However, objections were raised that such specificity would discourage teacher transfers and promotions and might also allow a board of education to focus unfairly upon and lay off particular people whom it desired to terminate.

### Reversion Rights

The statutory requirement for layoffs within particular tenure areas gave no credit for any previous seniority that an individual may have accumulated in other tenure areas. For example, guidance counselors normally were promoted into their positions after numerous years of service as classroom teachers. Under the existing statute they might be laid off because they had only two or three years service in the guidance tenure area, and with no right to revert to their previous teaching areas. Adoption of a concept of "reversion rights" would have the advantage of providing equity for those who had served for many years in the system, but it would also discount relevant experience for a particular job. Thus, reversion rights would tend to impact most heavily on recently hired teachers, including minority group personnel, and would also entail "bumping" of people from position to position, with resultant confusion and administrative difficulties within the school system.

### Computation of Seniority

Section 2585 had generally been interpreted to mean that only full-time regular service would be credited in computing relative seniority rights. This meant that no seniority credit would be given to those who had served for years as full-time or part-time substitute teachers or as paraprofessionals. Obviously, any change that would fully or partially give credit for prior substitute or paraprofessional service would be of advantage to thousands of teachers who had obtained such experience, but would be a disadvantage to those teachers

who had obtained regular appointments without such prior substitute
or paraprofessional service.

### Recertification

Education Law §2585.4 permitted the Board of Examiners and the
chancellor of the city school system to "recertify" teachers laid off from
certain positions in order to permit them to serve in other positions in
the system for which they were not licensed. Experienced teachers who
could take advantage of these provisions obviously sought to extend
them. But other persons, especially young teachers with special training for the preempted positions and parents insisting on appointment
of teachers fully qualified in specialized areas, argued that the procedures—both as prescribed and as practiced—already went too far.
Assemblyman Stavisky and his staff had uncovered evidence indicating
that this supposedly careful assessment process had become an "instant
recertification racket."[16]

### Reappointment Rights

Education Law §2585.5 provided that future vacancies must be filled
in the first instance in reverse rank order from names on a preferred
eligible list of candidates who had been laid off from similar positions in
the past. Seniority in these cases would be based on total service in the
system, rather than on service within the specific tenure area. Under
current New York City conditions, this meant that younger teachers
and minority group members who had been laid off or who had been
placed on existing eligible lists were unlikely to receive any appointments in the New York system in the foreseeable future.

During the months of February and March 1976, it had been made
known to the New York City school community that the Assembly
Education Committee[17] would be considering major revisions in the
seniority-layoff laws. As a result, the committee staff received numerous letters from a wide variety of individuals and groups. In addition,
approximately twelve member bills dealing with various aspects of
seniority had been formally introduced. By late March, most of the
attention of the committee staff, as well as of the public, was focused on
four major comprehensive legislative proposals in this area: the
Stavisky bill,[18] the United Federation of Teachers bill, the Board of
Education bill, and the Blumenthal bill, introduced by Majority Leader
Albert Blumenthal. The approach of each of these bills to the major
seniority-layoff issues discussed above is described in table 10.

Table 10
Summary of Major Provisions of Seniority-Layoff Bills

| ISSUES | STAVISKY BILL (A. 9983) | UFT BILL (A. 11860) |
|---|---|---|
| Definition of Tenure Areas | Same as existing law. | Same as existing law. |
| Reversion Rights | A laid-off teacher would have a right to return to a position in a previous tenure area and displace a person serving with lower seniority, calculated according to a complicated system of partial seniority credit for various relevant areas of service. | A laid-off teacher would have the right to return to a position in a previous tenure area and to displace a person with lower seniority based on "systemwide" seniority calculations, including all substitute and paraprofessional experience. |
| Computation of Seniority | Based on "systemwide seniority" rather than on seniority within tenure area. Systemwide seniority to include up to five years experience as a paraprofessional. | Based on full "systemwide" seniority calculation. *All* substitute and all paraprofessional experience to be included in computation. |

None of these comprehensive bills was specifically introduced or endorsed by black or Puerto Rican teacher groups, though each of them, of course, claimed to be considering the interests of this constituency along with those of others. Chairman Stavisky specifically

| Bᴅ. ᴏғ Eᴅ. Bɪʟʟ (A. 9862–A) | Bʟᴜᴍᴇɴᴛʜᴀʟ Bɪʟʟ (A. 10788) | Bɪʟʟ ᴀs Eɴᴀᴄᴛᴇᴅ (A. 13043) |
|---|---|---|
| Narrower "license areas" substituted for broad tenure areas. | Concept of tenure eliminated. | Narrower "license areas" generally substituted for broad tenure areas; Board authorized to propose additional groupings of related license "areas" to legislature. |
| A laid-off teacher would have the right to return to a position in a previous license area and to displace a person with lower seniority based on "systemwide" seniority, including full-time substitute service. | A laid-off teacher would have the right to return to a position in a previous license area and to displace another person if the laid-off teacher's seniority in the license exceeds the other person's seniority in the system. | A laid-off teacher would have the right to return to a position in a previous license area and to displace a person with lower seniority based on "systemwide" seniority, including full-time, substitute and paraprofessional service. Reversion rights of supervisors limited. No "bumpings" permitted after first 15 days of school term. |
| Based on seniority "within the license area." All full-time substitute service (but not prior paraprofessional service) within the license area to be included in computation. | Based on total seniority in the system, including 50% of paraprofessional experience, excluding experience in a supervisory position. | Based on full "systemwide" seniority calculation. All full-time substitute and all paraprofessional experience to be included in computation, except that a tenured incumbent in a position shall have priority over an untenured excessed teacher, regardless of amount of systemwide seniority. |

continued

acknowledged the importance of the affirmative action claims;[19] he believed that amending the statutory calculation of seniority credit to include paraprofessional experience would benefit the minority constituency. Similarly, the United Federation of Teachers, which had to

table 10 continued

| ISSUES | STAVISKY BILL (A. 9983) | UFT BILL (A. 11860) |
|---|---|---|
| Recertification | Continue present concept except that person seeking recertification must meet minimum education requirements established for the position, show satisfactory progression toward licensure, and meet full license requirements within five years of the appointment. | Essentially same as existing law. |
| Reappointment | Same as existing law. | Same as existing law, except systemwide seniority would be specifically defined to include *all* substitute and paraprofessional experience. |

sponsor a proposal acceptable to both its broad membership and its minority group constituency, appeared to favor minority interests by calculating seniority in terms of all previous paraprofessional and substitute service, although its sponsorship of the broad reversion rights and the systemwide definition of seniority probably would have impacted negatively on minority group interests. The Board of Education proposal gave full credit for all prior substitute service (but not all prior paraprofessional service), except for purposes of reappointment. Assemblyman Blumenthal, who represented a district with strong community control concerns and a large minority population, apparently was most interested in ensuring that supervisors and guidance counselors who lacked recent classroom experience would not be permitted to revert to previous licenses and displace young teachers. He also wanted to grant partial seniority credit for prior paraprofessional experience, a mechanism which might benefit 400 former paraprofessionals citywide.

| Bd. of Ed. Bill (A. 9862–A) | Blumenthal Bill (A. 10788) | Bill as Enacted (A. 13043) |
|---|---|---|
| Essentially same as existing law. | Essentially same as existing law. | Continue present concept except that person seeking recertification must meet minimum education requirements established for the position, show satisfactory progression toward licensure, and meet full license requirements within three years of appointment. |
| Same as existing law, except systemwide seniority would be specifically defined to include full-time substitute and paraprofessional experience. | Same as existing law, except seniority for reappointment purposes would be based only on the length of service in the position from which the person was laid off. | Same as existing law, except systemwide seniority is specifically defined to include all full-time substitute and paraprofessional experience. After reappointment of laid-off personnel, preference is to be given to those with recent substitute experience. |

In short, all of these major bills introduced early in the session assumed that the affirmative action problems could be adequately dealt with by giving full or partial credit for prior substitute and paraprofessional experience. The Gifford Report supported this position by its finding that there was a disproportionate number of minority teachers among the substitutes who were not rehired in September 1975. It is possible, however, that while a relatively large minority representation existed among recently hired substitutes, minorities were proportionately underrepresented among substitutes hired in earlier years. A bill granting seniority credit for substitute service in the distant past, therefore, might not benefit minorities. To make a reliable projection, one would need to analyze the amount of prior substitute experience for each ethnic group in the various categories of teachers threatened with layoffs.

There is no indication that any of the sponsors of the major bills had actual evidence as to the specific impact that their bills would have on minority group staffing. Indeed, it is not even clear that they were aware of the general statistics of the Gifford Report.[20] Nor is there any indication that direct consultations had been held with minority group representatives at the initial drafting stage to see whether credit for prior substitute service and prior paraprofessional service would satisfy their needs or whether gains in this regard might be offset by other provisions that were written to benefit other groups.

The first direct response from the minority group constituency to these proposals was contained in a position paper sent to Dr. Stavisky on March 15, 1976, by the Public Education Association, which had served as counsel in the *Chance* and *Rubinos* cases on behalf of the minority group personnel. The PEA had held meetings with a number of concerned educational groups to discuss the pending seniority bill proposals and concluded that the addition of paraprofessional service in computing systemwide seniority would be beneficial to minority groups, but the inclusion of prior substitute service would not. The PEA letter also objected to the generally accepted reversion principle because "far more minority personnel would be ousted through the bumping process than would be retained."

It is interesting to note that the PEA's response, like the initial formulation of positions by the other interests, did not contain any detailed backup or any statistical support for its general position. According to PEA, the Board of Education's inability and/or unwillingness to supply needed data made it impossible to speak in hard figures. However, it appears that the PEA and the coalition were in a position at least to present "soft" data. At meetings of the PEA seniority subcommittee, supervisors and teachers tried to re-create typical patterns of employment for teachers of different ethnic groups who entered the system at different times. Also administrators in the offices of community school districts selected a representative sample of teacher personnel files and calculated seniority credits under two formulas—with/without substitute service.[21] But no documentation of these fact-finding efforts was ever presented to the Education Committee—only the conclusions.

## III. The Legislative Process

As discussed above, routine bills are generally processed through the committee system in the New York State Legislature without extensive research or discussion. More important bills receive a certain amount of discussion in committee meetings, and proposed amendments may then be researched and drafted by committee staff. Citizen and interest-group input on legislative bills normally occurs through hearings, correspondence, statements of support or opposition, and informal discussions. Because of the importance of the seniority-layoff bill and the large numbers of people affected, Chairman Stavisky decided at the outset that extensive deliberations must precede its final formulation. The complexity and technical nature of many of the issues involved as well as the time pressures of a legislative session convinced Dr. Stavisky that it was best to schedule a number of working conferences in Albany. At these, members of the committee and representatives of the affected interest groups would be heard in an attempt to achieve a consensus on key points.[22]

Accordingly, preliminary conferences were held on March 17 and March 24, 1976. The first was attended by representatives of the groups that had filed comprehensive bills, who were informed that the committee would support an omnibus bill to be developed through consultation with an expanded group of interest group representatives. As part of this expansion, the list of groups and individuals invited to the next week's meeting included the New York City Board of Education, the United Federation of Teachers, the State Education Department, the Council of Supervisory Associations, the United Parents Association, the Community School Board Association, the Public Education Association, the Puerto Rican Educators Association, the Coalition of Concerned Black Educators and representatives of two black community school boards.[23]

At these preliminary discussions, the representatives of the various groups discussed their positions in general terms. The Public Education Association representative, however, did attack the thrust of the working drafts under discussion for not directly addressing the serious issues of minority employment. She proposed five specific changes: (1) that seniority be computed on a community district rather than a citywide basis; (2) that seniority rules be restricted to tenured personnel and that layoffs of probationary personnel be handled on a discretionary basis (the assumptions of the Blumenthal bill); (3) that additional limitations be placed on the recertification process; (4) that the preferred eligible list system for reappointments be replaced by a "pool" selected by community districts; and (5) that the legislature require the city to comply with integration orders on staff selection.

Dr. Stavisky stated that these preliminary discussions would serve as the basis for a comprehensive working draft of a bill that would reflect the concerns expressed by the various groups. Another meeting was planned as soon as this draft was ready. In the meantime, during the Easter recess, Dr. Stavisky received a letter at his home from a coalition of eleven minority group organizations, including the PEA and the Coalition of Associations of Black and Puerto Rican Educators and Supervisors. This letter stated that the discussions had focused almost exclusively "on remedial measures designed to iron out possible inequities as among different employees" and that there had been no attempt to "address the negative impact of seniority upon school administration, minority staff, or children's interest." Accordingly, these groups requested that the Assembly Education Committee hold hearings in New York City in order to document the effect of existing rules and regulations and to obtain information which "is within the exclusive control of the City Board of Education" and which, presumably, had not been made available to these groups. This request for on-the-spot hearings was subsequently endorsed by a number of established organizations, including the United Parents Association and the Citizens' Committee for Children.

After consulting with other committee members, Dr. Stavisky determined that the pressures of the five-day-a-week legislative session in Albany made any meaningful hearings in New York City impossible.[24] However, he took steps to ensure that representatives of all groups known to have an interest in this matter would be invited to the next working session in Albany. Accordingly, on May 10, approximately 40 people were in attendance, including all of the black and Puerto Rican members of the Education Committee, and five representatives of the coalition of black and Puerto Rican educators, the Public Education Association, and other identified minority group advocacy organizations.

At this meeting, a compromise document combining elements of various pending proposals was presented and explained by the committee staff to those present. Jose Pacheco, a spokesman for the coalition of black and Puerto Rican groups, maintained that the proposed draft provided almost nothing in terms of affirmative action. Granting credit for prior paraprofessional service in computing seniority, he said, would have limited impact because very few paras had gone on to become teachers. He called instead for bold action, including a total moratorium on further layoffs of minority personnel, residence within the city limits as a prerequisite for retention, and consideration of competence measures aside from seniority in determining layoffs.[25] The strong position taken by Mr. Pacheco, and supported in full or in part by many of those present, including some of the assemblymen themselves, made it necessary, probably for the first time, that direct attention be paid to the affirmative action issue.

At this point, Assemblyman Vann, a black member of the committee, referred to a separate bill which he had introduced in mid-February and which had not been discussed in previous sessions. Apparently taken from an original proposal of the Gifford Report, the bill provided that for future appointments, after recall of all laid-off personnel, priority would be given to persons on appropriate eligible lists who had previously served as regular substitutes in the particular subject area, regardless of their rank order on the list. The committee agreed to include this provision because, assuming that minority teachers represented a significant proportion of the substitute population, this approach would, in the long run, substantially increase minority representation in the teacher ranks.[26] The black and Puerto Rican teacher representatives, although favoring the proposal, still insisted on immediate affirmative action steps because the Vann proposal could have only minimal effect at a time when little new hiring was taking place. The UFT supported this provision as an affirmative action measure even though it was a departure from the union's strong historical commitment to rank-ordering hiring.[27]

The discussion then moved on to other issues, especially administrative problems of limiting "bumpings" and disruption at the beginning of the school term. However, before the meeting concluded, the representatives of the black and Puerto Rican coalition voiced their dissatisfaction with the general direction of events and with the fact that their substantive proposals were not being incorporated into the bill. Furthermore, they again requested that public hearings be held in New York City and, in fact, indicated that in the absence of a committee commitment to hold hearings, they themselves had scheduled a public meeting for the following Saturday and invited all members of the committee to attend. At the conclusion of the meeting it was decided that the Assembly Education Committee staff would revise the working draft and mail the revision to all participants, thereby hoping to again achieve a broad consensus. Because the legislative session was drawing to a close, they asked that each concerned party or group put its suggestions and comments on the new draft and mail them back to the committee.

On Saturday, May 15, 1976, the workshop "hearing" sponsored by the "coalition on seniority" was held. Assemblyman Stavisky, himself, took time to attend these sessions, as did several of the minority members of the committee. One speaker alleged that the percentage of black educators in the system had been reduced in the period June to October 1975 from 11% to 4% and Hispanics, from 4% to 1%.[28] As a result, those in attendance at the hearing endorsed, almost unanimously, the concept of a total moratorium on further minority layoffs.[29] Subsequently, a draft of a specific affirmative action statute which incorporated the moratorium concept was mailed to the Assembly committee, and the group indicated that it would have a representative available in Albany continuously for the next few weeks to work with the committee on the affirmative action points.

Over the course of the next few weeks, the negotiating process on the seniority-layoff bill continued in earnest, although on a more *ad hoc* basis. The committee staff prepared at least six versions of proposals for the bill, each of which was sent to the participants at the earlier conferences. Comments were received by mail, telephone, and through informal conferences with the lobbyists present in Albany and with representatives of the parties who came to the capital for special meetings. At this point, the committee's prime concern was to produce a compromise document acceptable to all interested parties.

Yet, despite constant adjustments and modifications, the minority coalition groups continued to express dissatisfaction with the general thrust of the bill. At times they indicated that they were skeptical of achieving any real results in the legislative process and were considering bringing the matter to the courts. Despite those protestations, most of the committee members, including Dr. Stavisky, apparently assumed that the consideration given to prior substitute and paraprofessional experience, combined with the hiring priorities under the Vann proposal, which all had agreed to accept, adequately met the needs for affirmative action. Also, given the types of bill that the legislature could be expected to consider, committee members assumed that the moratorium approach requested by the minority caucus would cause the defeat of the entire bill in the legislature. (Many also assumed that the approach was unconstitutional.)

In a draft issued at the end of May, however, Assemblyman Stavisky proposed a new clause to accommodate further the minority caucus. This clause required that the central Board of Education prepare, within six months, a "plan to promote the retention and hiring of personnel of Asian, American Indian, Hispanic, Black and other minority group ethnic origin," and, that such plan be submitted together with proposals for legislative enactments to the legislative leaders. By using a classic parliamentary technique, then, Assemblyman

Stavisky hoped to win support from the minority caucus for the present bill by promising that serious attention would be given to their most pressing concerns early in the next legislative session.

However, this proposal was politically unpalatable to many of the groups involved. After numerous new drafts were circulated, the working draft of June 9 had watered down the affirmative action plan language to require only "that the city board shall issue a report detailing steps taken and steps to be taken to promote the retention and hiring of personnel of ethnic minority group origins." In the June 17 draft, this clause was further revised to require only that "the city board shall issue a report disclosing the numbers of ethnic group minority personnel within the City School District by title and position."

Finally, on June 25, 1976, after three months of intensive work and negotiations, and at least twelve major rewritings of the bill, the final version, Assembly Bill 13043, was approved by the committee and was before the Assembly chamber for a vote. The details of the final bill, which, of course, was a compromise synthesis of the various proposals, are described in table 10 above.

As is indicated on the chart, on the major disputed points, the Board of Education position basically prevailed on the tenure issue, the union's position on the seniority calculations, and Assemblyman Stavisky's new approach on recertification. On the specific issues related to affirmative action, the bill included all prior substitute and paraprofessional experience in computing seniority and layoffs, and incorporated the Vann substitute-hiring-priority provisions. The final version also contained a watered-down rendering of the affirmative action plan clause requiring only a report disclosing the numbers of ethnic minority group personnel, as in the June 17 draft.

Assemblyman Stavisky believed that this package, although obviously a compromise of competing positions on many points, represented as fair a balancing of the issues as was possible under the circumstances.[30] Any bill more slanted toward the interest of any particular group would, he thought, be defeated on the floor. With the session coming to an end, it was imperative that *some* reasonable reforms be enacted to prevent another chaotic year for school staffing. Shortly before the bill reached the Assembly floor, the United Federation of Teachers issued a memorandum in support of the bill, and, somewhat unexpectedly, the Board of Education issued a memorandum in opposition.[31]

The bill also met opposition from the caucus of black and Puerto

Rican legislators. In the Assembly debates, Assemblyman Vann introduced the only significant opposition to the bill that was heard on the floor.[32] Vann complained of the bill's failure to provide meaningful affirmative action guarantees and proposed specific amendments to include a moratorium on layoffs of minority personnel and/or to reinstate the original proposal requiring a definite affirmative action plan to be presented to the legislative leadership.[33] Assemblyman Stavisky strongly resisted the Vann amendments, saying that he personally favored a stronger affirmative action plan provision and would support a "chapter amendment" after the main bill was adopted. At this point, however, he feared that a full reconsideration of the affirmative action points could endanger passage of the entire bill.[34] Ultimately, however, Assemblyman Vann's amendments were decisively defeated, the moratorium proposal losing by a vote of 11 to 110 and the affirmative action proposal losing by 42 to 70. Shortly thereafter, A. 13043, which was adopted by the Assembly by a vote of 132 to 13, was submitted to the Senate. After a vituperative debate on affirmative action amendments similar to those advocated by Assemblyman Vann, the Senate approved the bill by a vote of 34 to 7. It received the governor's signature shortly thereafter, and was enacted into law as Chapter 521 of the Laws of 1976.

## IV. SUMMARY PERSPECTIVES

### Principle/Policy Issues

The impact of New York City's fiscal crisis on minority teachers and supervisors presented largely similar constellations of principle and policy considerations which had to be addressed by both the legislature and the court. The principle claims arose out of indications that the layoffs disproportionately affected teachers who were black and Hispanic. The policy considerations included the competing individual equities of nonminority staff, the fiscal and administrative implications of any changes on the school system, and the educational program consequences of personnel changes.

But the differences in the judicial and legislative approaches to this complex mix of interrelated issues are striking. In the court, the focus of all the deliberations was the minority plaintiffs' principled claim. Because of the initial liability finding that the traditional examination system had discriminated against minority applicants, Judge Tyler, despite his stated disinclination to become involved in the intricacies of the excessing issues, felt duty-bound to fashion an affirmative action remedy for those members of the plaintiff class (whatever their number) who would be detrimentally affected by the proposed layoffs. When fashioning a final decree, he, of course, took into account all the relevant policy considerations. But he subordinated these policy factors to his primary goal—fashioning an affirmative action remedy. Despite its reversal of Judge Tyler's far-reaching order, the Court of Appeals agreed that the basic principle claims had to be met and therefore ordered a "constructive seniority" form of affirmative action relief.

By way of contrast, the legislature focused on all of the policy problems caused by the layoffs. None of the legislators (and, indeed, none of the interest groups involved) ever disputed the basic claim that recently hired minority teachers were disproportionately affected by the layoffs. But the minority claims were not viewed as principle issues entitled to preeminent consideration. Rather, they were seen as one legitimate interest to be weighted against other legitimate and competing policy claims in reaching a final workable (or at least politically acceptable) solution. Stated another way, the legislature made no initial "liability finding" of discriminatory impact that necessitated a remedy tailored to right the specific "wrong" suffered by the minority personnel; it had before it a broad, comprehensive problem that somehow had to be resolved.

In this situation, the institutional differences between the legislature and the court led to critical differences in results: the minority groups' position largely prevailed in the court but was largely ignored in the legislature. The outcome in a particular case cannot, of course, legitimize general involvement in educational policy making by a particular branch of government; nevertheless, the differences between the legislative and judicial approaches to similar constellations of principle and policy issues do provide an empirical basis for reaching some meaningful conclusions. Some of these conclusions will be set forth in chapter 10.

### Interest Representation Issues

One of the most interesting parallels to emerge from the comparative case studies of the judicial and legislative processes in New York is the fact that basically the same interest groups were active in the two forums. The legislative process, almost by definition, was of course "multipolar." Correspondence was received from a large number of individuals and groups, and representatives of at least a dozen organizations at one time or another participated in meetings and working sessions on the bill. Major input and participation in the critical negotiating process, however, was confined to three groups —the Board of Education, the United Federation of Teachers, and Coalition of Associations of Black and Puerto Rican Educators and Supervisors.[35] The Board of Examiners played no role in the legislative negotiation, but on the parallel issues under consideration in *Chance*, i.e., the layoff-excessing issues, the Examiners also did not participate.[36]

But, despite the parallel between the court and legislature with regard to the number and identity of the interest groups involved, and the variety and substance of the specific issues raised, important differences were evident in terms of the relative influence of the various groups in the deliberations.[37] In *Chance*, the minority plaintiffs basically framed the issues for litigation. In the legislature, by way of contrast, the minority representatives became involved at a time when the issues already had been initiated and partly defined by the UFT and the Board of Education. Furthermore, in the court deliberations, the minority groups' interests were forcefully and effectively articulated by experienced counsel. In the legislative process, however, the minority group was represented by an inexperienced, voluntary spokesman for the legislative coalition, while the union and the Board of Education were represented by professional lobbyists.[38]

In short, although formal access to the legislature was made fully available to minority interests, actual influence was a function of the political power of the constituency represented (including the number of sympathetic legislators on the committee) and the resources available to present a point of view. As Assemblyman Vann put it, "our ability to participate in committee deliberations was good—whether our input was seriously considered was another matter." From this position of weakness, the comparative advantage of being a plaintiff in a case like *Chance*, pressing claims of right in the "principled" judicial process, can help to explain our finding in chapter 3 that a disproportionate number of federal court challenges to educational policies are brought on behalf of minority interests. Joseph Pacheco, the spokesman for the coalition, made this same observation:

> My experience is that the federal courts still provide the quickest and the best relief for minorities. The political processes of

legislation are an uphill battle. Even when you get favorable legislation it is so watered down, it represents such a broad compromise of everything that the positive things you get out of it really have a minimum impact. I think that there is too much emotionalism attached to our particular issues for us to be successful politically. Just use the word reverse discrimination and that is it. You have polarization immediately ... The law sometimes cannot just go according to popular opinion ... That is why the best redress is in the courts where the results are not contingent on numbers or popularity.

## Fact-finding Issues

Assessing the ethnic impact of existing and proposed personnel practices on minority staffs was the threshold fact-finding task for both the court and the legislature. The initial question at the liability phase of *Chance* was the extent to which the Board of Examiners' system disproportionately excluded minority candidates from receiving supervisory licenses. On the excessing issue, the necessary factual base was the specific impact of anticipated excessings on minority personnel. Similarly, in the legislative process assessment of the minority group claims depended on information about the extent to which past and future layoffs and excessings adversely affected minority teachers.

Interestingly, in both forums the minority representatives presented general allegations that were not, initially, substantiated by hard evidence. Judge Mansfield, chiding the plaintiffs for their shortcomings in this regard, quickly fashioned a plan for obtaining the necessary evidence. Thus, the court, when confronted with evidentiary inadequacies, was able to compel the Board and the other parties to do whatever was necessary to obtain the necessary information; furthermore, a formal procedure was available for the plaintiffs in the case to challenge discrepancies in initial data put forward by the defendants. In the legislature, such mechanisms for compelling efficient discovery simply did not exist. Furthermore, at the excessing phase of the court proceedings, Judge Tyler required the defendants to come up with precise estimates of anticipated layoffs and excessings. Thus, the court compensated for its own lack of staff resources by inducing the parties themselves to gather and submit the necessary information.

It is often assumed in the separation-of-powers literature that legislatures, in comparison with the courts, possess an independent fact-gathering capability. Despite the New York State Legislature's high-ranking staff resources, it does not actually provide sufficient resources for substantive investigation and research.[39] Although the Assembly Education Committee devoted substantially more time and resources to its deliberations of the seniority layoff bill than to almost any other issue considered in the 1976 session, the committee staff considered it beyond their capability to obtain comprehensive primary data on discriminatory impact or other key issues.[40]

Consequently, the legislature, like the court, was left to rely on the parties to supply basic data.[41] In comparison with some of the court's complex information requests in *Chance* (i.e., for detailed survey of the pass rates on fifty examinations over a seven-year period), the information sought by the legislature was relatively straightforward: the data related primarily to ethnic breakdowns of staff members who had been or would be terminated and how various alternative proposals would affect these groups. At no time was such information actually obtained. The Board of Education, although amenable to providing whatever information was readily available, was apparently unwilling (and believed it had no obligation) to seek additional data or to engage in qualitative statistical analyses of available facts and relate them to the immediate issues.[42]

In addition to information gathering, the other basic issue concerning fact-finding capability is information assessment. In theory, expert testimony is presented to a legislative body at hearings; in fact, these hearings usually are oriented toward political and public relations concerns more than toward serious fact-gathering.[43] It is noteworthy that Assemblyman Stavisky decided to not even take the time to go through the formalities of convening such hearings. He organized the working sessions as forums where the political positions of the various interests and parties could be discussed and reconciled. There was no pretense that evidence or expert testimony would be considered objectively and dispassionately. Although our findings in chapter 4 indicated that judges often employ various "avoidance devices" in dealing with complex social fact issues, the legislature, by the very nature of its political approach, is even more strongly inclined toward avoiding basic social fact issues. As a result, in this case, no factual record that could be subjected to scrutiny was ever produced.[44] Thus, comparing the legislature's and the court's capabilities for comprehending expert testimony and social science data is largely beside the point, simply because the legislature did not even purport to obtain and assess such data.

## Remedial Issues

Although the basic issues to be addressed were approached from a principle direction by the court and from a policy direction by the legislature, once it became clear that some remedial action needed to be taken, the process of fashioning such a remedy was remarkably similar in the two forums. The working out of the details of an appropriate "plan" was left largely to the interested parties, with the court and the education committee serving as "arbitrators" in those limited areas where the parties could not achieve a consensus agreement. Thus, in the court setting, the basic workings of both the interim appointment procedures and the permanent licensing plan were largely hammered out by the parties. Similarly, in the legislature, the definitions of tenure areas, extent of reversion rights, etc., were worked out in a negotiating process. Impasses on particular issues (such as the role of the community boards in the on-the-job evaluations), were brought to the judge for resolution in *Chance*, while in the legislative setting similar critical blocking points (such as the method for computing seniority) were decided by the education committee, and ultimately approved by the full legislature.[45]

In terms of capacity to consider the broad, comprehensive implications of major educational reforms and to fashion appropriate structural mechanisms to obtain desired results in New York, the court and legislature were subject to the same strengths and weaknesses. Since in both forums the parties worked out the details of the remedies, there appears to be no basis for arguing that the court was less capable of comprehensively structuring complex systematic reforms than was the legislature.

When, however, the formulation of a remedy is viewed as a long-range process for effectively implementing social policy reforms, significant differences in the legislative and judicial approaches become apparent. Legislatures, unlike courts, do not usually purport to retain jurisdiction and monitor the results of their statutory enactments on an ongoing basis. If any of the interested parties here should become seriously aggrieved by problems arising out of the new reforms, they would be required to reconvene the entire legislative process, and the likelihood of obtaining the priority focus they achieved in the 1976 session would be small.[46] In *Chance*, however, the court exercised jurisdiction over an eight-year period and thereby provided an opportunity for the parties to modify elements of the orders and allowed plaintiffs to compel compliance from the Board of Examiners under pressure from the court. Plaintiffs also obtained the rights to specific reporting requirements which gave them precise data to lodge such compliance complaints.[47] The court process provided an ongoing, flexible mechanism for maintaining remedial compliance, which was not available in the legislature. Some might conclude, however, that this very flexibility and ongoing involvement contributed to the protracted length of the eight-year litigation and to the lack of final resolution of the problem.

# 8

## Colorado Judicial Case Study
### *Otero* v. *Mesa County Valley School District No. 51*

———————◆———————

In March 1974, a coalition of lawyers from the Mexican American Legal Defense Fund (MALDEF), the Chicano Education Project (CEP), and the Colorado Rural Legal Assistance (CRLA) filed a complaint in federal court on behalf of a class of Mexican-American parents and school-age children residing in Grand Junction, Colorado. The lawsuit alleged that District 51's educational program and its hiring practices discriminated against Chicanos. To correct this situation the plaintiffs asked the court to order the school system to institute a comprehensive bilingual-bicultural curriculum and to require affirmative action hiring programs for Chicano personnel. After extensive pretrial proceedings and a lengthy trial, Federal District Judge Fred Winner issued a decision entering judgment for defendants on each of the plaintiffs' claims.[1]

We selected *Otero* to be the second detailed judicial case study for the EPAC project primarily because it provides an excellent comparison to the *Chance* case study in chapter 6. In *Chance,* the plaintiffs prevailed; in *Otero,* the defendants. In *Chance,* negotiations among the parties were productive and (by and large) reasonably harmonious; in *Otero,* the interparty relationships were acrimonious and unproductive. The thrust of the *Chance* litigation was in its protracted remedial phase; in *Otero,* the important focus was on liability fact-finding.

This chapter is organized as follows: Section I describes the political background of the litigation, the reasons for plaintiffs' decision to bring their grievances to the courts, and the initial reactions of school officials. Section II considers the plaintiffs' framing and reframing of their legal claims against the background of evolving legal doctrines. Sections III and IV examine the fact-finding process during the discovery phase and at trial. Finally, Section V sets forth summary perspectives in terms of our fourfold analytic methodology.

## I. HISTORICAL BACKGROUND

Mesa County, over which District 51 has jurisdiction, is located in a semiarid, coal mining, and livestock raising region in central western Colorado. Its county seat is Grand Junction, population 24,000, the largest city in Colorado west of the continental divide. Driving through Grand Junction one finds neat and modest single-family homes, reflective of its working and middle-class population. Compared to other Colorado school districts, District 51 has a relatively small tax base and less than the average amount of state and local revenues to spend on each child. Nevertheless, the achievement test scores of its students have been significantly higher than the national norms.[2]

The "average" family in District 51 is middle class and "Anglo."[3] Slightly over 8% of the students are of Mexican-American ancestry, or in common parlance, "Chicanos."[4] Unlike the Anglos, large numbers of Chicano families have incomes below the federal poverty level.[5]

The majority of Mesa County's Chicanos have lived in Colorado—if not in this specific locale—for generations. Despite this longevity, however, the Chicano population has lagged significantly behind the dominant Anglos in both economic level and educational achievement. Yet until the 1970s, ethnic and racial issues were not in the forefront of public consciousness.[6] On those rare occasions when Anglo officials or journalists did reflect on the special problems of Chicanos in Mesa County, their perspective was strictly economic. No connection was ever made between the cultural and linguistic differences of Chicano children and their socioeconomic status or educational achievement.[7]

About 1970, there was a marked increase in Chicano political activism in Colorado. A group known as La Voz de la Raza ("The Voice of the Race") was formed at that time in Grand Junction. Ray Otero, its leader, was an energetic and independent individual who was described simultaneously as charismatic and effective by his supporters and as ambitious and volatile by his detractors. La Voz and Otero adopted as a key goal the reformation of the school system to meet the needs of Mexican-American children.

After contact was established between La Voz and the recently formed statewide Chicano Education Project (CEP), two CEP staff people visited Grand Junction and examined some of District 51's personnel records. They quickly became convinced that there was a clear pattern of discrimination against Chicano educators. As late as

March 1974, the Board of Education had never had a Mexican-American member; the entire administrative staff (with one exception) and all 31 principals were Anglo; and the teaching staff between 1967 and 1974 was always more than 99% Anglo. As the trial judge eventually found: "Statistically, District 51 doesn't look good."[8]

Armed with these figures, La Voz asked the Board to implement a bilingual-bicultural curriculum in grades K–12, to change the general social studies curriculum, to recruit Chicano administrators and non-professional staff, and to end allegedly unequal distribution of federal funds. These requests led to negotiations.

From the outset, the two sides were far apart. They disagreed about the Board's legal obligations, and about the educational value of a bilingual program. La Voz lawyers interpreted the 1972 decision of the federal district court in New Mexico in *Serna* v. *Portales Independent School District*[9] to mean that once it was established that Anglo children substantially outperformed Chicano children in a school system, the equal protection clause entitled Chicano children —even ones with substantial English-speaking abilities—to bilingual educational services adapted to their own special needs. The Board, on the other hand, maintained it was meeting its legal obligations as defined by the U.S. Supreme Court's 1973 decision in *Lau* v. *Nichols*.[10] *Lau*, the Board argued, required no more than transitional English instruction for Spanish dominant students, and the few District 51 students to whom this applied, it claimed, were already receiving it. The parties also were at loggerheads on the employment question, the Board rejecting the claims that their hiring practices were discriminatory, that Chicano children would learn better from Chicano teachers, and that, therefore, ethnicity should be a criterion for employment decisions.

What doomed the preliminary negotiations from the start, however, were not the differences (which were indeed profound) but rather the subjective perceptions of the participants. The Board of Education members and the administrators were proud of their school system and believed it was meeting the needs of Chicano children. They deeply resented being singled out for criticism and confrontation by state and national Chicano organizations. They believed that La Voz was controlled by outsiders and "agitators" who were less interested in what they could accomplish for Mesa County Chicanos, through compromise if necessary, than in winning a test case with broad national implications.[11] Moreover, these Anglo school officials thought that at least one of the local Chicano leaders was trying to institute a major lawsuit and polarize the community only in order to advance himself politically. Hence, the Board's response to Chicano demands was based on the assumption that "Litigation was inevitable from the way they [Chicanos] were approaching the situation."[12] The Board thought that nothing short of complete abdication of its legal responsibility to shape educational policy with the interests of "100% of the community in mind"[13] could ward off a suit.

The filing of the *Otero* complaint was an important event for all members of the traditionally low-key community, which had hardly been touched by the racial and antiwar activism of the 1960s.[14] Among the generally nonpoliticized Chicano population, *Otero* was called "the La Voz Case," and it was identified with militancy. (Of course plaintiffs' attorneys, being more politically aware, considered their working within established political and legal institutions to be quite moderate.) As for the Anglos, many sensed that the possibility of violence "lurked in the background." This heightened awareness of ethnic differences evoked some hostility,[15] but there was no explicit Anglo political backlash.[16]

The underlying problem, as the plaintiffs' attorneys defined it, was that neither Chicanos[17] nor Anglos realized the extent of the disparity between the educational achievements of the two groups of students. No one understood that the school was responsible for this disparity and that feasible methods existed to eradicate it. The plaintiffs saw the La Voz demands and the *Otero* lawsuit as vehicles for educating people about the Chicano experience in District 51 schools. Despite the ultimate dismissal of their complaint, this educational purpose may well have been achieved. The *Daily Sentinel* reported regularly and in detail the plaintiffs' arguments, on one occasion even giving the school-by-school dropout statistics. One established, politically moderate Chicano businessman decided to testify for the plaintiffs at the trial, indicating that the plaintiffs' ideas were gaining broader support in the Chicano community. And, at the close of the trial, the *Daily Sentinel* itself editorialized that no matter who won, the suit had taught the community much about the importance of educating individuals, rather than "cramming [all children] into a common Anglo mold."[18]

## II. Structuring the Plaintiffs' Case

To a certain extent, it must be said that the *Otero* case was brought before the federal court because the opposing interests read the few existing judicial precedents on bilingual rights in substantially different ways and therefore lacked legal parameters for negotiation. The plaintiffs emphasized the importance of the bilingual-bicultural education remedy ordered by the New Mexico Court; the defendants relied on the narrower liability language staged by the Supreme Court. These differing interpretations drove the parties apart and thereby fueled their mutual suspicions.

In retrospect, the defendants' perspective was largely upheld by the Tenth Circuit Court of Appeals' invalidation of a bilingual-bicultura! plan in *Keyes* v. *School District No. 1, Denver.*[19] However, at the inception of *Otero* and throughout the trial, the plaintiffs' position was plausible.[20] The basic facts and figures pertaining to Chicano students in District 51 were similar to those in the New Mexico district. Plaintiffs seemed confident that the equal protection theory used in that case would also stand up in Grand Junction, even if District 51 mounted a stronger opposition than the *Serna* school board (which had not put expert witnesses on the stand to challenge the findings and conclusions of plaintiffs' experts).[21]

Generally speaking, then, the bilingual issues[22] in *Otero* coalesced around two theories of educational rights—an "exclusion" theory emerging from *Lau* and an "equal benefits" theory emerging from *Serna*.

### *"Exclusion" from Meaningful Educational Opportunity*

Under Title VI of the Civil Rights Act of 1964[23] a person may not be excluded from the benefits of a federally funded program, or subjected to discrimination, on the basis of national origin. In *Lau* v. *Nichols*,[24] the Supreme Court applied this principle to bilingual education. It held that the plaintiff class, children of Chinese ancestry in San Francisco "who do not speak English," are foreclosed from any "meaningful education" if their language deficiencies are not remedied.

*Lau* left many questions unanswered. In terms of liability, it was unclear, first, at what level of English language proficiency a child is to be considered "English-speaking," and, second, how many non-English-speaking students must be enrolled in a school district to trigger an obligation to mount bilingual programs.[25] In terms of remedies, the court never attempted to address the educational policy questions of the appropriateness or the effectiveness of the various approaches to bilingual education. Instead, the case was remanded to the trial court for further consideration.

The *Otero* defendants read *Lau* as articulating a narrow exclusionary theory of rights to bilingual education. Only students who were unable to function in English (and were thereby constructively "excluded" from education) had a right to special language instruction. Also, they inferred from this right a very limited remedy—transitional remedial instruction aimed at developing English language proficiency to the degree where students could function in the regular school program. In other words, the right was based on a measure of educational inputs. It was the school's obligation to furnish children instruction in a language that they could understand; once having done so, the school had no obligation to ensure that the language-deficient children acutally achieved as well as other children.

### Entitlement to "Equal Benefits"

The *Otero* plaintiffs did not view the Supreme Court's decision in *Lau* as limiting bilingual education rights under Title VI (or under equal protection doctrines which were not reached by the Supreme Court) to a narrow exclusionary theory model.[26] Indeed, in *Serna,* the case most parallel to the Mesa situation, the judge had interpreted *Lau* much more broadly.[27] The *Otero* plaintiffs asserted that all "national origin" Chicanos, even those with functional English proficiencies, were discriminated against by a school curriculum that was not oriented to their linguistic and cultural needs and interests.[28] These were not arguments for opportunity or access in a narrow sense; rather they were centered on the comparative benefits received by Anglo and Chicano children—i.e., on educational outputs.

Specifically, the *Otero* plaintiffs alleged that the lower academic performance levels of Chicanos in District 51 were a direct result of the failure of the school's curriculum to meet educational needs of the Chicanos. The district court in *Serna* had held that a school district must consider cultural differences in its educational programming and take affirmative steps to provide equal educational benefits for all students.

Later, the district court opinion in *Keyes* gave additional currency to this concept of equal treatment, holding that "[a] school system must strive to make the 'opportunity' of an education something that *all* children in that system can avail themselves of" (380 F. Supp. 673, 695).

Thus, for the plaintiffs *Serna* and *Keyes* established a right of language minority students, as a group, to receive academic benefits equal to those received by Anglo students.

Conceptually, the equal benefits theory was more sophisticated than *Lau*'s exclusion theory. Linguists and educational experts were agreed that the cutoff mandated by the exclusion standard was arbitrary. In actuality, a child's mastery of the English language is a matter of degree. The impact of imperfect English proficiency on educational achievement is also a matter of degree. Therefore, the graduated, comparative measure of learning deficiency implied by the equal benefits approach is better calibrated than an approach based on somewhat arbitrary definitions of "exclusion."

From the standpoint of judicial manageability, however, the exclusion standard had definite advantages. It could easily be formulated as a legal rule, and its application was not dependent on technical, educational, or social science theories concerning correlations between degrees of linguistic or cultural deficiencies and educational achievement. The exclusion approach also would avoid the necessity for close scrutiny of the effectiveness of educational programs.[29] The effectiveness of bilingual-bicultural programs in improving overall academic achievement of Chicanos is much in dispute. By comparison, there is hardly any question that schools can effectively teach Chinese or Mexican-American children how to speak English.[30]

### III. DISCOVERY: A RUNNING FEUD

By almost any standard, the discovery process in *Otero* was a disaster. There was confusion, acrimony, and excessive litigation. "During eleven years as a litigator I have never seen a case so disorganized and chaotic in discovery and presentation," stated John Groves, defendants' lead attorney.[31]

The capstone of a successful discovery process is a joint pretrial order. In it, the parties set forth their areas of agreement and disagreement on the facts and on the law, and they briefly describe the documents and testimony they intend to introduce into evidence. This allows for an organized and efficient trial, focused on the major issues left unresolved by the pretrial negotiations. Not only were the parties unable to agree on a pretrial order in *Otero*, but instead of submitting a single integrated statement, they submitted a compendium of documents (on the second day of trial) which indicated that the discovery process had only proliferated, not narrowed, their areas of disagreement. This lack of coordination and cooperation caused repeated unnecessary delays at trial.

The discovery debacles seemed to occur in a regular pattern. One party would request information which the other could not or would not provide. In the words of one of plaintiffs' attorneys, "The usual ground rules did not apply. It was impossible to pick up the phone and say, 'Let's stipulate to A, B, and C and get down to the real issues.' "[32] The result was a sudden plethora of discovery motions for production of documents, answers to interrogations, protective orders against unnecessary or illegal discovery attempts, etc. The briefs were excruciatingly detailed. When various motion papers had piled up for several weeks or months, Judge Winner would hold a hearing and urge the parties to work out an agreement. Sometimes this brought results. More often a judicial order had to be issued. But almost no attempt was made to anticipate future problems.

A prime example of this litigiousness was the dispute over the defendants' demand that plaintiffs pay $1 per page for photocopying district records, the maximum fee allowed by state law. At that rate, copying would cost thousands of dollars. Also, the work space the district had made available for plaintiffs' representatives was a dimly lit hallway. The defendants finally agreed to offer better arrangements after Judge Winner said he was prepared to provide suitable office space for plaintiffs in the courthouse and to order the district officials to bring in all their files.[33]

The most important discovery controversy occurred in January 1975, when the defendants notified plaintiffs that they had hired an independent testing team (under the direction of Dr. Edgar Garrett) to administer language proficiency tests in Spanish and English to all Spanish-surnamed students. The plaintiffs violently objected, relying on a prior court direction that no language testing "in this case" would be conducted by any party except in accordance with procedural safeguards which would allow the opposite party an opportunity to monitor the testing. The defendants' reply was that the Garrett testing was "routine" and therefore not covered by the phrase, "in this case." The plaintiffs said this verbal distinction was meaningless, since the defendants were looking for a testing procedure that would bolster their position. Besides, the unprecedented hiring of an outside testing team hardly seemed routine.[34] Judge Winner backed off from issuing a clear decision on this issue, saying he would rule on the admissibility of the test scores if and when they were offered at trial. (In the meantime, he declared that the plaintiffs were free to conduct their own testing.)[35]

### *Reasons for Intransigence*

Several factors contributed to the excessive belligerency of the pretrial fact-gathering process. As has already been noted, hostility between the parties preceded the filing of the complaint. District 51 officials believed they had been unfairly selected for test litigation by militant Chicanos. Not surprising, then, was the coolness with which plaintiffs were received when they arrived at district headquarters to inspect records. Even the usual professional courtesy among lawyers failed to dampen this distrust or to limit its impact. In addition, the inexperience of plaintiffs' attorneys[36] made them reluctant to compromise. The defendants' attorneys, meanwhile, may have been relatively unaffected by the usual litigant's concern that a hard-nosed approach to discovery would alienate the judge. Judge Winner, they knew, had a reputation as a conservative on civil rights cases and had given indications early on (by a set of "interrogatories" he posed to counsel) that he would read *Lau* narrowly.

Political hostilities aside, inherent characteristics of the lawsuit hindered accommodation. *Otero* was a relatively novel case. The applicable law was unclear, and the *Serna* record too skimpy to serve as a model for trial preparation. The lawyers needed to consult with experts to find out which facts were significant and which were not. On at least two occasions attorneys for both sides were surprised by expert reports: first, when the tabulation of achievement scores showed Chicanos performing at national norms, and second, when District 51's language tests indicated that Chicano children knew more English and less Spanish than was generally assumed. However, the plaintiffs were told by their experts that the district's tests were not valid. Consequently, the existence of this potentially damaging but, in plaintiffs' eyes, misleading evidence, only strengthened the plaintiffs' determination to fight for every potentially helpful piece of information.

Judge Winner made little effort to deal comprehensively with these complex discovery problems and facilitate compromise. Court involvement was sporadic and did not provide a general framework for efficient resolution of specific discovery problems[37] If, for example, Judge Winner had conducted pretrial hearings concerning the validity of the Garrett tests prior to their being administered, plaintiffs' objections might have been taken into account and a major evidentiary issue removed from the trial phase. Instead, the two parties went to trial, one believing that the tests were flawless (defendants), and the other that they were completely invalid (plaintiffs), and with little proclivity toward compromise.[38]

## IV. Social Science on Trial

In his decision, Judge Winner stated that analysis of such social science issues as the comparative validity of educational tests was not "a function of a court."[39] Nevertheless, the *Otero* trial was "largely a battle of experts."[40] Extensive testimony and evidence were offered on a broad range of educational issues including the validity of educational programming. In few cases have basic educational issues been presented to a court in such detail. Thus, despite the judge's reservations, *Otero* turned out to be a highly suitable case for considering the capacity of the courts to deal with complicated social science evidentiary issues.

The extensive web of educational issues and testimony spun out at the *Otero* trial is summarized in table 11. We will focus on three major areas of conflicting testimony, each of which concerns different problems about the use of social science data by the courts. First, we will look at the evidence pertaining to the linguistic abilities of the Chicano schoolchildren. Second, we will consider the role played by the report submitted by the defendants' main expert, Dr. Gene Glass, concerning the causes of achievement difficulties. Finally, we will consider the plaintiffs' use of the Cardenas Theory of Incompatibilities to try to establish the validity of the need for extensive bilingual-bicultural programming.

### Linguistic Abilities of Chicano Children in Mesa County

Despite a year of discovery and investigation, the trial began with totally divergent positions on the most elementary statistical facts in the case. Plaintiffs claimed that 80% of their class were proficient in Spanish; defendants asserted that the true figure was a mere 2.7%, that only 19% of them came from homes in which Spanish was spoken, and *none* of them was fluent in Spanish. Plaintiffs claimed that as many as 70% of the Chicano children lacked proficiency in English; the defendants said that only 54 out of the 1,063 had significant English deficiencies.

### Plaintiffs' Evidence

THE COURT: [H]ow many [of the Mexican-American children] have the language barrier? The entire 8 to 8½ percent have a language barrier or just a portion of that percentage?

MR. PENA: At this point, Your Honor, we would say over fifty percent . . . it will probably be seventy percent.[41]

The thrust of the plaintiffs' evidentiary submissions concerning the linguistic abilities of their class can be summarized by two propositions: (a) Spanish is the dominant language in the Chicano community (as a result of which 80% of Chicano students were "Spanish-

## Table 11
### Expert Testimony in *Otero*

| Liability Theory | Main Factual Issues | Types of Expert/Social Science Evidence Relied on by Parties |
|---|---|---|
| A. Functional exclusion | 1. English language proficiency | 1. a. Psychometrics (validity of tests, test procedures)<br>b. Linguistics (content validity of tests)<br>c. Sociology, statistics (validity of plaintiffs' language surveys)<br>d. Geography/linguistics/sociology (patterns of language use in the Southwest) |
| | 2. Correctness of special education placements | 2. a. Psychology |
| | 3. Dropout patterns | 3. a. Statistics |
| | 4. Effectiveness of District 51 programs for Spanish-dominant students | 4. a. Bilingual-bicultural education<br>b. Educational evaluation theories<br>c. Administration |
| | 5. Effectiveness of program concepts proposed by plaintiffs | 5. a. Bilingual-bicultural education<br>b. Educational evaluation theories<br>c. Administration |
| B. Equal benefits | 1. Achievement scores, Anglo/Chicano comparison | 1. Statistics |
| | 2. Language characteristics: Spanish and English proficiency; home and community usage | 2. a. Psychometrics<br>b. Linguistics<br>c. Sociology/statistics<br>d. Geography/linguistics/sociology |
| | 3. Relation between language characteristics and reading achievement | 3. Reading development |

continued

table 11 continued

| Liability Theory | Main Factual Issues | Types of Expert/ Social Science Evidence Relied on by Parties |
|---|---|---|
| | 4. Relationship between socioeconomic status and school performance | 4. Sociology/psychology |
| | 5. Grouping by intellectual ability | 5. Psychology, psychometrics |
| | 6. Schooling in an "alien environment." Teacher role-model effects. | 6. a. Psychology<br>b. Sociology |
| | 7. Dropout patterns. | 7. Statistics |
| | 8. Effectivenes of District 51 remedial programs | 8. a. Educational evaluation<br>b. Bilingual education theories<br>c. Administration |
| | 9. Effectiveness of program concepts proposed by plaintiffs | 9. a. Educational evaluation<br>b. Bilingual educational theories<br>c. Administration |
| | 10. Soundness of Cardenas Theory of Incompatibilities | 10. All of the above |

proficient"); and (b) Chicano students in District 51 have limited English language skills that are educationally significant.[42] If proved, these facts, consistent with plaintiffs' "equal benefits" legal theory, would tend to substantiate a need for broad bilingual-bicultural programming to improve general achievement levels. Since plaintiffs' legal theory was not based merely on functional "exclusion," plaintiffs did not seriously allege that large numbers of children were so deficient in English that they could not minimally function in District 51 schools.

In support of these propositions, the plaintiffs introduced the results of three surveys. First, there was a school survey in which teachers asked their students whether Spanish was spoken at home. A second "survey" was a review of student cumulative folders, i.e., a search through miscellaneous notations made by teachers, counselors, specialists, and supervisors for remarks about a child's language use or his home language experience. The third survey, conducted under the auspices of the Colorado Civil Rights Commission and based on visits by Spanish-speaking surveyors to 125 homes of Spanish-surnamed schoolchildren, noted that Spanish was spoken in 122 of these households.

None of these surveys *directly* examined linguistic proficiencies. Furthermore, their results could not easily be cumulated because they used disparate methodologies and lacked a common set of definitional categories. Nevertheless, Dr. Steve Moreno, a psychologist and one of the plaintiffs' expert witnesses, did try to integrate this data and to draw an overall conclusion. He ultimately testified that the data showed that 800 children in the system had significant Spanish language abilities (i.e., 80% of the Spanish-surnamed children). In addition, several local residents testified about the extensive use of Spanish in Mexican-American homes and at church and social events.[43]

A classic legal argument was used to bolster these potentially vulnerable conclusions. The plaintiffs introduced official school district documents written prior to *Otero* which, they said, corroborated their points; they insisted that the district must now be foreclosed from making allegations inconsistent with those prior "admissions." The most important of these was an application for federal funding of a bilingual education program.[44] In it, school officials had described the unique linguistic and cultural characteristics of Mesa County Chicano students and had deemphasized the importance of standardized language test results (which, of course, were later to become the cornerstone of the district's defense in *Otero*): " . . . it is again our contention that Mexican-American children residing in a portion of the local community where Spanish language is at least used in part in normal communication, still have documented needs as shown in the test results of the district's standardized testing program discussed later in this proposal and may be termed *Spanish dominant*."[45] But while the application was undeniably an "admission" that the district had considered bilingual education to be a desirable policy (given adequate outside funding), its definitions (e.g., "Spanish dominant") did not really correspond to those used by the plaintiffs at trial and did not specifically admit to the existence of the types of linguistic problems (and to the need for the types of remedies) that the plaintiffs urged.[46]

## Defendants' Evidence

MR. GROVES: Plaintiffs claim to represent one thousand sixty-three Mexican-Americans, who . . . the complaint claims speak, read or write the English language with substantial difficulty or not at all or primarily speak, read and write Spanish. Your Honor, I am here today to tell you and tell counsel for Plaintiffs, to make this statement in front of representatives of the school district, if that claim is true, if we have miscalculated the needs and characteristics of the Mexican-American students in this community, then they can have this school district.[47]

Basing their arguments on standardized tests administered in 1974 and 1975, the defendants maintained that a miniscule number of Chicano children were actually proficient in Spanish, and that almost all of them were at least minimally proficient in English. If the district's allegations were accurate, they would undermine any argument for bicultural programming (since they would indicate negligible Spanish cultural influence). They would also imply that *only* remedial English language programs, and not maintenance "bilingual-bicultural" ones, were needed for the few children with problems, since even these children presumably would have relatively little Spanish background.

A test is "valid" if it actually measures what it purports to measure. Validity is a matter of degree. Psychometrics, the science of measuring psychological characteristics, does not provide absolute cutoff criteria. Consequently, courts have had a great deal of difficulty applying the either/or demands of judicial decision making to questions of test validation.[48]

Generally, test developers and publishers establish the validity of their tests through "validation study." The *Otero* plaintiffs claimed that the manuals for the tests administered by Dr. Garrett[49] did not cite any such studies to support their validity, nor was Dr. Garrett or any other of the defendants' experts able to refer to any such studies in the professional literature.

In response, Dr. Fallis, the defendants' expert in sociolinguistics, testified that her examination showed the "content validity"[50] of the tests to be satisfactory. Plaintiffs countered with Dr. Kjolseth's testimony that the tests were not content valid for use in Grand Junction because their "content" had been standardized in El Paso, Texas, where Mexican-American children spoke a different dialect (related to regional and socioeconomic differences).[51]

Turning to the actual administration of the test,[52] the plaintiffs raised serious questions concerning the qualifications of the testers. For example, under cross-examination, Dr. Garrett admitted he was unfamiliar with the testing guidelines published by the American Psychological Association, the most influential set of standards in the field. Also, although Dr. Garrett had said that the two tests (the Dos Amigos and the STACL) were the best available, he was unable to name a single other available test he had considered. Furthermore, he was unfamiliar with sixteen tests which plaintiffs asserted were alternative instruments for testing proficiency in Spanish and English. As for the testers themselves, some of the members of the testing team Dr. Garrett assembled could not speak Spanish and had to administer the test phonetically. Though Garrett testified that the phonetic training was carefully done, it was revealed later that much of it had been with the wrong test in mind.[53]

Judge Winner characterized the plaintiffs' points as "minor technical criticisms."[54] He apparently believed Dr. Glass, defendants' witness, that the APA standards should not be treated as legal rules demanding strict enforcement. Contrary to general professional opinion,[55] Dr. Glass had testified that the persons who formulated the APA standards had "a professional axe to grind," facetiously comparing these rules to an automobile manufacturer's directions that car owners use a certain brand of motor oil.[56]

Judge Winner's minimization of the plaintiffs' technical objections was also influenced by plaintiffs' failure to reinforce their criticisms either with their own rigorous survey data or with examples of evocative, common-sense errors in the defendants' results. For instance, the defendants identified exactly 54 children whose English language proficiency was too limited for full participation in the regular curriculum, but whose Spanish language skills, they claimed, were even *less* developed. If the defendants' tests were grossly inaccurate, one would think that the plaintiffs could have identified more children with limited English language skill, or at least proved that some of the children on the defendants' list had substantial Spanish language abilities.[57] Instead, they pointed out only a single example of a glaring inconsistency in the test results.[58]

In short, plaintiffs failed to impeach the defendants' tests, either by contradicting their general findings with independent comprehensive surveys or by finding embarrassing inaccuracies through spot checking. In this context, Judge Winner's acceptance of defendants' statistical submissions and rejection of plaintiffs' allegations of technical deficiencies appeared to be a reasonable judicial stance.

### The Glass Report on Causes of Achievement Deficiencies

As I read the data they [Chicanos in District 51] are achieving in accordance with their abilities and they are achieving at the national norm.[59]

Dr. Gene Glass, a professor of education at the University of Colorado,[60] prepared a report for District 51[61] which is a classic example of how the use of sophisticated statistical methods can challenge plausible, but untested, allegations about the harmful effect of particular educational policies. A major issue in *Otero* was whether disparities between the achievement scores of Chicanos and Anglos resulted from an "Anglo-oriented" curriculum. Dr. Glass's thesis was that the achievement differences could be entirely explained by the influence of intelligence (I.Q.) and socioeconomic status and that linguistic or cultural factors were insignificant.

The Premises of Glass's Analysis

Glass's analysis begins with the following assumptions about intelligence, socioeconomic status, and their relationship to academic achievement. "Intelligence" is a behavioral construct describing inherited mental capacities; it is distinct from the construct "achievement," which represents learned mental abilities. Both intelligence and achievement can be measured accurately enough, for the purposes of this analysis, through standardized tests. "Socioeconomic status" is determined by the income level of a child's family; its significance for educational evaluation is as a presumed indicator of the amount and quality of educationally enriching activities a child experiences in his home and his community. Based on studies of large populations of students, it has been found that intelligence (I.Q.) and socioeconomic status (SES) are the strongest predicators of achievements, and are, therefore, important determinants of achievement.

The Glass analysis also assumes that schools cannot be held responsible for achievement disparities determined by I.Q. and SES. The intelligence of a school-age child (in relation to the norm for his peers) is fixed. Family income levels (and the life experience presumed to go along with them) can, of course, change. Public schools, however, are not vested with authority to redistribute wealth or to intervene in family and community life. Furthermore, compensatory education programs intended to break the connection between low SES and poor achievement have been generally unsuccessful.

Replying to the assertion that failure to adjust to ethnic differences caused District 51's Chicano students to achieve less than Anglos, Dr. Glass argued as follows: As stated above, the most likely causes of achievement disparities are I.Q. and SES. Therefore, before one can make inferences concerning the impact of ethnicity or culture on achievement, one must first control for the effects of I.Q. and SES. This is done by classifying students by ethnicity, I.Q., and SES. If

Anglos and Chicanos with equivalent I.Q. and SES achieve at different levels, a causal link between ethnicity and achievement might be inferred. Since, however, the data here showed that achievement scores within the I.Q./SES groups were uniform, plaintiffs' ethnicity hypothesis was refuted.

### The Criticism and Defenses of the Report at Trial

Plaintiffs challenged the Glass report by maintaining that I.Q. tests (as well as achievement tests) were linguistically and culturally biased, and that any analysis based on grouping children by I.Q. scores was thus invalid. Moreover, plaintiffs noted, Glass himself had no role in designing or administering the defendants' tests; he prepared his report on the basis of figures supplied by the school district.

Glass generally replied by stating that the methodology of his analysis inherently compensated for the alleged bias. He said that the only pattern of distortion that would prejudice the plaintiffs' case would be one in which I.Q. tests were more biased against Chicanos than were achievement tests.[62] But this situation could not occur, he continued, because "environment and culture have a greater impact on achievement (reading and spelling) than on intelligence ..."[63] Glass based his assertion on a well-known research study,[64] but its applicability to the immediate issue was far from clear. The question was not whether environmental factors could cause larger variances in *actual* intelligence than in *actual* achievement, but whether such factors could cause ethnically biased patterns of distortion in the process of *measuring* intelligence and achievement.

Dr. Glass further argued that the I.Q. tests were geared to levels of English language proficiency that were well within the competence of Chicano students as indicated by the district's 1974[65] language testing. This was a substantial argument, but it left unexplained an anomaly in Glass's own data, one that supported plaintiffs' view that Chicano I.Q. scores were deflated because of the verbal content of the test.

After grouping the students by I.Q. and SES, and evaluating achievement scores, Glass had found that:

a. Anglos excell Chicanos by less than one month in reading;
b. Chicanos excell Anglos by approximately 3 months in mathematics;
c. Anglos excell Chicanos by approximately 1.8 months in language.[66]

The ethnic disparity in achievement on the math and reading/ language arts scores is striking. Why did Chicanos do better in math, but not in reading or language arts, than Anglos with comparable I.Q. and SES? Difficulties with the verbal content of the I.Q. tests would seem the most likely explanation.

Language and/or cultural interference was also indicated by an unexplained 10-point difference between the average I.Q. scores of Chicanos (who scored lower) and those of Anglos. Glass speculated that the disparity was caused by migratory patterns and other geopolitical peculiarities of Mesa County. When viewed together with the reading/math inconsistency in the analysis, however, it would, again, seem more plausible to conclude that the I.Q. tests underestimated the general intellectual ability of the Chicano children.[67]

Dr. Glass has admitted that the plaintiffs might have focused on this anomaly and "blown it into something large."[68] But instead, he and his report survived unembarrassed and unscathed. Why did the plaintiffs fail to exploit this promising point of attack? Limited resources, as well as relative lack of concentration on the concrete facts in the local community by plaintiffs' national experts, seem to be the answers.[69]

A written counteranalysis responding to the Glass Report would have been especially valuable. Using the anomaly in Glass's data, such an analysis could have assumed that the best available (though still inadequate) estimate of the actual intellectual ability of Chicanos in District 51 was their math achievement scores. One could then group children by math scores (instead of I.Q. test scores) and by socioeconomic status, with the result that significant disparities in language and reading performance between Chicanos and Anglos probably would appear. One could accentuate the differences even more by adding a factor based on the assumption that, because of language interference, the math score underestimated Chicano intelligence (though not as much as the I.Q. tests).[70]

How effective such a counteranalysis would have been is beyond the scope of this discussion. What is pertinent here is that the mechanisms of adversarial presentation of social science data apparently did not, on this occasion, elicit a well-balanced perspective on the critical issues. The defendants' preparation was apparently much more intensive than was the plaintiffs'. In addition to preparing his report, Dr. Glass spent many hours training the defendants' attorneys in all relevant technical areas.[71] Glass and the attorneys were determined not to repeat what they perceived to be a major mistake in *Serna:* the inability of otherwise able attorneys to challenge the plaintiffs' expert evidence because they lacked training in social science methodology.[72]

The force of the plaintiffs' social fact arguments was also weakened by mistakes in trial tactics. Glass was able to maintain his credibility at trial largely because Pena had deposed him at such great length during the pretrial discovery.[73] During these depositions, Glass recalls, Pena was "extremely sharp" and "really had me rattled." One cannot fault Pena for his thoroughness, which was intended to guard against surprise testimony at trial. But his care had an unintended effect. Coached through the depositions by the defendants' lawyers, Glass mastered the form of hostile interrogation. By the time of his first court appearance, he was a confident and clever witness.[74] When pressed to explain the math/reading anomaly in his report, for example, Glass managed to move the questioning to other areas with the blithe remark that the anomaly was "something of a mystery."[75]

### The Cardenas Theory of Incompatibilities
Three Theories in One: Descriptive, Explanatory, Prescriptive

The social science theory for judicially mandating pilot programs of bilingual-bicultural education in the *Serna* and *Keyes* cases was the Cardenas Theory of Incompatibilities.[76] "Incompatibilities" is an umbrella term encompassing three distinct elements that share interrelated assumptions. First, it is descriptive. Cardenas classified the educationally relevant characteristics of Mexican-American children under five headings: Poverty, Culture, Language, Mobility, and Societal Perceptions. The characteristics of schools, on the other hand, were grouped under ten headings: Philosophies, Policies, Scope and Sequence, Curriculum, Staffing, Co-Curriculum, Student Services, Noninstructional Needs, Community Involvement, and Evaluation. "Incompatibility" was the term describing a mismatch between a characteristic of a child and a characteristic of his school.

Some incompatibilities are self-evident. For example, a monolingual Spanish-speaking child cannot obtain adequate instruction in a science class conducted exclusively in English. Statements about the existence and significance of other incompatibilities are, however, more controversial—e.g., plaintiffs' assertion that a school lacking a specific percentage of Chicano teachers will generate an "incompatibility" between the children's societal perceptions and the schools staffing.[77]

By cross-referencing the 5 student characteristics against the 10 school system characteristics, 50 areas of potential incompatibility are identified (see figure 1). The role model debate referred to in figure 1 arises from only 1 of the single "cells," seen above, but each one of the

| | PHILOSOPHIES | POLICIES | SCOPE AND SEQUENCE | CURRICULUM | STAFFING | CO-CURRICULUM | STUDENT SERVICES | NONINSTRUCTIONAL NEEDS | COMMUNITY INVOLVEMENT | EVALUATION |
|---|---|---|---|---|---|---|---|---|---|---|
| POVERTY | 1 | 6 | 11 | 16 | 21 | 26 | 31 | 36 | 41 | 46 |
| CULTURE | 2 | 7 | 12 | 17 | 22 | 27 | 32 | 37 | 42 | 47 |
| LANGUAGE | 3 | 8 | 13 | 18 | 23 | 28 | 33 | 38 | 43 | 48 |
| MOBILITY | 4 | 9 | 14 | 19 | 24 | 29 | 34 | 39 | 44 | 49 |
| SOCIETAL PERCEPTIONS | 5 | 10 | 15 | 20 | 25 | 30 | 35 | 40 | 45 | 50 |

FIG. 1. Schematic presentation of 50 areas of "incompatibilities." Source: Plaintiffs Post-Trial Brief, p. 93.

50 cells contains areas of potential dispute about underlying facts, educational theories, and priorities among policies.

The second element of the incompatibilities theory consists of propositions about causal interrelationships among the variables identified in the descriptive theory. The central contention, of course, is that incompatibilities manifested in the school setting depress the academic achievement of Chicanos. However, direct testing of the theory's predictions is difficult because the approach purports to be holistic and indivisible. In *Otero*, Dr. Cardenas testified that the theory could not be verified by separate tests of its discrete parts. For example, eliminating 80% of the existing incompatibilities would not necessarily improve Chicano achievement by 80% or by any other amount.[78] Presumably, however, eliminating all 50 incompatibilities would equalize the performance of Anglos and Chicanos. Consequently, anything less than substantially comprehensive implementation of all the theory's aspects is deemed inadequate. The theory demands a leap of faith.

The prescriptive and third element of the incompatibilities theory deals with remedying the stated disparities in the learning environment. Dr. Cardenas testified that in order to "reduce the incompatibilities," District 51 should implement a comprehensive bilingual-bicultural program (with supporting noninstructional services). He indicated that current district efforts could not achieve this. Implicit in his approach was an important value judgment—a child's ethnic characteristics are not "handicaps" that lie outside the school's responsibility; therefore, a school's unwillingness to adapt to these characteristics is deemed "discrimination."[79]

In order for his "prescription" to be persuasive in regard to District 51, Dr. Cardenas needed to show that bilingual-bicultural programs had, at least in some degree, proven their effectiveness in comparable settings. He described his experiences with a comprehensive program he administered as Superintendent of Edgewood School District in San Antonio, Texas.[80] The defendants challenged the relevance of this anecdotal testimony, pointing out that Edgewood's, unlike District 51's, school population was 90% Chicano and was achieving below national norms. In addition, they referred to the national evaluation of Title I programs (which Dr. Glass had supervised) and the Coleman Report,[81] as evidence that educators had as yet failed to implement programs that effectively compensated for the educational disadvantages of poor and minority students. In reply, Dr. Cardenas objected to the Coleman Report, as well as to negative survey findings concerning some federal Title VII bilingual programs, on the grounds that the schools included in the surveys had never attempted any substantial reductions of incompatibilities.[82]

"Illogical, Unbelievable, and Unacceptable"

By the time Judge Winner issued his decision in *Otero*, the Tenth Circuit Court of Appeals had already reversed District Court Judge Doyle's order to implement the Cardenas plan in Denver, holding that, "[a]lthough enlightened educational theory may well demand as much, the Constitution does not."[83] In the light of this precedent, it would have been difficult for any district judge to justify its implementation. In *Otero*, however, Judge Winner emphasized that regardless of the appellate court ruling, he would not have "imposed the plan on the district." In blunt language, he stated, "I found the Cardenas plan to be illogical, unbelievable and unacceptable."[84]

Why was Judge Winner's rejection of the incompatibilities theory so forceful and so complete? Plaintiffs indicated that from the first he indicated great skepticism, if not outright hostility, about the merits of their claims.[85] But a brief consideration of the manner in which the

Cardenas theory was presented in *Otero* as compared with *Serna* and *Keyes*, where it was endorsed, indicates that any judge, even one sympathetic to plaintiffs' objectives, would have had great difficulty in accepting the *Otero* plaintiffs' reliance on the Cardenas theory.

In both *Serna* and *Keyes*, the Cardenas plan was pressed primarily at the remedial stage of the litigation. In other words, after the court had made a basic finding of constitutional violations, plaintiffs proposed the incompatibilities approach as an appropriate method for introducing programmatic changes to remedy these violations. In *Otero*, however, plaintiffs made the Cardenas theory an integral part of their basic liability theory. In essence, they claimed that a school system which was not organized to overcome Dr. Cardenas's 50 incompatibilities was *per se* in violation of the Constitution.

In other words, the court was being asked to find that the failure to adopt a controversial educational policy (and one which was highly theoretical and, admittedly, was not validated) violated the basic constitutional principle of equal educational opportunity. This it would not do.[86]

## V. Summary Perspectives

### *Principle/Policy Issues*

In order to invoke the jurisdiction of the federal district court, the plaintiffs in *Otero* defined the basic issue in their case as a denial of equal educational opportunity under the Fourteenth Amendment. Although framed in terms of a constitutional principle, the thrust of the complaint was an attempt to incorporate into the *Lau* principle of the right of non-English-speaking pupils to receive a meaningful education, a policy concerning an assertedly desirable means for improving the education of English-speaking Chicano pupils (i.e., the Cardenas Theory of Incompatibilities).[87] Thus, the "equal benefits" aspects of *Otero* would be categorized with the few "policy" cases under our threefold classification scheme described in chapter 2.[88] Here plaintiffs' lack of success on the merits is consistent with our caselet finding that plaintiffs almost always are denied relief on pure "policy" claims.

The distinction between the "exclusionary theory" articulated by the Supreme Court in *Lau* and the "equal benefits" approach inherent in the Cardenas plan clarifies the sometimes difficult distinction between principle and policy issues in the educational context. In *Lau*, the Supreme Court held that Chinese-speaking students who are unable to function in English were being totally "excluded" from their right to obtain a meaningful education. In articulating the *principle* of a right not to be excluded, the Supreme Court need not, and in fact did not, consider the competing policy considerations as to whether remedial English, bilingual, or bilingual/bicultural programming would be the most effective remedy for overcoming the students' educational deprivation. These remedial issues simply were not a necessary part of the basic principled judgment. In *Otero,* however, the plaintiffs sought to compel implementation of one type of bilingual program, a program based on the complex incompatibilities theory. The court was being asked in the first instance to consider the validity and remedial potential of a particular policy approach as an integral part of its liability determination.

The irony of the plaintiffs' situation in *Otero,* as noted in the previous section, was that the ultimate relief they sought was not fundamentally different, either in type or in magnitude, from the extensive educational programming innovations ordered by the court in *Serna* or the extensive personnel innovations implemented in *Chance.* The critical difference was that in the latter two instances, the policy considerations entered into the judicial process at the remedial stage, whereas in *Otero* the basic policy considerations were pressed at the liability stage.[89]

## Interest Representation

As with most of the cases in our caselet sample, *Otero* was brought to enforce the rights of minority group plaintiffs. But it was brought at a time when such plaintiffs had at least some hope of redress in the legislature. In the early 1970s several bicultural bills had been introduced—but killed—in the Colorado legislature.[90] Interest in the bilingual-bicultural issue was growing in Colorado, and the United States Office for Civil Rights was becoming increasingly aggressive in enforcing the *Lau* remedies. In 1975 a fairly comprehensive state bilingual-bicultural act was enacted. Still, in March 1974, when the *Otero* complaint was filed, it would not have been realistic to expect passage of such a law in the near future. As shown in the next chapter, the law was a direct consequence of fortuitous circumstances—the Democrats winning control of the House, a Chicano representative assuming the powerful position of Speaker, and a freshman Chicano senator obtaining a key position on the Joint Budget Committee. In short, *Otero* represents the use of a reform strategy that views the legislative and judicial forums as alternative strategic arenas for mobilizing political support and for achieving immediate results[91]—the courts were not an absolute "last resort" for these minority plaintiffs.

*Otero* was brought and certified as a class action. Although the case did not reach the remedy stage, the class action status was of significance, in terms of both the methods of presenting the evidence and plaintiffs' broader goal of educating the Chicano community. Early in the case, the defendants presented evidence that none of the individually named plaintiffs was substantially deficient in English, and that some of them had, in fact, attained a high level of achievement in school.[92] But because they had framed the case as a class action, the plaintiffs were allowed to persist in seeking information and developing evidence concerning the overall needs and level of achievement of the Chicano community.[93] Also, in terms of "educating" the Chicano community, it was important for La Voz to be able to present the court case as a crusade on behalf of the entire Chicano community, rather than as a more limited attempt to overcome specific problems of a few individuals.

Unlike most of the cases in our caselet sample, *Otero* was clearly a "bipolar" case in terms of party representation. Issue was drawn between the plaintiff Chicano student class on the one hand, and the school district administration on the other hand. No other groups sought intervenor or *amicus* status. Given the wide publicity and impact of this case in the local community, and its potential impact on other interests, this bipolarity was somewhat surprising since any substantial educational programming changes, and certainly any relief on the employment discrimination claims, would have affected the interests of teacher and administrator groups. However, neither the teachers' union nor any other employee groups sought to participate in the case. Nor did any groups or individuals representing the interests of the non-Chicano population, although these people may well have perceived the school board's strong stance as being fully representative of their perspectives.[94] It is, of course, conceivable that, if the plaintiffs had prevailed and the case had gone on to remedy stage, other groups would have sought involvement at that point.

The clear "party bipolarity" in *Otero*, did not, however, appear to result in "issues bipolarity." The issues raised in the case were broad and multipolar. Indeed, consideration of Cardenas's incompatibilities theory required an analysis of the functioning of the entire school system. And major claims and defenses that presumably would have been pressed by other affected interests (e.g., non-Chicano students and teachers, Chicano job applicants) were amply developed by the parties.

*Otero* also constitutes a classic example of a major and "novel" educational reform litigation that would not have been brought if the resources of public interest attorneys and advocacy groups had not been available. At the time of its initiation, the suit did not have broad support in the local community, and no disgruntled job applicants were poised to sue for better employment opportunities or back-pay awards. It is doubtful that the handful of plaintiffs would have had the inclination or the resources to hire private attorneys on their own.[95] On the other hand, it would be unfair to conclude that the *Otero* case was necessarily "manufactured" by public interest attorneys divorced from the concrete realities of the local scene. Federico Pena, plaintiffs' lead attorney, claimed he had not considered Grand Junction to present a good test case, but went to court because he felt a responsibility to provide good representation for clients who needed help with a specific grievance. Thus, in contrast with Professor Bell's thesis that civil rights attorneys in class action cases often overlook or ignore the specific subgroups within a plaintiff class,[96] the attorneys in *Otero* appeared to have shifted their strategies and abstract theories to fit the needs or the perceptions of the clients at the local level.

Despite the basic integrity of the lawyer-client relationship on the plaintiffs' side, however, representation by outside attorneys[97] undoubtedly created some practical problems. First, the very presence of these outsiders was deeply resented by the defendants' side and hardened their resistance to any possibility of accommodation, or even normal courtesies between attorneys. Secondly, the plaintiffs were at a disadvantage in presenting as evidence educational theories (e.g., the Cardenas theory) which were largely based on facts and assumptions that had been derived from experience in other areas. Their experts had not mastered the concrete facts of the local situation.

## Fact-finding Issues

### Information Collection

The amount of information submitted to the decision maker in *Otero* was extensive. The voluminous record in this case included approximately 3,000 pages of trial transcript testimony and 500 exhibits, complemented by an additional 3,000 pages of deposition transcripts, 250 pages of pleadings, 650 pages of interrogatories and answers, and 1,000 pages of briefs and other miscellaneous material.

Ironically, however, the apparent completeness of the evidentiary submissions raised serious problems. Any fact-finding mechanism obviously would stagger under the sheer weight of the volume of the submissions. The strength of the judicial process in terms of information-gathering capability lies not so much in its ability to obtain all relevant information, but rather in the courts' ability to shape the process and focus it on the seriously disputed points.

But in *Otero* the court neither shaped nor focused the voluminous evidentiary submissions. Throughout discovery, Judge Winner played a passive role, allowing the acrimonious confrontations to remain largely unrestrained, except when judicial intervention could not be avoided. Unlike Judge Mansfield in *Chance,* he did not attempt to establish a discovery plan; he did not compel the parties to formulate an effective pretrial order by stating agreed facts and disputed issues; and in comparison with Judge Mansfield's actions in inducing the parties in *Chance* to collaborate in the design and implementation of a racial impact survey, Judge Winner declined to deal with the language survey problems when they were presented in an early stage in discovery, and he allowed the language survey problem to linger and fester through both the discovery and the trial. In addition, in order to forestall potential challenges to his decision on the grounds of partiality or an underinclusive record, the judge allowed virtually all evidence proferred during the lengthy trial to be included in the record (a practice which largely benefited the plaintiffs).

The acrimonious attitude of the attorneys during the discovery process in *Otero,* was not, of course, reflective of the general pattern revealed in our caselet sample or in *Chance.* These attitudes, obviously would have hampered any effort to shape and organize discovery efficiently. However, Judge Winner's passive approach to these problems appeared to exacerbate the difficulties.

The judge's posture in this regard was inconsistent with his stated position that many of the policy issues raised in the pleadings should not have been brought before the courts. If from the outset he had clearly distinguished between principle-oriented issues that should be decided by the court, and pure policy or subsidiary policy issues that should not, the court might have been in a position to organize the relevant information efficiently and to discard the extraneous.

Information Assessment

Judge Winner strongly believed that courts generally should not engage in educational policy making, but should defer to the judgment of local school boards. Consistent with this view, he held that he would not substitute his judgment for the conclusions of the board and its expert on educational testing and achievement issues, so long as these conclusions were rendered in good faith. His holding in this instance is a good example of the type of avoidance device categorized under the heading of "burden of proof" in chapter 4. In other words, unless plaintiffs met the heavy burden of persuading the court that the defendants had not carried out their educational responsibilities "in good faith," the judge would refuse to analyze independently the validity of the board's testing methodologies and educational programming approaches.

Despite this, Judge Winner went on to say that although he deferred to the discretion of the board, "It just so happens that I thought the testimony of the school board experts as to testing procedures and the conclusions reached as a result thereof made good sense—much better sense than did the opposing testimony."[98] The judge then discussed in great detail his independent conclusions concerning many of the complex social fact issues raised during the trial. Thus, in his lengthy dicta, Judge Winner, unlike the overwhelming majority of judges in our caselet sample, did undertake a detailed assessment of the relevant facts. For that reason, *Otero* provides an important illustration of judicial fact-finding capabilities.

If, as Dr. Glass stated, the defendants' attorneys were given "what amounted to a graduate course in statistics"[99] in preparing for the trial, Judge Winner should also be given high marks for completing this course. For example, his decision contained a detailed analysis of the comparative validity of plaintiffs "home surveys" on student language proficiency as against defendants' STACL standardized tests. The judge's criticism of the methodology in plaintiffs' survey was both perceptive and accurate. The decision also reflected more than casual familiarity with test validation concepts. Although the judge specifically indicated that he upheld the credibility of defendants' experts on these points, the decision was based on independent analysis and understanding of the issues.[100]

Judge Winner dismissed plaintiffs' detailed allegations that Dr. Garrett's language proficiency testing methodology violated the norms of the American Psychological Association as being "minor technical criticisms." Since plaintiffs were never able to show any substantive errors in the testing results, the court's decision to give these arguments little weight and thereby avoid detailed consideration of their merits seems plausible. Thus it is evident that when complex and multiple evidentiary issues are presented in a case like *Otero,* a judge, no matter how adept at understanding intricate social science issues, must at some point make some basic judgments about which issues deserve full consideration. Such judgments will be made largely on a "common-sense" basis. In *Chance,* e.g., Judge Mansfield gave great consideration to technical psychometric arguments similar to those rejected for consideration by Judge Winner in *Otero,* because, in that instance, allegations of a lack of content validity were illustrated by compelling common-sense examples of absurd examination questions.[101]

Judge Winner's decision did not, of course, contain any discussion of the vulnerable points in Dr. Glass's student achievement report. Since these potential criticisms were not fully developed or forcefully argued, the judge was not in a position to consider them. This void in the fact-finding analysis clearly stemmed from the limitations of the adversary system, especially the resource deficiencies of the plaintiffs and the more extensive expert preparation by the defendants.[102]

# 9

## Colorado Legislative Case Study
### *The Bilingual-Bicultural Education Bill*

———◆———

In the mid-1970s, promoting implementation of a broad concept of bilingual-bicultural education in the public schools was a major reform priority of many of Colorado's Chicano leaders. As indicated in the previous chapter, in 1974 a test case litigation[1] was commenced in the federal court proceedings in the *Otero* case, attempts to gain passage of statewide legislation promoting or mandating bilingual-bicultural education were being pressed in the state legislature. The close correspondence between the issues considered by the two branches of government, and the simultaneous timing of their actions, make a study of the Colorado legislature's 1975 deliberations on the bilingual-bicultural education act an ideal point of comparison for the *Otero* study. In addition, the conclusions drawn from this comparison can themselves be compared to the findings from our New York judicial/legislative studies.

Surprisingly, despite the simultaneous timing[2] and overlapping of participants,[3] the judicial and the legislative decision-making processes hardly influenced each other. Although references to the *Lau* and *Serna* cases appeared sporadically in the legislative debates, *Otero* was barely mentioned. Indeed, when several of those legislators who were more involved in the passage of the bilingual-bicultural bill were interviewed three years later, they were totally unaware of *Otero* or of its holding.[4] Conversely, although the attorneys for the plaintiffs informed Judge Winner in their posttrial briefs that the bilingual-bilcultural act had been passed by the legislature and that, in essence, the bicultural programmatic relief they were seeking was now the official policy of the state of Colorado, Judge Winner seemed unimpressed and made no mention of it in his sixteen-page opinion.

This case study, like the New York legislative case study in chapter 7, is organized in five sections. Section I discusses the educational problem as defined by the minority constituency. Section II describes the legislative setting in the spring of 1975, when major attention became focused on bilingual education. Section III summarizes the basic issues contained in the major bill initially submitted by the Chicano legislators. Section IV traces the reactions, amendments, and deliberations as the bill wound its way through the various legislative stages. Finally, Section V gives summary perspectives based on the four-part analytic framework employed throughout this study.

## I. THE PROBLEM

In the state of Colorado, approximately 80,000 students, or 20% of the student population, are of Hispanic origin. During the 1974–75 school year, 6,588 Spanish-surnamed students were identified as being enrolled in bilingual or bilingual-bicultural education programs, and an additional 849 as enrolled in English-as-second-language programs.[5] The programs in which these students participated were located in 34 of Colorado's 181 school districts.[6] At the time, these programs were funded mainly through local school-district tax revenue resources or by federal moneys received under Title VII of the Elementary and Secondary Education Act of 1965. Simply stated, the aim of the proponents of the bilingual-bicultural education bill was to extend the scope of these programs to include all eligible Hispanic students, and to obtain substantial state funding so that the permanence of the programs could be assured.[7]

The chief sponsors of the bill, however, did not define the problem primarily in terms of a functional exclusion of non-English-speaking Chicano students from public education. It was generally known that the Chicano community had deep roots in Colorado and that for many families English was the primary language of both adults and children.[8] But, consistent with the Cardenas incompatibilities theory, discussed in the previous chapter, these leaders also believed that the Colorado public school environment was, by and large, an alien one for Chicano students, undermining their cultural aspirations and impairing their scholastic achievement.[9] Thus, Valdez, who was to become the Speaker of the House during the 1975 session, stated that ever since he was elected to the legislature in 1970, his "first priority" had been enactment of a bilingual-bicultural bill. It was "absolutely necessary for our kids; it would stop the 'non-achievement' cycle."[10]

The opponents of the legislation, like the defendants in *Otero*, took the position that mandating "bicultural" programming would be an improper use of the public schools to solve pervasive socioeconomic problems. Moreover, they were not convinced that this approach would actually improve student achievement.[11] Consequently, much of the legislative opposition was centered on alternative proposals for "tutorial" English-as-a-second-language remedial services for those children who could not speak English. Thus, like the *Otero* defendants, the legislative opposition favored the concept of requiring transitional language instruction for non-English-speaking children, but rejected the broader "incompatibilities" approach as the bilingual solution in Colorado.

## II. The Legislative Setting

In its study of the technical capabilities of the 50 state legislatures, the Citizen's Conference on State Legislatures ranked Colorado number 28, specifically emphasizing its limited staffing resources.[12] Unlike New York, where each legislator is allocated some individual staff resources and committee chairmen receive substantial staff appropriations, in Colorado neither the individual legislators nor even the committee chairmen are given direct staff assistance. Research for the legislature as a whole is done by the Legislative Council, consisting of approximately 30 staff members to serve the needs of all 100 legislators. In addition, a legislative bill-drafting office and the Office of the Revisor of Statutes, each with a staff of approximately 20–25, provide technical assistance in the drafting of bills and revising of statutes.

One Legislative Council staff member is usually assigned to serve two standing committees. Since this staff member is expected to arrange committee hearings, line up witnesses, and handle the administrative formalities of the committee's business, little time is allotted for actual research.[13] Since, generally speaking, the assistant's primary allegiance is to the committee chairman, individual legislators, as a practical matter, have little access to staff services, except perhaps when such services can be obtained from the four full-time or eleven part-time college interns who work with some of the members.[14]

Although in comparison to the situation in New York, the research resources available to individual legislators and to standing committees in Colorado are extremely limited, as is the amount of space available to them,[15] the legislative work load apparently leaves more time for consideration of bills by the members. For example, during the average long session, the Colorado legislature considers approximately 1,200 bills,[16] compared, for example, with 9,000 bills in New York. Standing committees in Colorado generally meet twice a week and consider an average of 4 to 5 bills per session, compared with an average of 20 bills considered by the New York education committee.[17]

### III. The Basic Issues

Bilingual education issues appeared on the legislative agenda at the insistence of Chicano representatives, but not because of an external crisis such as the fiscal crisis and massive layoffs in New York. On the contrary, the 27-page House Bill No. 1295 introduced early in the 1975 session by a coalition of Chicano legislators[18] was the culmination of several years of legislative consideration of bilingual-bicultural education issues.

In 1973, Representative Valdez had introduced a bilingual bill which was passed in the House but defeated in the Senate. As a substitute for a comprehensive bill, the legislature then appropriated a small amount of money for a study of the extent and operations of existing bilingual programs,[19] and granted additional appropriations to the State Education Department to expand its technical resources in this area. During the two years preceding the 1975 session, the Chicano legislators sponsored extensive meetings throughout the state so that educators, parents, members of the community, and lawyers expert in the field could provide specific input on the bill.[20] Senator Sandoval estimated that approximately 150 people participated in drafting the expanded version of the act which was introduced in 1975 as H.B. 1295.

This input resulted in a greater emphasis than in the 1973 bill on "bicultural" aspects of student eligibility and programming, and on community involvement. In other words, H.B. 1295 was an attempt to implement a program in line with the Cardenas incompatibilities theory. As such, it was innovative in comparison not only with existing programs in Colorado, but also with existing statutory and regulatory requirements of other states and of the federal government.

The consistent bicultural emphasis of the original version of H.B. 1295 and its reallocation of policy-making authority to local community groups can be seen from a brief summary of the bill's major aspects.

## Eligibility

The declaration of legislative intent was directed at those students "with linguistically different skills *or* culturally different environments due to the influence of another language in their family, community, or peer group, or due to their cultural environment..." (p. 2; emphasis supplied). The main significance of this broad definition of student eligibility was that it was not restricted to students who could speak no English but, consistent with the Cardenas theory, assumed that students from "culturally different environments," whatever the present extent of their English language proficiency, are entitled to special programming.[21]

A school district would be required to develop a program if 20 or more students or 5% of the student population in any of its schools met the above definition.[22] A district would also be permitted, though not required, to develop a program if a smaller number of students had been identified. Once a program was developed, additional students who were not eligible under the definitions would also be permitted to enroll.

## Programming

Once the requisite number of eligible students had been identified, the district would then be responsible for developing programs "of sufficient duration and scope to meet the educational needs of all pupils with linguistically different skills or culturally different environments" (p. 9). These programs were to fulfill the broad objectives for bilingual-bicultural education set forth in the legislative declaration, including the development of "cultural and ethnic pride and understanding" (p. 2). No specific limitations concerning the number of years in which a child would be enrolled in the program, or the number of hours per week to be devoted to it, were contained in the draft.[23]

## Staffing

In selecting teachers and teacher aides for this program, the school district would be required to "make an affirmative effort to seek, recruit and employ persons who are bilingual and who share or reflect the culture of the students with linguistically different skill or culturally different environments who enroll in the program" (pp. 14–15). Special certification procedures for such bilingual teachers were written into the act. In addition, a program in which 100 or more pupils were enrolled was required to appoint a director of bilingual and bicultural education; and in any community containing 50 or more students, one or more full-time "community coordinators" would have to be hired.

### Administrative Structure

On the local level, a parent committee, at least 75% of which was to consist of parents of students in the program, was to be established in each school district. This committee would have extensive powers, including the right to "approve and have full and effective participation in hiring, curriculum, and budgeting of the bilingual and bicultural program" (p. 20). In addition, the committee would have the right to receive information, to employ a staff member of its own, and to receive funds to allow its members to visit model programs throughout the state and make trips to recruit personnel.

On the state level there was a "state steering committee" whose members would be selected from a list of individuals recommended by the local parent committees. This state committee would have extensive powers to select the assistant commissioner for bilingual education and to adopt rules, regulations, timetables, and evaluative criteria for the effective implementation of the act. In addition, it would approve testing procedures for local school districts, consider appeals of local educational agencies whose programs were not approved by the State Education Department, and evaluate all bilingual and bicultural program plans.

### Enforcement

Any local school district that failed to identify eligible students and develop plans as required by the act could be penalized with loss of all its state funding and its accreditation. The draft was ambiguous as to whether a school district would be required to implement the program if, after its development and consideration by the State Education Department and state steering committee, sufficient state funds were not available to support it fully.[24]

## IV. THE LEGISLATIVE PROCESS

The saga of the Colorado Bilingual-Bicultural Education Act reveals how "political savvy and clout"[25] can engineer the passage of a highly controversial piece of legislation. That the 1975 Act was passed by both houses and signed into law, although the less controversial

1973 act had been killed, can be attributed to the skillful maneuvering of two key Chicano legislators who achieved positions of power in the 1975 legislative session.

The first was Representative Ruben Valdez. After an overwhelming Democratic majority took control of the House, Representative Valdez, "generally acknowledged as the most effective legislator in the . . . session,"[26] was elected speaker. As previously noted, Valdez had, for years, considered the bilingual-bicultural bill as his highest legislative priority. His newly acquired power now enabled him to bargain hard with the Senate Republican majority for passage of his priority bill. The second key figure in his political drama was Paul Sandoval, a freshman legislator and the sole Democrat appointed to the powerful Joint Budget Committee. Like Valdez, Sandoval considered the bilingual-bicultural bill as his highest legislative priority, and was willing to vote with the Republican chairman of the Joint Budget Committee, Senator Joe Shoemaker, on virtually every other item under the committee's jurisdiction, in return for Shoemaker's support of the bilingual-bicultural bill.[27] Table 12 summarizes the specific changes made to the original bill as it worked its way through the legislative process.

## Deliberations in the House

The House Education Committee undertook consideration of H.B. 1295 in early March. During the next four weeks, it devoted six meetings (a total of 7½ hours), to deliberations on this bill. The first three meetings brought testimony from thirty-five witnesses. Given the limited time available, few of these witnesses had an opportunity to present detailed arguments; the testimony of most of the individual citizens and educators lasted less than five minutes.

A handful of speakers, however, were granted more time to develop issues before the committee. Ernie Andrade, Coordinator of Minority Programs for the Greeley Public Schools and an expert witness in *Otero*, discussed for approximately a half hour the theoretical basis of bilingual-bicultural education and the specific programs operating in his particular district. Federico Pena, chief counsel for the plaintiffs in *Otero*, also testified for about a half hour; he discussed the legal precedents and the applicability of the Cardenas theory, and ended with a detailed section-by-section explanation of the bill. Dr. R. Kjolseth, another witness in *Otero*, testified for approximately twenty minutes on bilingual-bicultural programs in the United States and other countries and emphasized the importance of parental involve-

Table 12
Summary of Major Provisions of Drafts of
Colorado Bilingual-Bicultural Act

| LEGISLATIVE PROCESS | ELIGIBILITY | PROGRAMMING | ENFORCEMENT |
|---|---|---|---|
| Original Version | Students with "linguistically different skills *or* culturally different environments" District must establish a program if 20 students or 5% of population in any school are eligible | Full bilingual-bicultural K–12 | Penalty for noncompliance: complete termination of all state funding and withdrawal of accreditation. Additional private right of action |
| House Ed. Comm. | Same as original except: 50 students or 10% of population | Same as original | Development of plan declared mandatory. Private right of action (attorney fees). Attorney General right of action. No specific penalties. Clarification that district need not implement program if no state funding |
| Senate Ed. Comm. | Students "who speak only a language other than English" Permissive-grant applications | "Tutorial program" —nonmandatory details | Permissive—no enforcement |

ment. In addition, several representatives of federal civil rights agencies gave brief statements about relevant federal regulations and about the U.S. Civil Rights Commission study on the educational experiences of Mexican-Americans in five states in the Southwest.

Most of the testimony supported the bill. Several representatives of the State Education Department raised questions concerning specific

| APPROPRI- TION LEVEL | STAFFING | ADMINISTRATIVE STRUCTURE | |
| --- | --- | --- | --- |
| | | Parent Advisory Committee | New Division State Ed. Dept. |
| $8 million | Affirmative effort to seek teachers and aides who are bilingual and "share or reflect" the culture of the eligible students Requirements for hiring director (if 100 students), community coordinator (if 50 students), etc. | YES, with rights to approve programming, hiring, curriculum. Right to employ a staff member and receive travel expenses | YES, plus state steering committee, with power to set regulations, hear appeals, and evaluate plans |
| $8 million (Reduced to $6 million by House Appropriations Committee) | Same as original | YES, with specific consultative rights, staff member to be appointed by Board. Expenses may be paid by Board | YES, plus state steering committee, with specific consultative rights |
| $1 million | No specific provisions | No specific provisions | No specific provisions |

continued

details, but few argued with the basic concept of bilingual-bicultural programming. A major exception to this was Dr. Donald Oglesby, the Superintendent of the Mesa County School District. As might be expected from a defendant in *Otero*, Dr. Oglesby opposed the bill and raised the same objections that had been pressed in *Otero*. Specifically, he pointed to the absence of data concerning the functional profi-

table 12 continued

| LEGISLATIVE PROCESS | ELIGIBILITY | PROGRAMMING | ENFORCEMENT |
|---|---|---|---|
| Senate Appropriations Comm. | Students with "linguistically different skills" defined as students with English language difficulties who also come from culturally different environments 50 students or 10% of population in any school | Full bilingual-bicultural (but some provisions emphasizing bicultural aspects omitted) K–3 | Development of plan declared mandatory, but no specific penalties or references to right of action. Clarification that district need not implement program if no state funding |
| As Enacted | Same as Senate Appropriations Comm. | Full bilingual-bicultural K–3 | Same as Senate Appropriations |
| 1977 Amendments to Act | Students with "linguistically different skills" defined as students whose English language level is below district mean or student expectancy level who also come from a culturally different environment | "Transitional" bilingual-bicultural program of "necessary scope and duration" to meet specific objectives, which may not be required on a daily basis | No change |

ciency in English of Spanish-surnamed children; he emphasized the difference between bilingual and bicultural programs; and he stressed that no existing data indicated that such bilingual-bicultural programs increased student achievement. He also raised the issues of local control, costs and the inappropriateness of teachers having to "share or reflect" the student's culture. In other words, in his fifteen minutes of testimony, Dr. Oglesby put before the committee the three major evidentiary issues in *Otero:* the linguistic proficiencies of students, the validity of the incompatibilities theory, and the interpretation of Chicano achievement-test scores. But these substantial issues were not given great attention. Committee members did not cross-examine Dr. Oglesby,[28] later witnesses did not pursue his points, and

| Appropria-tion Level | Staffing | Administrative Structure | |
| --- | --- | --- | --- |
| | | Parent Advisory Committee | New Division State Ed. Dept. |
| $2.35 million | Same as original | YES, with specific consultative rights. Board to provide "technical assistance" to committee | Same as House Ed. Comm. |
| $2.35 million plus $200,000 for a tutorial program (Senate Ed. Comm. bill) | Affirmative effort to seek teacher and aides who are bilingual Director/Coordinator: Same as original | Same as Senate Appropriations | Same as House Ed. Comm. |
| $2.1 million (including $200,000 for a tutorial program) | No change | No change | No change |

the opponents of the bill did not arrange to have an educational expert such as Dr. Glass lend additional credibility to Oglesby's skeptical views.

Following the three sessions of public testimony, "work-up sessions" were held to amend or revise the bill on a line-by-line basis. Representatives of the State Education Department attended some of these meetings, providing technical drafting advice, and explaining some of the "understandings" that were behind the amendments now being adopted by the committee. These "understandings" had evolved out of long and detailed negotiations held outside the formal committee structure. Our interviews revealed that the main participants in these informal negotiations were Representatives Valdez and Lucero; Representatives Miller and Sears, the highest ranking Republicans on the Education Committee; attorneys from the Chicano Education Project; Robin Johnston, Chairwoman of the State Board of Education; and staff members of the State Education Department.

The state officials were mainly interested in eliminating or modifying the powers of the proposed parent and state steering committees. Chairwoman Johnston believed that the proponents of the bill were seeking to set up a parallel education system, and that this new structure "would destroy education in this state."[29] The Republican legislators concurred in the department's position on this, but were also concerned with the enforcement provisions (e.g., the total cutoff of funds) and the large numbers of children who would be eligible under a 20%–5% formula. At this early stage, the basic "bicultural" eligibility and programming aspects of the bill were as yet not the main focus of the challenge by the opposition. Representative Sears specifically stated that strong eligibility and programming rights were acceptable to her "if the other troublesome items were eliminated." The State Education Department did not aggressively contest the bicultural features, Commissioner Frazier having stated that, under the Colorado Constitution, the school system had a responsibility to "teach the cultures of all children."[30] Thus, this intensive negotiating process enabled the parties involved basically to achieve their primary goals. The proponents of the bill retained the innovative bicultural eligibility and programming formula, while the opposition substantially eliminated the "troublesome issues" of parallel administrative structures and mandatory enforcement powers.[31]

This compromise, ultimately endorsed by unanimous vote of the committee, was, however, obtained only after much travail and bitter confrontation. On the one hand, State Chairwoman Johnston related that initially feelings ran so high that she received death threats over the telephone: "You destroyed our children and we will kill yours." On the other hand, the Chicano coalition doubted the fairness and neutrality of the State Education Department since its commissioner, who had promised support for a bilingual-bicultural bill, now seemed, in their view, to be advising the Republican opponents.[32] Republicans also repeatedly alluded to the strong lobbying pressure mounted by members of the Chicano Education Project, who were seen as out-of-state "agitators" funded with foundation money. One representative characterized it as a new method of lobbying which bypassed the legislature. Instead of bringing its case to the members directly, the CEP stirred up the constituents in a local district and brought tremendous indirect pressure on members from their home area.[33] Interestingly, however, though the bill reflected strongly felt needs of the Chicano community, it did not otherwise arouse strong affirmative interest on the part of other groups or among the education community, as had been the case in New York. For example, the Colorado Education Association (the statewide teachers' organization) did not participate substantially in the deliberations, and simply went on record as generally favoring the concept of bilingual education.[34] Similarly, the Colorado Association of School Boards never took a strong stand on any of the issues. Thus, the political battle basically pitted the Chicano legislators and their supporters against the Republican opposition, with the State Education Department (called upon as a resource primarily by the Republican side) acting as a third force.

After being amended by the House Education Committee, H.B. 1295 quickly passed through the House Appropriations Committee, whose only change was a decrease in the appropriation from $8 million to $6 million. The measure then went to the House floor. Most of the brief floor debates were centered on the appropriations and on the question of the availability of sufficient funds. The $6 million figure was ultimately left intact, since the final decision on funding would, in any event, be made after consideration by the Senate Appropriations Committee and the Joint Budget Committee.

Discussion on the bill preceding the House vote was essentially anecdotal, rather than analytic. Representative Lucero stressed his own school experiences and made no reference to any of the specific evidence or data which had been introduced before the committee or which may have been made available in the original formulation of the bill. The only "experts" discussed in his speech were Pavlov and Skinner, whose relevance to the bill was not entirely clear. Representative Valdez did briefly allude to *Lau, Serna,* and statutes in other states, but only to show that "the courts and everyone else are saying that the time has come for equal education." Finally, on the third reading, and after bipartisan support for the concept of bicultural education was expressed by the Republican chairman of the Education Committee, the bill was passed by the House by a 50–3 vote.

### Deliberations in the Senate

H.B. 1295 was next sent over to the Senate, where the Republican-controlled Senate Education Committee undertook initial consideration of the bill. Five sessions, lasting altogether 4½ hours, were held by the committee. Witnesses, most of whom had already appeared before the House Committee, testified at three of these sessions. Predictably, the testimony before the Senate Committee was similar to that in the House, except that the time accorded to all witnesses was substantially reduced and the number of witnesses was approximately half.

That the Senate Committee would develop the evidentiary issues in a more limited matter was not unexpected since an extensive record of the House proceedings was already available. Yet, there is no indication that transcripts or even summaries of the testimony before the House were ever used. In general, the Senate Education Committee's official file on this bill was quite bare. Documentation was scanty, consisting primarily of the State Education Department's Resolution 20 report, certain budget notes, letters from interested parties, and analyses of some of the legal issues by staff members of the Legislative Council. No copies of the Civil Rights Commission's Mexican-American Study Report, no data on linguistic characteristics of children or their achievement levels, and no information concerning the Cardenas theory were contained in the file.

In its formal deliberations, the Senate Committee paid little attention to the specific details of H.B. 1295. Its chairman, Senator Hugh Fowler, had decided that the entire concept of the bilingual-bicultural bill was "revolutionary" and he was unalterably opposed to the concept of "using the schools as an agency of social change."[35] Under Senator Fowler's urging, the committee rejected the substance of H.B. 1295 and substituted an entirely different concept of a "tutorial program"—although the original title and bill number were retained. The "tutorial" bill would have provided $1 million for individual English-language remediation programs for children who "speak only a language other than English." Senator Fowler felt that, consistent with the *Lau* decision, the state was obligated to provide programs only to children who were effectively excluded from participation because of linguistic difficulties; in addition, from an educational viewpoint, he believed that an individualized language-remediation approach ("like a Berlitz crash course") was the soundest way to solve the bilingual problem.

The Democratic members of the Senate Education Committee adopted the substitute tutorial approach as a means of getting the bill (that is, the title and the number) out of committee. They were confident that the substance of H.B. 1295 could be put back by the Senate Appropriations Committee.[36] Since then, Senator Fowler has main-

tained that he was misled by the leadership of his own party on this
point, claiming there was agreement on his tutorial concept and that
he never would have let the bill out of committee if he had thought
that the leadership intended to reinstate its original substance.[37]

In any event, the bill was approved in its tutorial form by the Education Committee and then sent to the Senate Appropriations Committee which met on seven occasions, for a total of 9¼ hours. No
public testimony was taken at these sessions, except for a demonstra-
tion of a bilingual lesson by a class from the Johnston School District,
which made a deep impression on those committee members who had
never seen a bilingual program in operation.[38] In essence, the Senate
Appropriations Committee, which normally considers only fiscal aspects of a bill, played the analytic reviewing role that the Senate Education Committee might have played if its chairman were not totally
opposed to the bicultural concept.

The main concern in the Appropriations Committee's deliberations
was the bicultural concept and the definition of eligible students. The
committee decided to include cultural differences in the basic definition of "linguisitically different skill,"[39] and then to eliminate most of
the separate "bicultural" references throughout the body of the bill.
Senator Sandoval accepted this compromise in order to get the bill out
of committee, because, as he put it, so long as the title and legislative
declaration of the bill retained the explicit reference to "bicultural"
considerations, the courts would understand the clear legislative intent in implementing the bill.[40]

Other major changes of the Appropriations Committee were a limitation of the program to the kindergarten through third grade (K–3)
level and a reduction of appropriations from $6 million to $2.35
million. These changes were not strongly resisted by the proponents
of the bill because the K–3 limitation "makes sense educationally,"
and, because as Representative Valdez admitted, given the fiscal realities, a reduction to the K–3 level was a necessary "gimme" to assure
the bill's passage.[41] It is interesting that there was little opposition to
the strong affirmative-action hiring aspects, and the Appropriations
Committee draft retained the requirement to seek teachers and aides
who "share or reflect the culture" of the students.

On June 14, the bill moved to the Senate floor for what was to
become the most extensive debate in that chamber's history.[42] During
the eighteen hours of grueling consideration, almost 200 amendments to the Appropriations Committee version of the bill were intro-

duced, mostly by Republicans seeking to weaken its bicultural aspects. Through most of this debate, lawyers from the Chicano Education Project were present to provide technical assistance to the Democratic proponents, while Commissioner of Education Frazier's advice was frequently sought by the Republican legislators.[43]

The thrust of the Senate debate was centered on the critical bicultural issue. Early on, Senators Sandoval and Cisneros proposed an amendment to reinstate the numerous references to "biculturalism" eliminated by the Appropriations Committee. This was a shift from Sandoval's previous position that technically these references were not necessary. Later, however, he and the other supporters came to believe it was important to bring this issue out in the open and to focus on the explicit bicultural element.[44]

In advocating the new program, Senators Sandoval and Cisneros, like their colleagues in the House, stressed their own personal educational experiences. They referred, also, to various court cases, including *Serna* and *Keyes,* to prove the courts' acceptance of "bilingual-bicultural programming," but they did not emphasize the Cardenas theory or statistics concerning achievement scores, etc. Senator Fowler, leader of the opposition, focused on the average citizens' feelings that this bicultural orientation was "un-American." Other opponents also expressed concern that the word "bicultural," as opposed to "multicultural," implied that only Chicanos, but not other linguistic or cultural groups, would be able to take advantage of this program.

In the end, the Senate Appropriations Committee's version of H.B. 1295 was adopted by the Senate with a number of technical amendments: specific references to biculturalism throughout the bill were reinstated, while the original emphasis on biculturalism in the legislative declaration, the definition of eligibility, and the explicit requirements for bicultural programming remained intact. The most significant change that Senate opponents of the bill achieved was the elimination of specific references in the affirmative action hiring provisions to individuals who "share or reflect the culture" of the eligible students. The basic funding was maintained at $2.35 million, although an additional $200,000 was appropriated for the type of pilot "tutorial program" outlined in Senator Fowler's substitute proposal.

On the final vote, Senator Shoemaker and five other Republicans voted with all the Democrats but one to enact the 1975 bilingual-bicultural education act. The next day, the Senate version was accepted without modification by the House, and the bill was sent on to the governor for his signature.*

## V. Summary Perspectives

### *Principle/Policy Issues*

The basic issue before both the court and legislature in Colorado in 1975 was whether a bilingual-bicultural program based on the Cardenas Theory of Incompatibilities should be implemented for students who generally were proficient in English but came from "culturally different environments." Approaching the question from the perspective of principle, the court held that Chicano students were not entitled to such a program. Approaching the same question from the perspective of policy, the legislature decided that such a program should be put into effect. Thus, as with our New York case studies, the institutional differences between the legislature and the court led to strikingly different substantive results.

The clear principle perspective in the *Otero* case was the "exclusion-

---

*Passage of H.B.1295 in 1977 did not, however, end legislative consideration of these issues in Colorado. During the 1977 session, major amendments were made in the law. These amendments specified that the program funded under the act would be "transitional" and that eligible students with "linguistically different skills" would include only those whose English language skills were "below the district mean or expectancy level *and* who come from an environment of different customs and traditions" (emphasis supplied). These changes have reduced the extent of mandatory bicultural programming in Colorado. Nevertheless, the Colorado act still maintains a strong bicultural thrust when compared to the legislation of other states.

These changes were clearly not unrelated to the Republicans' full control of the legislature in the 1977 session. In addition, the State Education Department had found that the definitional inconsistencies within the bill made it extremely difficult to specify who was eligible and who had a right to the limited funding provided under the act. Apparently, in some districts it had been assumed that all Spanish-surnamed students were automatically eligible.

Despite the renewed legislative battles in 1977, most of our interviewees agreed that, by and large, the act has now been widely implemented, and many local superintendents who were initially skeptical have now endorsed the programs; in some cases they have provided local funding to supplement the limited state appropriations. According to Representative Valdez, an important feature of the implementation is the mechanism for parental and community participation at the local and state levels (even as modified). This consultative apparatus has been meaningful and is currently the strongest in Colorado law. The seriousness with which it has been taken is exemplified by the fact that a proposal by one school district which did not "seriously consider" parental recommendations was rejected by the State Board of Education, and the attorney general was instructed to institute appropriate court proceedings to bring that district into compliance.

ary" approach, which, under the *Lau* precedent, would have entitled plaintiffs to relief if they had been able to show that a significant number of non-English-speaking students were being denied access to meaningful education. Their inability to prove this led the court to consider their attempts to press the complex Cardenas theory as raising extraneous policy considerations which should be left to the discretion of the local school board.

The Colorado legislators, by way of contrast, were not focused on such general principles of liability as the exclusion concept. From the outset, the Republican opponents in the House accepted the premise that broad bilingual-bicultural programming was a legitimate educational policy approach, and they focused their objections on the bill's fiscal and administrative implications. Even when the bicultural approach was directly attacked in the Senate, the debate centered on the instrumental advantages of bicultural programming, and not on the "legitimacy" of treating entitlement to such programming as a legal right.

The two Colorado case studies illustrate the reasons why courts do not easily accept broad new policy approaches as the basis of liability determinations, even when a strong need for reform has been shown. Judicial liability decisions have important precedential impact which legislative enactments do not. If the *Otero* case had ruled that Chicano students were entitled to educational benefits geared at raising their achievement levels to that of Anglo students, other courts would have found it difficult to deny analogous relief in cases raising similar challenges to school financing systems and to numerous health, welfare and other public services. Furthermore, a finding of liability under an equal benefits theory would have logically enabled plaintiffs to argue for a complete remedy that would fully rectify the wrong, whatever the costs involved. Judge Winner had warned that such widespread implementation of the plaintiffs' approach would bankrupt local school districts.

By way of contrast, in the Colorado legislative process, the problems of precedent, effectiveness, and financing were not obstacles to adoption of the equal benefits theory as a policy goal. Chicano underachievement was seen as an educational problem—a symptom of a *need*—not as evidence of a violated *right*. Consequently, the legislature could try to remedy the achievement gap by partial funding without committing itself to remedy every instance of underachievement. In so doing, it was not establishing broad principles which could then be applied to numerous other public service issues.[45]

The difference in principle/policy roles of the courts and the legislature was readily articulated by the Colorado legislators. Throughout the House and Senate debates, speakers periodically invoked the *Lau, Serna,* and *Keyes* decisions to establish the legitimacy of the claims of Chicano children to educational "rights." As Representative Lucero put it: "The courts state the basic principle, and the legislature fills in the details."[46] Although resentful of any suggestions of direct court interference with legislative prerogatives,[47] Representative Sears admitted that the *Lau* decision clearly was an "impetus to passage of the bill."

Thus, it seems reasonable to conclude that, although no court had mandated the enactment of the bilingual-bicultural bill, known court decisions had established in the minds of the legislators the basic legitimacy of the type of educational rights for which the Chicano legislators were pressing.[48] In the context of the court decisions, or at least of the legislators' perception of them, the principle of bilingual-biculturalism was widely accepted, and the Republican opponents of the bill were unable to overcome the weight of these legitimacy assumptions (despite references to widespread citizen concern and "revolutionary" implications). In short, though the enactment of the bilingual-bicultural educational concept into law can be attributed to the political power of Chicano legislators, the success of this interest group cannot be separated from the influence on the political climate of prior court decisions that had given currency to the idea of a principle of entitlement to bilingual education.

### Interest Representation Issues

The Colorado Bilingual-Bicultural Education Act is an exception to our general hypothesis that, due to insufficient political power in the legislature, minority group interests tend disproportionately to bring their grievances to the courts. Although the Chicano legislators were a minority (7%), their key power positions in the 1975 Colorado legislature allowed them to promote passage of their priority bill.[49] These unique circumstances, though perhaps fortuitous, do indicate that, when effective political power is mobilized, minority interests can gain substantial results from the legislative process—at least on high-priority issues.

The Colorado case study confirmed the finding of our New York study that the breadth and depth of interest representation seem to be determined largely by the political nature of the controversy, rather than by inherent institutional characteristics of the judicial or legislative forums. The same groups, such as the teachers association and the school boards association, which had remained silent during *Otero,* did not participate actively in the legislative process either.[50] Consequently, the main protagonists were the Chicano legislators (backed by the organizational and legal expertise of the Chicano Education Project) and a coterie of Republican legislators. Thus, the legislative process, like the judicial process in *Otero,* was basically a bipolar confrontation between two parties with essentially adversary positions.[51]

Similarly, in terms of "issue" polarity, it seems clear that all major issues and perspectives considered in the legislature were also before the court, and indeed the major issues (whether phrased in terms of equal benefits vs. exclusion, or bilingual-bicultural vs. tutorial English language instruction) were framed in remarkably similar terms.[52]

### Fact-finding

The findings in the case study of the New York legislative process in chapter 7 disputed assumptions prevalent in the literature concerning the superiority of legislative, as compared with judicial, fact-finding capabilities. The legislative experience in Colorado revealed a similar pattern of lack of capacity for systematic fact-gathering or analytical fact analysis. Particularly striking in this regard is the contrast between the legislative deliberations and the *Otero* trial. The litigation compiled an extensive record and developed detailed expert testimony (on both sides) which included the preparation of one substantial social science report specifically addressing the issues in dispute.[53] The court's decision was, for the most part, attentive to the evidence and based on specific factual findings.

Although the legislative hearings accumulated much detailed testimony from a wide number of concerned citizens and experts,[54] they primarily served a showcase function; the facts accumulated were not scrutinized by the legislators and did not appear to have major impact on the votes of individual legislators or on the final outcome. For example, in the debates, the Chicano legislators elaborated on their own educational experiences, rather than on the details of the Cardenas theory; the opponents emphasized the widespread feelings about the "revolutionary" bicultural concept, rather than the issues of functional exclusion or the feasibility of biculturalism as a method for raising Chicano achievement levels. In addition, almost all the legislators admitted in their interviews that fundamental positions were taken on the basis of political judgments, and that the evidentiary record did not significantly shape the final outcome.[55] As an assistant to the Senate Education Committee bluntly put it: "On a scale of one to ten, the substantive use of factual information in the passage of this bill was zero."[56]

As was true with the New York legislative case study, then, there is no basis for directly comparing the information assessment capacity of the court and the legislature on the relevant social fact issues because the legislature simply did not purport to engage in fact-finding assessments. In short, the legislative process reflected a political decision-making pattern in which the detailed consideration of specific social science issues that were at the core of the court's analytic policy making process was a secondary factor.[57]

### Remedial Issues

The legislative process in Colorado supports the hypothesis put forward in chapter 7 that the structure and details of far-reaching educational policy reforms are likely to be formulated largely by negotiations among interested parties, whether these decisions are made in the legislative or judicial forums. Although the Colorado proceedings included substantially more "on the record" committee hearings and conferences than can be seen in the New York legislative case study, in both situations most of the substantive work in modifying the original version of the bill and formulating the authoritative final version (i.e., "the remedy") was in in *ad hoc* negotiating sessions in which representatives of the main interest groups worked together with the key legislators.[58] Compared to the New York story, this negotiating process went smoothly, and there were few "requests for arbitration" to either the full committees or the legislature. Apparently, the relatively even balance of political power among the main parties in Colorado permitted compromises to emerge more readily.

Though the legislature's capability to develop a "comprehensive" approach to a policy problem is illustrated in the Colorado deliberations, the Colorado experience also demonstrates that such comprehensiveness can be undermined as the process unfolds by the particularistic concerns of various political interests. In its initial version, H.B. 1295 attempted to provide a broad solution to the problem of underachievement by Chicano students. It not only defined in broad terms the eligible population and delineated the nature of the programming, but it also established elaborate structural mechanisms for citizen input and governance, and included such details as the hiring of teachers and the methods for identifying eligible students. As the political process unfolded, however, the comprehensive interrelationship of the various aspects of the bill was not maintained. The original broad definition of eligibility had apparently been coordinated with funding appropriations to allow for some amount of programming for all eligible students. At a later stage, the amount of funding was substantially reduced from $8 million to approximately $2.5 million. But strict time deadlines prevented a precise calculation of the number of students eligible for the program under the new eligibility criteria and the relationship of this figure to the $2.5 million appropriation.[59] Thus, what had originated as a comprehensive, fully funded program, was finalized as a more limited initiative whose funding basis was not directly related to its needs.

Contrary to the situation in New York, where the legislature appeared to lack a ready capability to monitor the impact on minorities of implementation of the new law and to consider revisions in it, the Colorado legislature, in 1977, made important revisions in the Bilingual-Bicultural Education Act. Two years of experience under the 1975 law provided an impetus to the amendment process, and, in this sense, the modifications were analogous to the amendments to decrees that we noted in several court cases. The two major changes—limiting the definition of eligible students and specifying the transitional nature of the program—were drawn from recommendations contained in a memorandum dated March 31, 1977, entitled "Needed Clarification in the Bilingual-Bicultural Act," submitted by Commissioner Frazier.[60] However, the 1977 amendments, like the original passage of the bill, were primarily influenced by political considerations, rather than by a close analysis of newly obtained facts. The paring down of bicultural programming resulted after the Republicans had regained control of both houses, thereby removing Representative Valdez and other Democratic legislators from their commanding political positions.

# PART IV

## Conclusion

# 10

## Legitimacy and Capability
## Reconsidered

◆

The search must be for a function which might (indeed, must) involve the making of policy, yet which differs from the legislative and executive functions; which is peculiarly suited to the capabilities of the courts; which will not likely be performed elsewhere if the courts do not assume it; which can be so exercised as to be acceptable in a society which generally shares Judge Hand's satisfaction in a "sense of common venture"; which will be effective when needed; and whose discharge by the courts will not lower the quality of the other departments' performance by denuding them of the dignity and burden of their own responsibility.[1]

Our empirical investigations of 65 representative education reform cases was presented in a format that would test most of the countervailing hypotheses and allegations raised by the critics and the defenders of judicial activism. Many of our specific findings supported particular contentions raised in the literature. For example, judicial discovery mechanisms provided efficient information-gathering processes, and there was a high rate of compliance with judicial decrees.

On many of the larger questions, however, we concluded that the issues as framed in the judicial activism debate did not adequately confront the realities of the judicial process. Traditional principle/ policy categorizations, for instance, do not adequately explain the more complex "principle/policy balancing" situations that constituted the bulk of our sample. And allegations of judicial capacity or incapacity to evaluate complicated social science data shed little light on the actual, prevalent pattern of "avoidance devices" in judicial fact-finding. In short, the wrong questions often were being asked, and the complexity of the courts' actual role in educational policy-making situations was being masked.

199

For these reasons, the major purpose of this concluding chapter is to explore the implications of our specific findings and to recast the underlying issues in the judicial activism debate in certain areas into more useful and relevant concepts. The comparative perspective gained from our New York and Colorado case studies will be integrated with the specific caselet findings to accomplish this result. For continuity, we retain the fourfold analytic categorization of issues used throughout the study.

## I. Legitimacy

### *Principle/Policy Issues*

The main legitimacy issue emerging from the judicial activism debate summarized in chapter 1 was whether judges have been exercising policy-making prerogatives which properly belong to the executive and legislative branches. The starting point for our study, therefore, was an assessment of the essential character of the claims asserted by plaintiffs who sought court orders enjoining school board policies. Were these claims based on arguments of principle, or of policy?

The major conclusion drawn from the caselet analysis in chapter 2 was that in remarkably few cases did plaintiffs base their requests for court intervention on "pure policy" arguments. By our count, there were only 2 pure policy suits among the 65 caselets; in addition, 1 of our major case studies, *Otero*, fits that description. Alternatively, accepting the trial judges' characterizations of the claims, we can identify 8 policy cases altogether (including our 3). It is interesting that plaintiffs were denied relief in every one of these situations.

The overwhelming majority of cases in our sample involved situations of "principled" adjudication. Eighteen percent of the cases in the entire sample were strict principle cases, such as allegations of intentional racial discrimination. Another 80%, according to our categorization, relied on qualified priniciples which we termed "principle/policy balancing" cases. These claims were framed as general principles subject to exceptions. Although the criteria for the exceptions were described with enough generality to exclude *ad hoc* instrumental policy judgments, they nonetheless integrated factual analysis of selected policy arguments into the adjudication of rights. For example, in the many student speech and appearance caselets the judges had to consider the validity of administrators' claims that the plaintiffs' challenges unavoidably would lead to substantial disruption of the educational program.

Thus, in order to assess properly the basic claims of principle, courts must become involved in factual and policy issues directly subsumed in the principle issues. In addition, once a finding of liability has been made against a defendant for violation of an applicable "neutral" principle, numerous "pure policy" issues inevitably come into the case at its remedial stage. In such situations, critics can pinpoint judicial involvement in "policy" issues. As we see it, however, what is significant in such cases is not whether policy arguments are ever involved in court decisions, but whether the "crux" of the case involves matters of principle that properly belong before the courts.

Aside from policy matters integrally related to the basic principle questions, litigants tended also to raise additional "subsidiary policy issues" in 59% of the cases. If distinctions among the policy-making roles of the different branches of government are to retain any substantial significance, it would not be legitimate for subsidiary arguments concerning the political, social, or fiscal implications of the controversy to be brought before the courts in a liability phase of a case.[2] Our findings indicated that by and large the courts tended to reject subsidiary policy arguments or to ignore them altogether in articulating the grounds for their liability decisions.

The judges' tendency to reject subsidiary policy arguments, together with the repeated dismissal of "pure policy" claims, was consistent with a pattern of widespread judicial concern about the courts' role in policy making, a concern which was explicitly articulated in 23 cases.[3] We infer from these patterns that the dichotomy between principle and policy issues was the basic frame of reference used by judges to assess the legitimacy of court review of challenged public policies.[4]

Our conclusion that district court judges generally tread cautiously in policy-oriented cases and maintain a reasonably workable principle/policy distinction in applying constitutional and statutory standards is not, of course, a complete answer to those who do not agree on the content of these standards, and who believe that the principles announced in such major decisions of the United States Supreme Court as *Tinker, Goss,* and *Lau* were themselves too broad and usurped the prerogatives of school boards or legislators. An immediate answer to this position is that when courts are properly operating within the sphere of principle as defined by the Supreme Court, the institution of American government that has been acknowledged (at least since *Marbury* v. *Madison*[5]) to have the responsibility for determining ultimate constitutional principles, they cannot be said to be violating separation-of-powers limitations or to have

usurped policy roles of other branches.[6] Beyond this doctrinal answer, however, we believe that an important consideration, which is
not often recognized in the discussions of legitimacy, is that much of
the increased judicial activity in social policy areas appears to stem
from a dramatic increase in the number of substantial "principle"
claims brought to the courts, rather than to a shift in judicial orientation from the traditional concentration on "principle" issues toward a
new willingness to consider cases based on "policy" claims. We shall
return to a reconsideration of these problems of assessing the basic
"legitimacy" of judicial activism later in this chapter, after discussing
our specific conclusions on the capability issues.[7]

### Interest Representation Issues

The prevalent assumption that most educational policy litigations
are brought by minority group plaintiffs was substantiated by our
caselet analysis. Depending upon the breadth of the definition of
"minority group," between 50% and 74% of our sample caselets were
initiated by minority plaintiffs. Since specific constitutional and statutory principles were often enacted to protect the rights of minorities,
these findings are consistent with our basic conclusion that principle,
rather than pure policy, issues tend to be brought to the courts. Also,
the minority group plaintiffs in our sample prevailed in 71% of the
cases they brought, whereas nonminority plaintiffs won only 35%.
These striking statistics indicate that claims brought by minority
plaintiffs generally have substantial validity (at least in terms of statutes and constitutional provisions which may have been promulgated
largely for their benefit).

But the quantitative data, taken alone, cannot answer the larger
question as to whether, under contemporary circumstances, minority
interests can obtain a full and fair hearing in the legislative and
executive forums. Further insights into this issue were provided by
our comparative judicial-legislative case studies. In the New York
legislature, the principle claims asserted by minority interests were
treated in the same manner as policy claims asserted by other groups.
Although the minority groups were included in the deliberations,
their limited political influence and lack of resources resulted in only
token recognition of their claims in the final version of the bill. In the
court's deliberations in *Chance,* by way of contrast, these minority
groups participated as equals, and their claims, considered as basic
matters of principle, could not be deemphasized.

The Colorado studies, however, showed a different dynamic.

Chicano interests established a substantial political presence in the legisltature and were able to achieve their major policy objectives. The circumstances causing this substantial Chicano influence in the Colorado legislature may have been fortuitous. But the results in this situation are a reminder that minority groups can protect their interests in political forums when they are able to achieve a degree of representational equality in the political arena that is comparable to the representational equality they can usually expect in the context of civil rights litigations. As (or if) such political equality is achieved in the future, special judicial solicitude of minority rights and its attendant impetus toward judicial activism may substantially decrease.

Our study also generated a number of findings relevant to the issues of depth and breadth of representation in education law litigations. Most cases were brought as class actions, a factor which should have activated specific judicial mechanisms that might assure that the plaintiffs fully and adequately represented the interests for whom they purported to speak. However, the courts neglected to apply these class action protections by essentially ignoring in 34% of the cases the request for class action certification. In both of our major judicial case studies, where class action certification was granted, the evidence indicated that the plaintiffs did represent the interests of the large number of minority group individuals for whom they purported to speak.

In terms of the breadth and variety of social interests represented in court proceedings, our caselet data indicated a substantial pattern of "multipolar" party representation. Additional participation beyond a single plaintiff or defendant occurred in 57% of the cases, and motions for joinder, intervention, and *amicus* status were approved by the courts at exceptionally high rates. But, although the judges posed few obstacles to expansion of the party structure, they did not appear to encourage additional interests to become involved in the cases.

The presence of multiple parties, however, did not always lead to the presentation of a wide variety of substantive issues. Often, multipolar party representation was accompanied by a bipolar articulation of the issues. These results may indicate that the primary issues in educational litigations tend to align themselves in bipolar form. On the other hand, it may be that the inherently bipolar orientation of the adversary process discouraged a broad, multipolar approach, even when it was needed for effective, comprehensive policy making.

Our comparative judicial-legislative case studies provided important insights on this point. In both of these, virtually the same parties which appeared before the courts also participated in the legislative deliberations, and all of the issue viewpoints raised in one forum were also clearly articulated in the other. In New York, where a broad variety of interest groups appeared as parties, intervenors, or *amici* in the *Chance* litigation, the same varied set of groups took part in the legislative discussion. Similarly, in Colorado, representation both in the court and in the legislature was bipolar.

In other words, in neither state did the forum determine the extent of party polarity. Rather, participation seemed to be determined by the willingness of certain groups to take a public stand in areas of intense controversy (involving, in these instances, highly charged racial and ethnic issues). In Colorado, for example, the teachers' association and other potentially affected groups did not become involved in either the judicial or legislative consideration of the bilingual-bicultural education issues because the highly controversial nature of the issues might have split their membership. Pending further empirical research, we would tentatively conclude that the assumption that the relatively narrow party representation in some public policy cases stems from inherent limitations of the judicial process may be overemphasizing institutional factors and minimizing consistent patterns of public behavior by the groups interested in the underlying controversies.

The final interest representation issue considered in our study was the question of the role of public law advocacy centers. The critics' assertion that a substantial number of education litigations are brought by public interest attorneys was substantiated by our caselet data. More than half of the cases in our sample were, in fact, brought by the public interest bar; furthermore, public interest attorneys tended disproportionately to be involved in the cases resulting in major reform decrees and in the cases raising novel and relatively novel legal issues.

The claim, however, that public interest lawyers often generate abstract lawsuits unrelated to the concrete aggrievements of their clients was not borne out by our data. Public interest attorneys requested and obtained class action certification (with its attendant protective mechanisms) substantially more often than did private attorneys. Furthermore, we concluded in both *Chance* and *Otero* that the specific positions advocated by the public interest attorneys appeared to emerge from the felt needs of their clients.

The reason for the predominant involvement of public law advocacy centers in the major education reform cases is apparent. The substantive degree of expertise and resources needed to sustain a protracted reform litigation is beyond the normal means of most individuals or minority groups. Indeed, in *Otero,* even the resources of the Chicano Education Project were insufficient for countering the defendants' expert studies and testimony. If our tentative finding that public interest attorneys do speak for concrete, felt aggrievements of their clients is correct, then the real issue here is whether it is desirable for society (or certain foundations) to provide minority group interests with legal resources to bring major reform cases. If so, the public law advocacy centers would appear to be an appropriate (and perhaps the only) mechanism for doing so.[8]

Assuming that education reform litigations, whether initiated by public interest attorneys or by private attorneys, will continue to be a prevalent trend in the future, we would reiterate our recommendations concerning the importance of the courts' invoking more assiduously available class-action procedural mechanisms which offer promise of enhancing the quality of interest representation. Also, we would stress the importance in new model cases of broad multipolar party participation, both from the point of view of legitimacy (maximizing perceptions of the openness of judicial deliberations) and of capacity (increasing resources for fact-gathering and implementation of relief). Although in the overwhelming number of instances judges readily approved requests for participation, in certain cases (e.g., *Chance*) the court strictly applied formal intervention rules at an early stage in the litigation, without explicitly giving full consideration to the breadth of relevant issues in the case, and to the possible need for broader group participation, especially at later remedial stages. Judicial authorization of class action status and multipolar participation do not appear to have interfered with the efficient functioning of the judicial process in the cases we studied.

## II. Capacity

### Fact-finding Issues

The initial fact-finding issue raised in the judicial activism debate concerned the courts' ability to obtain sufficient information on complex social fact issues. Our caselet data indicated that the judicial discovery process was an effective information-gathering technique. Formal discovery mechanisms were utilized in most of the cases, and the adversary parties normally cooperated in supplying requested information. The courts were required to decide disputes about discovery requests in only 11% of the sample cases.

Since there is no objective measure of completeness, it is impossible to state definitively whether this efficient discovery process actually resulted in submission of a "complete" evidentiary record in any particular case or number of cases. However, it seems reasonable to conclude that in educational policy cases, where most of the relevant information is in the possession of the school board defendants, efficient discovery procedures would result in the accumulation and submission of most of the available data. Furthermore, because of the public nature of these disputes, defendants seem inclined to accede to requests for information more readily than would corporate defendants in private litigations. A public defendant tends to be sensitive to its obligation (or the public's perception of its obligation) to cooperate in providing basic facts. In the end, noncooperation is also probably pointless, since much of the information sought may be obtained under freedom-of-information-act procedures.[9]

Our judicial-legislative case studies provided further perspectives on comparative fact-gathering capabilities. For example, in Colorado where identical factual issues were relevant to both the judicial and legislative deliberations, the evidentiary record submitted to the court clearly was more complete than the parallel submissions in the legislature. In New York, where inquiry into the critical question of discriminatory impact required not merely access to raw data possessed by the defendants, but also substantial analytic compilations of that data, the federal court (but not the legislature) was able to induce the parties to undertake detailed, costly surveys and statistical compilations.

The judiciary's substantial fact-gathering capability may be self-defeating, however, if not properly managed. In *Otero* Judge Winner's disinclination to organize discovery, his postponement of the pupil testing issue, and his failure at the outset to distinguish principle-related from subsidiary policy issues, led to a cumbersome trial and to the accumulation of a staggeringly voluminous record. In addition to the fact that a passive judicial stance at the discovery stage may be inconsistent with the information-gathering needs of "new model" litigations, such an approach also fails to organize the issues around major, principle-oriented questions and to identify issues involving extraneous subsidiary policy questions in advance of trial. In other words, active judicial involvement in discovery and in the organization of the factual record may, in the long run, help to ensure that courts do not become embroiled in extraneous policy issues.

Assuming that substantial information has been obtained, the remaining fact-finding issue concerns the courts' ability to assess competently the social science submissions that are before them. First, let us note that the assumption that complex social science information is involved in almost all new model litigation cases was not borne out by our caselet data. Social fact evidence was actually introduced in only 42 of the 65 cases in our sample (most commonly in suits based on novel legal issues). Only 10 of these cases were found to involve "complex" social fact issues. Furthermore, in very few of these complex cases did judges have to resolve conflicts in social science evidence by a direct evaluation of source materials and expert reports. Instead, the judges predominantly utilized various "avoidance devices" and based their decisions on such factors as "admissions" by a party or its witnesses or the failure of one party to satisfy its legal burden of proof. In the minority of cases where arbitrating between expert social science opinions was inescapable, the judges tended to utilize "traditional" fact-finding methods such as evaluating witness credibility. Competent assessment of witness credibility, however, usually required the judges to achieve a basic working understanding of sophisticated social science issues.[10] Our impressions of the performance of the judges in *Chance* and *Otero,* as well as the general perception of attorneys interviewed in our caselet sample, indicated that by and large the judges did a reasonably good job of educating themselves on the issues in this fashion.[11]

In the final analysis, both the strength and the weakness of the courts as a fact-finding mechanism depend on the adversary system, which is its motor force. If the opposing adversary parties place before the court a complete factual record which puts in contention the major social science issues, the court seems reasonably well equipped to undertake competent assessments of the conflicting social science data.[12] If, however, one of the parties fails to present potentially significant countervailing arguments or information (as with the discriminatory impact statistics in *Chance* and the Glass report on student achievement disparities in *Otero*), the court, lacking an independent specialized knowledge of the area, will naturally base its decision on the facts and arguments before it and on its own "common-sense judgments."[13]

In assessing the significance of the strengths and weaknesses of the judicial adversary process, it is, of course, important to place the issue in a comparative perspective. Our case studies of the legislative process in two states indicates that legislators rely on interest group representatives to compile the "evidentiary record," in almost the same manner as judges rely on parties to a litigation. Also, it appears that on a given issue the same interest groups are likely to participate in deliberations, regardless of the forum. Consequently, any deficiency in an evidentiary presentation by an adversary in a court proceeding is likely to be repeated by that party if and when it appears before a legislature.

Furthermore, state legislators, like judges, are essentially "generalists" in the controversial policy areas in which school reform suits typically are brought. This is due to the rapid turnover of the legislative committee memberships, the relative novelty of contemporary educational issues for "legislative experts," and the fact that the comparative expertise of specialized committee members may not be relied upon by the legislature as a whole. Thus, legislators are not likely to have any greater capability than judges for rectifying "adversarial distortions."

Our comparative judicial-legislative case studies also yielded other significant findings. Much of the critical commentary on judicial fact-finding capability assumes that the legislative branch is superior in this area, because of the theoretical advantages of open access, extensive staff resources, and investigative hearings. In fact, however, the research resources of both the Colorado and New York legislatures were found to be limited, hearings were conducted largely for the purpose of marshaling political support, and little focused analytic fact-finding was actually undertaken. These conclusions are not surprising when one realizes that legislative decision making is predominately based on a process of "mutual adjustment"[14] which attempts to reconcile the positions of competing interest groups through political bargaining.[15] Factual information may be incorporated into this interest-balancing process, but such information need not be explored systematically nor related logically to the final outcome.

In contrast to the "political decision-making" model of the legislative forum, the judicial pattern might be described as an "analytical decision-making" model. The latter approach leads to judgments "reached and supported by fact and analysis in the light of explicit standards of judgment."[16] Thus, courts feel bound to attempt to justify their decisions with reasoned analysis that takes account of all the relevant facts in the record.[17]

In addition to the fact that some criticisms of judicial fact-finding are based on unfounded assumptions about the legislature's superior capabilities,[18] additional criticisms of judicial performance by certain social scientists are also largely inapplicable. A case in point is Dr. Eleanor Wolf's critical review of the trial court's performance in a major desegregation case in Detroit. Wolf, a sociologist, expressed concern about the number of potential sources of distortion in the courts fact-finding process, including miscitations of social science literature, use of tenuous social fact arguments, and the court's deference to agreements between the adversary parties about factual premises, the validity of which was apparently the subject of dispute among educators and researchers.[19]

Wolf's specific points and analogous critiques by other social scientists are consistent with some of the limitations of the adversary fact-finding process discussed above. Nevertheless, the critical consideration seemingly overlooked in this approach is that neither a court nor any other decision-making body should properly be viewed as an "educational" forum. Leaving aside the fact that many academic social scientists, too, are often influenced by political considerations when espousing positions,[20] the fact remains that in policy-making contests any decision-making body composed primarily of laymen, whether it be a court, a legislature, or an administrative agency, is likely to exhibit the type of deficiencies that Wolf has described. If social science evidence has, indeed, become inextricably involved in the consideration of basic public policy issues, it seems inevitable that one or another of the imperfect branches of government will have to be entrusted with these responsibilities.[21]

In short, we believe that assessments of judicial performance based on comparisons to the theoretical fact-finding abilities of the legislature or to the analytical capabilities of academic and scientific work groups are essentially misplaced. In fact, courts appear to be better equipped than legislatures to evaluate social fact evidence systematically and to render analytically reasoned decisions.* On some issues, of course, (and especially those on which available information is

---

*Of course, this is not to say that certain changes might not improve the judicial fact-finding process in complex new model cases. For example, it might be reasonable to relax the normal rules limiting a witness's ability to be recalled to "rehabilitate" prior statements after hearing testimony from the other side, in order to permit the most comprehensive presentation of an expert's overall opinion. Similarly, submission of summary social fact reports on critical issues (similar to posttrial legal briefs) prepared by opposing experts, and procedures for encouraging formal admission of basic social science texts (with appropriate opportunity for explanatory comment by attorneys and expert witnesses), might be useful innovations. Acceptance of the appropriateness of the court's fact-finding role, especially with the addition of the foregoing innovations, might also spark a reconsideration of the prevalent use of "avoidance devices" by judges. Despite the courts' shortcomings, it may be that more controversial social fact issues should be subjected to direct scrutiny. See Davis, "Facts in Lawmaking," 80 Colum. L. Rev. 931 (1980); M. Frankel, Partisan Justice (1978).

highly inadequate or where political reconciliation is of critical importance[22]), the rational-analytic judicial mode may be inappropriate, and such issues might best be resolved by the mutual adjustment process of the legislative forum. The question of judicial fact-finding capability therefore should be reframed: What are the relative advantages for resolving particular types of public policy issues through the "analytical fact-finding" processes of the court and through the mutual adjustment, political bargaining mode of the legislature.[23]

### Remedial Issues

The judicial activism debate raised questions about the remedial implementation capabilities of the courts, and, in particular, their ability to formulate broad reform decrees and then to deal in a flexible, comprehensive fashion with the myriad administrative and policy problems that inevitably arise when major institutional reforms are undertaken. Our caselet studies focused on readily measurable elements of judicial implementation of remedies—the number and degree of intrusiveness of remedial orders, the extent and nature of defendant participation in decree formulation, the amount of compliance, and modifications of decrees. In addition, the *Chance* case study provided an in-depth analysis of an eight-year implementation process involving the restructuring of major features of the largest school district in the country.

Our data largely rebutted the criticism that the judiciary lacks the resources, expertise, or comprehensive perspective needed to implement educational reform successfully. In the caselet survey, we found two main patterns of behavior by which courts compensated for their institutional limitations. First, the judges found relatively "nonintrusive ways to vindicate plaintiffs' rights. In most cases where defendants were found liable, the courts, instead of entering extensive "reform decrees," utilized the less intrusive relief of "self-executing injunctions." The latter did not call for on-going court supervision and active involvement in school district affairs (although the overwhelming majority of these cases did result in systemwide reform). Specifically, while remedial orders were entered in 41 of the 65 cases, only 15 reform decrees were issued. Even in these 15 cases, the courts tended to adopt the least intrusive monitoring mechanisms that were available. Thus, the assumption that a decision in favor of plaintiffs generally leads to broad, direct judicial intervention into school administration and policy deliberations was not born out by our evidence.

In those cases where extensive reform decrees were issued, defendants or relevant public agencies participated substantially in the formulation of the policy content of the decrees.[24] We found only one clear instance of a judge, alone, drafting an extensive reform decree. As a practical matter, this participation meant that the staff resources and other implementation tools of the parties automatically became available to the court. The roles played by the Task Force and by the Chancellor's Advisory Counsel in *Chance* were dramatic illustrations of the pooling of the resources of public bureaucracies, citizen groups, unions, and *ad hoc* consultants (paid for by foundation grants) to formulate, administer, monitor, and modify a major reform decree.

This pattern of participation by school boards and other affected agencies in the remedial process also tended to rebut the allegation that judicial remedies are insufficiently "comprehensive." When the courts serve largely as catalysts and mediators for processes that basically are undertaken by affected school officials themselves, the policy review capabilities of the education agencies become available to the court and may, for all practical purposes, be considered an integral part of the judicial process. While it is true that the courts' central concern with the rights being violated establishes boundaries and priorities for the decision-making process in which the parties will engage under the courts' auspices, it is interesting to note the remarkable similarity between remedial mechanisms in the legislative process and those utilized in the courts. After defining basic policy objectives, the legislators also tended to leave the same interest groups and their representatives the responsibility for fashioning acceptable operational mechanisms to implement them.

Our statistics further revealed that modifications of judicial decrees occurred in 27% of the cases in which plaintiffs prevailed. Although the need for these modifications might be attributed to failures of the judges to anticipate foreseeable implementation problems, we believe that in most instances the problems to which they responded could not have been anticipated better by a legislative or executive decision maker. For example, no one could have predicted the intricate combination of transfer and layoff issues that arose over the course of the eight-year *Chance* litigation. A legislature may also have to reconsider a "remedy" it designed, as it did in our Colorado case study in regard to the 1977 amendments to the Bilingual-Bicultural Education Act. But courts would appear to have some important institutional advantages for undertaking necessary adjustments of remedial processes at the implementation stage. They are able to retain jurisdiction, to require periodic reporting, and to assemble on short notice diverse institutional resources to design flexible responses to unexpected problems.[25] In addition, courts, because of their rational-analytical orientation, are in position to achieve goal clarification and to apply effective pressures for completion of necessary tasks which are often lacking in other implementation settings.[26]

Our generally positive conclusions concerning judicial remedial capabilities may seems, at first, to contradict recent case study findings about school desegregation litigation. For example, Kalodner and Fishman's recent compendium of eight major desegregation cases revealed substantial compliance problems.[27] The courts in these cases had become isolated and "abandoned" by the school boards and other agencies and groups. Left alone to enforce plaintiffs' rights in this acrimonious environment, the courts increasingly adopted highly intrusive mechanisms[28] and interfered substantially with the operational spheres of school boards, as was exemplified by Judge Garrity's placing South Boston High School in trusteeship under direct court jurisdiction.

To some extent, the dramatic difference between the generally successful remedial experience in the cases in our sample as compared to the substantial difficulties encountered in desegregation cases may be attributed to the sheer scope and complexity of school desegregation. Implementation of effective remedies for racial segregation can require extensive revamping of an entire school structure.[29] By comparison, many of the remedial tasks presented by our sample of educational policy cases were relatively straightforward.

Nevertheless, this complexity factor alone does not provide a satisfactory explanation of the different compliance patterns. After all, the major special education cases in our sample required extensive institutional changes; although implementation was far from perfect, substantial compliance was effected, and nothing like the grudging resistance evidenced in desegregation cases was experienced.[30] Similarly, the remedial process in cases involving extensive reform of professional standards and specific practices in state mental hospitals did not result in substantial compliance problems similar to those described in the desegregation situations.[31]

We believe that the more fundamental reasons for the differing remedial experiences encountered in desegregation as opposed other education law litigations stem from the characteristics of the social contexts in which these principle dispute arise. We perceive two basic patterns. When a public policy dispute is generally viewed by most segments of society as involving ambiguous or changing moral standards calling for authoritative clarification, there is a social situation of "moral flux."[32] On the other hand, when there are significant numbers of people who are unequivocably committed to conflicting moral and legal positions, the social situation is "confrontational."

In moral flux controversies, although the adversaries may be deeply concerned about their point of view, they generally accept the idea that the courts are an appropriate forum for clarifying the legal or moral ambiguities. Unsuccessful litigants speak the language of dissent, not of civil disobedience; the issues are not of such overriding personal concern that they would persist in strong resistance to the courts' position. Most of the cases in our study were litigated in such a context of moral flux. The special education cases provide a particularly good example. Historically, mentally retarded persons were institutionalized and excluded from participation in "normal" social activities and schooling. But in recent years psychological and humanitarian attitudes have begun to shift on these issues. The courts' declaration of a right to education for handicapped children (and right to treatment for institutionalized persons) has articulated and galvanized moral attitudes on this point, and the public and education/health professionals generally have appeared willing to accept the guidance of courts in defining society's basic obligation for providing educational services and treatment to handicapped persons.[33]

Desegregation cases, however, are the paradigmatic example of litigation involving principle issues that are "confrontational." The essence of such a situation is that the stakes are high.[34] Public perceptions on these issues, by and large, are not in a state of moral flux; on the contrary, strongly divergent views on these questions are entrenched. The opposing camps perceive the issues as involving intensely valued personal interests and social practices. Judicial involvement in such situations is not viewed as a clarification; on the contrary, it is seen as endorsement of the position of one of the competing camps. Moreover, public officials who choose to resist judicial orders can count on relatively strong political support from a large segment of the community who similarly feel aggrieved and threatened by the court's stance.[35]

In short, the difference between our own findings on remedial capacity and the findings of other researchers reporting on desegregation litigation results from the differences between judicial in-

tervention in moral flux controversies as compared to judicial intervention in confrontational situations. The main implication of this
distinction is that the difficulties courts have encountered in effectuat-
ing relief under circumstances of entrenched resistance should not be
considered a criticism of the capability of judicial institutions, *per se.*
Comparatively speaking, in such situations courts experience substantially the same problems as would any governmental agency attempting such thoroughgoing systemwide reforms.[36] (In many of the
instances, the courts become involved precisely because the other
branches are unable or unwilling to handle such confrontational issues.) Our findings have shown that in situations where the parties
(and the public) are inclined to cooperate (or at least to avoid strong
resistance), courts are capable of fashioning effective relief. Thus, in
the areas of remedies, as in the area of fact-finding and interest representation, many of the arguments that have been used to criticize
judicial capabilities are, we believe, more reflective of the social, political, and technical characteristics of particular public policy controversies than of any comparative judicial incapacity to deal with those
issues.*

### III. A Final Perspective

Our empirical investigation has indicated that courts do not act in
strict accordance with certain assumptions of classical separation-of-
powers theory. We have found that in public law litigations, courts

*The model of largely effective judicial supervision of extensive reform decrees
which emerged from our study may call for a reconsideration of the traditional judicial
attitudes toward the remedial process. For example, although we would conclude that
the intricate pattern of negotiation, testing of "interim remedies," and revisions of a
permanent plan in *Chance* was largely effective, the court clearly was unhappy with its
role. Judge Tyler, in particular, seemed uncomfortable with any deviation from the
traditional right-remedy of the traditional lawsuit and felt it unseemly for the court to
share its jurisdiction with outside political forces not completely subsumed under its
control. But the realities of the untidy remedial process in new model cases would
appear to call for precisely such a role (note in this regard the serious implementation
problems in the Philadelphia "Areawide Council case" where the court ignored these
realities. Horowitz, *supra* note 25, at ch. 3). From this perspective, one would disagree
with the court of appeals' decision in *Chance* to terminate jurisdiction at a point when
the parties had apparently reached the culminating stage of their long deliberations on
the Permanent Plan.

Of course, the effectiveness of judicially supervised remedial processes (as with any
other human endeavor) will, to some extent, depend upon the intellectual, administrative, and political skills of the particular judge. (Note in this regard that in *Chance* Judge
Mansfield made a specific request to the assignment committee of the Southern District
Court to designate Judge Tyler as his successor, instead of allowing the assignment to

operate in a fashion that is more political than the role contemplated under the traditional model of court adjudication, but less political and more "rational" than the decision-making processes of legislative bodies. Thus, we determined that the courts are able to accommodate diverse and vigorous interest representation; that judicial procedures facilitate information gathering and focus presentation of opposing expert viewpoints in an "analytical" fact-finding format that is distinct from the "political bargaining" patterns of legislative deliberations; and that, in implementing remedies, courts have been able to employ effectively the full panoply of resources available to the litigants themselves in fashioning and implementing policy reforms.

Our findings indicate that the basic issues in the judicial activism debate need to be reformulated. Repeatedly, we have found that the most notable defects in judicial performance, whether they concern interest representation, fact-finding, or remedies, are often caused not by comparative incapacities of the judiciary vis-à-vis other governmental agencies, but by the social, political, and technical characteristics of the particular controversies; or by the limitations of the participants in resources, skill, and motivation, which manifest themselves similarly regardless of whether a given dispute is addressed by a court or by another governmental institution. Seen in this light, the critical question, we now believe, is not whether the courts are "better" or "more capable" fact-finders or implementers of remedies than are legislatures, but whether particular aspects of social problems should be handled through the principled, analytic judicial process or through the instrumental, mutual adjustment patterns of the legislatures.[37]

Although all three branches of American government have become more activist and interventionist in the post-New Deal era, we believe that certain significant social trends of recent years have particularly affected the sphere in which the judicial branch operates—i.e., the domain of the principle—and have accelerated thrusts toward judicial activism. Because of the demise of traditional religious, communal, and familial value-creating institutions,[38] it appears that contemporary Americans have increasingly come to look to the rational-analytic processes of the courts to satisfy their need for definitive clarification of basic values and principles.[39]

---

be made by the usual randomized procedure. See ch. 6, p. 81 *supra.*) Increased attention to the realities and requirements of new model cases could, of course, influence the way judges approach these tasks, their training, and even the abilities considered in the judicial selection process.

Indisputable as these trends toward judicial activism are (indeed, in many areas, the legislative and executive branches have themselves[40] specified that particular types of social controversy should be relegated to the courts), their desirability or ultimate "legitimacy" remains a more complex and difficult question. From an empirical perspective, any final assessment of the propriety of the movement toward increased judicial activism, particularly in "confrontational" issues, must consider the long-term consequences of court involvement in social policy issues. Have important rights been vindicated to an extent great enough to outweigh the possible cost of such intervention in terms of the institutional authority of the courts?[41] Will the courts prove capable of finding solutions to major confrontational problems, or are they delving into issues that are beyond the "limits of social policy," i.e., beyond the power of any governmental institution to handle effectively?[42] Only when the answers to these sweeping empirical questions are answered can a final position be taken on the ultimate legitimacy issues. Our study will have served its purpose if it helps to shift the focus of the judicial activism debate toward research and analysis that will provide better grounded—if not conclusive—answers to these fundamental questions.

# Appendix A

## Citation to Court Opinions
## From the EPAC 65-Case Sample

———————◆———————

*Opinions addressing preliminary motions and peripheral issues (e.g., attorney fee awards) are omitted.

York City), 370 F. Supp. 42 (S.D. N.Y.) *aff'd per curiam,* 495 F. 2d 1090 (2d Cir. 1974).

16    Conrad v. Goolsby, 350 F. Supp. 713 (N.D. Miss. 1972).

17    Copeland v. Hawkins, 352 F. Supp. 1022 (E.D. Ill. 1973).

18    Dameron v. Tangipahoa Parish Police Jury, 315 F. Supp. 137 (E.D. La. 1970).

19    Demkowicz v. Endry, 411 F. Supp. 1184 (S.D. Ohio 1975).

20    Dixon v. Beresh, 361 F. Supp. 253 (W.D. Mich. 1973).

21    Dostert v. Berthold Public School District, 391 F. Supp. 876 (D. N.D. 1975).

22    Fabian v. Independent School District No. 89, 409 F. Supp. 94 (W.D. Okla. 1976).

23    Frederick L. v. Thomas, 419 F. Supp. 960 (E.D. Pa. 1976), *aff'd,* 557 F. 2d 373 (3d Cir. 1977).

24    Gambino v. Fairfax County School Board, 429 F. Supp. 731 (E.D. Va.), *aff'd,* 564 F. 2d 157 (4th Cir. 1977).

25    Georgia Association of Educators v. Nix, 407 F. Supp. 1102 (N.D. Ga. 1976).

26    Gilpin v. Kansas State High School Activities Assoc., 377 F. Supp. 1233 (D. Kans. 1974).

27    Givens v. Poe, 346 F. Supp. 202 (W.D. N.C. 1972).

28    Graham v. Knutzen, 351 F. Supp. 642, *decree modified,* 362 F. Supp. 881 (D. Neb. 1973).

29    Gurmankin v. Costanzo, 411 F. Supp. 982 (E.D. Pa. 1976), *aff'd,* 556 F. 2d 184 (3d Cir. 1977).

30    Heath v. Westerville Board of Education, 345 F. Supp. 501 (S.D. Ohio 1972).

31    Hernandez v. Hanson, 430 F. Supp. 1154 (D. Neb. 1977).

32    Horton v. Orange County Board of Education, 342 F. Supp. 1244 (M.D. N.C. 1971), *modified,* 464 F. 2d 536 (4th Cir. 1972).

33    Hosier v. Evans, 314 F. Supp. 316 (D.V.I. 1970).

34    Houston v. Prosser, 361 F. Supp. 295 (N.D. Ga. 1973).

35    Hunt v. Board of Education (Kanawha), 321 F. Supp. 1263 (S.D. W.Va. 1971).

36    Huntsville City Board of Education v. Brown, 379 F. Supp. 1092 (M.D. Ala. 1974).

37    James v. Beaufort County Board of Education, 348 F. Supp. 711 (E.D. N.C. 1971), *aff'd per curiam,* 465 F. 2d 477 (4th Cir. 1972).

38    Jinks v. May, 332 F. Supp. 254 (N.D. Ga. 1971), *aff'd in part (back pay), remanded in part (attorney fees),* 464 F. 2d 1223 (5th Cir. 1972).

39    Johnson v. New York State Education Department, 319 F. Supp. 271 (E.D. N.Y. 1970), *aff'd,* 449 F. 2d 871 (2d Cir. 1971), *vacated and remanded for determination on mootness,* 409 U.S. 75 (1972).

40    King v. Civil Service Commission (New York City), 382 F. Supp. 1128 (S.D. N.Y. 1974).

41    Kruse v. Campbell, 431 F. Supp. 180 (E.D. Va.), *vacated and remanded,* 434 U.S. 808 (1977).

42    Local 858 of the American Foundation of Teachers v. School District No. 1 (Denver), 314 F. Supp. 1069 (D. Colo. 1970).

43  Lopez v. Williams, 372 F. Supp. 1279 (S.D. Ohio 1973), *aff'd sub nom*, Goss v. Lopez, 419 U.S. 565 (1975).
44  Usery v. Board of Education (Salt Lake City), 421 F. Supp. 718 (D. Utah 1976), (formerly entitled "Marshall v. Board of Education").
45  Mills v. Board of Education (District of Columbia), 348 F. Supp. 866 (D.D.C. 1972).
46  Minarcini v. Board of Education (Strongsville), 384 F. Supp. 698 (N.D. Ohio 1974), *aff'd in part, rev'd in part*, 541 F. 2d 577 (6th Cir. 1976).
47  National Indian Youth Council v. Bruce, 366 F. Supp. 313 (D. Utah), *aff'd*, 485 F. 2d 97 (10th Cir. 1973), *cert. denied*, 417 U.S. 920 (1974).
48  Natonabah v. Board of Education (Gallup-McKinley), 355 F. Supp. 716 (D.N.M. 1973).
49  Nicholson v. Pittenger, 364 F. Supp. 669 (E.D. Pa. 1973).
50  Parker v. Fry, 323 F. Supp. 728 (E.D. Ark. 1971).
51  Paxman v. Wilkerson, 390 F. Supp. 442 (E.D. Va. 1975).
52  Pennsylvania Association for Retarded Children (PARC) v. Commonwealth of Pennsylvania, 334 F. Supp. 1257 (E.D. Pa. 1971), *decree modified*, 343 F. Supp. 279 (E.D. Pa. 1972).
53  Pervis v. LaMarque Independent School District, 328 F. Supp. 638 (S.D. Tex. 1971), *rev'd*, 446 F. 2d 1054 (5th Cir. 1972).
54  Peterson v. Board of Education (District No. 1), 370 F. Supp. 1208 (D. Neb. 1973).
55  Press v. Pasadena Independent School District, 326 F. Supp. 550 (S.D. Tex. 1971).
56  Romeo Community Schools v. U.S. Dept. of Health, Education and Welfare, 438 F. Supp. 1021 (E.D. Mich. 1977).
57  Schwartz v. Galveston Independent School District, 309 F. Supp. 1034 (S.D. Tex. 1970).
58  Sims v. Board of Education (District No. 22), 329 F. Supp. 678 (D.N.M. 1971).
59  Sims v. Waln, 388 F. Supp. 543 (S.D. Ohio 1974), *aff'd*, 526 F. 2d 686 (6th Cir. 1976), *cert. denied*, 431 U.S. 903 (1977).
60  Smith v. Smith, 391 F. Supp. 443 (W.D. Va. 1975), *cert. denied*, 423 U.S. 1073 (1976).
61  Wallace v. Ford, 345 F. Supp. 156 (E.D. Ark. 1972).
62  White v. Dougherty County Board of Education, 431 F. Supp. 919 (M.D. Ga. 1977), *aff'd*, 439 U.S. 32 (1978).
63  Whitfield v. Simpson, 312 F. Supp. 889 (E.D. Ill. 1970).
64  Williams v. Albemarle City Board of Education, 5 EPD ¶8592 (M.D. N.C. 1973), *aff'd*, 508 F. 2d 1242 (4th Cir. 1974) (en banc).
65  Zoll v. Anker, 414 F. Supp. 1024 (S.D. N.Y. 1976).

# Appendix B

## Methodology for the Selection and Analysis of the 65 Caselets Analyzed in Part II

---

### I. SAMPLING PROCEDURES

#### Defining the Sample

The 65 caselets in the EPAC study constitute a carefully selected sample of the broad "universe" of educational policy litigations. Generally speaking, this universe consists of federal cases commenced by plaintiffs in order to change systemwide practices, policies, or rules in the public schools. This general definition was operationalized as follows:

1. Structural criteria:
   - *a)* Dismissal order, or liability determination (preliminary or final) made between January 1, 1970, and December 1, 1977.
   - *b)* Complaint requesting an injunction that would replace, modify, or forbid enforcement of a systemwide educational policy.
     - (1) "Systemwide" was defined to include rules, policies, and patterns or practices in effect throughout an entire school or in any larger unit of school administration (e.g., districtwide, statewide, national).
2. Subject-matter exclusions:
   - *a)* School desegregation cases. (Litigations alleging segregated assignments of students. Also included in this category were lawsuits by school districts to enjoin federal authorities from terminating funding for failure to desegregate.)
   - *b)* Nonpublic school cases, including challenges to programs of financial assistance to sectarian schools.

The rationale for the above "structural criteria," we assume, are self-evident, except for the decision to include only cases seeking injunctive relief. While it is true that in some school reform cases plaintiffs do not seek injunctive relief, a plaintiff's formal request that a court order a policy change is a workable and objective indication of a reform goal. The use of this criterion admittedly excludes from our sample what might be called individual "test cases" and "declaratory cases." In the former, a plaintiff seeks only individual relief, but his suit may intend to establish (or may unintentionally establish) a legal precedent that will have a broad impact on school politics. Attempting to include such individual test cases in our sample would have been problematic, since the researcher could not ascertain reform objectives or results without detailed analysis of the background of the case and interviews of individuals involved. In the typical declaratory case, the plaintiff seeks a declaration of the general unlawfulness of a policy, but does not seek judicial orders to compel the defendant to change its rules and practices to conform to the declaration. Although in many such cases the plaintiff may have a reform objective, the declaratory complaint is a much weaker clue to this intent. For these reasons, we decided to concentrate the study on the more reliable sample—injunctive cases—leaving for future research the question as to whether there are any substantial differences in the school reform litigation process resulting from noninjunctive cases.

The subject-matter exclusion criteria were established primarily to assure that our analysis would cover the largest number of cases possible without unnecessarily duplicating work done by others. Suits involving segregation and aid to nonpublic schools have been subjected to extensive doctrinal analysis and to some empirical study.[1] If included in our sample, the quantity and complexity of these cases would have required a substantial commitment of resources which, we believed, would be better utilized in the study of other types of education policy cases which have not received broad attention. Indeed, one of the important questions the project has addressed is whether the "lessons" of the widely publicized segregation cases have been applied inappropriately to all "educational policy" cases.

### Selecting the Sample

The objective of the sampling process was to identify a group of 50–70 federal cases representative of the defined universe of educational policy litigation. This sample size was considered large enough from which to draw generalizations and small enough to facilitate relatively detailed study.

A computerized law research system—LEXIS—was the primary sampling tool used. The memory bank of the LEXIS federal library includes the full text of most federal district court opinions.[2] For us, the system's most valuable feature was its capacity to conduct full text searches. Thus, we were able to formulate a search request consisting of several alternative configurations of words and phrases and to have the computer scan the full text of every federal district court opinion in its memory to see if it met these criteria. Specifically, our search request screened for opinions that contained (a) the words "public school" or "education" in combination with "policy," and (b) phrases such as "equitable relief" and "injunctive relief."[3] Each opinion containing the relevant set of search words was then listed on a printout.[4]

We considered the possibility that a judge who uses phrases like "educational policy" in an opinion is more likely to have a particular approach to the kinds of cases we are studying. For example, the sample might underrepresent cases in which either the judge failed to see the policy implications of his decision—although arguably he should have considered them—or in which the judge may have considered policy issues but was unwilling to reveal his policy concerns on the record. We could think of no method of precluding this potential bias without relinquishing the unique advantage of LEXIS and being forced to adopt alternative, less objective methods. In any event, we discovered no concrete indications of bias from this source. Our final caselet sample included a broad distribution of both "activist" and "passivist" judges.

Also, the plaintiff/defendant breakdowns of wins and losses in the LEXIS cases were similar to the percentages in a sample of educational policy cases screened through other means.[5]

In response to our request, LEXIS listed 236 federal district court citations. A perusal of the cited opinions indicated that 113 citations were not relevant to our area of interest. For example, a number of cases involving prisoner rights, welfare, and higher education issues were on the list because the text of the cited opinions coincidentally used one of the word configurations in our computer program. The balance of 123 cases was narrowed down to 60 by excluding 32 desegregation and nonpublic education cases; 18 teacher dismissal and 5 student conduct cases that did not include substantial claims for systemwide injunctive relief; and 1 tax assessment case deemed irrelevant to educational policy making. One of the 60 cases, *Otero*, was set aside to be used for a detailed case study. An updating screening seven months later (following the same procedure) yielded 6 new cases, so that the final sample size was 65.

After completing the LEXIS screening, we checked a second time for the presence of systematic subject-matter bias by manually surveying 119 volumes of West's *Federal Supplement*[6] covering the same time period as the LEXIS search. Each volume contained a subject-matter digest with case abstracts. All entries headed "Schools and School Districts" were reviewed, together with the published opinions corresponding to those abstracts that met our screening criteria. Since complaints were not available, questions as to whether plaintiffs had requested injunctive relief were resolved in accordance with a standard set of presumptions devised for this purpose. Cases meeting the screening criteria were then classified by subject matter.

We then compared the subject matter distribution of the LEXIS and the *Federal Supplement* cases.[7] Table 13 provides a summary comparison of the groups of cases identified by the two methods. The table shows that the subject matter distributions are substantially similar.[8] This result strongly suggests that the LEXIS sampling procedure was not systematically biased with regard to subject-matter distribution.

Our sample was drawn from those cases meeting our defined educational reform criteria for which written decisions were available. Assuming that judges issue written opinions to explain their orders in cases which raise important public policy issues (and that the reporting services publish such opinions), the available body of published opinions is likely to reflect the substantial bulk of judicial activity in this area. However, it is also possible that for a variety of reasons (including predecisional settlements, pronouncements of oral decisions from the bench, or lack of affirmative steps to assure publication of written decisions), a larger number of cases are actually handled by the courts than is reflected by the published decisions.

Enough information exists to make it possible, in theory, to identify and screen individually each of the cases in this "larger universe." But such a screening would clearly be grossly impractical. During the period 1970–77, there were 790,000 civil cases terminated in the federal courts;[9] about 100,000 of them have been classified by the Administrative Office of the United States Courts into two subject categories in which one would expect to

## Table 13
### Subject Matter Breakdown of LEXIS—*Federal Supplement* Samples
### (Period: 1/1/70–12/31/76)

| Subject Matter of Case | Number in F. Supp. Survey | Number as a Percentage of F. Supp. Survey (Total 175) | Number in LEXIS Survey | Number as Percentage of LEXIS Survey (Total 59) |
|---|---|---|---|---|
| A. Regulation of Student Speech and Conduct (Subtotal) | (90) | (51) | (25) | (42) |
| 1. Grooming and dress | 38 | 22 | 8 | 14 |
| 2. Speech and association[a] | 18 | 10 | 7 | 12 |
| 3. Corporal punishment | 10 | 6 | 2 | 3 |
| 4. Eligibility to participate in school activities. | 12 | 7 | 3 | 5 |
| 5. Fairness of disciplinary procedures[b] | 12 | 7 | 5 | 8 |
| B. Professional Staff (Subtotal) | (37) | (21) | (16) | (27) |
| 1. Maternity-related | 8 | 5 | 6 | 10 |
| 2. Race discrimination (general) | 9 | 5 | 4 | 7 |
| 3. Race discrimination (challenges to employment selection procedures) | 6 | 3 | 3 | 5 |
| 4. Other[c] | 14 | 8 | 3 | 5 |
| C. Handicapped Students | 7 | 4 | 3 | 5 |
| D. Curriculum (not including special education) (Subtotal) | (15) | (8) | (6) | (10) |
| 1. Religious content | 9 | 5 | 2 | 3 |

continued

table 13 continued

| SUBJECT MATTER OF CASE | NUMBER IN F. Supp. SURVEY | NUMBER AS A PERCENTAGE OF *F. Supp.* SURVEY (TOTAL 175) | NUMBER IN LEXIS SURVEY | NUMBER AS PERCENTAGE OF LEXIS SURVEY (TOTAL 59) |
|---|---|---|---|---|
| 2. Racial ethnic minorities | 3 | 2 | 2 | 3 |
| 3. Other | 3 | 2 | 3 | 5 |
| E. School finance | 9 | 5 | 6 | 10 |
| F. Electoral process | 12 | 7 | 2 | 3 |
| G. Other | 5 | 3 | 1 | 2 |
| Totals | 175 | 99[d] | 59 | 100[d] |

[a]This category also includes cases involving regulation of speech and free association activities of nonstudents such as parents, guest speakers, religious organizations, and commercial advertisers.

[b]This category applies to cases in which there is no serious challenge to substantive rules, but only to procedures for enforcement, or in which there is a claim of arbitrary discriminatory patterns of enforcement.

[c]Residency requirements; alien status; physical/mental examinations; handicapped applicants; life style/immorality (e.g., unwed mother status); grooming; free speech.

[d]Total does not equal 100% because of rounding off.

find virtually all educational policy cases.[10] Thus, specific analysis of this larger universe would require the screening of 100,000 cases and the accumulation of pleadings in thousands of cases from courts all over the country.[11] This would be a monumental task. (Furthermore, the research value of such a sample, which presumably would include many minor cases and discontinued actions,[12] may be subject to question.) Under these circumstances, we believe that the representativeness of the sample we utilized has been verified by the best available methodology.[13]

## II. CASELET ANALYSIS PROCEDURES

### *The Content Analysis Coding Instrument*

Once a representative sample of cases was obtained, it was necessary to devise a procedure to review objectively the voluminous data available in the records of the 65 cases and to analyze and code the information in terms of the basic judicial activism issues set forth in chapter 1. Three main factors had to be considered in designing an instrument for these purposes—balancing quantitative and qualitative information, logistics, and objectivity.

With regard to the first factor, we constructed sets of questions that progressed from discrete quantifiable facts to more open-ended judgmental facts. To deal with the logistical problem of producing 65 caselet reports with a finite amount of resources, we structured our instrument (which we call the caselet[14] questionnaire) on the assumption that a researcher would be working with a file containing the court opinions and copies of key pleadings, briefs, and other materials from the court file; that the attorneys involved in the case could be reached by telephone for short interviews; and that the average amount of time available to review a file and complete a caselet report would be two and one-half days.[15] Finally, in pursuit of objectivity, we tested initial drafts of the questionnaire against a subset of sample cases, revised the format to maximize clarity in the drafting of questions, and conducted training sessions, staff meetings, and editorial reviews to try to ensure intercoder reliability, i.e., to make sure that the classifications were being applied consistently by our three researchers.

### Applying the Instrument

The survey was carried out over a one-year period. The research staff consisted of an attorney and two second-year law students who were supervised by two principal investigators (both of whom are also practicing attorneys). The first survey task was to assemble individual document files for the 65 sample cases. To do this, the researcher reviewed the complaint, court opinion, and docket sheet of each case and compiled a list of the relevant pleadings, briefs, orders, affidavits, etc., to be requested from the courts.[16] When the documents were received the researcher studied the file and drafted a caselet report. One of the principal investigators then reviewed the report and met with the researcher to discuss it and to consider plans for attorney interviews. The researcher then conducted the attorney interviews and submitted a revised report.

Attorney interviewing initially posed some logistical problems. Several attorneys were difficult to locate since many of the court decisions were five to seven years old. Through persistence and a little detective work, the researchers ultimately succeeded in interviewing 130 attorneys for the principal parties in 60 of the 65 caselets (92%).

Once the 65 caselet studies were complete—amounting to about 1,000 pages of data—the caselet analysis phase began. Answers to certain concrete questions were tabulated and their implications considered. For example, we quickly discovered that constitutional claims predominated in the sample, and that plaintiffs had won a majority of their cases. The analysis of the responses to questions involving judgmental factors was more complicated. In some areas the responses were both complete and in a suitable form for immediate analysis. In others, there was adequate information, but, as the analysis proceeded and hypotheses were formed, reorganization and reinterpretation of the data became necessary. Finally, there were some areas in which information remained incomplete and the data could only be used for illustrative purposes.

The questions dealing with the administration of orders serve as a good example of a questionnaire section yielding responses translatable into useful findings.[17] The answers to these questions were the basis for the finding that complete compliance occurred in almost all cases of remedial orders[18] and that contempt proceedings were rarely invoked.[19]

The assessment of the concept of the "novelty" of the plaintiff's claim is an example of the process of reformulation that sometimes had to be undertaken. Until all the caselets were completed it was difficult to set precise standards for judging the relative novelty of a claim. Furthermore, the researchers' ratings were not always consistent. However, because the researchers had been instructed to explain their ratings in some detail, the principal investigators were able to formulate and apply a consistent definition of "novelty." In other areas, we found that the informationrevealed by the responses called for changes in terminology to describe the actual research findings more specifically. For example, the term "legislative fact-finding," used in three questions, was discarded in favor of "social fact-finding."[20] A distinction in the questionnaire between "negative injunction" and "affirmative injunction" was replaced by the concepts "self-executing injunction" and "reform decree."

Analysis of the caselet data led to new perspectives in some areas of inquiry. For instance, our study of the information obtained through the responses to about 20 questions concerning the role of social fact evidence led to a realization that the ways in which courts dealt with such information would best be described by the term "avoidance device." Consequently, most information from these questions was reanalyzed and set forth within the framework of that hypothesis.

In many areas, our quantitative findings revealed interesting patterns which called for more interpretative prerogatives. In these instances, we amplified the numerical patterns set forth in the tables with a qualitative analysis (often going beyond our caselet report back into the actual case files) of the detailed events of the particular litigations. For example, cases identified as having compliance problems were specifically scrutinized in order to obtain concrete insights into the workings of the remedial process.

Many of the findings in the EPAC report were expressed in terms of numerical percentages or other types of quantitative comparisons. The identification of patterns of behavior in a relatively large number of representative cases was, of course, one of the major purposes of our empirical study and distinguished its findings from many prior effects based on small numbers of selective litigations. But despite the attempts made in this project to broaden the data base for analyzing judicial activism, one still may reasonably question the degree of confidence with which inferences can be made about educational policy litigations in general from observations of the 65-case sample. One answer to this question is that if one applied a formal statistical test to the quantitative comparisons that were specifically relied upon in the EPAC report, one would find that they satisfied the conventionally accepted confidence level of 95%.[21] The more fundamental answer, however, is that our conclusions are based on well-informed judgments. That is, in the process of forming those judgments numbers were merely a part of the vocabulary of discussion; they were employed as a coherent way of summarizing results whose implications could be understood without technical statistical analysis.

# Appendix C
## *Caselet Data Summary*

| Caselet | Subsidiary Policy Arguments (1) | Novelty of Claim (2) | Class Action Status (3) | Plaintiff Attorney Affiliation (4) | Incidence of Discovery (5) | Discovery Motions (6) | Compliance with Court Decrees (7) | Modifications to Remedial Orders (8) |
|---|---|---|---|---|---|---|---|---|
| 1 | D | RN | DC | PI* | S | | | |
| 2 | | NN | | Pr | N | | P[3] | M |
| 3 | | N | | Pr | S | | C | |
| 4 | P/D | N | | Pr (U) | E | | P | S |
| 5 | P/D[1] | NN[2] | C/DC[1] | PI* | S | | C | |
| 6 | | NN | NR | Pr | N | | | |
| 7 | P | NN | | G | N | | | |
| 8 | | N | | PI | S | | | |
| 9 | | NN | C | Pr (PI) | E | S | | |
| 10 | D | N | | Pr [PI] | M | | | |
| 11 | | NN | DC | PI* | M | | | |
| 12 | D | NN | DC | PI | N | S | | |
| 13 | | NN | | Pr | N | | | |
| 14 | P/D | N | NR[4] | Pr | N | | | |
| 15 | P | RN | NR | Pr [PI] | N | | C | |
| 16 | | NN | NR[5] | Pr | N | | C | |
| 17 | | NN | | PI-LS | N | | C | |
| 18 | | NN | AW | Pr | N | | C | |
| 19 | | NN | DC | Pr | M | | C | |
| 20 | D | NN | C | Pr | N | | C[1] | |
| 21 | P/D | NN | | Pr | S | | P | |
| 22 | | NN | C | Pr | M | | C | M |
| 23 | P/D | RN[1] | C | PI-LS (PI) | E | S | C | M |
| 24 | D[2] | NN | C | Pr (PI) | S | | C | |
| 25 | D | NN | | Pr | M | | C | |
| 26 | D | RN | | Pr | N | | C | |
| 27 | P | NN[2] | C | PI-LS | E | Ct | C | |
| 28 | | NN[2] | NR | PI-LS | E | Ct[1] | C | S |

227

| Caselet | (1) | (2) | (3) | (4) | (5) | (6) | (7) | (8) |
|---|---|---|---|---|---|---|---|---|
| 29 | P | RN | NR | PI-LS | M | Ct | C | S |
| 30 | D | NN | | PI-LS | N | | C | |
| 31 | | NN | C | PI-LS | M | Ct[2] | C | |
| 32 | D | NN | C | PI | M | | | |
| 33 | P/D | N | C | PI-LS | N | | C | |
| 34 | P/D | NN | DC | Pr | N | | C | |
| 35 | P/D | RN | | PI | N | | | |
| 36 | P/D | N | | G[1] | N | | | |
| 37 | | NN | C | PI* | M | Ct[1] | P[4] | |
| 38 | | RN | C | PI* | M | | C | |
| 39 | P | N | NR | PI-LS | N | | | |
| 40 | D | NN | NR | Pr | S | | | |
| 41 | | RN[1] | C | PI (PI-LS) | E | S | C | VS[1] |
| 42 | P | N | NR | Pr | S | | | |
| 43 | | NN[2] | C | PI* | S | | C | |
| 44 | | N | | G | E | Ct | C | |
| 45 | P/D | N[1] | C | PI (PI-LS) | M | Ct[2] | P | S |
| 46 | P | N | C | PI | E | Ct[3] | | |
| 47 | P/D | N | DC[3] | PI | N | | | |
| 48 | D | RN | C | PI (PI-LS) | E | | P | |
| 49 | | N | DC | PI-LS | E | S | P[5] | VS |
| 50 | P | NN | | Pr | N | | C | |
| 51 | | NN | C | U | M | | C | |
| 52 | P | N | C | PI | E | Ct | P | VS |
| 53 | | NN[2] | NR | PI* | N | | | |
| 54 | D | RN | C[2] | Pr | S | | C | |
| 55 | | NN | NR | PI* | N | | | |
| 56 | | N | | G[1] | N | | C | M |
| 57 | P | NN | | Pr | N | | | |
| 58 | P/D | N | NR | PI | S[1] | | | |
| 59 | P/D | RN | DC | PI | S | | | |
| 60 | | NN | NR | PI* | N | | C[2] | |
| 61 | D | NN | NR | Pr | N | | C | |
| 62 | D | NN | | Pr [PI] | S | | C | |
| 63 | | NN[2] | NR | PI | N | | | |
| 64 | | NN | C | PI* | S | | P[4] | |
| 65 | | N | NR | Pr | M | Ct | | |
| | | | | | | | | |
| Totals | Pl. = 23 | N = 18 | C = 21 | Pr = 27 | N = 27 | Ct = 10 | C = 32 | M = 4 |
| | 37% | 28% | 32% (45%) | 42% | 42% | | | |
| | Def. = 27 | RN = 11 | DC = 9 | PI = 23 | S = 14 | S = 5 | P = 9 | S = 4 |
| | 43% | 17% | 14% (19%) | 35% | 22% | | | |
| | Pl or Def = 37 | NN = 36 | NR = 16 | PI-LS = 10 | M = 13 | | | |
| | 59% | 55% | 25% (34%) | 15% | 20% | | | VS = 3 |

| Caselet | (1) | (2) | (3) | (4) | (5) | (6) | (7) | (8) |
|---|---|---|---|---|---|---|---|---|
| | | | AW = 1<br>2% (2%) | Gov. = 4<br>6%<br><br>Union = 1<br>2% | E = 11<br>17% | | | |

## EXPLANATION AND NOTES: APPENDIX C
### CASELET DATA SUMMARY
### *Column 1: Subsidiary Policy Arguments*

A. Explanation

This column locates subsidiary policy arguments raised in the 63 "principle" or "principle/policy balancing" cases listed in columns 1 and 2 of table 1, at page 26. Double entries indicate cases in which both plaintiffs and defendants made subsidiary policy arguments. Percentage figures are computed on a base of 63.

B. Coding

P = plaintiff

D = defendant

C. Footnotes

1. Plaintiff policy argument related to procedural due-process claim; defendant policy argument related to flag salute claim.

2. Arguments made by *amicus curiae* which supported defendant's position.

### *Column 2: Novelty of Claim*

A. Explanation

Cases are distinguished by the degree of novelty of plaintiff's claim. "Novel" indicates that plaintiffs primarily (or solely) relied on a novel claim. "Relatively novel" indicates that plaintiffs relied upon a moderately novel claim, or else substantial claims both of a novel and not-novel nature were litigated.

B. Coding

N   = novel

RN = relatively novel

NN = not novel

C. Footnotes

1. The earlier special education cases were considered novel; the later ones, although they still broke some new legal ground, were rated relatively novel.

2. Although all of the student procedural due-process cases were decided prior to the Supreme Court decision in *Goss* v. *Lopez*, 419 U.S. 565 (1975), C. 43, there already was considerable lower court precedent in this area. See R. Butler, "The Public High School Student's Constitutional Right to a Hearing," 5 Clearinghouse Review No. 8 (December 1971); D. Kirp and M. Yudof, Educational Policy and the Law 190–97 (1974). Alternatively, if these cases were tabulated in column 2 as "relatively novel," then the following changes would occur:

(a) "relatively novel" would increase from 17% to 26%.

(b) "not novel" would decrease from 55% to 46%.

## Column 3: Class Action Status

A. Explanation

This column indicates the disposition (or lack of disposition) of class action allegations in 45 cases. C. 5 has two entries because it included two distinct claims which were treated differently for class action purposes. Consequently, a total of 47 dispositions were listed. "Totals" are expressed first as a percentage of the total sample and second (in parentheses) as a percentage of the 47 cases with class action allegations.

B. Coding

C   = certification granted.

DC = certification denied.

NR = no ruling on class certification

AW = class action application withdrawn

C. Footnotes

1. See explanation above.

2. Three out of 4 alleged classes were certified, and the fourth one was of minor importance.

3. Denial of certification was implicit in the opinion.

4. The circuit court had the same difficulty as we do in ascertaining how the district court treated the class action status of the claim. "[P]laintiff . . . moved to amend to allege a class action [but] the case appears to have been tried as an action for the benefit of the plaintiff only." 449 F. 2d 781, 782.

5. The court referred to this case as a class action, but no certification order was entered.

## Column 4: Plaintiff Attorney Affiliation

A. Explanation

Main entries indicate primary representation at the trial court level. Entries in parentheses indicate secondary representation at the trial court level. Entries in brackets show changed primary representation at the appeal court level. (Computation of totals does not include entries in parentheses or brackets.) An asterisk (*) indicates an attorney in private practice affiliated with a public interest organization for the purposes of a given case.

In Cs. 11, 32, 37, and 64, the attorney for plaintiffs had a relationship with a union (North Carolina Teachers Association) in addition to an affiliation with the NAACP.

B. Coding

Pr     = private attorney

PI     = public interest attorney

PI-LS = federal legal services public interest attorney

G      = government attorney

U      = union attorney

C. Footnote

1. School board plaintiff using private attorneys.

## Column 5: Incidence of Discovery

A. Explanation

Cases are distinguished by the extent of use of discovery procedures for information gathering. A case is classified as "None" if neither the docket sheet nor attorney interviews indicated that formal discovery procedures were used to attempt to obtain information from an adversary. (Also listed is C. 12, a case in which the court dismissed the complaint before the plaintiffs apparently received any information in response to discovery requests.) Absent specific indications to the contrary, it was presumed that a party which filed copies of discovery requests with the court received at least "some" information in reply.

B. Coding

N = none
S = some
M = moderate
E = extensive

C. Footnote

1. Classification is based solely on attorney recollection. No discovery activity was indicated on the docket sheet.

## Column 6: Discovery Motions

A. Explanation

This listing includes all cases in which discovery motions were filed, divided between cases in which motions were decided by court order and ones in which the motion was either settled, withdrawn, or mooted before decision. In some of the cases there was more than one motion; if at least one motion was resolved by the court, then it is categorized as "Ct."

B. Coding

Ct = motion(s) decided by court
S  = settled, withdrawn, or mooted before decision

C. Footnotes

1. No formal motion was docketed, but the court nevertheless resolved objections to interrogatories (C. 28), or objections to answers to interrogatories (C. 37).
2. The motions in these cases were technical, e.g., setting dates for depositions; shortening or lengthening the usual time period for replying to discovery requests.
3. There were at least seven discovery motions in this case primarily divided between motions to compel answers to interrogatories and motions for protective orders.

## Column 7: Compliance with Court Decrees

A. Explanation

This listing includes every case in which plaintiffs were granted relief. Initially, cases were rated under four headings: complete compliance, partial compliance, token compliance, or no compliance. However, since no cases were found in the latter two categories, only the former two remain.

B. Coding

C = complete compliance
P = partial compliance

C. Footnotes

1. Plaintiffs alleged noncompliance, but the court determined that defendants had not violated its order.

2. The relief order was reversed on appeal.
3. Defendants did not violate the letter of the relief order, but plaintiffs contended that they did not carry out its full intent. After further proceedings, a modified order was entered embodying more detailed instructions to the defendants, with which they complied.
4. Opposing attorneys disagreed about whether there had been full compliance.
5. Partial compliance with 1973 order; full compliance with 1975 order.

### Column 8: Modifications to Remedial Orders

A. Explanation

Modifications to remedial orders occurred in 11 cases. Here the modifications are classified as minor, substantial, or very substantial.

B. Coding
  M  = minor
  S   = substantial
  VS = very substantial

C. Footnote
  1. In *Kruse* (C. 41), the Supreme Court vacated the original liability decision and remanded the case to the district court for a determination as to whether a remedy was "practicable" within the meaning of an applicable federal statute. That is, the High Court's decision did not foreclose relief, and did not even formally reverse the lower court's initial legal conclusions. This classification is based on the district court's decision on remand to deny injunctive relief, rather than to reinstate substantially the same relief it previously had ordered under a different liability theory.

# Appendix D

## *Interviews:* Chance *Case Study,* New York *Legislative Case Study,* Otero *Case Study,* and *Colorado Legislative Case Study*

———◆———

*Chance* CASE STUDY (CHAPTER 6)

| ABBREVIATION | DATE | IDENTIFYING INFORMATION* |
|---|---|---|
| Arricale Interview | 1/77 | Frank C. Arricale, II. Executive Director, Office of Personnel, Board of Education of the City School District of New York, 1974–1978. |
| Bernikow Interview | 2/28/77 | Leonard Bernikow. Assistant Corporation Counsel. He represented the Board of Education almost from the inception of the suit, until he was appointed United States Magistrate on December 1, 1975. |
| Cohen Interview | 2/9/78 | Saul Z. Cohen. Chief attorney for Board of Examiners. Partner, Kaye, Scholer, Fierman, Hays and Handler. |
| DuBois Interview | 4/7/78 | Elizabeth Bartholet, formerly Elizabeth DuBois. Lead counsel for plaintiffs. Staff attorney, NAACP Legal Defense Fund; Director, Legal Action Center. Presently, Assistant Professor, Harvard Law School. |
| Lewis Interview | 4/28/77 | Mrs. Blanche Lewis. Chairperson, Chancellor's Advisory Council. |
| Quinones Interview | 5/6/77 | Nathan Quinones. Member, Board of Examiners (provisional appointment, July 1972–September 1974). Presently, Executive Director, High School Division, New York City Board of Education. |
| Rockowitz Interview | 6/28/77 | Dr. Murray Rockowitz. Member and Chairman, Board of Examiners. Pres- |

*The first identifying information which is given refers to the person's position during the phase of the litigation about which he or she was questioned. In some cases additional information also is given.

|                         |          | ently, Director of Research and Information, American Association for Jewish Education. |
|-------------------------|----------|----------------------------------------------------------------------------------------|
| Schiff Interview        | 5/5/77   | Harold Schiff. Education Director of the Anti-Defamation League, B'nai Brith, and member, Chancellor's Advisory Council. |
| Seeley Interview        | 3/23/77  | David Seeley. Director, Public Education Association. |
| Siegel Interview        | 7/25/77  | Harold Siegel. Executive Secretary, Board of Education of the City School District of New York. |
| Stein Interview         | 5/9/77   | James Stein. Grievance Director, Council of Supervisory Associations, Local No. 1, National Supervisors' Union, AFL-CIO. |
| Tractenberg Interview   | 7/30/77  | Paul Tractenberg. Special Counsel to the Human Rights Commission of the City of New York for its investigation of personnel practices of the city Board of Education; one of plaintiffs' five representatives on the Task Force. |
| Tyler Interview         | 7/19/77  | Honorable Harold R. Tyler, Jr., United States District Judge, Southern District of New York. Presiding judge in *Chance*, January 1974–April 1975. Subsequently, Deputy United States Attorney General. Presently, partner in the firm of Patterson, Belknap, Webb & Tyler, New York City. |
| UPA Interview           | 5/20/77  | Field staff of the United Parents Association of New York. Betty Felton, Director. Valerie Harty, Betty Goldklang, May Devlin, and Ida Clark, staff members (Group interview). |
| Williams Interview      | 5/25/77  | Frederick H. Williams. Executive Director, Office of Personnel, the Board of Education of the City School District of New York, 1971–73. Presently retired. |

### New York Legislative Case Study (Chapter 7)

| ABBREVIATION       | DATE     | IDENTIFYING INFORMATION* |
|--------------------|----------|--------------------------|
| Arricale Interview | 10/12/77 | Frank C. Arricale, II. Executive Director, Office of Personnel, Board of Education. |

*At the time of the 1976 session.

| Flemming Interview | 10/18/77 | Joseph Peter Flemming. Attorney in private practice and consultant to the Coalition of Associations of Black and Puerto Rican Educators and Supervisors. |
| PEA Interview | 10/12/77 | Jean Silver Frankle and Carol Ziegler. Attorneys on the staff of the Public Education Association. |
| Goosen Interview | 10/20/77 | Frederick Goosen. Staff director, Education Committee of the New York State Assembly. |
| Pacheco Interview | 10/5/77 | Joseph Pacheco. New York City school principal and representative of Coalition of Associations of Black and Puerto Rican Educators and Supervisors. |
| Shannon Interview | 11/4/77 | Joseph Shannon. Associate Legislative Representative, United Federation of Teachers and New York State United Teachers. |
| Stavisky Interview | 11/7/77 | Leonard P. Stavisky. Chairman, New York State Assembly Education Committee. |
| Vann Interview | 10/27/77 | Albert Vann. New York State Assemblyman and Chairman of Black and Puerto Rican Assembly Caucus. |

### *Otero* CASE STUDY (CHAPTER 8)

| ABBREVIATION | DATE | IDENTIFYING INFORMATION |
|---|---|---|
| Baller Interview | 11/18/77 | Morris J. Baller. Staff Attorney, Mexican-American Legal Defense and Education Fund, San Francisco, California (plaintiffs' lead counsel for appeal to Tenth Circuit). |
| Glass Interview | 1/24/78 | Dr. Gene Glass. Professor of Education, and Director of Laboratory of Educational Research, University of Colorado (defendants' expert witness). |
| Groves-Getz Interview | 1/25/78 | John W. Groves and Jon E. Getz. Members of the firm Nelson, Hoskin, Groves and Prinster, Grand Junction, Colorado (attorneys for defendants). |
| Jackson Interview | 1/20/78 | Dr. Gregory Jackson. Staff Member, United States Commission on Civil Rights (assisted plaintiffs at trial as expert on educational evaluation and statistics, in his individual capacity). |
| Johnson Interview | 1/26/78 | Kenneth Johnson. Publisher, The |

|                      |            | Daily Sentinel, Grand Junction, Colorado. |
| -------------------- | ---------- | --------------------------------------- |
| Lippoth Interview    | 1/26/78    | Mrs. Peggy Lippoth. Member, Board of Education, School District #51 (1972——). |
| Marquez Interview    | 1/26/78    | Jose D. L. Marquez. Staff Attorney, Colorado Rural Legal Services (plaintiffs' lead counsel at trial on employment discrimination issues). |
| Oglesby Interview    | 1/25/78    | Dr. Donald Oglesby. Superintendent, School District #51 (1970——). |
| Pena Interview       | 1/23/78    | Federico Pena. Staff Attorney, Chicano Education Project, Lakewood, Colorado (plaintiffs' lead counsel on bilingual-bicultural programming issues). |
| Reeder Interview     | 1/26/78    | Dr. Wayne Reeder. Director of Elementary Education, School District #51. |
| Swearingen Interview | 1/24/78    | Jay Swearingen. Counsel, Colorado Association of School Boards, Denver, Colorado. |

### Colorado Legislative Case Study (Chapter 9)

| Abbreviation       | Date               | Identifying Information* |
| ------------------ | ------------------ | ----------------------- |
| Comer Interview    | 1/25/78            | Senator William J. Comer. Democrat, Member, Senate Education Committee. |
| Emerson Interview  | 1/26/78            | Joyce Emerson. Legislative Council, staff person assigned to Senate Education Committee. |
| Fowler Interview   | 1/24/78, 1/25/78   | Senator Hugh C. Fowler. Republican, Chairman of Senate Education Committee. |
| Johnston Interview | 1/26/78            | Robin Johnston. Chairwoman, State Board of Education. |
| Kjolseth Interview | 1/25/78            | Dr. Rolf Kjolseth. Professor, Department of Sociology, University of Colorado. |
| Knox Interview     | 1/24/78            | Representative Wayne Knox. Democrat, Member of House Education Committee. |
| Lucero Interview   | 1/24/78            | Representative Leo Lucero, Democrat, Chairman, House Education Committee. |
| Pena Interview     | 1/23/78            | Federico Pena. Staff Attorney, Chicano Education Project. |

*The identifying information which is given refers to the person's position during the legislative deliberations of 1975.

Sandoval Interview     1/25/78     Senator Paul Sandoval. Democrat, Member, Joint Budget Committee.

Sears Interview     1/24/78     Representative Virginia Sears. Republican, Member of House Education Committee, 1977.

Shoemaker Interview     4/24/78     Senator Joe Shoemaker. Chairman of Senate Appropriations Committee and and Joint Budget Committee.

Showalter Interview     1/24/78     Representative Carl Showalter. Republican Member of House, Proponent of 1977 legislative amendments.

Strickland Interview     1/25/78     Senator Ted Strickland. Republican, Member of Senate Appropriations Committee, Chairman, Joint Budget Committee, 1977.

Swearingen Interview     11/11/77     Jay Swearingen. Legal Counsel, Colorado Association of School Boards.

Valdez Interview     1/24/78     Representative Ruben Valdez, Democrat, Speaker of the House.

# Notes

## CHAPTER 1

1. 411 U.S. 1, 42–43 (1973).
2. Goss v. Lopez, 419 U.S. 565 (1975).
3. Cleveland Board of Education v. La Fleur, 414 U.S. 632 (1974).
4. Lau v. Nichols, 414 U.S. 563 (1974).
5. Morgan v. McDonough, 540 F. 2d 527 (1st Cir. 1976), *cert. denied*, 429 U.S. 1042 (1977). Cf. Milliken v. Bradley, 433 U.S. 267 (1977).
6. See, e.g., Glazer, "Towards an Imperial Judiciary?" 41 Pub. Interest 104, 106–7 (1975). The specific holding in *Rodriguez*, a case dealing with education finance reform, however, has meant that federal courts have terminated their involvement in this particular area. Federal inaction, though, appears to have accelerated activism by state courts. See, e.g., Serrano v. Priest, 557 P. 2d 929 (Sup.Ct. Cal. 1977), Robinson v. Cahill, 303 A. 2d 273 (Sup.Ct. N.J. 1973), *on rehearing*, 339 A. 2d 193 (Sup.Ct. N.J. 1975) *injunction granted in part*, 358 A. 2d 457 (Sup.Ct. N.J. 1976).
7. See, e.g., Rizzo v. Goode, 423 U.S. 352 (1976); Milliken v. Bradley, 418 U.S. 717 (1974); cf. Mt. Healthy City Board of Educ. v. Doyle, 429 U.S. 274 (1977); Paul v. Davis, 424 U.S. 693 (1976); Bishop v. Wood, 426 U.S. 341 (1976). See generally, Gelfand, "The Burger Court and the New Federalism" 21 B.C.L. Rev. 763 (1980). However, Prof. J. H. Ely argues that the Burger Court's "value imposition" in many cases, especially in those dealing with abortion and family matters, is more far-reaching than the Warren Court approach. See Ely, "Forward: On the Discovery of Fundamental Values," 92 Harv. L. Rev. 5 (1978); Ely, Democracy and Distrust (1980).
8. The right to equal educational opportunities for handicapped children was first articulated by the federal district courts in 1972. See, e.g., Mills v. Board of Education, 348 F. Supp. 866 (D.D.C. 1972), Pennsylvania Association for Retarded Children v. Commonwealth of Pennsylvania, 343 F. Supp., 279 (E.D. Pa. 1972). It has since been extensively developed by the lower courts. See, e.g., Panitch v. State of Wisconsin, 444 F. Supp. 320 (E.D. Wisc. 1977); Frederick L. v. Thomas, 408 F. Supp. 832, 419 Supp. 960 (E.D. Pa. 1976), *aff'd*, 557 F. 2d 373 (3d. 1977); cf. New York State Association of Retarded Children v. Rockefeller, 357 F. Supp. 752, 763–64 (E.D. N.Y. 1973). The Supreme Court has not as yet ruled on the merits of a claim of

equal educational opportunity for handicapped children. But cf. Kruse v. Campbell, 434 U.S. 808 (1977) (lower court constitutional ruling vacated and remanded), and Davis v. Southeastern Community College, 442 U.S. 397 (1979) (interpretation of rights of the handicapped under §504 of the 1973 Rehabilitation Act). For an analysis of activism by state trial judges see Galanter, Palen, and Thomas, "The Crusading Judge: Judicial Activism in Trial Courts," 52 S. Calif. L. Rev. 699 (1979).

9. See, e.g., Title VI of the Civil Rights Act of 1964; Title IX of the Education Amendments of 1972; and the Education of the Handicapped Act of 1975. Statistics reflecting the federal judiciary's activity show that the total number of reported education law cases decided by the federal courts was 15 between 1897 and 1906, 112 between 1946 and 1956; and 729 (an increase of almost 700%) between 1956 and 1966. For the four-year period thereafter (1967–71) the total was 1273. (Source: J. Hogan, The Schools, The Courts, and The Public Interest 7 [1974].) Although comparable figures are not available for recent Burger Court years, the findings discussed at p. 37 *infra* indicate that these long-term trends have not substantially abated. See also Hellman, "The Business of The Supreme Court Under the Judiciary Act of 1925: The Plenary Docket in the 1970's," 91 Harv. L. Rev. 1709, 1756–58 (1978).

10. See, e.g., cases cited in note 6 *supra.*

11. See Wyatt v. Stickney, 344 F. Supp. 373 (M.D. Ala. 1972), *aff'd in part sub nom.* Wyatt v. Aderholt, 503 F. 2d 1305 (5th Cir. 1974).

12. Pugh v. Locke, 406 F. Supp. 318 (M.D. Ala. 1976), *aff'd in relevant part sub nom.;* Newman v. Alabama, 559 F. 2d 283 (5th Cir. 1977), *reh. denied;* James v. Wallace, 564 F. 2d 97 (5th Cir. 1977), *cert. denied,* 438 U.S. 915 (1978); Rhem v. Malcolm, 371 F. Supp. 594, 377 F. Supp. 995 (S.D. N.Y. 1974), *aff'd and remanded,* 507 F. 2d 333 (2d Cir. 1974), *on remand,* 389 F. Supp. 964, *amended,* 396 F. Supp. 1195 (S.D. N.Y. 1975), *aff'd,* 527 F. 2d 1041 (2d Cir. 1975), 432 F. Supp. 769 (S.D. N.Y. 1977), 432 F. Supp. 769 (S.D. N.Y. 1977).

13. See, e.g., Metropolitan Housing Development Corp. v. Village of Arlington Heights, 469 F. Supp. 836 (N.D. Ill. 1979), *aff'd,* 618 F. 2d 1006 (7th Cir. 1980).

14. 89 Harv. L. Rev. 1281 (1976).

15. *Id.* at 1302.

16. For a more detailed discussion of "blending," see Sharp, "The Classical American Doctrine of 'the Separation of Powers,' " 2 Chi. L. Rev. 385, 427 (1935). Sharp maintains that the constitutional convention explicitly rejected James Wilson's call for a rigid model of separation of powers. *Id.* at 412. In Federalist No. 4 James Madison states that Montesquieu's theory of the separation of powers clearly contemplated "blending."

17. R. Berger, Government By Judiciary 249–50 (1977). An exploration of the theory that the judiciary is following the "Iron Law of Emulation" in taking on executive and legislative functions inconsistent with the traditional doctrine of separation of powers appears in Moynihan, "Imperial Government," Commentary, June 1978, 25, 26.

18. R. Berger, Congress, v. Supreme Court 184 (1969). In Federalist No. 78, Alexander Hamilton stated that "the judiciary, from the nature of its functions, will always be the least dangerous to the political rights of the Constitution."

19. Of course, according to Rousseau, basic authority was not even to be delegated to elected representatives, but was to remain vested in an assembly of all citizens. See, e.g., J. Rousseau, The Social Contract (Frankel ed. 1947).

20. Glazer, "Toward An Imperial Judiciary?" note 6 *supra*, at 106 (1975); P. Kurland, Politics, The Constitution, and the Warren Court 203 (1970) (judges acting as "Platonic Guardians").

Paul Mishkin describes the subtle process by which the judiciary allegedly oversteps its proper bounds in a majoritarian system: "I challenge the acceptance of the set of mind that, having identified a real social problem, too easily concludes (a) that if there is a problem, there must be a solution, (b) that the continued existence of the problem establishes both that the other parts of government cannot be relied upon and that courts' traditional remedies are not efficacious, and (c) that judges must therefore act in a wholesale fashion to reform government to bring about the 'cure'!" Mishkin, "Federal Courts as State Reformers," 35 Wash. & Lee L. Rev. 949, 950 (1978). See also Nagel, "Book Review: *American Constitutional Law* by Lawrence H. Tribe," 127 U. Pa. L. Rev. 1174 (1979), for discussions of the limits of rationalistic social problem solving, and A. Wise, Legislated Learning: The Bureaucratization of the American Classroom (1979).

21. Glazer, "Should Judges Administer Social Services?" 50 Pub. Interest 64, 78–79 (1978).

22. See, e.g., R. McCloskey, The American Supreme Court (1960); A. Cox, The Role of the Supreme Court in American Government 2 (1969); J. Choper, Judicial Review and the National Political Process (1980). Historically, the separation-of-powers theory dealt with the division of authority among the branches of a *single* governmental unit. More recently, the principles underlying the theory have become the touchstone of a more generalized set of criticisms of an alleged pattern of "anti-democratic" judicial actions which includes instances of federal judicial intervention into the policy-making processes of state and local legislative, executive, and administrative bodies; see e.g., Nagel, "Separation of Powers and the Scope of Federal Equitable Remedies," 30 Stan. L. Rev. 661, 663 (1978); cf. A. Bickel, The Morality of Consent (1975). Technically, where the federal judiciary is enforcing against state governments or local school districts statutory or regulatory policies established by Congress or the federal executive, "federalism" concerns—rather than strict "separation of powers" or "popular sovereignty"—are at play. But since most instances of direct federal intervention in local school affairs occur through the judicial branch (which, according to the critics, creates new rights or unreasonably expands existing ones), the critics are primarily concerned with the basic separation-of-powers issues.

23. As James Madison stated in Federalist 10: "When a majority is included in a faction, the form of popular government . . . enables it to sacrifice to its ruling passion or interest both the public good and the rights of other citizens. To secure the public good and private rights against the danger of such a faction, and at the same time to preserve the spirit and form of popular government, is then the great object to which our [Constitutional] inquiries are directed."

24. Johnson, "Judicial Activism Is a Duty—Not an Intrusion," The Judges Journal (ABA, Fall 1977) at 5; see also Johnson, "The Constitution and the Federal District Judge," 54 Tex. L. Rev. 903 (1976); Johnson, "The Role

of the Federal Courts in Institutional Litigation," 32 Ala. L. Rev. 264 (1981); Kaufman, "Chilling Judicial Independence," 88 Yale L. J. 681, 689 (1979).

25. R. Rist and R. Anson, eds., Education, Social Science, and the Judicial Process viii (1977); see also H. Kalodner and J. Fishman, Limits of Justice (1978), for a discussion of the difficult, exposed position of courts in desegregation situations where school boards and other political institutions refuse either to initiate action or to cooperate with judicial attempts to find workable solutions.

26. Hobson v. Hanson, 269 F. Supp. 401, 517 (D.D.C. 1967). For a further discussion of the judge's views see Wright, "Professor Bickel, The Scholarly Tradition, and The Supreme Court," 84 Harv. L. Rev. 769 (1971).

27. Levi, "Some Aspects of Separation of Powers," 76 Col. L. Rev. 371, 376 (1976). See also Rostow, "The Democratic Character of Judicial Review," 66 Harv. L. Rev. 193, 197 (1952), and R. Nealy, How Courts Govern America (1981). Indeed, even Continental notions of popular sovereignty may need to be reconsidered in light of contemporary conditions. Rousseau, the originator of the classical popular sovereignty doctrine, forcefully stated that "No state has ever been founded without having religion for its basis." Rousseau, *supra* note 19, at 119, and his discussion therein of the need for a "civil religion," indicates that the "general will" could be given commanding authority only because it would be expected to operate within the restraints of a higher religious law. With the breakdown of traditional religious institutions, these popular sovereignty notions may need reexamination.

28. Chayes, *supra* note 14, at 1315. Interestingly, between 1937 and 1972 the United States Supreme Court declared only 32 acts of Congress unconstitutional, and most of these dealt with relatively technical issues. See G. Schubert, Judicial Policy-Making (1974).

29. When courts finally do take a stand in a new area, there appears, however, to be a "progressive logic of constitutional positions once taken [propelling] courts beyond the point where they can retreat from a dynamic role in policy debates." R. Lehne, The Quest for Justice 5 (1978). See also D. Horowitz, The Courts and Social Policy 10 (1977). See generally L. Fuller, The Morality of Law (1964); Pennock, "Law's Natural Bent," 79 Ethics 222 (1969).

30. See also Schubert, *supra* note 28, at 199: "It is inevitable that in the *long* run the Supreme Court will follow the election returns." Dahl, "Decision-Making in a Democracy: The Supreme Court as a National Policy Maker," 6 J. Pub. Law 279 (1957); but cf. Casper, "The Supreme Court and National Policy Making," 70 Am. Pol. Sci. Rev. 50 (1976).

31. L. Tribe, American Constitutional Law 51 (1978).

32. "The root of this evil [the conception of the judge as an automaton] is preoccupation with the separation of powers and Blackstone's 'childish fiction' (as Austin termed it) that judges only 'find,' never 'make,' law." Hart, "Positivism and the Separation of Law and Morals," 71 Harv. L. Rev. 593, 610 (1958); see Note, "Formalism, Legal Realism, and Constitutionally Protected Privacy Under the Fourth and Fifth Amendments," 90 Harv. L. Rev. 945, 948–51 (1977).

33. "Legal realism" refers here to several related bodies of twentieth-century legal theory, bearing such various labels as "realism," "positivism,"

and "pragmatic instrumentalism." For an insightful, comprehensive overview of legal realism and the implications of its rejection of formalism and natural law theories, see E. Purcell, The Crisis of Democratic Theory: Scientific Naturalism and the Problem of Value (1973). See also Linde, "Judges, Critics and the Realist Tradition," 82 Yale L. J. 327 (1972); R. Dworkin, Taking Rights Seriously, ch. 2 (1977); Summers, "Professor Fuller's Jurisprudence and America's Dominant Philosophy of Law," 92 Harv. L. Rev. 433 (1978); H. L. A. Hart, The Concept of Law (1961); Llewellyn, "Some Realism about Realism," 44 Harv. L. Rev. 1222 (1931). For an important study of the role of the judiciary in shaping social policy in the early nineteenth century through its basic common-law jurisdiction, see M. Horowitz, The Transformation of American Law 1780–1860 (1977).

34. "The life of the law has not been logic: it has been experience." O. Holmes, The Common Law 1 (1946). See also K. Llewellyn, The Bramble Bush (1960).

35. See Hart, "Positivism and the Separation of Law and Morals," *supra* note 32, at 593.

36. Cf. R. Dworkin, Taking Rights Seriously, ch. 4 (1977), originally published as Dworkin, "Hard Cases," 88 Harv. L. Rev. 1057 (1975).

37. Note, however, that there was divergence among the realists themselves about the nature of and justification for judicial lawmaking. Considering respect for majoritarian decisions to be the essence of separation-of-powers theory, realists such as Holmes and Hand argued for judicial restraint and deference in overruling political decisions. See, e.g., L. Hand, The Bill of Rights (1958). In contrast were legal writers such as Jerome Frank, who asserted that judges decide cases largely on the basis of personal policy predilections. See, e.g., Law and the Modern Mind (1930). Many political scientists, accepting realist premises, argue that the judiciary must be seen, empirically, as "a special kind of political forum" in a public-policy-making process that integrates the activities of courts, legislatures, and executives. P. Nonet and P. Selznick, Law and Society in Transition: Towards Responsive Law 96 (1978). From this perspective judges do act, and should act, as social engineers, the scope of their discretion being limited only by the consideration that severe adverse public reactions might sap their overall institutional power. See, e.g., M. Shapiro, Freedom of Speech. The Supreme Court and Judicial Review (1966); J. Peltason, Federal Courts and the Political Process (1955); Dahl, *supra* note 30.

38. For a detailed discussion of these issues, see Yudof, "School Desegregation: Legal Realism, Reasoned Elaboration, and Social Science Research in the Supreme Court," 42 Law & Contemp. Prob. 57 (Autumn 1978); Purcell, *supra* note 33.

39. Wechsler, "Towards Neutral Principles of Constitutional Law," 73 Harv. L. Rev. 1 (1959). See also Wechsler, Principles, Politics, and Fundamental Law (1961), and Greenawalt, "The Enduring Significance of Neutral Principles," 78 Col. L. Rev. 982 (1978).

40. See, e.g., McDougal, "The Application of Constitutive Prescriptions: An Addendum to Justice Cardozo," 33 Record of the Association of the Bar of the City of New York 255, 263 (1978). In The Least Dangerous Branch 49–65 (1962), A. Bickel argues for a pragmatic middle course, between principled justifications and realistic political constraints. Citing *Brown* v. *Board of Educa-*

*tion,* he states that judges must be attuned to the shifts in social relations, politics, and morality when choosing and applying principles. He deals with separation-of-powers issues in advising the courts to engage in a "colloquy" with other branches as an alternative to withdrawing completely or to over-extending the courts' jurisdiction. But cf. Bickel, The Supreme Court and the Idea of Progress (1970).

41. See, e.g., Greenawalt, *infra* note 44, at 1006–13; see also, the summary of pragmatic instrumentalism in Summers, *supra* note 33.

42. See Dworkin, *supra* note 36. Using a somewhat different approach Harry Wellington has reached similar conclusions. See Wellington, "Common Law Rules and Constitutional Double Standards: Some Notes on Adjudication," 83 Yale L. J. 221 (1973). For a related attempt to establish a consistent principled basis for legal rights, see C. Fried, Right and Wrong (1978).

43. "[T]he theory of democracy provides objections to judges deciding cases on grounds of policy that do not hold when the judge decides on grounds of principle." Dworkin, "Seven Critics," 11 Ga. L. Rev. 1201, 1237 (1977).

44. Greenawalt, "Policy, Rights, and Judicial Decision," 11 Ga. L. Rev. 991, 1036 (1977). Wechsler's concept of "neutral principles" is inherently neither "conservative" nor "liberal." But it tends to be favored by conservatives (and critics of judicial activism) because neutral principles that give deference to other branches of government or that rely on original historical intent are easier to construct than principled departures from precedent based on social facts and other "progressive materials." See e.g., Bork, "Neutral Principles and Some First Amendment Problems," 47 Ind. L. J. 1, 8 (1971): "Where constitutional materials do not clearly specify the value to be preferred, there is no principled way to prefer any claimed human value to any other. The judge must stick close to the text and the history, and their fair implications, and not construct new rights."

45. United States v. Carolene Products Co., 304 U.S. 144, 152–53 note 4 (1938). See generally Kurland, *supra* note 20, at 174; Bickel, The Supreme Court and the Idea of Progress (1970), *supra* note 40, ch. 4; O. Fiss, The Civil Rights Injunction 60 (1978). For differing analyses of the relationship between democratic theory and the concept of special constitutional protection for minority rights, see Ely, "Toward a Representation-Reinforcing Mode of Judicial Review," 37 Md. L. Rev. 451 (1978); and Sandalow, "Judicial Protection of Minorities," 75 Mich. L. Rev. 1162 (1977). Ely, in Democracy and Distrust (1980), maintains that the entire questioning of the legitimacy of judicial activism relates to the issue of representation of minority rights and that judicial intervention into legislative policy making can only be justified if "discrete and insular" minorities have been excluded from participation in legislative processes. This view has been sharply criticized in Tushnet, "Darkness on the Edge of Town: The Contributions of John Hart Ely to Constitutional Theory," 89 Yale L. J. 1037 (1980), and Tribe, "The Puzzling Persistence of Process-Based Constitutional Theory," 89 Yale L. J. 1063 (1980).

46. In a proper case, the "minority" interest would not include every group that has failed to prevail in the majoritarian political process. Cf. citations in note 45 *supra* with Shapiro, note 37 *supra*.

47. Horowitz, *supra* note 29, at 42–43.

48. Glazer, "Towards an Imperial Judiciary?" *supra* note 6, at 120. Paul

Mishkin adds that judges are "susceptible to the views of a specific, relatively small, elite group of the society" because of their training, social contacts, frames of reference, etc. Mishkin, *supra* note 20, at 966. Reaching the opposite conclusion, Martin Shapiro indicates that judges are more sensitive to the full range of public opinion because they are not tied to particular constituencies. Shapiro, *supra* note 46, at 28. See also Nealy *supra*, note 27.

49. D. Bell, "Serving Two Masters: Integration Ideals and Client Interests in School Desegregation Litigation," 85 Yale L. J. 470 (1976).

50. K. B. Clark, "Social Science, Constitutional Rights, and The Courts," in Rist and Anson, *supra* note 25, at 9.

51. Chayes, *supra* note 14, at 1311–12. See also Dienes, "Judges, Legislators, and Social Change," 13 American Behavioral Scientist, 511, 513 (1970). For an analysis of the evolution of traditional modes of party participation into a public law litigation "consultative process," see Eisenberg, "Participation, Responsiveness and the Consultative Process: An Essay for Lou Fuller," 92 Harv. L. Rev. 410 (1978). See also Tribe, "Seven Pluralist Fallacies: In Defense of the Adversary Process—A Reply to Justice Rehnquist," 33 U. Miami L. Rev. 43, 53 (1978). Proposals for further strengthening the courts' ability to promote participation by all affected interests (including appointment of an "absentee advocate") are contained in Special Project, "The Remedial Process in Institutional Reform Litigation," 78 Col. L. Rev. 784, 870–927 (1978).

52. The issues of legitimacy and capacity are, of course, interrelated. Montesquieu and Blackstone both justified the separation-of-powers doctrine by referring to a need both to ensure the liberty of the people and to enhance efficiency through a specialization of functions. Sharp, *supra* note 16, at 391. Moreover, under a system of "blended" powers, one branch's ability to handle certain problems more efficiently helps to establish the legitimacy of that branch's extension of its activities. The relevance of "efficiency" arguments to basic legitimacy concerns, however, has its limits. Robert Nagel, e.g., argues that "[h]ighly effective measures . . . can be unconstitutional . . . Some constitutional doctrines, including separation of powers, were *designed in part to make government less efficient,* and they cannot be disregarded merely because they have their intended effect" (emphasis supplied; footnote omitted) (see Nagel, *supra* note 22, at 686).

53. Damaska, "Presentation of Evidence and Fact-finding Precision," 123 U. of Pa. L. Rev. 1083 (1975); Frankel, "The Search for Truth: An Umpireal View," 123 U. Pa. L. Rev. 1031, 1052 (1975).

54. 5 Wigmore, Evidence §1367, at 29 (3d ed. 1940).

55. Cf. Davis, "Facts in Lawmaking," 80 Colum. L. Rev. 931, 940 (1980).

56. Horowitz, *supra* note 29, at 48 (1977). The hearsay rule is an example of a rule of evidence that is intended to *promote* truth-seeking but, the critics allege, may have the opposite effect when social facts rather than historical facts are in dispute. In addition, there are other rules that are intended to protect certain societal values even if that means *sacrificing* the accuracy of judicial findings, such as attorney-client or husband-wife privileges of confidentiality. Relevant evidence may also be excluded—particularly in criminal trials—in order to deter misconduct by government agencies in the gathering of information. See, e.g., Frankel, "The Adversary Judge," 54 Texas L. Rev. 465, 482 (1976).

57. See Dienes, *supra* note 51, at 515; Mishkin, *supra* note 20, at 964.

58. Miller and Barron, "The Supreme Court, the Adversary System, and the Flow of Information to the Justices: A Preliminary Inquiry," 61 Va. L. Rev. 1187 (1975); Davis, *supra* note 55.

59. Horowitz, *supra* note 29, at 45; see also B. Levin and P. Moise, "School Desegregation Litigation in the Seventies and the Use of Social Science Evidence: An Annotated Guide," 39 Law & Contemp. Prob. 59 (Winter 1975).

60. Traditional adjudication is also restricted to two-sided fact issues, as contrasted with "polycentric" issues, i.e., ones with interacting points of influence that defy solution by any single criterion. See Fuller, "The Forms and Limits of Adjudication," 92 Harv. L. Rev. 353, 394–404 (1978). Prof. Fuller's concept is reformulated in terms of public law litigation in Eisenberg, *supra* note 51.

61. Levin and Hawley, "Forward," 39 Law & Contemp. Prob. 1, 3 (Winter 1975). See also Horowitz, *supra* note 29, at 25.

62. The comparative advantage of the impartial adversary fact-finding process to the inquisitional modes of Continental legal systems is discussed in Thibaut, Walker, and Lind, "Adversary Presentation and Bias in Legal Decisionmaking," 86 Harv. L. Rev. 386 (1972), and Damaska, *supra* note 53.

63. Chayes, *supra* note 14, at 1308.

64. For an example of the trial judge's techniques in this regard in a complex educational finance reform case, see Lehne, *supra* note 29, at 36–37.

65. For a detailed discussion of the Supreme Court's long involvement in social fact issues see P. Rosen, The Supreme Court and Social Science (1972). See also Doyle, "Social Science Evidence in Court Cases" in Rist and Anson, eds. *supra* note 25, at 10; Wisdom, "Random Remarks on the Role of Social Sciences in the Judicial Decision-Making Process in School Desegregation Cases," 39 Law & Contemp. Prob. 135, 137 (Winter 1975). Cf. Eisenberg and Yeazell, "The Ordinary and the Extraordinary in Institutional Litigation," 93 Harv. L. Rev. 465, 481–94 (1980).

66. Chayes, *supra* note 14, at 1308.

67. See, e.g., Levin, "Education, Life Chances, and the Court: The Role of Social Science Evidence," 39 Law and Cont. Prob. 217, 237 (Spring 1975); Yudof, *supra* note 38. Ronald Dworkin has argued that courts not only should, but typically do, avoid basing decisions on social science causal theories; instead they tend to make "interpretive judgments" that closely integrate moral and factual viewpoints. Dworkin, "Social Sciences and Constitutional Rights—The Consequences of Uncertainty," in Rist and Anson, eds., *supra* note 25, at 21.

68. B. Cardozo, The Nature of the Judicial Process 113 (1921).

69. Wellington, *supra* note 42, at 240.

70. Chayes, *supra* note 14, at 1298–1302. For a detailed overview of the complex mechanics utilized by courts in a wide variety of new model cases, see "Special Project, *supra* note 51.

71. Wellington, *supra* note 42, at 240.

72. Horowitz, *supra* note 29, at 35.

73. *Id.* at 35.

74. Lehne, *supra* note 29, at 4.

75. " . . . it does not have before it either information as to the total amount of resources available or information on the competing claims for those re-

sources." B. Levin, The Courts As Educational Policymakers and Their Impact on Federal Programs 7 (1977); see also Horowitz, *supra* note 29, at 3.

76. Kalodner and Fishman, *supra* note 25.

77. Chayes, *supra* note 14, at 1309. See also Goldstein, "A *Swann* Song for Remedies: Equitable Relief in the Burger Court," 13 Harv. C.R.–C.L.L. Rev. 1 (1978).

78. Note in this regard the broad scope of a district court's remedial powers once a plaintiff's right to a remedy has been established. "Once a right and a violation have been shown, the scope of a district court's equitable powers to remedy past wrongs is broad, for breadth and flexibility are inherent in equitable remedies." Swann v. Charlotte Mecklenburg Board of Education, 402 U.S. 1, 15 (1971). Although the *Swann* doctrine still stands, several post-*Swann* decisions by the Supreme Court have complicated obtaining injunctive relief. Milliken v. Bradley, *supra* note 7 (interdistrict desegregation plan); Rizzo v. Goode, *supra* note 7 (police conduct review procedures); Gilligan v. Morgan, 413 U.S. 1 (1973) (training of National Guard); cf. Ingraham v. Wright, 430 U.S. 651 (1977) (even assuming a liberty interest affected by corporal punishment, child is not entitled to federal remedy, only state tort remedy); but see Milliken v. Bradley, *supra* note 5 (comprehensive intradistrict education plan to remedy effects of segregation); Hills v. Gautreaux, 425 U.S. 284 (1976) (metropolitan remedy for housing discrimination); Dayton Board of Education v. Brinkman, 433 U.S. 406, 417–18 (1977), 443 U.S. 526 (1979) (systemwide busing remedy vacated and remanded in 1977 decision, but similar order upheld in 1979). These developments are discussed in relation to separation-of-powers and legitimacy issues in Nagel, *supra* note 22, and in Goldstein, *supra* note 77; see also Special Project, *supra* note 51, for a discussion of intrinsic and extrinsic limitations on judicial remedial authority.

79. There is a growing social science literature that attempts to describe and analyze such generic implementation problems. See, e.g., E. Bardach, The Implementation Game (1977); J. Pressman and A. Wildavsky, Implementation (1973); M. Derthick, New Towns in Town: Why a Federal Program Fails (1972); E. Hargrove, The Missing Link (1975); Berman, "The Study of Macro and Micro Implementation," 26 Public Policy 157 (1978); Van Meter and Van Horn, "Policy Implementation Process," 6 Administration and Society, 445 (1975).

80. See, e.g., Van Meter and Van Horn, note 79 *supra* at 462 (degree of consensus on goals most important factor for successful implementation); Majone and Wildavsky, "Implementation as Evolution: Exorcising the Ghosts in the Implementation Machine," Russell Sage Discussion Paper, no. 2 (1978) (ambiguity in policy goals).

81. Such has been the finding of other studies of desegregation situations not involving court decrees. See, e.g., the analysis of desegregation attempts in 91 cities contained in D. Kirby. T. Harris, R. Crain, C. Rossell, Political Strategies in Northern School Desegregation (1973); United States Commission on Civil Rights, Fulfilling the Letter and the Spirit of the Law (August 1976), and related Commission Staff Report entitled "Reviewing a Decade of School Desegregation, 1965–75: Report of a National Survey of School Superintendents" (1977).

82. Accordingly, many commentators—even ones quite critical of court

performance—have suggested tactics and reforms for making better use of these abilities. A note entitled "Implementation Problems in Institutional Reform Litigation," 91 Harv. L. Rev. 428 (1977), recommends increasing nonparty input; establishing "implementation estimates"; monitoring standards and resolution dispute panels; appointing masters for enforcement; and adopting comprehensive implementation plans. Kalodner recommends early appointments of experts to assist the courts' efforts to clarify the functions of the participants in the process, the establishment of monitoring agencies, and a clarification of the lawyers' roles in aiding the court in its implementation concerns. Betsy Levin suggests the requirements of a "judicial impact statement" in public law litigations to avoid "unintentional consequences." Levin, *supra* note 75, at 92–93. See also implementation devices surveyed in Special Project, *supra* note 51.

83. In recent years some serious efforts have been made to bridge the large gap between theory and extensive empirical analysis—as in *The Courts and Social Policy,* by Horowitz and *Limits of Justice* by Kalodner and Fishman. But although these works contain valuable insights and raise important questions, their general conclusions about many key issues in the judicial activism debate are based on data drawn from mere handfuls of cases which on the whole seem selected without objective criteria. See Yudof, "Essay Review of H. Kalodner and J. Fishman, Limits of Justice: The Court's Role in School Desegregation," 1 W. New Eng. L. Rev. 691 (1979). In the "Role of Judge in Public Law Litigation," *supra* note 14, Chayes synthesized a number of descriptive generalizations to show that the traditional theory of adjudication does not fit the facts of judicial activity in the public sector. The article, however, does not attempt to validate systematically the generalizations on which the model is based. The report of the Columbia Law School Special Project on "The Remedial Process in Institutional Reform Litigation," *supra* note 51, is styled as a "survey of representative cases," in contrast to the detailed case study approach. However, the authors do not explain their survey methodology or their definition of "representative." Their data is used to formulate a typology of variables that is illustrated by string citations.

84. See Linde, *supra* note 36, at 229.

85. The methodology utilized in this study is described in more detail in appendix B.

## CHAPTER 2

1. Since we selected our cases from among trial court decisions, we anticipated fewer "hard cases" raising controversial principle/policy categorization issues than might be anticipated from the normal scholarly concentration on the more controversial Supreme Court cases.

2. Dworkin, "Seven Critics," 11 Ga. L. Rev. 1201, 1229 (1977). Dworkin also states at 1203: "[W]e must ask whether judges try to enforce the rights they think the parties have, or whether they create what they take to be new rights to serve social goals." The great importance that Dworkin attaches to the question of judges' perceptions of their own actions is shown in his interpretation of M. Horwitz's book, The Transformation of America Law (1977), found *Id.* at 1207–11.

3. We recognize that the conclusions reached in this chapter are less definitive and less concrete than the empirical findings reported in chs. 3–5. The critical importance of these issues, however, justifies even a search for tentative answers.

4. These definitions were derived from the principle/policy literature discussed in ch. 1, and especially from Dworkin's concepts.

5. Tinker v. Des Moines Independent School District, 393 U.S. 503 (1969).

6. Cf. R. Dworkin, Taking Rights Seriously 92 (1977); Dworkin, "Seven Critics," *supra* note 2, at 1204; A. Bickel, The Least Dangerous Branch 58 (1962) ("A true principle may carry within itself its own flexibility . . . flexibility on its own terms"); C. Fried, Right and Wrong (1978) (comparison of absolute norms and categorical norms); Greenawalt, "The Enduring Significance of Neutral Principles," 78 Colum. L. Rev. 982, 988 note 25 (discussing whether Wechsler considered Holmes's clear-and-present-danger test to be a neutral principle).
Another kind of norm found between the principle and policy poles is illustrated by a statutory guarantee that handicapped children receive "appropriate education." In this case the right grows out of prior legislative balancing of competing policies (e.g., weighing the needs of handicapped students against resource limitations and limits of federal intervention, judging the effectiveness of educational programs, etc.). Consequently, when litigation questions the application of the statutorily created right to "appropriate" education, the court must reconstruct (and perhaps extrapolate from) the lawmakers' policy-balancing process in order to implement the right at issue. Cf. Greenawalt, "Policy, Rights and Judicial Decision," 11 Ga. L. Rev. 991, 1009 note 49, and Dworkin's reply in Dworkin, "Seven Critics," *supra* note 2, at 1233 note 26 (policy considerations in equal protection analysis).

7. This definition applies to balancing within the parameters of an articulated principle, rather than to "exegetic" balancing between two principles. See Henkin, "Infallibility Under Law: Constitutional Balancing," 38 Colum. L. Rev. 1022 (1978); Fried, *supra* note 6.

8. Hereafter, caselets usually will be identified by their numbers on the list. For example, *Caplin v. Oak,* which is listed as case 12 in appendix A, will be referred to as "C. 12," and string citations will be in the form "Cs. 5, 10, and 15."

9. The one exception was C. 44, a suit solely based on the Federal Age Discrimination in Employment Act. However, there were 3 cases in which the plaintiffs, although pleading a constitutional claim, placed primary reliance on federal statutory rights (Cs. 49, 56, 62); 3 cases in which constitutional and federal statutory claims were stressed about equally (Cs. 36, 47, 48); and 4 cases in which constitutional and state statutory claims were about equally important (Cs. 23, 33, 39, 65).

10. Such claims are usually not pursued seriously because they rely on totally unprecedented legal theories or, if the claim is not novel, because the facts may be hard to prove. A party may nevertheless include such a claim in order to retain the option of taking advantage of subsequent legal and factual developments. Such claims also can provide a vehicle for a more detailed and sympathetic picture of the plaintiff's grievance.

11. If a claim with ample authority was properly pleaded, but the party did

not seriously pursue it, the claim was omitted from our classification. In other words, although we did not make judgments about the weight of the evidence on contested issues of fact, we did decide whether the party had actually placed the pleaded claim in contention.

12. For example, our sample included five cases challenging mandatory maternity-leave policies. All of them were filed before the Supreme Court's decision in Cleveland Board of Education v. La Fleur, 414 U.S. 632 (1974), which struck down Cleveland's maternity-leave practices on a basis which would fit under our classification of principle/policy balancing analysis. (In *La Fleur*, the teacher's interest in having an opportunity to prove her fitness to teach, and to continue teaching if she was able, was treated as a right not subject to divestment on the grounds of asserted goals such as preventing embarrassment to teachers and students. However, it was specifically subject to balancing against the educational goal of continuity of instruction.) We classified the five mandatory maternity-leave cases in our sample as principle/policy balancing claims because at the time when they were filed, the weight of recent legal authority, although not definitively clarified until *La Fleur*, strongly pointed in this direction, and there would have been no colorable precedent for attempts to frame the issue in strict principle terms (e.g., by arguing that classification by gender required strict equal protection scrutiny).

Our standard for assessing the weight of precedent is analogous to a federal court's inquiry into whether a claim presents a "substantial federal question." As in that evaluative process, our conclusions could not be narrowed to the point of objective scientific certainty. However, we believe that consistency in applying our definitional categories resulted in meaningful distinctions among the case sample as a whole. In any event, definitional disagreements concerning a small number of close cases should not substantially affect the basic findings.

13. The prevailing interpretation of Supreme Court doctrine during the relevant time period considered alienage to be a suspect classification, invoking the strict equal protection test. Subsequent Supreme Court decisions, however, have applied a less strict standard of review. See Ambach v. Norwick, 441 U.S. 68 (1979) (aliens barred from teaching in public schools); Foley v. Connellie, 435 U.S. 291 (1978) (aliens barred from state police officer positions).

14. We would note that free exercise claims often are resolved through principle/policy balancing, e.g., when a parent or child's interest in religious practice conflicts with the state's interest in compulsory education. Wisconsin v. Yoder, 406 U.S. 205 (1972). However, this case was classified as strict principle because there was an established Supreme Court precedent (West Virginia v. Barnette, 319 U.S. 624 [1943]) which had already resolved the main balancing issues involving school flag ceremonies in school. Similarly, establishment clause claims may require policy balancing, (e.g., regarding allegations of "excessive entanglement" of church and state), but such issues were not present in the religion cases in the sample.

15. The U.S. Supreme Court had repeatedly refused to review the legal issues in these often emotionally charged disputes.

16. See L. Tribe, Constitutional Protection of Individual Rights 963 note 37 (1978). Within this consensus the appeals courts did differ about such matters

as allocating burdens of proof between plaintiff and defendant, and deciding whether inculcating conventional norms of appearance could ever be considered a legitimate policy objective. Although often acknowledging that applicable judicial precedents established principle/policy balancing as the requisite mode of decision, the trial judges expressed considerable discomfort at having to balance plaintiffs' putative rights of personhood, expression, and privacy against the state's interest in setting educational policies. Three judges abstained; two said they thought abstention would be desirable, but could not justify it under existing law; two expressed doubts about controlling appellate decisions requiring them to conduct balancing tests. Ultimately, the judges upheld the plaintiffs in five out of six cases in which they undertook balancing (Cs. 16, 17, 21, 50, 61).

17. The four race discrimination cases in column 2 are contrasted with the race cases listed in column 1, because, in addition to claims of discrimination, plaintiffs also claimed that school district practices were irrational or denied due-process procedures. For example, in *Horton* (C. 32), a challenge to North Carolina's probationary teacher employment procedures was combined with a race discrimination claim. *Georgia Association* (C. 25) and *King* (C. 40) challenged the rationality of the standardized employment examinations as well as their discriminatory impact.

18. The Supreme Court has not ruled on the issue as to whether handicapped persons constitute a "suspect classification" entitled to strict scrutiny analysis under the equal protection clause. Cf. Fialkowski v. Shapp, 405 F. Supp. 946 (E.D. Pa. 1975).

19. See, e.g., P.L. 94–142, 20 U.S.C.A. §1401 et seq.

20. At issue in *Bobilin* (C. 8) was a rule promulgated by state education officials in Hawaii requiring public school children to work in school cafeterias for up to seven times each year. The plaintiffs' claim that their children were being impressed into involuntary servitude, in violation of the Thirteenth Amendment, was totally without legal precedent. A further argument that the rule represented an abuse of discretion because it served no valid educational purpose was, on its face, asking that the court second-guess the board's educational judgments.

21. The present discussion is limited to the liability phase of the litigation. In the remedial phase which occurs after a court determines that a plaintiff is entitled to some form of relief, policy issues necessarily become more extensive because a prime consideration in designing any remedy is its efficacy in eliminating the unlawful practices which the court has identified.

22. Additional examples are C. 46 (professional staff control over selection of reading materials will improve quality of curriculum); and C. 21 (permitting girls on boys' teams would impede development of comprehensive girls' athletic program).

23. On the other hand, we found that a wealth of potential policy arguments were not used by the parties.

24. In some instances, of course, the opposite effect may have been intended. Pointing out policy problems may be a way for school boards to state that a broader, more complex set of issues than the plaintiffs put forth are involved and that the court should not try to second-guess the school board's judgment.

25. Cs. 47, 55, 57, 58, 59. The other two divergent cases were C. 40, which the court treated solely as a race/principle claim, but which contained testing issues which we would classify as principle/policy; and C. 3, in which race/privacy principle issues was emphasized but the court focused on irrationality of policy.

26. Two cases which we, too, rated as policy, plus the five cases, listed in the footnote above.

27. It is, of course, impossible to determine objectively the extent to which subsidiary policy concerns may have consciously or subconsciously influenced judges' decisions. However, an analysis of cases in which judges explicitly stated their concern about the collateral consequences of court intervention indicates that these considerations played a secondary role to principle and principle/policy balancing analysis. In our questionnaire we asked: "Did the court express any knowledge or concern about the policy or administrative consequences of its decision?" In 47 of the 65 caselets (72%) the answer was "yes." In the large majority of these 47 cases, the courts noted the potential hardships on defendant school systems (e.g., the practicality of administering a relief order, the impact of imposing legalistic procedures on a traditionally informal school environment, etc.). Nevertheless, the defendants' success rate in these 47 cases is 38%, almost precisely the same as in the remaining 18 cases, in which judges did not mention these factors (39%). The recognition of the school board's subsidiary problems, therefore, did not appear to dispose the courts more favorably toward sustaining the school board's legal positions, provided plaintiffs' claims were based on controlling principles.

28. Judicial commentary on separation of power was relatively *ad hoc*. There was no commonly accepted conception of how this institutional principle was to be integrated with other principles of decision. Some important areas of concern were: reluctance to second-guess the judgment of local school officials; the proper allocation of responsibility among the three federal branches of government; availability of relief through other governmental agencies; and the resource allocation impact of court orders.

29. See p. 3 *supra*.

30. The main impact of *Rodriguez* may have been to divert into state courts one specific type of litigation—challenges to state and local school financing systems. Even in this regard, however, the decision did not signal a contradiction of the prevailing concept of the limits of "manageability" for principles of educational reform, since the courts of several large states (e.g., California, New York, New Jersey) have accepted the very principle claims that failed in *Rodriguez*.

*Rodriguez* did not even affect the finance-related cases in our group of federal cases. In the pre-*Rodriguez* decision, in *Johnson* (C. 39), the court held that the defendants' policies served a "compelling state interest." In *Brown*, (C. 9) the plaintiffs pleaded a fundamental rights claim in their pre-*Rodriguez* complaint. After the Supreme Court decision, however, they were still on firm ground with a race discrimination claim and a traditional equal protection claim.

31. Subsequent to *Rodriguez*, the Supreme Court itself has specifically extended such principles to the education domain. The *Rodriguez* precedent made it easier for the court to dispose of the plaintiffs' claims in *Zoll* (C. 65),

but we expect that the same result would have been reached even if education *had* been deemed "fundamental" by the Supreme Court.

32. See, e.g., Kirp, "Law, Politics and Equal Educational Opportunity: The Limits of Judicial Involvement," 47 Harv. Ed. Rev. 117 (1977). Judicial activism arising out of the enforcement of statutes will neutralize the classic legitimacy arguments stressing the finality of judicial rulings based on the Constitution. (A legislature can overrule a statutory, but not a constitutional decision.) But new objections are beginning to be heard which challenge the legitimacy of the courts' willingness to accept the delegation to them by legislatures of broad policy-making powers. See J. H. Ely, Democracy and Distrust 131–34 (1980); Industrial Union Department v. American Petroleum Institute, 448 U.S. 607 (1980) (concurring opinion of Justice Rehnquist).

## Chapter 3

1. Each of the three subcategories which we have included in our definition of "minority groups" represents a group of citizens who arguably meet the criterion of suffering from substantial limitations on their ability to participate fully in the majoritarian political process. These claims, therefore, are entitled to special consideration by the courts, according to those who accept the proposition that protection of constitutionality guaranteed rights for groups lacking full access to majoritarian processes is the special responsibility of the judicial branch. See J. H. Ely, Democracy and Distrust (1980); Tribe, "Seven Fallacies of Pluralism: In Defense of the Adversary Process—A Reply to Justice Rehnquist," 33 U. of Miami L. Rev. 43 (1978). Our categorization does not include groups who are temporarily "minorities" on a specific issue because they "have failed to obtain their objectives through the political process." Sandalow, "Judicial Protection of Minorities," 75 Mich. L. Rev. 1162 (1977). The extent to which each of our subcategories meets the classic definition of a "discrete and insular minority" entitled to special protection varies, however; "suspect class" minority groups qualify most clearly, and "nonconformists" least clearly.

2. First Amendment cases brought by nonminority persons who were not identified with strongly unconventional ideas or lifestyles were categorized as "other."

3. On the other hand, plaintiffs may avoid class action certification because of the difficulties in defining the class and possible onerous notification requirements or because ample relief may be available without class certification.

Class action allegations and their disposition did not, in fact, appear to be expecially important for relief in our sample. In 16 of the 21 cases in which class certification was granted, the court entered a systemwide injunctive order. However, systemwide injunctions were also entered in 13 other cases: of these 7 were not even styled as class actions; 5 cases had no certification ruling, and in 1 certification was denied. This finding reflects the fact that in educational policy cases, if a single plaintiff obtained an order enjoining the enforcement of a policy, the relief would benefit similarly situated persons whether or not they are called members of a class. See, e.g., *Banks* (C. 5), 314 F. Supp. 285, 288.

It is difficult to determine how class action procedures may have affected the quality of relief. In all but two of the cases which resulted in major "reform decrees" (a term defined in ch. 5), the plaintiff class had been certified. But lack of certification in the two exceptional cases—*Armstead* (C. 4) and *Nicholson* (C. 49)—did not appear to affect the nature of relief. For example, in *Nicholson,* despite the denial of class action status the court held public hearings which were similar to those held in *PARC* (C. 52), where certification was granted prior to approval of the consent decree.

4. An *amicus curiae,* or "friend of the court," is an individual or group that is granted permission to file a brief or otherwise present information to the court. Technically, an *amicus* is not an actual party and does not have the right to raise new issues, or to appeal, if he is dissatisfied with the decision.

5. In three of these instances, intervention requests by other persons were approved. One of these, a request by a teachers' union for intervention in the remedial stage of *Frederick L.* (C. 23) was denied because of "untimeliness." Another judge in the same court, however, permitted union intervention in a case that was already six years old (*PARC,* C. 52); see also *Nicholson* (C. 49) (two out of five intervention applications granted in remedial phase); *Brown* (C. 9) (teachers' union intervention denied in liability stage). In public law litigation, the need for multipolar representation tends to increase at the remedial stage. Groups which earlier shared a common interest during the liability stage often diverge on the specifics of the remedy. It would therefore seem that the traditional understanding of the doctrine of "untimeliness" under Federal Rule of Civil Procedure 24 is in need of reconsideration under these circumstances. See Note, "The Remedial Process in Institutional Reform Litigation," 78 Col. L. Rev. 789, 924–26 (1978).

6. A striking exception was Judge Becker during the later remedial phase of *PARC* (C. 52). He approved an unusual "at large" intervention by the Philadelphia Federation of Teachers (which was not designated as a plaintiff or defendant), and repeatedly encouraged persons with an interest in, or information about, the remedial issues in *PARC* to take part in negotiating sessions. Also, in C. 36 the court told the parties they should bring county school officials into the case. In C. 41, the judge said he favored the joining of the U.S. Department of Health, Education and Welfare, but he did not pursue the matter when the parties disagreed with him. In C. 18, the judge asked counsel to canvass opinion in the locality about the desirability of various possible reapportionment remedies.

7. For example, in *National Indian Youth Council* (C. 47), a suit brought by an Indian advocacy organization to close an off-reservation Indian school, parents of Indian schoolchildren and representatives of the Navajo tribe were not included in the plaintiff class. In *Minarcini* (C. 46), a suit challenging a school board's censoring of the high school English department's reading list, the teachers' union of a neighboring school district asked for (and was granted) *amicus* status, while the teachers employed by the immediately affected district did not try to participate.

8. Cs. 6, 15, 23, 41, 48, 52.

9. Cs. 15, 18, 23, 41, 45, 48, 49, 52.

10. In the legislative process, the *issues* may also be "bipolar," but a large number of groups may seek to participate in order to register the size of their following and the intensity of their concerns.

11. The public interest bar here means attorneys affiliated (either full-time or in connection with a particular lawsuit) with a not-for-profit organization engaged in legal action. A private attorney who offered his services without charge was considered a "public interest attorney" only if he acted in affiliation with a public interest group, such as the American Civil Liberties Union, or the Lawyers' Committee for Civil Rights Under Law. Federally funded legal services offices were also classified as public interest organizations. Private attorneys representing school boards were listed as "governmental."

12. *Banks* (C. 5) is included in this total; it was a hybrid religion/due process case.

13. This figure becomes 70% if student due process cases are categorized as "relatively novel" rather than "not novel."

14. Assuming that a lawyer's use of class action mechanisms indicates that he is in contact with the people he purports to represent and actually reflects positions they espouse, it is significant that public interest attorneys seek and actually obtain class action certifications substantially more often than do private attorneys. Correlating "Class Action Status" with attorney affiliation (appendix C, cols. 3 and 4), we found the following: Public interest attorneys requested class action certification in 88% of their cases, whereas private attorneys filed such requests only 59% of the time. Public interest attorneys obtained certification for 50% of such claims, were denied in 13%, and received no ruling in 56%. The deficiencies in present judicial application of class action procedures, however, preclude any firm conclusions on these points. (See p. 38 *supra*.)

## CHAPTER 4

1. In this chapter "social fact" information is used to refer to the products of either basic or applied social science research, and also to the testimony of persons whom courts recognize as "experts." For example, on the question of corporal punishment—its educational value and psychological consequences—social fact submissions could take such varying forms as (a) survey statistics about the frequency of corporal punishment; (b) studies by research psychologists concerning children's responses; and (c) opinion testimony by principals or school psychologists about the effects of corporal punishment on academic achievement and classroom discipline.

2. This latter function is especially useful in educational policy cases where a plaintiff can often obtain critical data concerning the operations of the school system only through access to the school district's files.

3. This finding is based on a search of the docket sheets for entries of interrogatories, depositions, and other discovery-related materials, as well as attorney interviews. Discovery procedures were not used in the remaining 27 cases mainly for the following reasons: (a) the parties easily stipulated to the accuracy of the relevant facts (particularly in speech and grooming cases); (b) mutually satisfactory information exchanges were worked out informally; and (c) evidentiary materials had already been prepared in a related administrative proceeding or court suit.

4. Interview with attorney for school district.

5. Discovery appeared to have contributed to important stipulations in Cs. 23, 24, 25, 41, 44, and 52. This list may not be exhaustive because it is based only on explicit attorney statements and on explicit statements in the record.

6. When asked whether discovery procedures had been abused, attorneys in only four cases (Cs. 27, 29, 46, 49) responded that they thought their opponents had acted unreasonably. In C. 29, each attorney stated that the other had acted unfairly in what was generally a bitter litigation.

7. The larger issue involved here is whether it is possible in any context to define the type and the quantity of social fact evidence that is "optimal" for the determination of social policy disputes. See ch. 10, pp. 208–9 *infra*.

8. See ch. 3 *supra*, for a definition and discussion of multipolarity.

9. For further description and analysis of shifting party alliances and their effect on judicial process, see the detailed case study of *Chance* v. *Board of Examiners*, ch. 6 *infra*.

10. This hypothesis is, of necessity, addressed to signs of distortion that are measurable and comparable over a large number of cases. More subtle factors contributing to distortion, such as the difference in the qualifications and forensic skills of opposing experts, are considered in the context of our detailed case studies.

11. Cs. 5, 26, 36, 46, and 47. For example, in C. 26, the court rejected the defendants' evidence about physical and psychological differences between boys and girls as irrelevant to the question of why it was necessary to exclude a qualified girl runner from competing in interscholastic cross-country races. A more detailed analysis of how judges avoid the necessity to analyze social fact evidence is presented in the following subsection of this chapter.

12. Cs. 17, 21, 31, 44, and 61 (student appearance [3 cases], student speech, age discrimination).

13. Cs. 11, 32, 38 (race discrimination [2 cases] and mandatory maternity leave).

14. C. 34 (where the issue concerned the comparative sexual precociousness of married and unmarried students).

15. In C. 49 the main defendant essentially conceded liability. In Cs. 33 and 37, the employment statistics and census figures at issue were straightforward and subject to a "common-sense" analysis.

16. In C. 25 the plaintiffs presented strong testimony by experts from the Educational Testing Service that the National Teachers Examination which they had developed was being used for a purpose for which it was not validated, but it is possible that a countervailing expert might have convinced the court that the district's practices were reasonable and that validation arguments were overly technical and unrealistic. In C. 27 the court accepted the plaintiffs' statistical evidence of discriminatory suspension patterns; a statistical expert for defendants might have drawn different inferences. Finally, in upholding a grooming regulation, the court in C. 57 relied on testimony by defendant school district's witness concerning the cultural value of the rules and the dangers of disruption if they were not enforced; countervailing testimony might have changed the outcome (the courts in Cs. 21 and 31 rejected the same kind of unopposed defendant testimony).

17. Doyle, "Social Science Evidence in Court Cases," in R. Rist and R. Anson, Education, Social Science and the Judicial Process 10 (1977).

18. The remaining 23 cases involved "historical facts" which are the subject of traditional forms of judicial inquiry: i.e., did specific actions actually occur or were specific statements made? Social facts involve recurrent patterns of behavior relating to general policy issues. See generally p. 12 *supra.*

19. D. Horowitz, The Courts and Social Policy 47 (1977).

20. The 11 "complex" social fact cases consisted of all 4 special education cases, 3 race discrimination cases involving testing issues, 2 corporal punishment cases, 1 intradistrict finance case, and the 1 handicapped teacher case.

21. There also was some overall correlation in the sample between novelty and social fact evidence. Such evidence was introduced in 72% of the "novel" cases, but in only 61% of the "not novel" cases (appendix B, col. 2; table 6, col. 2).

22. Both decisions antedated the Supreme Court ruling in Ingraham v. Wright, 430 U.S. 651 (1977). Parties also attempted to introduce social fact evidence in two-thirds of the grooming cases, another area of unsettled doctrine.

23. Cf. Cs. 22, 30, 38, and 51 with Cs. 19 and 56. The social fact evidence was introduced in C. 22 at a hearing that antedated *La Fleur,* and the case was finally decided after *La Fleur.*

24. See ch. 2 *supra,* at 28.

25. Note that the court in this complicated case also employed a social fact precedent avoidance device (see *supra,* at 53–54) and made an independent fact-finding judgment on another issue (see *supra,* at 55).

26. An especially aggressive use of a tacit admission occurred in the remedial phase of *Kruse* (C. 41). The issue in dispute was the level of services to be provided to learning disabled children prior to the effective date of new federal statutory standards. The attorneys drafted a compromise plan, but the state declined to accept it. Then, when the plaintiffs proposed the same terms of this plan to the court, the court incorporated them into a remedial decree over the state's objections. The court apparently was influenced by the state's attorney's willingness to recommend the terms of the plan to state officials.

27. Five more of the complex fact issue cases were decided through avoidance devices (Cs. 9, 40, 41, 58, and 59), and one involved a single-party submission (C. 25).

28. In our interviews, almost none of the attorneys indicated that he or she thought a judge was blatantly incapable of comprehending the social fact issues. In C. 44 one attorney did express mild reservations about the judge's understanding of the statistical methodology, but was contradicted by the opposing attorney. In C. 15 the appellate judges' opinion showed a lack of understanding of the technical workings of the proportional representation system of elections, but the district court judge's opinion reflected full grasp of these details. In C. 48 both attorneys agreed that the judge understood the liability facts, but one attorney thought he got "lost" in the remedial phase.

In certain cases the judges were especially well qualified to address the disputed social fact issues arising in education policy cases. For example, in C. 9, both attorneys pointed out that the judge, a former antitrust lawyer, had easily understood complex statistical data. Another judge who had served as a state civil rights commissioner was now ruling on a federal anti-discrimination regulation (C. 56). By a trick of fate, the judge in C. 39, a case challenging the constitutionality of a state statute, had helped to enact that very law when he was the majority leader in the state senate. (Plaintiffs did not move to disqualify him.) Thus, judges sometimes have a background in the social fact-finding problems that arise in educational policy cases. Cf. Chayes, "The Role of the Judge in Public Law Litigation," 89 Harv. L. Rev. 1281, 1307–8 (1976).

29. Application of relatively straightforward reportorial statistics and other data also tended to be undertaken.

30. The court also treated as an admission a statement by the school superintendent that the standards and the policy "had nothing to do with determining teacher competency."

31. The court's minimizing of the relative importance of knowledge of the urban school district came back to haunt it in the remedial stage of the case. For months it was caught in a bitter dispute about the particular teaching assignment to which the plaintiff was entitled, consistent with her court-decreed seniority.

32. 411 F. Supp. 982, 987.

33. For the next phase of remediation, the court appointed a special master to monitor the defendants' compliance. The master's responsibilities included (among others) investigation of the suitability of educational programs and of the adequacy of screening/placement procedures; review of interagency coordination efforts; scrutiny of budget procedures to determine means for curing budgetary shortages; and assistance to defendants in preparing a comprehensive plan: During the master's tenure, the court twice again found that the defendants' efforts were inadequate (7/75, 8/77). These findings were based primarily on the master's reports.

## CHAPTER 5

1. Implementation theorists might call this the organization of cooperative behavior through the playing of "implementation games." See, e.g., E. Bardach, The Implementation Game (1977).

2. For reasons stemming from the history of equity jurisprudence, courts sometimes will frame what is, in substance, a reform order in "negative" terms that appear to make it a self-executing order. For example, a court might order a school district with no facilities for teaching mentally retarded children to "refrain from denying" appropriate educational services to that class of students. Notwithstanding the negative language, the court has in fact ordered the defendant to embark on major institutional reform, i.e., establishing diagnostic and programmatic services for a unique class of children. To avoid confusion, we will not distinguish, as in some legal literature, between "negative injunctions" and "affirmative injunctions," or between "prohibitive injunctions" and "mandatory injunctions."

Prof. Owen Fiss has defined three broad categories of injunctions: "preventive," "reparative," and "structural." See O. Fiss, The Civil Rights Injunction 7 (1978). All of Fiss's structural injunctions would fit our definition of a reform decree, but his reparative injunctions could fall on either side of our basic dichotomy (between reform decrees and self-executing judgments), depending on how potentially intrusive each one was. Therefore, we believe that a distinction between reform decrees and self-executing judgments is the better framework for analyzing our data with regard to the primary issue in the chapter, namely, the nature and extent of direct judicial intrusion in school district policy-making prerogatives.

3. As discussed in appendix B, our sample excluded cases in which plaintiffs *requested* only declaratory judgments. However, in a few cases, despite requests for coercive injunctions, the court saw fit to issue only a declaratory judgment.

4. As indicated in ch. 1, some commentators have hypothesized that in social policy cases the courts are prone to undertake institutional reform on the basis of unrepresentative individual cases. Our data, however, calls attention to a viable alternative to the two extremes of dismissal or extensive judicial policy making. As was done in each of the individual self-executing cases, courts can distinguish between meritorious institutional claims and less compelling claims for institutional reform by granting relief to plaintiffs as individuals but denying them institutional changes.

5. The exception is C. 6, a student publication case in which the court did not merely prohibit a course of conduct but also entered a consent order establishing a new set of institutional standards and procedures.

6. Eight out of the nine liability judgments in these categories resulted in reform decrees.

7. These three modes of participation in themselves represent a continuum along the plane of intrusiveness. For example, a defendant who negotiates a plan with the plaintiff is generally subject to greater outside pressure and influence than one who drafts the plan on its own. Any mode of defendant participation, however, will generally be less intrusive than a remedy wholly or largely formulated by outside agents.

8. By way of contrast, there was a negative legislative reaction in *Givens* (C. 27), another discipline case. The North Carolina legislature passed a statute, in clear contradiction of the court's ruling, that purported to increase the discretionary authority of school officials in discipline matters.

9. Ironically, *PARC* and *Mills* (Cs. 52, 45), were specifically cited by Congress as establishing the basic principles for legislative action (see Senate Report #94–168, 1975 U.S. Code Cong. & Admin. News, p. 1432), but the remedial stages of these cases were still continuing after the passage of the act.

10. Legislation supportive of prior judicial decisions in self-executing order cases occurred in C. 30 (Title VII employment discrimination requirements) and C. 43 (Ohio Rev. Code Ann. §3313.66).

11. Whereas defendants' drafting of a basic plan can be considered the primary mode of decree formulation in five cases, plaintiff formulation (which generally would connote a high degree of intrusiveness) was predominant, at least in major stages, in three (Cs. 4, 15, 37).

12. In *Hosier* (C. 33) the court ordered the admission of alien children in the Virgin Island public schools and set forth the principles for dealing with the threat of school overcrowding.

13. Twelve out of fifteen cases.

14. Eleven out of fifteen cases.

15. Six out of fifteen cases.

16. Although we believe that the filing of contempt motions, generally speaking, constitutes a valid indication of compliance, sometimes plaintiffs

may fail to bring allegations of noncompliance because they lack either resources to compile proof of violations or sustained interest in implementation.

17. In *Frederick L.* (C. 23) the plaintiff's attorney reported that he drafted a
contempt motion, but decided against filing because he concluded that forces
beyond the school district's control (strikes and budget crises) were responsible for the latter's temporary noncompliance with the decree. In *Dixon* (C. 20)
the court specifically found that the defendant had not violated the court
order. In the other 2 cases, the court took the allegations of contempt seriously, but found means other than formal adjudication to resolve them. An
off-the-record warning by the judge convinced school officials in *Alexander*
(C. 2) to reverse an alleged retaliatory action against an individual plaintiff. In
*PARC* (C. 52), after presiding over several days of testimony on the contempt
motion, the judge discontinued the hearing and established a unique, ongoing negotiation forum to deal with the compliance difficulties. (See pp. 68–70,
*supra.*)

18. Our present focus is on the later implementation phase of *PARC*. For a
description of the complex remedial efforts in the early period of implementation, see Kirp, Buss and Kuriloff, "Legal Reform of Special Education: Empirical Studies and Procedural Proposals," 62 Calif. L. Rev. 40
(1974).

19. The conference of April 24, 1978, was observed by one of the authors.
Counsel confirmed that it was a representative meeting.

20. This matter was pressed by a group of parents who were pleased with
the program at the threatened school and did not want their children transferred, as they had been many times before. After listening to the parents'
grievances, Judge Becker explained in lay language that his authority to order
changes at that level of administrative detail was limited by the doctrine of
federalism. However, at the same time that he disclaimed formal jurisdiction
in the situation, he elicited a detailed explanation of the school closing decision from school officials present at the conference.

## CHAPTER 6

1. See, e.g., D. Ravitch, The Great School Wars 161–63 (1974). New York
City was the only school district in the state required to maintain such a
specialized testing body. All other school districts could appoint as a supervisor any candidate having appropriate state certification, normally issued on
the basis of completion of course requirements rather than scores on a written
test.

2. The four permanent members of the Board of Examiners themselves
obtained their positions through competitive civil service examinations. The
chancellor of the City School District of the City of New York (or his representative) held the fifth position on the board, ex-officio (N.Y. Ed. Law
§§2569, 2573, 2590).

3. According to the *Chance* plaintiffs, 19% of the city's *acting* principals were
black or Hispanic. The disparity was attributed to the discriminatory impact
of the exam. Brief submitted by plaintiffs-appellees, 1971 Appeal to the Second Circuit Court of Appeals, at 3.

4. See Chance v. Board of Examiners, 458 F. 2d 1167, 1172 (2d Cir. 1972).

5. In 1971, the community school board wanted to appoint 37 minority acting principals and 131 minority acting assistant principals lacking the city license. Chance v. Board of Examiners, 330 F. Supp. 203, 224 (S.D. N.Y. 1971). A graphic example of this phenomenon of widespread acting appointments was set forth in the facts of Board of Education (New York City) v. Nyquist, 31 N.Y. 2d 468 (1973). Mrs. Adele Timpson had served as acting principal of a racially segregated Harlem elementary school for eleven years because no "eligible" person could be found to take the position. Mrs. Timpson, who had "been highly praised by her supervisors for her performance of a difficult job" (31 N.Y. 2d 471), had failed to pass the license examination on *six* occasions.

6. See, e.g., Strayer and Yavner Report (2 Mayor's Committee on Management Survey, Administrative Management of the School System of New York City 755 [1951]); Shinnerer Report (Report by Dr. Mark C. Schinnerer to the New York State Department of Education [1961]); Cresap, McCormick and Paget Report (Management Study for the New York City Board of Education [1962]); Griffiths Report (Teacher Mobility in New York City: A Study of Recruitment, Selection, Appointment, and Promotion of Teachers in New York City Public Schools, New York University [1963 and 1966]); Theobald Report (in Agenda for a City, Institute for Public Administration [1970]).

At the very time the NAACP was preparing *Chance,* the City Human Rights Commission was instituting a broad-based investigation of the city school system's personnel practices. The investigation, which included public testimony by top-ranking school officials, union leaders, civic group representatives, educators, and testing experts, concluded that the low rate of minority hiring was not due to any conscious or deliberate discrimination, but to a *de facto* exclusion of minority groups that resulted from inefficiencies and inflexibilities of the personnel system. The evidence pertaining to educational policy issues was summarized by the commission's special counsel as follows: "The clear weight of informed opinion at the commission's hearing favored elimination of elaborate, locally created, written testing procedures. For those procedures have not recently demonstrated great worth, even toward the realization of their most commonly stated advantages. Screening out incompetents? Eliminating patronage and a 'spoils system' by objectivity and professional development and administration? Upgrading the professional status of teaching? All are worthy goals certainly. But the record of mandatory, centralized written testing procedures in helping to reach them is spotty indeed" (P. Tractenberg, Testing the Teacher 188–89 [1973]). In 1972, the New York State Commission on the Quality, Cost and Financing of Elementary and Secondary Education (the "Fleischmann Commission") recommended the abolition of the New York City Board of Examiners.

7. For discussion of the political events leading to passage of the Decentralization Law, see D. Rogers, 110 Livingston Street (1968); M. Berle and M. Gittell, Confrontation at Oceanhill-Brownsville: The New York School Strikes of 1968 (1969); N. Levin and R. Cohen, Ocean Hill-Brownsville: A Case History of Schools in Crisis (1969). For a general overview of the Decentralization Law, see Rebell, "New York's School Decentralization Law: Two and a Half Years Later," 2 J.L. & Educ. 1 (1973).

8. They often admitted that the licensing system could be improved, but

claimed the Examiners themselves could be counted on to undertake any necessary reforms. For example, Dr. Murray Rockowitz, the examiner in charge of research, stated that prior to *Chance* he had already begun studying modern personnel assessment techniques used in the industrial sector and had planned to incorporate them into the Examiners' procedures. Although the litigation speeded up the timetable, according to Rockowitz many of the reforms ordered in *Chance* were already being developed. Rockowitz Interview. This view has been sharply disputed, however, by Paul Tractenberg, Special Counsel to the Commission on Human Rights, who was primarily responsible for conducting its investigation and who later represented the *Chance* plaintiffs in negotiations with the Examiners. Based on these experiences, he concluded that no substantive positive reform would have been carried out if the *Chance* suit had not been brought. Tractenberg Interview.

9. The Examiners' critics argued, however, that the existing system had spawned its own substantial web of patronage through the hiring of supervisors to conduct examinations. In 1969, 4,500 persons were used as temporary examination assistants, and 3,500 of them came from within the school system. The Examiners informally selected the examination assistants who were then paid at the rate of $13.23 an hour. No training in test construction was required. In a three-year period, only 8 out of 4,500 assistants were removed because of unsatisfactory performance. Furthermore, the Examiners' budget was $3.5 million, all but $61,000 of which was expended for the services of full-time and part-time staff. P. Tractenberg, *supra* note 6, at 253–54. Affidavit of Arnold Webb, October 1970.

10. Examiners' regulations prevented the scorer of written tests from knowing the name, race, sex, or religion of the person being graded. The plaintiffs admitted that these safeguards prevented discrimination in the mechanical aspects of grading the *written* tests. They did charge, however, that discrimination against blacks and Puerto Ricans was practiced in the grading of the *oral* phase of the examinations.

11. A large proportion of incumbent white teachers and supervisors were Jewish. Some widely publicized anti-Semitic statements during the decentralization confrontations of the late sixties convinced many Jewish educators that the only likely alternative to the Examiners would be a system of community selection that would discriminate against them. On the other hand, many strong critics of the Examiners, both from within and without the school system, were Jewish. Jewish civic organizations took varying positions. Schiff Interview.

12. See discussion, *supra* at note 6.

13. Reported court decisions:
    1. Opinions of the United States District Court in *Chance* v. *Board of Examiners* that were reported in *Federal Supplement* (F. Supp.) or in *Employment Practices Decisions* (EPD) are listed below in chronological order.
    3 EPD ¶8020 (1970)
    330 F. Supp. 203; 3 EPD ¶8286 (1971)
    4 EPD ¶7600 (1971)
    6 EPD ¶8976 (1973)
    6 EPD ¶8977 (1973)

8 EPD ¶9520 (1973)
6 EPD ¶8978 (1973)
7 EPD ¶9084 (1973)
8 EPD ¶9521 (1974)
8 EPD ¶9663 (1974)
11 EPD ¶10632 (1975)

2. Decisions of the Second Circuit Court of Appeals in *Chance* v. *Board of Examiners* reported in the Second Series of *Federal Reporter* (F. 2d) are listed below in chronological order.:

458 F. 2d 1167 (1972)
496 F. 2d 820 (1974)
534 F. 2d 993 (1976)
561 F. 2d 1079 (1977)

14. She continued in that role when she left the Legal Defense Fund to become the Director of the Legal Action Center, but finally withdrew as counsel in September 1978 when she joined the faculty of the Harvard Law School.

15. Bernikow withdrew from the case when he was appointed United States Magistrate in December 1975.

16. Under city regulations, a conflict between two public agencies, such as the Examiners and the Board, entitled one of them to retain outside counsel.

17. Partial intervention was granted in December 1973 with respect to the effect of the injunction on transfer rights under the union contract, and in July 1974 on the issue of seniority rights in a period of threatened layoffs. A further intervention motion with regard to testing issues was denied in May 1976.

18. See note 52 *infra*. Also denied intervention were two individual principals who opposed the Examiners' settlement with plaintiffs.

19. 458 F. 2d 1167 (1972); 496 F. 2d 820 (1974); 534 F. 2d 993 (1976); 561 F. 2d 1079 (1977). Additional appeals were denied without opinion. A full listing of all reported decisions of the District Court and the Court of Appeals is set forth at note 13 *supra*.

20. The complaint and motion papers were filed on September 24, 1970, and the temporary restraining order was issued on November 4, 1970.

21. A trial is a full evidentiary hearing during which the court determines disputed issues of material fact and issues a final order determining the legal relationships between the parties. A preliminary injunction hearing, by way of contrast, is an abbreviated trial, often based on affidavits or short oral testimony. If the judge, after considering the factual materials, finds that the plaintiff will probably prove his case when a trial finally is held, and that without some immediate relief the plaintiff will suffer irreparable harm (which is not outweighed by the equities of the defendants), he will issue a preliminary injunction. By definition, such a preliminary order is not final, and each party is still entitled to a full trial and adjudication.

22. The fifth member was the chancellor's designee.

23. The Board of Education, which had never filed an answer and declined until the last minute to participate in the Task Force, now strenuously opposed the interim plan, arguing that its implementation would weaken the incentives, and called for delineating and instituting a permanent regular

testing and appointing procedure. Judge Mansfield disagreed, maintaining that the interim procedures were necessary to "restore some degree of confidence in the system" (6 EPD para. 8977, p. 6147). He approved entry of a consent judgment ("the Final Judgment") settling plaintiffs' claims against the Examiners and imposed the exact terms of this judgment upon the Board in the form of a modified preliminary injunction. At first, the Board appealed the injunction, but later it retracted its objections and joined in the Final Judgment.

24. Although the law relating to racial hiring goals was unsettled in 1970, when *Chance* was filed, plaintiffs in employment discrimination class actions commonly sought orders for affirmative action in hiring. A few years later clear precedents for such goals were established in cases involving nonmanagerial positions. See, e.g., United States v. Wood, Wire and Metal Lathers International Union, 471 F. 2d 408, 412–13 (2d. Cir.), *cert. denied,* 412 U.S. 939 (1973); Rios v. Enterprise Association Steam Fitters Local 638, 501 F. 2d 622, 628–33 (2d. Cir. 1974).

25. This chapter is based on intensive research inquiring into the period September 1970 through June 1978. Important events which occurred from June 1978 through December 1981 have been summarized in a postscript and addendum at pp. 120–22, *supra.*

26. Judge Mansfield, Court Transcript 12/18/70, p. 48.

27. Court Transcript 11/19/70, p. 4 (emphasis supplied).

28. "I have examined your claims of certain questions being culturally biased, and so far I do not find myself very persuaded. I find on the very self-same examination questions that would probably be easier for a person of black or Puerto Rican background and color to answer than a white person." Court Transcript, 11/19/70, p. 8.

29. Court Transcript, 12/18/70, p. 46. This initial estimate was based in part on the affidavit testimony of one of the Examiners. Court Transcript, 11/9/70, p. 7.

30. Court Transcripts, 11/19/70, pp. 17–18; 12/8/70, p. 42.

31. 330 F. Supp. 203, 210.

32. The Examiners' decision to accede to Judge Mansfield's request for extensive survey data—instead of objecting to the scope of the discovery—was described by the Examiners' counsel as a "critical moment." The officials, he said, felt both obligated to make information available to the public, and confident that the statistics would validate the fairness of their tests. Defendants would have presented a stronger case, however, if the survey had been limited only to the more recent exams, which were said to be much more job-related and more racially neutral. Cohen Interview.

33. The federal legal basis for such litigations was Title VII of the 1964 Civil Rights Act, 42 U.S.C. §2000e. When *Chance* was filed in 1970, Title VII prohibited racial discrimination in private employment only (and was not amended to include public employees until 1972). *Chance,* therefore, was initially filed under the general constitutional provisions of the equal protection clause of the Fourteenth Amendment. Nevertheless, Judge Mansfield, like most judges at the time, assumed that the spirit, if not the letter, of Title VII concepts should be applied to cases involving public employees. In 1975, the *Chance* plaintiffs moved to amend their complaint to include a claim

under Title VII. Their sole purpose was to lay the basis for an award of attorney fees under Title VII. The motion was denied. In 1976, the United States Supreme Court held, in Washington v. Davis, 426 U.S. 229, that a constitutional equal protection claim based on racial discrimination required proof of *intentional* discrimination could be established if a challenged employment selection instrument or practice had a disproportionate impact on the hiring of minority candidates, whatever the employers' intent. The implication of *Davis* became an issue in the 1977 appeal. See 561 F. 2d 1079 (2d Cir. 1977).

34. Court Transcript, 5/21/71, p. 3. One should bear in mind that differential rates of 5–1 or 10–1 were common in Title VII cases won by plaintiffs.

35. 330 F. 2d 203, 212. The court was also impressed by arguments concerning the cumulative impact on minority candidates of successive supervisory examinations. Prior to 1970, eligibility for taking the principal examination depended on passing the assistant principal examination. Therefore, the racial impact of the Examiners' procedures on licensing principals had to be computed from figures, which integrated the prescreening effects of the first test.

The court regarded as irrelevant, evidence about the cumulative impacts of factors outside the control of the Examiners (e.g., college admissions practices) or within its control but not challenged in the instant complaint (e.g., teacher examinations). The latter omission was challenged in a later suit that is still pending. See Rubinos v. Board of Examiners, Civ. No. 2240/74 (S.D.N.Y.). Similar comparisons of minority representation in the supervisory corps were also disregarded.

36. Relying on this statistical form of proof, Judge Mansfield never had to identify any specific practice that caused the racial impact.

The Examiners, disenchanted with their statistical expert witness, hired a new statistician to help them supplement the hearing record. Rockowitz and Cohen Interviews. First, they introduced new data showing that the November 1970 elementary principal examination (the target of the plaintiffs' preliminary injunction motion) had little, if any, discriminatory impact. Second, they reanalyzed the facts already in the record. The central argument in the reanalysis of the old data was that the "one in one billion" probabilities were based on false assumptions, because the pool of white applicants and the pool of minority applicants included in the survey were not comparable. The white groups scored better on the tests because they contained, overall, more experienced and better qualified individual applicants.

Judge Mansfield refused to reopen the record. He said the proffered evidence was untimely, noting also that the racial survey for the 1970 examination was very incomplete and that the plaintiffs had had no opportunity either to undertake discovery or to conduct cross-examination. The Court of Appeals upheld Judge Mansfield. Its decision pointed out that the Examiners' contention that the allegedly nondiscriminatory outcome of the 1970 test was due to the reform of past examination practices, amounted to an admission that the prior examinations were biased. (There was, however, at least one plausible explanation for these alleged improvements in minority performance—substantial participation by minority candidates in the Board of Education's tuition-free coaching courses modeled after the coaching classes white candidates had taken for years.)

37. The trial court ruled that they had to make a "strong showing" that their examinations were a necessary part of the licensing system. The court of appeals avoided the issue of defining the burden of proof by sustaining the trial court's holding on the grounds that the Examiners had not even shown their tests to be "minimally rational." 330 F. Supp. 203, 216.

38. Criterion-referenced validation would require statistical correlations showing that supervisors who had done well on past exams actually performed better on the job.

39. See 458 F. 2d 1167, 1169; and 330 F. Supp. 203, 217.

40. See, e.g., 458 F. 2d 1167, 1175.

41. Final Judgment, section III.C. (emphasis supplied).

42. Memorandum decision, 3/6/74, pp. 3–4.

43. Court Transcript, 3/21/74, pp. 11–12 (emphasis supplied). Resolving the "in conjunction with" dispute was not the sole problem in administering the interim performance tests. Because the Examiners repeatedly failed to complete tests within the 60-day period prescribed in the Final Judgment, in December 1974, the plaintiffs moved the court to modify the Final Judgment to provide that any candidate whose application was not processed within 60 days would be deemed to have passed the exam, unless the community school board he was serving objected. After listening to detailed assurances from the Examiners that they would meet pending deadlines, Judge Tyler denied the motion without prejudice to its being renewed should the assurance be breached.

44. Court Transcript, 3/21/74, p. 39.

45. Court Transcript, 3/21/74, p. 38.

46. "[T]he defendants need not agree with plaintiffs' suggestions and plaintiffs will be impotent to force their views through Court orders. The only Court review will be of the new system itself (rather than of its development), as each new test is implemented, to determine whether it is constitutional, *not to determine whether it is the best test or the fairest test which could be conceivably created.*" Memorandum, April 1, 1975, p. 4 (emphasis supplied).

47. Memorandum, April 1, 1975, p. 4.

48. At the January 14, 1975, hearing, Judge Tyler emphasized that he did not believe the court had remedial authority comparable to that of a court which had rendered a final judgment of liability, and on that basis refused to impose on the defendants a participatory role for the plaintiffs. Plaintiffs argued that the defendants' willingness to negotiate resulted only after "extensive findings, conclusions and repeated iterations by lower and higher courts that of a strong likelihood that the plaintiffs would prevail on the merits." Letter-memorandum 1/28/75). They cited a recent decision in which Judge Frankel of the same federal court warned that absolving defendants who had settled under pressure from the normal obligations of losing parties would be an invitation to intransigent litigation by plaintiffs. Judge Tyler must have given this argument some weight since he reversed his original decision adverse to plaintiffs on the issue of reporting requirements in response to this memorandum.

49. Memorandum, April 1, 1975, p. 4.

50. "Excessing" is a term used in the New York City School District to refer to the reassignment of pedagogical personnel when enrollment reduction,

reorganizations, or budgetary cutbacks require the elimination of existing positions. A layoff occurs when the district is unable to reassign to another position a person whose position has been abolished.

51. Former New York Ed. Law §2585.3.

52. The Board of Examiners did not participate in these proceedings. The CSA was granted limited intervention for the purpose of participating in the excessing proceedings and, in general, supported the Board of Education's positions. The New York City School Boards' Association, representing 23 of the 31 community school boards, participated in the excessing proceedings as an active *amicus curiae*, after having been denied intervenor status. The association had not reached a consensus about whether to support or oppose the plaintiffs' basic request. Consistent with the decentralization concerns of its members, however, the association urged that any excessing regulations the court might approve be limited to the *intra*-district context. *Inter*-district excessing would have permitted the central Board to assign excessed supervisors into community districts without the school boards' consent, and outside of the Circular 30 hiring procedures.

53. In the meantime, Judge Tyler had issued a limited temporary order prohibiting interdistrict excessing and temporarily maintaining the status quo.

54. Court Transcript, 11/8/74, p. 3.

55. *Id.* at 28.

56. Letter, Board's counsel to Judge Tyler, December 17, 1974. Board officials have stated on many occasions that centrally administered interdistrict excessing is a valuable tool for racially integrating school staffs. Response of the Board of Education of the City of New York to the November 9, 1976, letter from the Office for Civil Rights, April 22, 1977, p. 19. Arricale Interview. The association, however, repeatedly argued that any such positive effects were not worth the educational detriment of forcing community boards to accept supervisors not of their choosing.

57. Court Transcript, 11/8/74, p. 8.

58. "I have raised a lot of questions and I get no answers from any of you people. You do not agree on anything. That is why I am trying my best to practice law here in order to get this thing done." Court Transcript, 11/8/74, p. 19.

59. "Bumping" is a term used to describe the situation where a supervisor excessed because of the abolition of his position displaces a supervisor with less seniority in another position, with the result that the less senior supervisor is bumped into excess. He may, in turn, exercise seniority rights against a yet less senior supervisor and so on down the line, in what the parties often refer to as a game of "musical chairs."

60. Judge Tyler, Court Transcript, 9/13/74, p. 14.

61. The Appeals Court panel vote was 2–1; the quoted phrases are from Judge Oakes's dissenting opinion; 534 F. 2d 993, 1001.

62. See, e.g., Bridgeport Guardians Inc. v. Bridgeport Civil Service Commission, 482 F. 2d 1333 (2d Cir. 1973); Vulcan Society v. Civil Service Commission, 490 F. 2d 387 (2d Cir. 1973).

63. 534 F. 2d 993, 998–99.

64. This concept was similar to the original Board of Education proposal. It

would give individual incumbent minority supervisors additional seniority credit but would not guarantee their retention as against any white supervisors who had accumulated more seniority. It appears that because of delays in implementing any layoffs pending resolution of these issues in court (and through negotiations) following the Court of Appeals decision, the immediate crisis passed without any substantial invocation of this new system.

65. It was difficult to draw the line between the Board of Education/ chancellor's function of describing the qualifications required for a position, and the Examiners' job of devising the examinations to test for those qualities. If the Board of Education and the chancellor maintained that the only qualifications necessary for licensing were the possession of specific credentials, then the Examiners would have been left with merely a clerical function. Would that invade the province of the Examiners, i.e., its discretion to develop appropriate assessment tests?

66. This term, referring to the combination of imposed and consensual features, was used by Judge Pollack, who took over the case in 1975 when Judge Tyler became United States Deputy Attorney General.

67. D. Rothman, counsel to Board of Education, Court Transcript, 6/1/76, p. 17.

68. Court Transcript, 5/21/71, pp. 98–99. Early on, some key supporters of the plaintiffs also believed that a structured examination at entry level probably was impracticable. But they thought the plaintiffs had "nothing to lose" by attempting to develop a practicable job-related test. If they succeeded, that would be fine. If the problem proved impracticable, however, the failed attempt would show the impossibility of developing an adequate test of this type. Seeley Interview.

69. D. Rothman, Court Transcript, 6/1/76, p. 19. An early symptom of this problem was seen in the job analysis prepared by the Boards' consultants which was criticized, *inter alia,* for being based on observations on how supervisors on the job presently performed, with little attention as to how they should perform under changing conditions.

70. *Id.* at 20.

71. S. Cohen, Court Transcript, 6/1/76, p. 71.

72. Affidavit of E. Fitzgerald, member of the Board of Examiners, dated May 5, 1976, para. 3. The report of the Chancellor's Advisory Council supporting the Board of Education's position was derided as the product of nonprofessionals worked up for the purpose of rubber-stamping the Board's intentions. The latter contention seems unfounded, since the Advisory Council minutes show that long before the Board's change of position, the council had, in fact, opposed the hiring of AIR without better assurances of its capabilities. The council's later decision to reject the AIR report was made after study, discussion and dialogue with an AIR representative. *See* pp. 106–7 *supra.*

73. Court Transcript, 6/1/76, pp. 39–40.

74. *Id.* pp. 60–61.

75. *Id.* p. 31.

76. Court Transcript, 6/1/76, p. 64.

77. 561 F. 2d 1079, 1091.

78. "The Board of Education may promulgate its plan, subject to challenge in the state courts, and the Examiners may take their own action, subject to proper review by the state courts." *Id.* at 1092.

79. The Examiners' representatives were the Examiners themselves, and their lead attorney, Saul Cohen. The plaintiffs were initially represented by Paul Tractenberg (a professor at Rutgers Law School and former Special Counsel to the New York City Commission on Human Rights during its investigation of personnel selection in the city school system); Rhoda Karpatkin (an attorney and community school board member); Boston Chance and Louis Mercado (the named plaintiffs); and their attorney Elizabeth DuBois. The services of Tractenberg and Karpatkin were paid for by a foundation grant. One participant's description of the early phases of the Task Force is found in Tractenberg, Testing the Teacher 317–21 (1973).

80. Other issues needing resolution included adoption of continuing eligible lists (i.e., allowing names to be added to an existing list before its exhaustion); establishment of scientific validation techniques; upgrading the qualifications of the Examiners' staff; hiring consultants to work on prototype tests; and reporting requirements.

81. The hard-fought history of this compromise explains the outraged tenor of the Examiners' objections to the proposed 1976 modifications to the Permanent Plan. Judge Pollack swept away the Examiners' "gatekeeper" role at Step 1—the authority to cut off persons who failed minimal competence tests—and reduced their service function at that stage to little more than a clerical role. In essence, the Examiners lost what they had bargained for; the plaintiffs recouped what they had bargained away.

82. Participants give different accounts of the atmosphere and dynamics of the negotiation process. On the Examiners' side, sessions were described as being long, disorganized, and predominantly adversarial. Rockowitz, e.g., said that the sessions were like meetings of the "victors and the vanquished." Cohen stated that public policy making through "endless consultation" was a "dreadful" process. (According to Frederick Williams, once the Task Force meetings were underway, Cohen influenced Rockowitz to moderate his position and to accept, at least in part, the idea that the plaintiffs had a role to play in designing the new system through negotiation. This suggests that a lawyer's perspective and negotiating experience in a bitter policy dispute may have lessened, rather than promoted, an adversary position.)

The plaintiffs' representatives, by and large, emphasized the positive aspects of the experience. DuBois, e.g., felt that the time and energy devoted to the Task Force negotiations were actually quite small in comparison to the resources which had been devoted to numerous commission investigations, studies, and inquiries on the school district personnel policies, all of which resulted in "virtually zero product." *Chance,* on the other hand, had revolutionized the examination system in a relatively short period of time. Rockowitz, Cohen, Williams, and DuBois Interviews.

83. See note 45 *supra.*

84. King and Quinones relied upon the plaintiffs' representatives in the Task Force for technical support to help them work for reforms from within the Examiners' organization. For example, even prior to the establishment of

the Task Force, Quinones had accepted a briefing on *Chance* from a staff person of the Public Education Association, because he had not heard from Chairman Rockowitz for weeks following his nomination.

85. "All we could have won by trial was essentially what we had already won with the preliminary injunction—an order to develop a new constitutional system. Most trials in employment discrimination cases do not produce an order that is very different from the Mansfield original order." DuBois Interview.

86. As set forth in Special Circular No. 42, 1971–72 (not to be confused with the *later* procedures of Special Circular 30, 1972–73; see pp. 82, 105 *supra*), this circular also promulgated mandatory citywide rules and three general community standards pertaining to: eligibility; public notice of vacancies, involvement of parent associations; interviewing and establishment by community boards of methods for evaluating candidates; setting performance objectives for the persons hired; and evaluating performance of acting supervisors within six months of the date of the assignment.

87. Lewis Interview. These groups included the PEA, the supervisors' and teachers' unions, the Anti-Defamation League of B'nai B'rith, and the community school boards. The Executive Director of Personnel served as the Secretary to the Council, but no city district official was an official member.

88. By contrast, the Board of Examiners' Ad Hoc Advisory Council convened in January 1974 for the stated purpose of consulting with community representatives about examination procedures, but generated no new ideas, concrete proposals, or substantive modifications to the Examiners' position. The council ceased to exist after its fourth meeting, in May 1974.

89. However, in considering grievances and making recommendations about them to Board officials, the council never acted in a quasi-judicial capacity, i.e., no adversary evidentiary hearings were conducted.

90. Also, the community boards had to list their basic criteria for selecting supervisors, e.g., teaching record relative to student growth and achievement; empathy for children; recommendations of supervisors, peers, and students; community involvement; and receptivity to new educational concepts and ideas. In the evaluation phase, each community district had to describe performance objectives and make them available to candidates.

91. Council Minutes, May 31, 1972; June 8, 1972. One possible sanction would be to revoke the salary certificate of an acting supervisor appointed under unapproved procedures.

92. Circular 30 (of school year 1972–73) was ready in draft in June. It took the chancellor and the Board of Education another four months to approve it, without substantive change.

93. Group Interview with Betty Felton, director, and field workers Valerie Hart, Betty Goldklang, May Devlin, and Ida Clark.

94. However, by 1977, the pressure on the chancellor succeeded in prompting a restoration of the previous evaluation form.

95. According to the UPA field staff, the degree to which the spirit of Circular 30 was implemented varied greatly from borough to borough and from district to district.

96. In this general context, discrimination is hard to define. According to Frederick Williams, minority communities tended to favor minority candi-

dates, "all other things being equal," because they were compensating for a long period of being "starved" for minority candidates. Until the racial composition of the supervisory staff was adjusted, minority background *per se* was considered an educational advantage because it demonstrated to minority students that minority persons could attain positions of status and responsibility, and therefore increased the students' motivation to achieve. Williams Interview.

97. In May 1974, the council asked the chancellor to allow it to become involved in the Task Force negotiations, but the idea was not accepted.

98. AIR was the consulting firm the Board of Education selected to write a job analysis under the Permanent Plan. See pp. 93–94 *supra*.

99. Some council participants not only rejected the AIR job analysis, but concluded that probably no job analysis could be written that could be used to develop a meaningful written examination to select candidates for supervisor positions. In other words, the Step 1 tests should be eliminated from the Permanent Plan. Frank Arricale stated: "The report has been an extraordinarily useful tool to convince me that this is not the route we should take." CAC Minutes, Sept. 17, 1975.

100. The momentum toward the resignation was checked largely by an impassioned plea by the Executive Director of Personnel, Frank Arricale. (This description of the April meeting is based on firsthand observation by one of the authors.)

101. Circular 30R provides for the continuation of a Chancellor's Advisory Council.

102. Similarly, the resolution had readopted the central contribution of the Task Force—the concept of two-step licensing using on-the-job performance evaluations.

103. "I don't think we ever took a vote. On every important question we reached a consensus." James Stein Interview.

104. As was stated by a number of interviewees (Frederick Williams, Blanche Lewis, and Harold Siegel), it is likely that any person appointed chancellor at the time would have created a body like the council. James Stein stated, however, that Dr. Scribner created the council because he had isolated himself from the support of professional groups and other established education organizations.

105. Executive Director of Personnel Frank Arricale recently stated: "Community district would not have understood the *Chance* case without the Chancellor's Advisory Council." Statement at council meeting, 4/28/77.

106. Quinones Interview. Harold Siegel, Executive Secretary of the Board of Education, indicated that in many instances (and especially in the excessing situation) the availability of the court—as a forum that could cut through conflicting laws, regulations, and contract rights and render a clear decision—was an asset for the Board's policy planning. On the other hand, Rockowitz, Quinones's colleague (who was chairman of the Examiners throughout most of the litigation period), thought that on various particulars the judges had "arrogated to themselves a responsibility for which they really had no competence" (Rockowitz Interview). The Examiners' counsel, Saul Cohen, expressed similar concerns during the remedial proceedings.

107. Arricale Interview. David Seeley, Frederick Williams, the UPS staff,

and Blanche Lewis, while admitting to the speculative nature of the question, thought that without the promise of possible court action, minority communities would probably have turned to confrontation politics, and possibly violence, to resist the supervisory licensing system. The flash point could have been refusals by local boards to replace persons serving as acting elementary school principals with persons on the eligible list from the November 1971 examination.

108. Note, however, that although those arguments did not raise "subsidiary policy issues," the actual materials submitted were not, according to Judge Mansfield, persuasive (or even in some instances, legally admissible) "hard" evidence of racial discrimination.

109. See ch. 2 *supra*.

110. See ch. 2, pp. 30–31 *supra*.

111. One critical separation-of-powers issue that did not arise in *Chance* was court intrusion into the realm of taxation and appropriations. As noted in ch. 2, in cases where courts have ordered remedies, defendants frequently argue that the judiciary is infringing upon jealously guarded fiscal powers. In *Chance*, however, the plaintiffs favored reforms that were not expected over the long run to increase the cost of licensing supervisors. Indeed, simplifying the Examiners' tests would reduce the costs, a fact used in 1976 by the plaintiff and the Board of Education defendants as an explicit policy argument supporting modification of the Permanent Plan.

112. Arguably, since the Court eventually utilized the "rational relationship" test for its equal protection analysis rather than the "strict scrutiny" approach traditionally applied in cases of racial discrimination, the threshold finding of discriminatory impact may not have been necessary. The validation issues might well have been raised even by nonminority individuals who had failed an "irrational" examination.

113. Class action certification was given to a class which included all blacks and persons of Puerto Rican origin or descent who (1) have failed examinations for supervisory positions in the New York City School System; or (2) have failed to apply for or take such supervisory examinations because they reasonably believed the supervisory system to be discriminatory and unrelated to job performance; or (3) have taken such supervisory examinations and have been or are in the process of being evaluated for eligibility lists to be promulgated; or (4) are eligible or will be eligible for supervisory examinations to be given in the future. 6 EPD ¶8976, at 614–15. Note that the fourth clause created a constantly expanding class.

114. In the preliminary injunction phase of *Chance*, the following organizations submitted *amicus curiae* briefs to the district court, in support of plaintiffs: New York Association of Black School Supervisors and Administrators; ASPIRA of America, Inc. (a Puerto Rican organization); and the Public Education Association (PEA). On appeal, these groups again supported the plaintiffs, but, in addition, the following groups filed briefs opposing the injunction: the CSA; the Anti-Defamation League of B'nai B'rith, jointly with the Council of Jewish Organizations in Civil Service, Inc., and the Catholic Teachers Association of Brooklyn; and the United Federation of Teachers (UFT). Out of these organizations, only the CSA and the PEA remained active throughout the remedial proceedings. (A staff attorney of the PEA

became part of the plaintiffs' legal team, and primarily represented them in the seniority layoff issues.) However, individuals directly associated with B'nai B'rith, UFT, CSA, PEA, and directly or indirectly associated with the interests of minority supervisors, participated through the Chancellor's Advisory Council.

115. At the very beginning of the suit Judge Mansfield ruled that the CSA, as bargaining representative of persons holding supervisor licenses, did not have sufficient "interest" because the suit related to the future hiring of personnel. The opinion did not discuss the arguable interest of incumbent supervisors in the role of selecting their future colleagues, or mention the expertise the CSA could contribute to the evidentiary presentations.

When the plaintiffs later asked the court to abrogate provisions of the CSA contract dealing with transfer and seniority, the rights of incumbent supervisors were clearly implicated, a conflict Judge Mansfield probably had not anticipated when he wrote his 1970 intervention opinion. Now, the CSA was made a defendant, but only with respect to the issues of transfer and seniority. The CSA was later granted limited intervenor status on the excessing issues. At that time the association was also permitted to appear as *amicus*.

116. Little direct judicial precedent existed for the *amicus* role played by the association, which, unlike traditional *amici*, was not limited to the filing of briefs, but was permitted to speak at hearings, present witnesses, oppose motions, etc.

117. See discussion in ch. 3, pp. 38–41 *supra*.

118. However, it could be argued that one affected "interest group" did not appear in the proceeding. This group consisted of white supervisors appointed under the interim procedures who, like the minority plaintiffs, may have been previously denied licenses because of the irrationality of the old examination system. Apparently, this unrepresented group contained a disproportionate number of Italo-Americans and Orthodox Jews. The CSA ostensibly represented the interests of the postinjunction white supervisors, but it was disinclined to base any arguments for relief on the assumption that the examination system was irrational, since it (and previously appointed white supervisors it represented) vigorously maintained that the prior examination system was a highly job-related, nondiscriminatory merit selection procedure. According to Executive Director of Personnel Frank Arricale, "[T]he group that was proportionately greatest hit, was Italo-American because they came in after the blacks. Italo-Americans are the product of open admissions, whereas blacks had been coming into the system via black colleges and other earlier black-related experiences . . . The Italo-American drop-out rate comes very close to the black drop-out rate. The number of Italos in the system is about the same as the number of blacks, both in terms of teachers and in terms of supervisors." Discussing the excessing order, Arricale indicated that Italo-American leaders in New York were not clearly for or against quotas *per se*, but they believed that if there is to be affirmative action, Italo-Americans should not be classified as "other." Cf. Landi v. Board of Education (New York City), 93 Misc. 2d 21 (S.Ct.N.Y. Co. 1978). Arricale also noted that Orthodox Jews were latecomers into the system who had suffered special hardships and discrimination en route to becoming supervisors.

119. Arricale Interview.

120. When it came time to fashion relief on the excessing issue, the inability of the parties to present any hard information concerning the impact of alternative proposals on affected individuals and on the system as a whole became more significant.

121. Tyler Interview. For example, when Tyler remarked that his role as a trial judge was to try any unsettled issues, DuBois replied: "We can't try the nature of the future examination system." See p. 93 *supra.*

122. The shifting position of the parties and their experts on test validation issues, such as the Board of Education's reversal on the feasibility of conducting systematic job analyses for supervisory positions, illustrates the unresolved state of many critical social fact issues on the public policy agenda.

123. Or legislatively, as in the case of the legislation creating "continuing" eligible lists, which emanated from a Task Force proposal.

124. The plaintiffs were not alone in pressing these major policy questions. The defendant Board of Education, or at least certain forces within the Board, also apparently had an interest in having the court redefine the relative positions of the Board of Education, the community boards, and the Board of Examiners, and looked to the court to diminish or eliminate effectively the powers of the Board of Examiners, a position which predecessor Boards had pressed unsuccessfully before the legislature.

125. Note, of course, that the overall impact of *Chance,* and especially the implementation of the Circular 30 procedures, nevertheless had the effect of substantially increasing the powers of the community school boards.

126. Note in this regard that each time the case came before the Second Circuit Court of Appeals, the appellate judges expressed bewilderment and impatience that *Chance* had not yet been resolved. Both Judges Tyler and Pollack, when the case was reassigned to them, pressured the parties to reach an immediate resolution of all outstanding issues. Saul Cohen, the Examiners' attorney, commented that he was frustrated because unlike large antitrust cases on which he had worked, no judge or master imposed firm working deadlines on the parties. He indicated, however, that his clients accepted the desultory pace of negotiation because they recognized the need at times to avoid forcing the court to decide extremely volatile issues which were not yet ripe for resolution.

127. The Second Circuit decision overruling Judge Pollack seemed intended to discourage trial judges from becoming too easily involved in the political maneuverings that are often connected with broad and long-lasting remedial orders. While the appellate panel did not accept the Examiners' extreme characterization of a consent judgment as a contract which may be altered only with the full consent of all parties, it did state that revision of such a judgment other than by consent was a "vital" action that must be preceded by a hearing based on specific findings about the necessity for the changes.

128. Court Transcript, quoted at 354 F. 2d 993, 996.

129. These percentage figures are approximations supplied by the Office of the Chancellor. The test was taken by 689 persons of whom 266 passed, an overall failure of 61%. Since 106 of the candidates did not identify their race, no conclusive statements about racial impact can be made at the present time. *New York Times,* December 11, 1980, p. B2, col. 5.

130. Index No. 18719/78, Supreme Court, Kings County.

131. Order of February 15, 1980. See also Board of Education Special Circular 45, 1979–80. Another action necessary to implement the settlement was the enactment of a state law extending the life of supervisory licenses based on the pre-*Chance* examinations. 1981 N.Y. Laws ch. 697.

132. *New York Times,* note 129 *supra.*

133. Memorandum of Understanding between: The Board of Education of the City of New York and the Office for Civil Rights, United States Department of Health, Education and Welfare, dated September 7, 1977, at para. 6. The issue of the validity of this memorandum has been the subject of extensive litigation. Most recently, on September 22, 1980, the Second Circuit Court of Appeals upheld its validity. Caulfield v. Board of Education, 632 F. 2d 999 (2d Cir. 1980), *cert. denied,* 101 Sup.Ct. 1739 (1981).

134. The authors currently are engaged in a research project funded by the National Institute of Education, which is studying the effectiveness and legitimacy of administrative enforcement of civil rights laws. The project is centered around a detailed case study of OCR's enforcement effort in New York City, including the Memorandum of Understanding.

## CHAPTER 7

1. Rubinos v. Board of Examiners, Civ. No. 2240/74 (S.D.N.Y.).

2. One reason for the slow pace of litigation was that the reduction in force cause by the fiscal crisis had made disputes about hiring much less pressing.

3. Apparently, another consideration was a scarcity of available resources, particularly legal resources, since many of the attorneys representing the minority group interests were already heavily committed by the involvement in *Chance, Rubinos,* and other cases. Flemming and PEA Interviews.

In any event, the reversal of Judge Tyler's excessing decision in January of 1976 further limited the validity of the judicial option. At best, a lawsuit focused on teacher layoff problems would, under the Court of Appeals' decision, provide only "constructive seniority," a form of relief which the minority interests felt was inadequate.

4. PEA, Pacheco Interviews. Mr. Pacheco, the spokesman for the Coalition of Associations of Black and Puerto Rican Educators and Supervisors, expressed his attitudes toward the legislature as follows: "The legislature is basically anti-New York City and anti-minority, with the exception of minority legislators and some New York City white legislators. They view all the problems of New York City as being insoluble, as being caused by minority people who are non-Americans, who can't succeed in our way of life."

5. These statistics, as well as all others cited in this section, were obtained from "Seniority and Layoffs: A Review of Recent Court Decisions and Their Possible Impact on the New York City Public School System" (November 1975), prepared by Dr. Bernard Gifford, Deputy Chancellor of the New York City Board of Education. Hereinafter, "Gifford Report."

6. New York Education Law §2590–j.5. The original decentralization proposals of Mayor Lindsay, as well as the original proposals of the Board of Education, totally eliminated the Board of Examiners and left all hiring to the discretion of the local school boards, subject only to state certification procedures. Strong opposition from the United Federation of Teachers and other

groups induced the legislature to adopt the compromise system discussed above.

7. Ironically, the NTE alternative system was attacked by the U.S. Office of Civil Rights as being a prime cause of staff segregation in New York City since it led to a concentration of minority teachers in the "45%" schools. Letter to Irving Anker, Chancellor, from Martin H. Gerry, Director, OCR, November 9, 1976.

8. A large number of unlicensed teachers, working on "per diem certificates," many of whom were minority, also were not rehired for the 1975–76 term. PEA Interview.

9. As indicated at p. 144, *infra,* statistics concerning the proportionate impact of layoffs on all minority teachers in the system apparently were never compiled, although throughout the legislative deliberations, all parties assumed there was a disproportionate impact on minorities. Half a year after the 1976 legislative session, OCR Director Gerry indicated in his November 1976 letter to Chancellor Anker that there "may not have been" a disproportionate impact. He did not, however, cite any supporting statistics or sources.

10. See Board of Education v. City of New York, 41 N.Y. 2d 535 (1977). The N.Y. Court of Appeals upheld the validity of the bill and the procedures by which a governor's veto was overridden for the first time in 101 years. A settlement fixing the precise amount of the city's obligation to the Board was later negotiated by the parties.

11. Out of a total of 10,841 bills introduced in the assembly in 1976, 520 passed both houses and 473 were signed into law by the governor (Source: 1976 Legislative Index).

12. Citizen's Conference on State Legislatures, State Legislatures: An Evaluation of their Effectiveness (1971).

13. A member of the U.S. House of Representatives is permitted a personal staff of 18; a U.S. senator's staff is determined by the population of his state, with the minimum staff payroll at $508,221 and the maximum at $2 million (J. Reston "Backstairs at Congress," *New York Times,* January 12, 1979, p. A 23).

14. By way of contrast, the staff for the House of Representatives Education and Labor Committee in November 1976 numbered 101, of whom approximately 65 were professionals (Source: Chief Clerk, House Education and Labor Committee). In general, state legislative standing committees are considered "but pale shadows of their congressional counterparts" (G. Blair, American Legislatures, 174 [1964]). "During a recent biennium, Congress spent some $630 million on itself for 535 members in two houses; state legislatures spent about $350 million on themselves for 7,600 members in 99 houses" (A. Rosenthal, Legislative Performance in the States, 5 [1974]). A large portion of the appropriations available for staffing in the New York State Legislature has traditionally been made available for central staff controlled by the Speaker and the minority leader, who under the legislature's tradition of strong party discipline, and tight central organizational control, often tend to dominate lawmaking in most controversial areas. See generally A. Moffat, "The Legislative Process," 24 Cornell L. Q. 223 (1939); Citizen's Conference on State Legislatures, *supra* note 12, M. Milstein and R. Jen-

nings, Educational Policy-Making and the State Legislature: The New York Experience 35–38 (1973).

A federal trial judge ordinarily has two full-time law clerks, who are recent law school graduates. The professional staff assistance to state trial judges varies from state to state.

15. Baer v. Nyquist 34 N.Y. 2d 291 (1974). In a decision issued after the committee's action on the seniority layoff bill, the Court of Appeals somewhat narrowed the implications of *Baer*, at least in the case of guidance counselors. Steele v. Board of Education 40 N.Y. 2d 456 (1976). At the time the bill was under consideration, however, a broader reading of *Baer* had been adopted by the lower courts. Generally speaking, legislators were familiar with these pre-*Steele* decisions and considered it imperative for the legislature to overrule them. Stavisky Interview.

16. Opening statement by Leonard Stavisky, Committee Hearing on the Impact of Fiscal Crisis on the Quality of Education in the New York City School System, October 31, 1975.

17. The Assembly Education Committee, controlled by the Democratic party which drew most of its strength from New York City, had entered into an informal understanding with the Republican leadership of the Senate Education Committee, that the Assembly would take primary responsibility for drafting a bill on the city's seniority problems, while the Senate would concentrate on seniority problems in the rest of the state.

18. In point of fact, the bills referred to herein as the "UFT" and the Board of Education bills also had been formally introduced, as a courtesy, by Chairman Stavisky. The bill identified herein as the "Stavisky bill (A9983) had been personally drafted by Dr. Stavisky, as "a basic working draft," with expert assistance from the State Education Department.

19. At oral conferences and in legislative memoranda, Dr. Stavisky repeatedly stated his intent to come up with a bill that would deal equitably with three major concerns: the legitimate claims of teachers subject to layoffs, the interest of schoolchildren who had been subjected to serious staffing disruptions, and the affirmative action concerns of minority group spokesmen.

20. Goosen Interview.

21. It was still difficult to reach conclusions about many issues. "Differences of perspective about the impact of certain provisions just haunted our seniority subcommittee deliberations." PEA Interview.

22. Dr. Stavisky stated that he tries to hold such conferences on various topics during each session and often considers them even more productive than hearings. Cumulative testimony is eliminated; speakers can be interrupted to pursue points in dialogue; direct confrontations between opponents help to clarify the relative importance each group attaches to the various issues; attendance and substantive participation by committee members increase. Stavisky Interview.

23. Of the various groups invited which would be expected to represent the minority teachers, only the PEA attended these initial conferences.

24. Stavisky Interview.

25. Note that these broad proposals differed substantially from the specific five points raised by the PEA in March.

26. After 4,500 teachers were hired at the beginning of the 1977–78 terms, Executive Director Arricale reported that almost 25% of those hired were minority teachers, who had obtained their appointments "usually under the two-term substitute priority State Law." "Minority Rehires and New Hires," Memo to Chancellor Anker, October 19, 1977, p. 1.

27. Among UFT members, it was "a little controversial." Shannon Interview.

28. It was again stated that granting seniority credit for paraprofessional service was a step in the right direction, but would have little impact on basic minority concerns, and that the counting of prior substitute service might not be helpful to black and Hispanic minorities. Since no accurate statistics were readily available on this issue, the group, therefore, requested that further action be delayed until "competent statistics can be pried out of the Central Board—even if this means no action on this one point until next year."

29. The hearing went on most of the day, with 20–40 people in attendance at any given time or a total of 80–100 people overall. Pacheco Interview.

30. Stavisky Interview.

31. The Board had prevailed on the tenure area issue and had obtained concessions in the concept of systemwide seniority as originally proposed by the UFT (the bill contained a prohibition against a nontenured person bumping a person in a position, regardless of his or her comparative systemwide seniorities). Nevertheless, the Board claimed that a systemwide seniority rule requiring the layoff of the more experienced persons in a given license area, was educationally unsound and rendered the bill unacceptable. The Board also continued to oppose the inclusion of paraprofessional service in the computation of basic seniority. The committee chairman considered this opposition to be a breach of a prior pledge of support by a high Board official. Goosen Interview.

32. An attempt by a special interest group to have an administrative tenure area specifically defined in the law was the only other issue seriously raised in the debate.

33. It is interesting to note that even in the final Assembly debate, no hard statistics on the *impact* of the bill were available. Assemblyman Vann stated that the ranks of black teachers had been depleted from 11% to 4% (Transcript of debate 6/25/76, p. 10, 688); Assemblyman Eve alleged that 44% of the blacks in the system had been laid off (Transcript at 10, 696), but no one attempted to trace the statistical impact of any of the pending proposals. The lack of statistical evidence was cited by Assemblyman Vann as his final reason for recommending that the bill be defeated (Transcript at 10, 737–38).

34. Transcript of debate 6/25/76, p. 10, 690.

35. There is no indication that correspondence from various individuals and outside groups substantially affected the deliberative process. Many of the groups which filed *amicus* briefs in *Chance* also participated peripherally in the legislative process.

36. The Community School Boards Association, although denied formal party status as an intervener, actively participated in *Chance*. Although specifically invited to attend the working sessions of the Education Committee, the association declined to send a representative. However, representatives of several individual boards did attend. Majority Leader Blumenthal,

whose home district encompassed Community Board 3, the initiator of community board involvement in *Chance*, played an active role in the legislative process and was generally perceived as representing a strongly pro-community board perspective.

37. The parallel representation of similar groups and issues in the court and the legislature also undermines the argument that public interest advocacy organizations artificially create issues to be presented to the courts. At least in regard to the excessing issues considered here, the attorneys in *Chance* cannot be said to have overstated the concrete aggrievements felt by the minority faculty members; on the contrary, the coalition spokesman took a much more extreme position in the legislature, pressing for a total moratorium on minority layoffs, rather than a proportionate quota retention plan.

38. The union's state organization had four full-time lobbyists resident during the legislative session in Albany, and the Board of Education also had a two-person lobbying staff. The black and Puerto Rican coalition, essentially an *ad hoc*, one-issue group, had no regular staff, much less an Albany representative. When coalition representatives first visited Albany, they were surprised to learn that even sympathetic legislators expected the coalition to provide the basic drafts and data to support their position.

39. In addition, as indicated at note 22 *supra*, few hearings devoted to objective fact-gathering were actually held. The legislative process described by Professor Moffat in 1939 still applied in general terms in New York in 1976: "Each committee specializes in a particular field, but unlike the Congress, where committees are in session throughout the legislative term, in state legislatures the committees disband at the end of the session and, of necessity, are not especially expert in their subjects. Seldom does a committee itself draft legislation or even undertake to improve or change a bill that comes before it. It either accepts or rejects the proposals. Occasionally, a member will indicate to the introducer what objections were raised, and if he is sufficiently interested he himself will prepare amendments to overcome these objections. It is also important to bear in mind that almost no legislation originates within a legislative body. Requests come from citizens, agencies, organized groups and administrative officials . . . The member takes the letter to the bill drafting commission, an official agency of the legislature, for the preparation of legislation in proper form." Moffat, "The Legislative Process," 24 Corn. L. Q. 223, 224 (1939).

Increases in staff appropriations, and the opening up of weekly committee meetings to the general public, have modified Dr. Moffat's description to the extent that some major program bills are drafted by committees or central staff; staff members are available to engage in drafting refinements and amendments of major bills, and limited general discussions of major issues can take place. Nevertheless, the inherent limitations of the part-time legislative process, and minimal staffing appropriations, especially for the individual members, necessarily preclude extensive original research or fact-finding.

40. Chairman Stavisky and Executive Director Goosen indicated that it had been difficult to provide the necessary time to conduct the investigation of fiscal and recertification practices. Although the seniority bill was considered at least the second most important bill reviewed by the committee during that

session, no resources were available to conduct independent research on this issue.

41. Our findings on this point are consistent with those of a study of the 1969 session of the New York legislature which emphasized the dependence of legislators on information provided by interest groups. M. Milstein and R. Jennings, *supra* note 14, at 101.

42. For example, when the attorney for the black and Puerto Rican coalition requested 27 items of information from the Board (under the Freedom of Information Act), it supplied answers to only six of his questions. In regard to most of the remaining items the Board's letter of response stated: "These items are not available and at present there appear to be no plans in the immediate future for their compilation." Letter from Ellis Mott, Office of Public Affairs, Board of Education, to Joseph Peter Flemming, Esq., May 11, 1976. Flemming and the PEA claimed to have attempted to calculate the net loss of teachers in the previous year from the partial figures supplied in this letter, together with additional information contained in the Gifford Report. However, there were substantial inconsistencies in the data provided by the two sources, and the PEA had no means of compelling the Board to clarify the discrepancies.

43. As Philip R. Lochner concluded in "Some Limits on the Application of Social Science Research in the Legal Process," 1973 Law and the Social Order 815, careful consideration of social science evidence is not the point of legislative hearings, which are held to rally public opinion for positions that have generally already been taken. Even if evidence is presented, it is the person who presents the facts, not the data itself, that matters. See also Blair, *supra* note 14, at 216; Jewell and Patterson, The Legislative Process in the United States, 478 ff. (1974). As a general practice, few hearings are held on specific bills in the New York legislature, although informational hearings on major issues are sometimes convened. Although almost 11,000 bills were introduced in 1976, only 146 hearings were held by all Assembly committees that year (Source: N.Y. Assembly Public Information Office).

44. Another aspect of the general assumption of legislative fact-finding superiority is that legislators are "specialists" on the substantive issues they consider, while judges remain "generalists." In this regard, we should note, however, that although Dr. Stavisky is by profession a college professor, and a number of members of the committee had previously been public school teachers or school board members, the majority of the committee members had no professional background in education. Stavisky Interview. Furthermore, none of the legislators had any particular background or experience on the intricate seniority and layoff questions which were before them. Wahlke has pointed out that "the constitution of legislative bodies makes practically impossible any explicit attempt to recruit or develop specialists among the membership." Wahlke et al., The Legislative System 194–95 (1962). Wahlke further states that although legislatures develop "experts" in certain subject areas among their members, these members are "experts" only in comparison to "other legislators, rather than to lobbyists or bureau people." *Id.* at 214–15. See also Jewell and Patterson, *supra* note 43, at 245, Rosenthal, *supra* note 14, ch. 8, Milstein, *supra* note 14, at 56.

Note also the rapid turnover in committee memberships which impedes the accumulation of specialist expertise (see generally Blair, *supra* note 14, at 173).

For example, the 27 members of the Assembly Education Committee in 1976 had an average tenure in office of five years, and only half of them (14) had been assigned to that committee for more than two years (Stavisky Interview, New York Legislative Index 1973, 1976—Dr. Stavisky, however, had been on the committee for eleven years, although he had become chairperson only two years before).

45. The difficult affirmative action issues raised by the excessing situation in both forums constituted the major exception to the general pattern of resolving remedial issues through negotiations with the interested parties. In *Chance,* after the parties failed to reach any agreement on an excessing plan, an order had to be issued by the judge. Similarly, in the legislature the parties did not negotiate any substantive affirmative action solution to minority layoffs.

46. As in this situation, claims of footdragging or noncompliance, of course, tend to be taken by aggrieved parties to the state courts rather than to the legislature. See, e.g., Dinerstein v. Board of Education 409 N.Y.S. 2d 23 (2d Dept. 1978), Landi v. Board of Education 93 Misc. 2d 21 (S.Ct. N.Y.Co., 1978).

47. Assembly Bill 13043 as enacted also contained two specific provisions for "reporting requirements." The Board of Education was required (1) to present at the next legislative session a report on actions taken to combine analogous license areas into broader "tenure areas"; and (2) to provide certain limited information concerning the numbers of ethnic minority group personnel working in various positions in the school system. The Board, however, did not even see fit to supply the minimal ethnic data called for, since none of the parties interviewed could recollect that such data was submitted. Unlike the plaintiffs in *Chance,* the minority interests had no formal mechanism for assuring compliance with these reporting requirements.

## CHAPTER 8

1. Otero v. Mesa County Valley School District No. 51, 408 F. Supp. 162 (D. Colo. 1975). Later, on October 31, 1977, the Court of Appeals for the Tenth Circuit remanded the case to Judge Winner for more specific findings of fact on the employment discrimination issue. (Plaintiffs had not appealed the dismissal of the educational programming claims.) On remand Judge Winner adhered to his original determination. See 568 F. 2d 1312 (10th Cir. 1977), *on remand,* 470 F. Supp. 326 (D. Colo. 1979), *aff'd* 628 F. 2d 1271 (10th Cir. 1980).

2. Oglesby Interview.

3. "Anglo" generally refers to English-speaking Caucasians, usually of European descent.

4. In combination, blacks, Orientals, and Native Americans make up only an additional 2% of the school population.

5. 408 F. Supp. at 162.

6. Johnson and Marquez Interviews.

7. Johnson Interview.

8. 408 F. Supp. at 176.

9. 351 F. Supp. 1279 (D.N.M. 1972).

10. 414 U.S. 563 (1973).

11. In light of the Board's perception of events, it is ironic that the plaintiffs' lead attorney, Federico Pena, told us he thought Grand Junction was a poor setting for a test case. He felt Colorado's San Luiz Valley had districts with "better facts"—i.e., more non-English-speaking children and more overt acts of discrimination. He decided, however, that his primary obligation was to La Voz, a local client attempting to overcome what it saw as concrete aggrievements, rather than to a more abstract national litigation strategy. Even if District 51 was not an ideal test case, Pena still believe the Board was violating the law. When the dispute could not be settled, he sought judicial remedies. Pena Interview.

12. Oglesby Interview.

13. Lippoth Interview.

14. Johnson Interview. Johnson, the publisher of the *Daily Sentinel,* could not recall any comparable court suit against a major public or private institution in Mesa County.

15. Lippoth Interview. No reported political violence actually occurred in Mesa County in connection with the controversy. However, two Chicanos who had planned to testify on behalf of the school district claimed they had received anonymous phone threats. Also the courtroom had to be cleared more than once in response to bomb threats following accusations that the trial judge was biased against the Chicano litigants.

16. For example, opposition to bilingual education never became a substantial issue in school board elections. Lippoth and Johnson Interviews.

17. Early in the case, La Voz called for a one-day student boycott and scheduled a protest meeting where bilingual-bicultural education issues would be discussed. Only 50 Chicano students attended, out of approximately 1,200. *Daily Sentinel* (5/31/74).

18. May 1, 1974. The same article also stated: "We have little faith that the courts or the legal maneuvering can; in the long run, solve these problems..."

19. 521 F. 2d 465, 480–84 (1975).

20. The Tenth Circuit had, in fact, previously affirmed the *Serna* decision, albeit on narrow factual grounds which avoided the basic equal protection issue. 499 F. 2d 1147 (1974). Furthermore, prior to the later reversal by the appeals court, the Colorado District Court had embraced the *Serna* theory in including a bilingual component to the integration remedies it ordered in *Keyes.*

21. It is interesting that the one significant point of agreement that emerged from interviews with the *Otero* attorneys was that *Serna* and *Otero* were analogous in their basic facts. The critical divergence in perceptions stemmed from the defendants' belief that the *Serna* trial court's conclusion that substantial numbers of students were being totally denied access to meaningful education was unsupported by the *Serna* record, or, at least, could not be proven for Mesa County. The court of appeal's affirmance of *Serna* had relied on that exclusion finding, noting that it made *Serna* "almost identical" to *Lau.* 499 F. 2d 1147, 1153.

22. Upon filing their case, the plaintiffs issued a press release that described *Otero* as a lawsuit intended to force the school district to hire more Chicano

teachers. Later, after the *Keyes* bilingual education order, the complaint was amended to allege that the plaintiffs were entitled to a comprehensive program of bilingual-bicultural education. From that point on, the curriculum claims dominated the court proceedings—until, of course, the appeal and remand in which employment was the only issue.

The shift in emphasis from employment to curriculum multiplied the number of policy issues presented to the court. The case was even further complicated by the plaintiffs' unconventional structuring of the employment claim itself. They did not sue under Title VII of the Civil Rights Act of 1964, which was, by 1974, the primary instrument for employment discrimination litigation. Instead, they relied solely on Title VI, a statute which was aimed at the rights of children, not teachers. The employment claim, therefore, hinged on plaintiffs proving that a pattern of employment discrimination existed which adversely affected the educational services received by Chicano children.

This roundabout fashion of approaching the employment discrimination issue (stemming from the pragmatic problem of finding potential employee plaintiffs because of their fears of being blacklisted by other school districts), complicated the plaintiffs' already formidable litigation tasks. It did, however, provide them the opportunity to establish the principle that students may have standing to challenge employment discrimination. 568 F. 2d 1312, 1314–15.

23. 42 U.S.C. §2000d.

24. 414 U.S. 563 (1974).

25. Justice Blackmun, in his concurring opinion, spoke of "substantial numbers." 414 U.S. 563, 572. This phrase was reiterated by the Tenth Circuit in its *Serna* affirmance. 499 F. 2d 1147, 1154.

26. Indeed, their initial complaint, filed two months after the *Lau* decision, did not even allege that substantial numbers of District 51 students were predominantly Spanish-speaking. The complaint was, however, later amended to include the facts which would be needed to establish a claim under the narrow exclusionary theory.

27. The judge in *Serna* referred generally to children with "language difficulties," rather than to "non-English-speaking" children: "Testimony by an educational psychologist established that in his opinion language difficulties accounted for 80% to 85% of differences indicated in achievement testing." 351 F. Supp. 1279, 1282. However, without making any reference to the record, the court of appeals in *Serna* found: "There is substantial evidence that most of these Spanish surnamed students are deficient in the English language . . ." 499 F. 2d 1147, 1153. Therefore, it concluded that "the factual situation in the instant case is strikingly similar to that found in *Lau*." 499 F. 2d 1147, 1153.

28. In the summer of 1975, the Office for Civil Rights (OCR) of the U.S. Department of Health, Education and Welfare issued a set of *"Lau* Remedies" ("Task Force Findings Specifying Remedies Available for Eliminating Past Educational Practices Ruled Unlawful Under *Lau* v. *Nichols*"). These guidelines mandate services not only for non-English-speaking children but also for children who speak "some English" and for bilingual speakers who are found to be underachievers. Although OCR thus took a broad approach in line with

the plaintiffs' perspective on *Lau* remedies, it does not necessarily follow that the Supreme Court would have found liability and ordered any remedies on a factual record like that in *Otero*. (In August 1980, the Department of Education published proposed new rules for nondiscriminatory treatment of children with limited proficiency in English. 45 Fed. Reg. 52052 [August 5, 1980]).

29. It is interesting that, in 1974, Congress enacted a law that could be read as favoring the equal benefits approach. Unlawful discrimination was defined so as to include: "the failure of an educational agency to take appropriate action to overcome language barriers that impede equal participation by its students in its instructional programs" 20 U.S.C. §1703 (f).

One of the first major decisions under this statutory provision was based on claims that a school district was not taking appropriate action to overcome the language barrier existing for children who speak black English. Martin Luther King Jr. Elementary School v. Ann Arbor School District, 473 F. Supp. 1371 (E.D. Mich. 1979). The court analyzed extensive expert testimony and professional literature from linguistics and educational research and also examined the teaching practices in the school district. This scrutiny led it to conclude that, despite the district's many efforts to remedy the reading problems of black students, it still had fallen short of the statutory mandate by failing to train teachers "to recognize the existence of the language system used by children in their home community and to use that knowledge as a way of helping the children to read standard English." 473 F. Supp. 1371, 1383.

30. The distinction in the legal analysis between the defendants' "exclusionary" theory and plaintiffs' "equal benefits" approach is analogous to the distinction in educational terms between "transitional" bilingual programs (teaching remedial English to allow a transition into regular school programming) and "maintenance" bilingual programs (maintaining proficiency in the native language and interest in the native culture in order to maximize creativity and performance). For a recent review of the rights of children with limited English abilities, focusing on statutory and administrative rules, see Roos, "Bilingual Education: The Hispanic Response to Unequal Educational Opportunity," L. and Contemp. Problems 111 (1978).

31. Groves-Getz Interview. Mr. Groves once served as chairman of the Board of Directors of Colorado Rural Legal Services, one of the legal groups representing the plaintiffs.

32. Marquez Interview.

33. Court Transcript, 12/20/74, p. 2.

34. In retrospect, this testing procedure became "routine" in the sense that it was repeated, after trial had been completed, to reassess the language abilities of Chicano youngsters for instructional purposes. Reeder Interview. However, in initially deciding to bring the outside team the defendants clearly considered the litigation value of employing credible outside experts and applying the test to all Chicano children, not merely to a small sample tested by the district itself in 1974. Glass Interview.

35. Order of February 12, 1975.

36. None had ever tried a major case before. Pena and Marquez Interviews.

37. Judge Winner did initiate one important organizational decision. He insisted that all employment discrimination evidence be presented and

briefed separately from the bilingual education claims. Plaintiffs, who opposed this approach, ultimately benefited from it by producing a much more manageable record for an appeal limited to the discrimination claim.

38. Dr. Glass and Dr. Jackson speculated that reputable experts for the opposing sides could probably have worked out mutually agreeable solutions to many of the testing problems if urged to do so by the court prior to the testing. Glass and Jackson Interviews. That result would have been comparable to the mutually acceptable, independent survey procedure worked out in *Chance* at Judge Mansfield's instigation. See ch. 6, pp. 87–88 *supra*.

39. 408 F. Supp. 162, 167.

40. *Id.* at 164.

41. Court Transcript, vol. 1, p. 14.

42. Plaintiffs' Post-Trial Brief, at 2 and 12.

43. Dr. George Keating, one of the plaintiffs' outside experts in reading, testified on the basis of his observations of public meetings in Grand Junction and conversations with community persons that the Spanish language "although perhaps suppressed, is still very much alive, present, and active in the community . . ." Court Transcript, vol. 8, p. 87.

44. The application was submitted to state authorities but was never actually filed with the federal government.

45. Plaintiffs' Trial Exhibit G, at 8 (emphasis supplied). The document defined "Spanish-dominant" in terms of at least partial use of Spanish in normal conversation.

46. This issue of an alleged "prior admission" arose also with respect to dropout statistics. Defendants' expert, Dr. Glass, showed that the school district staff had made numerous errors in compiling official statistics for the state Board of Education. The recomputed data was much more favorable to the district. The plaintiffs took the position that defendants were bound by their prior formal "admissions." But, although the plaintiffs may have been prejudiced by their reliance on the original, misleading statistics, the court could not be expected to order a prospective remedy for a problem that, in fact, could be shown to be nonexistent. On the other hand, it might be argued that if a public agency makes drastic changes in its policy position during a litigation, it may be appropriate under some circumstances to foreclose it from contradicting the assumptions of its prior policies or from arguing against remedies that may assume continuation of the new policy direction.

47. Court Transcript, vol. 1, p. 17.

48. Although the plaintiffs' attorneys demonstrated a good knowledge of psychometric principles, neither they nor their experts ever clearly and systematically summarized for the court the important concepts in the field and the legal authority for applying them to the instant tests. By comparison, the initial expert affidavits in *Chance* (where, of course, these issues were more central to the case) began with an exposition of these definitional and conceptual problems and then proceeded to analyze the tests and state conclusions.

49. See p. 154 *supra*.

50. Content validation is one of the three basic psychometric validation approaches. The others are criterion-referenced and construct validation. Content validation focuses on the factual correlation of the "content" of a test

question to the characteristics under study. It is a "lesser" standard than criterion-referenced validation, which emphasizes statistical predictive correlations of test questions to characteristics.

51. Dr. Kjolseth further stated that the test was not content valid because the question format used to illicit responses from the children was phrased in terms of a game which the children learned in school, in English, and which the children by and large had not practiced in Spanish. Consequently, use of this questioning would artificially inflate the measures of proficiency.

52. Deficiencies in test administration constitute an independent ground for impeaching test results. That is, even if a test design has been proven valid under proper administration, it cannot be assumed to be valid under improper administration. Of course, if the test design has not been validated, proper administration procedures cannot rehabilitate its acceptability.

53. At approximately 11:00 P.M. on the night before the test, Dr. Garrett learned that the team was supposed to give the short form rather than the long form of one of the tests. A late-night, crash retraining session had to be mounted.

54. 408 F. Supp. 162, 168.

55. Dr. Jackson (who assisted Attorney Pena in the cross-examination of Glass) believes that Dr. Glass minimized the importance of the APA standards in an attempt to save Dr. Garrett's credibility. When interviewed, however, Dr. Glass (a member of one of the committees that approves the standards) reiterated the points made in his testimony. Jackson and Glass Interviews. Despite general professional acceptance of the APA standards by psychometricians (Dr. Glass's trial statement being a minority view), Judge Winner's refusal to incorporate the technical APA standards into the law was consistent with recent legal trends that are moving away from earlier indications of strict application of the APA standards. Cf. Griggs v. Duke Power Company, 401 U.S. 424 (1971) and Albermarle Paper Company v. Moody, 422 U.S. 405 (1975) with Washington v. Davis, 426 U.S. 299 (1976). Cf. also Guidelines (29 C.F.R. Part 1607, November 1976) with Uniform Guidelines on Employee Selection Procedures (1978), 43 Fed. Reg. 38290 (10/25/78). See, generally, Lerner, "Washington v. Davis: Quantity, Quality and Equality in Employment Testing," 1976 Sup. Ct. Rev. 263. Within some limits, opinions about the importance to be given to the APA standards are not so much a professional psychometric judgment as a judgment of political and social philosophy. No one disputes the fact that following the APA standards increases the probability that a test will be valid. But how great a degree of risk of error or invalidity is unacceptable? The courts have to answer this question in concrete situations.

56. Court Transcript, vol. 19, p. 18.

57. Attorney Pena stated that plaintiffs' attorneys were too overwhelmed with other trial preparations to doublecheck this kind of information. Had it been done, he believed, they could have produced this kind of evidence. Pena Interview.

58. Dr. Kjolseth noted that one child had scored 0 on the Spanish Dos Amigos test and a 3 on the English Dos Amigos test, indicating that the child was either alingual or spoke a language other than Spanish or English. The same child, however, scored 20 on both Spanish and English on the STACL tests, which showed he was a strong bilingual speaker.

59. Dr. Glass, Court Transcript, vol.18, p. 58.

60. At the time of the trial, Dr. Glass was the author of over 100 papers for professional journals and a statistical methods textbook used in 100 colleges and universities. He was then serving as the president of the American Educational Research Association.

61. "Ethnic Group Differences in Educational Achievement in Mesa County Valley School District #51," by Gene Glass and Daniel Klinger, January 1975, Defendants' Exhibit 1-E (hereinafter, "Glass Report").

62. Consider this example. At a given level of SES, a student with an I.Q. of 110 has a normal expectancy for achievement in math of 110. Chicano student "A" has a true I.Q. of 110 but, because of test bias, is measured at I.Q. 100. His actual math achievement level is 105, but again, because of test bias, he is measured at 100. The bias in the I.Q. test was 10 points, whereas in the achievement test it was only 5 points. In actuality, student "A" is underachieving; but because of his distorted I.Q. score he is grouped in the Glass analysis with students of I.Q. 100 and is found to be precisely at his expectancy level of 100. Thus, if I.Q. tests *are* more biased against Chicanos than are achievement tests, Chicano underachievement will be obscured, making it *harder* for the plaintiffs to prove they suffered educational detriment. However, if the achievement tests are the more biased of the two, then the analysis will indicate the Chicanos are performing less than they actually are. These results, of course, would make it *easier* for plaintiffs to produce "evidence" of harm. The third possibility, equal bias in the two tests, would not provide an advantage to either party.

63. Glass Report at 15.

64. C. Burts, "The Genetic Determination of Differences in Intelligence: A Study of Monozygotic Twins Reared Together and Apart," British Journal of Psychology, 1966, pp. 57, 137–53.

65. The report was written prior to the 1975 tests. Although Dr. Glass admitted that the 1974 testing methodology was open to criticism, he testified that the 1975 testing was completely sound and confirmed the conclusions reached from the 1974 tests. (Court Transcript, vol. 19, pp. 27–28.)

66. Glass Report at 25.

67. When interviewed after the case, Glass observed: "I would say that nine out of ten psychometricians or statistical researchers to whom you presented all aspects of that case would probably assent to the conclusion that the I.Q. tests had a very strong verbal content, and that there was some language interference for the Chicanos . . ." He was, however, convinced that even if such error existed, an analysis corrected for it would still reveal that the amount of language interference suffered by the Chicanos was insufficient to justify ordering District 51 to implement compensatory programs.

68. Glass Interview.

69. Financial limitations forced the plaintiffs to depend on experts who were willing to donate their time to the case. Not surprisingly, such persons were (with the exception of Dr. Gregory Jackson) strong advocates of bilingual-bicultural programming. Their personal leanings were quite apparent and probably hurt their image as independent experts objectively analyzing the particular case. Note also that plaintiffs' experts generally denied the validity of using I.Q. tests for Chicano students, referencing to supportive research studies or to policies in other jurisdictions (such as decisions in

California to limit the use of the tests). But no written summary of the relevant literature was presented, much less a study and evaluation that attempted to apply existent research studies specifically to the situation in District 51.

70. This analysis is based on interview comments of Dr. Gregory Jackson. Dr. Jackson's spontaneous decision to become a volunteer expert for the plaintiff dramatized the inequality of social science research in the case. In Glass's opinion, "Plaintiffs were poorly served in general by their expert testimony, with the exception of Greg Jackson who was well trained and competent." At the time of the trial, Jackson was a staff member of the U.S. Commission on Civil Rights. At the plaintiffs' request, the commission originally sent him to the trial for the limited purpose of describing the preparation of the commission's report on Mexican-Americans in the Southwest and helping to lay the foundation for its introduction into evidence. As a witness and as an observer, he was strongly impressed with the value of Glass's assistance to the defendants, and with the plaintiffs' inability to counter it. He arranged to take several vacation days that week in order to assist the plaintiffs in the capacity of a volunteer. Getting involved as late as he did, Jackson's ability to counterbalance Glass's report was severely limited. The plaintiffs' lawyers were working "sixteen hours a day" trying to keep pace with each day's developments and did not have the luxury of rethinking positions or receiving instruction in the intricacies of social science methodology.

71. "I estimated that they mastered what would amount to the material for a graduate course in statistics." Glass Interview.

72. Glass and Grove/Getz Interviews. Also, it enhanced Glass's credibility that he was not publicly identified as a staunch supporter or opponent of bilingual programs. Ironically, Dr. Glass himself has noted the dangers of judicial reliance on any one or more "so-called independent experts." Although it is more difficult, he says, to label the biases of educational experts than to classify a sociologist as a Marxist or an economist as a Keynesian, political inclinations inevitably shape professional reading and research selections. He, himself, was comfortable in the role of advocate in *Otero* because, after analyzing the school data, he concluded that the school's position coincided exactly with his own educational and political policy viewpoints about government's responsibility in these areas. Glass Interview.

73. Pena and Glass Interviews.

74. Glass had learned, e.g., how to use the very limitations of social science as a defensive weapon. During cross-examination, an attorney usually tries to lead the witness through a series of yes/no questions that culminate in a contradiction of the witness's direct testimony. When social science materials are being discussed, however, almost any question can be truthfully answered either yes or no, so long as the answer is qualified. Thus, when Pena questioned Glass at trial, Glass answered "no" to questions where a "yes" answer was anticipated and vice versa. Pena's timing sometimes was thrown off, and Glass used these moments to discourse as long as possible about his views, turning the focus away from the cross-examiner's trend of thought.

75. Court Transcript, vol. 19, p. 91. Pena elicited agreement from Glass that there were only three plausible explanations of the results: (a) the District 51 math curriculum was better suited for Chicanos than for Anglos;

(b) Chicanos have a special knack for math, or (c) the I.Q. scores used in the Glass Report were inaccurate. Pena wanted Glass to reject the first two possibilities, thereby trapping him into admitting the third was correct. Glass did rule out the first possibility, but then surprised Pena by saying the second was indeed the best explanation. Pena and Jackson were stunned and did not recover in time to make Glass admit that he had no empirical support for the second hypothesis. Indeed, when interviewed, neither Jackson nor Glass knew of any reputable findings indicating that Chicanos are more adept than Anglos at math.

76. See Cardenas and Cardenas, "The Cardenas-Cardenas Theory of Incompatibilities," Today's Education (National Education Association, February 1972); Cardenas, An Education Plan for the Denver Public Schools (National Education Association Task Force de la Raza, January 1974). In Keyes, the court of appeals reversed the portion of the district court plan that was based on the Cardenas theory.

77. The defendants denied that failure to provide (any given number of) "role models" significantly impeded Chicano achievement; they strenuously argued that abstract standards governing role-model representation could not justify the hiring of an otherwise less qualified Chicano. Dr. Cardenas recognized in his Otero testimony that even if one assumes this incompatibility exists, the weight to be given to this factor can be troubling:

BY DEFENDANTS' COUNSEL: "Do you think that, given the basic level of qualifications . . . a school district in that situation (with a deficiency of Mexican-American teachers) should ignore more qualified Anglos to hire a qualified Chicano?"
DR. CARDENAS: "I think that is a value judgment, sir."
Q: "Well, do you have . . . ? I'm asking for your value judgment."
A: "It's one that I find is difficult to make, sir."
Court Transcript, vol. 10, pp. 116–17.

78. At the time of the Otero trial, however, the theory's proponents were unable to cite any empirical studies which proved any degree of causal relationships even among smaller groupings of the variables.

79. "[B]eing raised in poverty is not necessarily a handicap unless the school makes no allowance for the type of economic background in which the kid was raised and, therefore, handicaps him in going through school program." Dr. Cardenas, Court Transcript, vol. 10, pp. 20–21.

80. Another witness for plaintiffs, Ernesto Andrade, testified about programs in Colorado.

81. U.S. Office of Education, Equality of Educational Opportunity (1966).

82. These objections, of course, were more a basic rejection of the assumption of most broad survey research in education than criticisms of other specific findings of Coleman or other researchers.

Approximately two and a half years after the Otero trial, the debate about the value of survey research for showing the effectiveness of bilingual-bicultural education programs based on the theory of incompatibilities was still far from settled. In February 1977, the interim report of a national study of Title VII bilingual programs conducted by American Institutes for Research (AIR) for the U.S. Office of Education was released. By comparing students in Title VII and non-Title VII classrooms on the basis of Spanish and English language proficiency, math achievement, and attitudes toward school, the study reached the conclusion that the Title VII programs, for the most part, were not effective. In a recent article, Dr. Cardenas pointed out methodological defects and stated that those program failures were caused by poor administration. He said: "In general, funds for bilingual education have been dispersed throughout the country without regard to staff adequacy, availability of materials, evaluation designs and accountability procedures. Even special research studies such as the aforementioned A.I.R. Office of Education Study were unbelievably bad." Cardenas, "Responses," in Noel Epstein, Language, Ethnicity, and The Schools (1977), pp. 80–81.

83. Keyes v. School District No. 1, 521 F. 2d 465, 482 (10th Cir. 1975).

84. 408 F. Supp. 162, 170.

85. Pena Interview. Both specific statements in his *Otero* decision and analysis of his prior rulings lend credence to this view. For example, Judge Winner stated: "The recent proliferation of lawsuits against school districts, schools and school officials suggests that some people think the courts should assume overall supervision of the nation's educational system, but I disagree, although I confess that I wonder if school personnel should not be awarded combat pay for their efforts in trying to educate in today's climate." 408 F. Supp. 162, 170 note 3. Note also his reference to Cardenas as "an expert in curriculum, bilingual-bicultural education and all sorts of other things." 408 F. Supp. 162, 165.

A search request to a computerized law library (LEXIS) for civil rights cases decided by Judge Winner yielded six decisions in addition to *Otero:* Alexander v. Gardner-Denver Company, 346 F. Supp. 1012 (1971); Evans v. State Board of Agriculture, 325 F. Supp. 1353 (1971); Goodloe v. Martin Marietta Corp., 7 EPD ¶ 9198 (1972); Joslin Dry Goods Co. v. Equal Employment Opportunity Commission, 336 F. Supp. 941 (1971); Salton v. Western Electric Co., 7 EPD ¶ 9193 (1972); Spurlock v. United Airlines, Inc., 330 F. Supp. 228 (1971). A consistent theme in Judge Winner's opinions in these cases was that statutes and procedures established to provide equal opportunity are subject to abuse by minority complainants who are seeking not merely equal rights but special advantages. See, e.g., Judge Winner's warning in *Spurlock* that anti-discrimination statutes could be used as "a means of coercion" against employers. 7 EPD, ¶ 9197, p. 7514.

86. If the Cardenas theory had been accepted as the basis for a liability finding, the court might logically have felt compelled to order full implementation of the Cardenas plan in fashioning relief, since only full adoption of the entire plan would overcome constitutional violations premised on its absence. According to Dr. Cardenas's testimony, this would require District 51 to provide Chicano students, among other things, with dental care, allergy examinations, glasses, clothing, and even full legal services in appropriate circumstances. Court Transcript, vol. 11, pp. 17–18. By contrast, the judges in *Serna* and *Keyes* were free to modify the total Cardenas perspective and order steps to eliminate some, but not all, of the incompatibilities alleged in those circumstances. For example, in *Serna,* the court ordered that minimum programs of 30–60 minutes per day be implemented at the elementary level, but noted that additional programming might be desirable.

87. Commenting on the framing of the class definition in the complaint, Judge Winner specifically pointed out that the definition "stems directly from the so-called 'Cardenas Plan' . . . and it was obviously phrased by plaintiffs' counsel in anticipation of the testimony of Dr. Cardenas in the trial of this case." 408 F. Supp. at 160.

88. Although it was alleged that large numbers of the plaintiffs spoke virtually no English and were functionally excluded from education, the evidence in support of this claim was too meager to warrant classifying the case as principle or principle/policy balancing.

89. This distinction also explains the decisions of the Tenth Circuit Court of Appeals in *Serna* and *Keyes*. In *Keyes*, implementation of the Cardenas plan was reversed because no "principle" basis for such relief had been established at the liability stage; in *Serna*, on the other hand, the same court affirmed the Cardenas approach because the record was seen as showing a pattern of exclusion "almost identical" to *Lau*. In this context, it is interesting to speculate on the implications of the plaintiffs' decision in *Otero* to frame their employment discrimination claims as subsidiary aspect educational benefits claim, in contrast to the major emphasis on employment discrimination in the *Chance* complaint, to which remedial educational policy issues were later attached by the plaintiffs. Perhaps if greater emphasis had been placed initially on the employment discrimination principle claims in *Otero* (the aspect of the case that the Tenth Circuit remanded to Judge Winner for more explicit fact-finding), the plaintiffs may have met with a greater degree of success.

90. There is no indication that the Mesa County Chicanos had been directly involved in the attempts in the early 1970s to pass a bilingual-bicultural bill in the legislature. The statewide and national advocacy groups that participated in the lawsuit, however, may be presumed to have played a liaison role in this regard.

91. See generally, S. Schengold, The Politics of Rights (1974).

92. See excerpts from depositions of named plaintiffs in Brief and Memorandum in Support of Defendants' Motion for Summary Judgment (filed 11/13/74). The plaintiffs' rebuttal is found in their reply brief filed 12/13/74.

93. Ironically, it turned out that the named plaintiffs were very typical of the plaintiff class—which spelled defeat for the class claims.

94. Also, striking for their lack of participation in this case were representatives of Chicano educators seeking employment in District 51. Plaintiffs apparently could not obtain even one such individual to assert the employment discrimination claims. They therefore had to frame their stance in terms of the indirect impact of hiring discrimination on the students' learning under Title VI.

95. Indeed, the costs of undertaking independent surveys and obtaining expert assistance to present the complex social science issues of the trial were even beyond the resources of the statewide legal advocacy groups. As indicated above in Section IV, this limitation put the plaintiffs at a disadvantage.

96. See ch. 1, p. 10 *supra*.

97. Plaintiffs' counsel included one local attorney, Mr. Jose D. Marquez, who was principally responsible for trial of the employment discrimination claim.

98. 408 F. Supp. at 167.

99. Glass Interview.

100. Note in this regard the following statement by Judge Winner: "Certainly if the expert testimony proved anything, it proved that educational theory is not an exact science, and an expert can be found who will testify to almost anything." 408 F. Supp. 162, 164.

101. Of course, judicial resort to common sense in dealing with complex social science issues sometimes can lead to inaccurate or misleading conclusions. For example, in analyzing plaintiffs' argument that children brought up in homes where Spanish is regularly spoken will experience "incompatibilities" in an Anglo school environment, Judge Winner alluded to anecdotal information concerning the family life of one of the plaintiffs' expert witnesses, Dr. Rolf Kjolseth. Dr. Kjolseth had indicated that although his native tongue is English, he and his wife make a conscious effort to speak only Spanish in the home. Judge Winner stated that "Dr. Kjolseth's children are doing quite well in school, but if the arguments of Dr. Cardenas be accepted, they shouldn't be." Clearly, however, it is stretching a point to say that the educational progress of the children of a college professor (whose native language is English) is representative of the situation of the average Chicano child in Mesa County. (It should be noted that Judge Winner's rejection of plaintiffs' home language theories, however, was also based on specific examples concerning educational achievement of members of the plaintiff class.)

102. On the other hand, Dr. Glass himself indicated that from another perspective, the adversary process enhanced the quality of his testimony. When interviewed after the trial, Dr. Glass stated that knowing that his testimony as defendants' expert in this case would be dissected by a skillful adversary motivated him to intensify his preparation to such an extent that he put more work into this task than he normally would devote to writing an article, preparing to deliver a paper before his colleagues, or giving a statement before a legislative committee. Glass Interview.

## CHAPTER 9

1. A case similar to *Otero* was also filed in the Montrose school district and was also assigned to Judge Winner. At the judge's request, this suit was held in abeyance pending the outcome of *Otero*. Pena Interview.

2. The complaint in *Otero* was filed in March of 1974, and the case went to trial in April 1975. The bilingual-bicultural education bill was introduced in the Colorado House of Representatives at the January 1975 session. Major committee hearings began in March, and the bill was passed in mid-June.

3. Several key actors did appear in both places—most notably, the Chicano Education Project attorneys who litigated the *Otero* case. They actively consulted for the bill's proponents and were instrumental in the drafting of many of its specific provisions.

4. One explanation why proponents of the bill did not specifically discuss *Otero* was that Judge Winner's preliminary statements indicated that the outcome of the suit was not likely to favor the Chicano interests. Rep. Valdez, however, expressed surprise "that the other side did not mention it." Sen. Strickland, a Republican leader, was aware of *Otero*, but did not press its

relevance. He maintained he "[was] not an attorney" and expressed his belief that activities of the judicial branch "provide no basis for legislation."

5. Colorado Department of Education, "Report on Senate Joint Resolution 20 Study," Part II, Bilingual-Multicultural Education Programs (1975), p. 12. Although the report gave no breakdown of students enrolled in bilingual as opposed to bilingual-bicultural programs, it did indicate that of 27 districts operating bilingual programs, only 6 also had a bicultural dimension. Some students were also enrolled in "multicultural" programs which "may or may not include second language teaching."

6. *Id.* at 8. Forty-two of the school districts surveyed, however, either did not return the questionnaire to the Education Department or submitted it after the deadline.

7. According to data in the fiscal note of the Executive Budget Office, dated April 24, 1975, the broad eligibility definition of the original draft of the bill would encompass approximately 60,000 Hispanic students.

8. For example, in Denver most Spanish-surnamed children spoke English as their primary language. Valdez Interview.

9. As Sen. Sandoval told his colleagues, on a personal level, "after four or five years in the public schools, I didn't have a culture left."

10. Valdez Interview.

11. Fowler and Strickland Interviews.

12. Citizens' Conference on State Legislatures, State Legislatures: An Evaluation of Their Effectiveness (1971).

13. Showalter, Emerson, Sears Interviews. To the extent that substantive research on particular issues is undertaken, it does not extend beyond writing to the State Education Department or to other sources within or without the state for statistics and other information that they may already have. Lucero, Sears Interviews.

14. The one exception to this pattern of highly limited staffing resources is Colorado's Joint Budget Committee, the powerful agency whose responsibility is to review all appropriation requests and the budgets of all its state agencies. Strickland Interview.

15. Unlike New York, where each member has a private office suite, the thirty minority members of the Colorado House have desk space in one large office complex in the basement: the majority members also share space on the basis of three or four to a room.

16. Emerson Interview. The "long" session, held every odd year, is a full legislative session permitting consideration of all bills and proposals. Each even year the legislature convenes for a shorter period to consider only those particular items on the governor's "call."

17. Knox Interview.

18. There were seven Chicano legislators in the 1975 legislature, five representatives, and two senators, all of whom were Democrats. Although a large number of other legislators became cosponsors of the original bill, the seven Chicano legislators took primary responsibility for pressing its enactment.

19. This study culminated in the Department of Education's "Report on Senate Joint Resolution 20 Study," discussed above at note 5. It was considered inadequate and was received too late to influence the deliberations of the 1975 bill. Lucero Interview.

20. Valdez, Lucero, Sandoval Interviews.

21. Compare the definition of eligibility under the Massachusetts Transitional Bilingual Education Act, Mass. Gen. Laws Ann. Ch. 71A (1971) (West), generally regarded as the pioneer statute in this field: " 'Children of limited English-speaking ability,' (1) children who were not born in the United States whose native tongue is a language other than English and who are incapable of performing ordinary classwork in English and (2) children who were born in the United States of non-English speaking parents and who are incapable of performing ordinary classwork in English." See also Texas Ed. Code §21.452(3). The HEW standard upheld by the Supreme Court in *Lau* was "inability to speak and understand the English language which excludes national origin-minority students from effective participation in the educational program . . ." 35 Fed. Regis. at 11595.

22. In contrast, the Massachusetts law (cited note 21 *supra*) required development of a program if there were 20 or more eligible students in the *district,* but no 5% alternative was provided. In addition, it specified that the 20 or more children were to be in one particular language classification. Similar requirements were also contained in the Federal Office of Civil Rights Regulations (the *"Lau* Remedies") promulgated in the summer of 1975. Strictly speaking, the anti-discrimination requirements of Title VI of the 1964 Civil Rights Act and the regulations issued thereunder (45 CFR Part 80) would apply even if a single eligible individual had been identified in a particular school district; but because of "staff limitations and priorities," OCR had indicated that it would enforce these requirements only when a district had 20 or more eligible students.

23. Compare the program endorsed by the court in *Serna, supra,* ch. 8, which specifically stated that children in grades 1, 2, 3 as a minimum "shall receive 60 minutes per day bilingual instruction" and students in grades 4–6 "shall receive 45 minutes per day bilingual instruction." Note, also, the specific limitations in §2 of the Massachusetts act (cited note 21 *supra*), which provided for a "transitional" bilingual program in which students would be enrolled for three years or until such time as they achieved a requisite level of English language skills, *whichever should occur first.*

24. Rep. Lucero, one of the bill's prime sponsors, believed that the first draft mandated full implementation, whether or not state funding was provided. It contained a recommended appropriation of $8 million; the fiscal note data analysis of the Executive Budget Office, dated April 24, 1975, put a $19.9 million price tag on this bill. It is not clear whether the sponsors of the bill knew that, even if their request for an $8 million appropriation was passed, half the eligible districts could not be funded.

25. Earle, "How to Pass an Education Bill," *Denver Post,* June 29, 1975, reprinted in *Un Nuevo Dia,* July 1975 (Chicano Education Project, Golden, Colorado).

26. *Ibid.*

27. Most interviewees indicated a belief that Sens. Sandoval and Shoemaker had an explicit or implicit "trade-off" understanding. See also Earle, *supra* note 25, at 10. Sen. Sandoval maintained that his support of Sen. Shoemaker on other bills was not a difficult compromise since the other bills were not really "controversial." Sen. Shoemaker, however, denied that a trade-off was

made, asserting that he would never support "any bill that costs money unless a case can be made for it."

28. Commentary or questioning by the committee members in general was almost nonexistent. Although several witnesses were asked to clarify statements, few were directly challenged. An exception was Mr. Moldo, the representative of the U.S. Civil Rights Commission, who presented statistics on Chicano dropout rates and related issues covering the six states of the U.S. Civil Rights Commission's Mexican-American Study. The committee asked him to provide specific data on the situation in Colorado. There is no indication, however, that such specific breakdowns were provided.

29. Johnston Interview.

30. Johnston Interview. Later, after having visited programs in other states, Chairwoman Johnston began to realize the more radical implications of the bicultural aspects of the Colorado bill, and therefore urged the committee to limit the program to a "transitional" rather than a "maintenance" approach. These "transitional" features were eventually included in the 1977 amendments to the act. See table 12, p. 184 *supra*.

31. The Education Committee revised the powers of the local parent committees (renamed "community committees") and the state steering committee. Both of these agencies were recast as consulting bodies that could advise, but not overrule, the decisions of the local school board and the State Education Department. Also, the 20–5% eligibility formula was modified to 50–10%. In addition, funding cutoff enforcement rights were revised, although additional incentives to private enforcement (attorney's fees) were added. The amendments also specified that a local school district would be required to implement a program only if funding was available from the state. The basic bicultural aspects of the eligibility definitions and the programmatic content were, however, left largely intact.

32. The department had apparently specifically promised to support a re-introduction of the 1973 bill. Johnston Interview. But, as indicated above, the 1975 bill was substantially different. Several members of the Chicano coalition maintained vehemently that Dr. Frazier had addressed a Republican caucus and sat on the Republican side of the chamber during the Senate debates. Sensitive to allegations of partiality, Commissioner Frazier appeared on April 3 before the House committee to "clarify the role of the department." He stated that the department was available to provide information and drafting assistance for *all* 100 legislators, "regardless of how we feel." He told proponents that the department was not seeking to undermine the bill, but was obligated to pinpoint educational or legal problems when asked for its opinion.

33. Showalter Interview.

34. Valdez, Comer Interviews. Apparently, the association's membership was split on the issues, although some concern was expressed on the affirmative-action hiring aspects of the bill.

35. "Senator Fowler Terms New Law Revolutionary," *Un Nuevo Dia,* July 1975 (Chicano Education Project, Golden Colorado), p. 3, Fowler Interview.

36. Comer Interview.

37. Fowler Interview. Sen. Shoemaker, the Republican chairman of the Appropriations Committee, thought the tutorial approach was inadequate

because its implementation was too expensive and its coverage not broad enough. Shoemaker Interview.

38. Shoemaker Interview. Transcripts of testimony brought before the other legislative committees were not transmitted to or considered by the Appropriations Committee. Sen. Shoemaker did indicate, however, that his personal decisions were strongly influenced by Chicano dropout rates presented to his Joint Budget Committee in previous years. He also said that he supported the bill because he knew of no other approaches which would remedy the serious dropout problem, a problem which translated itself into substantial long-term welfare and penitentiary costs to the state.

39. The committee's draft deemphasized the specific reference to "culturally different environment" in the House bill by incorporating it into an expanded definition of "students with linguistically different skills," which was now defined as: "students who are not able to take full advantage of present educational programs taught in English *and* who come from an environment of different customs and traditions which may include the influence of another language in their family, community, or peer group" (emphasis added).

40. Consistent with Sen. Sandoval's interpretation, the Appropriations Committee version continued specifically to require "a full-time program . . . in which the history, culture, and cultural contributions associated with the language of the students with linguistically different skills and the history and culture of the United States are presented to the students in the languages which reflect the cultures of the students in the classroom."

41. Valdez, Sandoval Interview. Sen. Sandoval indicated that the Republican leadership originally suggested limiting the bill to K–6 and he had counterproposed the K–3 limitation.

42. Sandoval Interview.

43. Despite the fact that the commissioner and State Chairwoman Johnston were generally perceived by the proponents as providing assistance to the Republican opponents, their indication that they could "live with" the bicultural orientation apparently greatly influenced and conciliated some of the Republicans on this key issue. Johnston Interview. See also Earle, *supra* note 25, at 10.

44. Sen. Shoemaker, the Republican chairperson of the Appropriations Committee, indicated that he personally never had any problems with the bicultural references, although "it was hard to understand exactly what biculturalism means." He agreed with Sen. Sandoval that the deleting of the bicultural references was a tactical necessity to get the bill out of committee.

45. Of course, it can be argued that the lack of any compulsion to shape a precise remedy for a specific right allowed the legislature to adopt a somewhat casual approach toward analyzing the number of eligible Chicano students, their particular needs, and the exact manner in which the bilingual-bicultural program would respond to those needs.

46. Lucero Interview. Sen. Sandoval also remarked: "It is easier to break through a principle in the courts; the legislature deals in politics."

47. Several of the Republican legislators, in particular, reacted strongly to the suggestion that they might be operating under court pressure. As Rep. Sears put it, "When we were threatened with court action at one stage in the negotiations, I saw red." Sen. Shoemaker expressed similar sentiments.

48. Ironically, of course, the district court in Colorado denied the legitimacy of a right to bilingual-bicultural education of the type being considered by the legislature, but this decision came after the legislative action. Apparently, no one pointed out the limited support for a broad concept of *biculturalism* in the *Lau* or *Serna* decisions, and the Tenth Circuit's reversal of the Cardenas plan in *Keyes* was not issued until after the bill had been enacted.

49. One might also view the Colorado events as the exception that proves the rule. Since Chicano representation in the legislature, in and of itself, was too small to effect bargaining, obviously the power positions held by two Chicano legislators were the critical factors. Furthermore, the success of the bilingual-bicultural bill was also influenced by prior court victories of minority interests in the *Lau* and *Serna* cases, which had established an aura of legal legitimacy that the legislature felt obligated to respect.

50. Generally speaking, the Colorado Education Association was viewed as being favorably inclined toward the bill (but concerned about such aspects as the affirmative-action hiring requirements), while the Colorado School Boards Association was viewed as being somewhat opposed (at least on the community control issues). Neither of these major lobbying organizations, however, took active part in the deliberations. As Rep. Knox put it, "the usual lobbyists were absent from the scene; most of the communication we received was from citizen types."

51. This view of the legislative process as being essentially bipolar must be qualified by reference to the role of the State Education Department and the State Board of Education. On several occasions Commissioner Frazier went out of his way to emphasize the department's neutral role. It is clear, however, that many of the Chicano activists saw the department as being aligned with the opposition. Despite this perception, the fact remains that the department was never officially in opposition to the concept of a bilingual-bicultural bill: in fact, the commissioner's acceptance of the concept of bicultural programming was a major factor in the Republicans' willingness ultimately to adopt this major innovation. If it is accepted that the State Education Department took a neutral posture on administrative and implementation questions, its role might fairly be analogized to the role it might have played in *Otero* if the case had gone to the remedial stage. In such a remedial situation, the expertise of the state department may well have been sought by the court in working out implementation details of a proposed remedy.

52. It might even be said that a broader range of issues was addressed in the judicial forum. Note, e.g., the strong attention to the employment discrimination points in the court compared with the relative neglect of any specific focus on the affirmative action issues in the legislature. The community control issues involving the local parent advisory committees that were of central concern in the House Education Committee's deliberations were not directly considered in the *Otero* trial, but these questions were inherently remedial and may well have been raised if *Otero* had reached a remedy stage.

53. I.e., the Glass Report, see ch. 8, pp. 161–65 *supra*.

54. In comparison to the court proceedings, both quantitatively and qualitatively, less relevant social science information entered into the legislative deliberations. Most of the numerous documents and reports submitted into evidence at the *Otero* trial were not formally included in the legislative committee records.

55. "The factors leading to passage of this bill were political and were not rational, well thought out, or scientific." Knox Interview. Sen. Shoemaker was a primary exception to this view, insisting that his decision to back the bill was based on dropout statistics submitted in previous years to his Joint Budget Committee. Although these statistics may have been influential in Sen. Shoemaker's mind, there is no indication that they were formally introduced before any of the committees or directly affected the general deliberations.

56. Emerson Interview.

57. Our characterization of the decision-making process as essentially divorced from focused social fact-finding should be considered in light of Wahlke's theory that legislators tend to rely on the recommendations of the "experts" within their party in deciding how to vote on particular bills. Wahlke et al., The Legislative System 194–95 (1962). Some indications of such reliance were present here. For example, during the debates, Sen. Cisneros referred to the "experts who devoted hundreds of hours to [the bill's] drafting." Rep. Valdez and Sen. Shoemaker also revealed considerable knowledge of relevant factual issues. Nevertheless, indications of strong reliance on available expertise is completely lacking. Indeed, neither the bill's proponents nor opponents felt it necessary or desirable during the debates to invoke any studies or expert perceptions. Apparently, the key information the legislative "experts" communicated to their colleagues concerned not the factual basis of the policies incorporated into the bill, but rather the position taken by the party leadership and the acceptability of the bill to affected constituencies. Cf. Davis, "Facts in Lawmaking," 80 Colum. L. Rev., 931, 932 (1980) ("They [legislators] may legislate, if they choose, with a bull-in-a-china-shop ignorance, without facts, without reasons, and with minds closed to reasoned arguments, as long as what they enact is sufficiently reasonable to meet due process requirements"). Note also that, although about 20% of the education committee's members were teachers or educational professionals, their specialist backgrounds were not a significant factor in the legislative process. The prime sponsors of the bill, in the House and the Senate, were not these educational experts, and it was these sponsors, rather than the "experts" among the committee members, who carried the bill.

58. No representatives of the school districts participated in the remedial negotiations, although in some sense the State Education Department did articulate their interests, especially on the issue of limiting parental rights in decision making at the local level. Republican legislators were also sensitive to these school district perspectives.

59. Also, as a result of the political compromises, the bill was clarified to state explicitly that if a local district's program was not funded, the district would not be required to carry it out; no consideration was given to the consequences of raising and then disappointing expectations of parents and students in this way.

60. According to Sen. Strickland, data concerning actual costs of the programs under the eligibility criteria first became available in 1977. Democratic legislators fought the amendments because, despite the indications of implementation problems, they deemed it unfair to revise substantially a major new program before it had adequate time to be fully developed; the governor also took this position and vetoed the first version of these amendments (governor's veto of May 16, 1977). He later relented and signed a modified version.

## CHAPTER 10

1. A. Bickel, The Least Dangerous Branch 24 (1962).

2. Of course, the distinction between basic policy and subsidiary policy may not be easily discernible, particularly in "novel" cases, or ones presenting principle/policy balancing claims. The correlation we found between "novelty" and subsidiary policy suggests that if the scope of a principle issue is unresolved, more such policy arguments will be asserted. (It is interesting to note that defendant school boards—who are generally critical of judicial involvement in educational policy matters—tended to raise subsidiary policy arguments, which would draw the courts into a detailed consideration of daily school affairs, at least as often as did plaintiffs.)

3. Such comments, however, did not correlate with any pattern of defendants' success. This suggests that even judges who recognize the potential policy impact (especially for the remedial stage) of a liability decision will nonetheless uphold a plaintiff's liability theory if it appears fundamentally grounded in a valid principle.

4. The comparative judicial/legislative studies provided specific illustrations of how the courts' principled orientation to social issues differs significantly from the legislature's policy approach. See, e.g., the court's rejection in *Otero* of the Cardenas incompatibilities theory, an approach which was largely accepted in the legislature. Note also, the legislators' explicit acknowledgment of an operational principle/policy distinction between the courts and the legislature (see p. 193 *supra*).

5. 1 Cranch 137 (1803).

6. This position recognizes that, on many close questions, issues proclaimed as matters of fundamental "principle" by the Court may be fairly perceived by commentators, or even by previous court majorities, as being matters of nonjusticiable "policy." Cf. West Virginia State Board of Education v. Barnette, 319 U.S. 624 (1943) with Minersville School District v. Gobitis, 310 U.S. 586 (1940). The point is that, under our system, ultimate authoritative decisions on such close questions rest with the Supreme Court majority (or with the rarely successful constitutional amendment process).

7. Some may also question our attempt to bridge the gap between theoretical literature on constitutional interpretation and empirical study of trial court behavior by objectifying the concepts of "principle" and "policy." Admittedly, these concepts are somewhat elusive, as reflected in our own decision to create a middle category of principle/policy balancing. We believe, however, that despite the necessary limitations and qualifications, the strong patterns which are revealed by our empirical findings are instructive. Even if one were to conclude that we were totally unsuccessful in our painstaking attempts to establish empirical principle/policy distinctions, that in itself would be significant for the legitimacy aspects of the judicial activism debates, since the concepts we sought to operationalize are those put forward by constitutional scholars involved in that debate. In any event, the conceptual difficulties inherent in the "principle/policy" segment of our study do not undercut the independent validity of the other three segments of our analytic framework—interest representation, fact-finding, and remedies.

8. See generally Rabin, "Lawyers for Social Change: Perspectives on Public Interest Law," 28 Stan. L. Rev. 207 (1976).

9. A possible additional factor is the sheer volume of litigation costs that can result from vigorously contested discovery. City and state attorneys tend to be short-staffed, and boards employing private counsel are usually very cost conscious.

10. Although private law litigation (e.g., medical malpractice) sometimes involves fact-finding informed by conflicting scientific opinions, these cases usually are significantly different from public law cases in that the fact-finder is a jury (not a judge), the relevant events have already occurred (unlike the prospective inquiry in many public law cases), the "expert" issues are usually less complex, and the direct impact of the decision is confined to private parties.

11. This unique mode of credibility inquiry raises the question of whether appellate judges should defer to credibility judgments reached in social science fact-finding to the same extent that they defer to the trial judge's fact-finding in traditional litigation. It may be argued that appellate judges (who often served as trial judges themselves), working with a paper record, are as capable of assessing the evidence as the judge who presided over the trial; therefore, their review should be more searching than in traditional cases.

12. Actually, our caselet data indicated that even when evidentiary submissions are one-sided, the courts often seem capable of compensating for the apparent "adversarial distortion" by ascertaining, on their own motion, weaknesses or contrary implications of evidence offered by one party. Specifically, we found that in the majority of cases involving one-sided evidentiary submissions, the party which presented the evidence actually lost on the merits of the case.

13. Furthermore, some of the "avoidance devices" utilized by the courts may reflect deficiencies in the adversary process, rather than an objective appraisal of the facts. For example, the "admissions" upon which courts focus when they base their decisions on "agreements among the parties" may, at times, result from strategic errors in an attorney's presentation or preparation of his witnesses, rather than from an intended acknowledgment by the party that it accepts the implications of a major position articulated by its opponent.

14. See generally C. Lindblom, The Intelligence of Democracy (1965).

15. See generally R. Dahl, A Preface to Democratic Theory (1956), A. Cox, The Role of the Supreme Court in American Government 108 (1976). See also Lochner, "Some Limits on the Application of Social Science Research in the Legal Process," 1973 Law and Social Order 815, 843. ("[T]he whole process is much less rational than the organizational decision making model assumes . . . In contrast to bureaucratic organizations, the legislature is by its very nature, compelled to be routed in conflict. For just this reason, the criteria used in appraising administrative behavior—efficiency and effectiveness—seems out of place." Wahlke et al., The Legislative System 379 [1962]).

16. H. Laswell, quoted in Mayo and Jones, "Legal-Policy Decision Process: Alternative Thinking and the Predictive Function," 33 G.W.L. Rev. 318, 338 (1964); see also Dienes, "Judges, Legislators, and Social Change," 13 American Behavorial Scientist 511, 514 (1970); cf. Fullilove v. Klutznick, 448 U.S. 448 (1980) (Powell, J. concurring). "But Congress is not expected to act as though it were duty bound to find facts and make conclusions of law . . . Congress has no responsibility to confine its vision to the facts and evidence adduced by particular parties."

17. A striking example of the "enforcement" of this regime was the court of appeals' remand of Judge Winner's *Otero* decision (on the employment discrimination issues) with the direction that he explain his fact-finding analysis in more detail.

18. Similarly, the distinction drawn in the literature between "adjudicative" and "legislative" fact-finding is misleading. The process that is denoted "legislative" fact-finding actually is a nontraditional mode of analytic fact-finding that includes analysis of complex social science materials. Our research indicates that the courts are, in fact, better positioned to undertake such "legislative" fact-finding than are the state legislatures.

19. E. Wolf, "Social Science and the Courts: The Detroit School Case," 42 Public Interest 102 (Winter, 1976); Wolf, "Courtrooms and Classrooms," in R. Rist and R. Anson, eds., Education, Social Science, and the Judicial Process 97. Compare, on this point, Rosen's indications that the complex social science presentations in *Brown* v. *Board of Education* "were neither misconstrued nor misused . . ." P. Rosen, The Supreme Court and Social Science 187 (1972).

20. In making this point during his interview for the *Otero* case study, Dr. Glass, former president of the American Educational Research Association, also noted that political biases are more easily camouflaged in the education field than in such social sciences as economics and sociology. As we reported earlier (ch. 8, note 102 *supra*), Dr. Glass said that the *Otero* trial inspired him to prepare more rigorously for his final testimony than he would ordinarily prepare for an academic presentation.

21. An additional consideration here is the fact that social science evidence is often inconclusive and divergent, rendering definitive "fact-finding" by any decision maker problematic and elusive. See Levin, "Education, Life Chances and the Court: The Role of Social Science Evidence," 39 Law & Contemp. Prob. 217, 232 (1975); Cohen and Weiss, "Social Science and Social Policy: Schools and Race," in Rist and Anson, *supra* note 19; Moynihan, "Social Science and the Courts," 54 Pub. Interest 12, 17 (1979). Interestingly, some natural scientists and social scientists have been advocating the use of quasi-judicial procedures to arrive at more authoritative answers to such divergent questions as the effect of schools on student outcomes, and the dangers of recombinant DNA research. Jackson, "Toward Expediting the Resolution of Debates in the Social Sciences," 12 Educational Psychologist No. 3, 324 (1978); Weinberg, "The 'Science Court' Controversy: Are Our Courts and Agencies Adequate to Resolve New and Complex Scientific Issues?" Record of the Bar Association of the City of New York 8 (January–February, 1978).

22. See Lindblom, note 14 *supra*, at 133 ff.; C. Lindblom and D. Cohen, Usable Knowledge (1979); H. Simon, Models of Man (1957).

23. Of course, in practice the judicial and legislative processes do not operate in total isolation from one another. At least in regard to nonconstitutional decisions, legislators have the option of amending the relevant statute if they are strongly opposed to a judicial result. Courts also can influence the practical outcome of legislative deliberations by the interpretations they give to key statutory phrases.

24. Our findings on this point were similar to the conclusions noted in a broad survey of new model cases discussed in Special Project, "The Remedial Process in Institutional Reform Litigation," 78 Colum. L. Rev. 784, 797 (1978).

25. Thus, Horowitz's criticisms of the shortsightedness of the court's decree in *Hobson* v. *Hanson* would probably also have pertained to a legislative attempt to solve similar problems (although a legislative infusion of additional funds may have mitigated the impact of the fundamental planning problems). See D. Horowitz, The Courts and Social Policy (1977), ch. 4. Courts might be said to be inherently limited in their ability to fashion fully "comprehensive" decrees by the strictures of the "right-remedy" correlations and time pressures on their deliberations; but legislatures are analogously limited by the strictures of the political process and the time pressures under which they operate. An example of a highly effective legislative oversight in monitoring and modifying policies concerning institutions for the mentally retarded is chronicled in E. Bardach, The Implementation Game (1977). But the "fixer role" of Assemblyman Lanterman in that situation was highly unusual, and, in fact, one might argue that the effectiveness of his one-man monitoring role (which is closer to the monitoring process of a single judge than of a legislative committee) provides support for the rational-analytic judicial role in supervising complex implementation schemes.

26. A whole literature has recently developed which analyzes the problems inherent in the attempt to implement social policy by any governmenal agency. See, e.g, references cited in ch. 1, note 79 *supra*. Ambiguity about the meaning of policy goals and lack of consensual support for policy objectives are cited there as major impediments to effective implementation. Also, some theorists view policy implementation as a competitive political process that can easily result in the fragmenting of whatever consensus supported the original policy goals. Cf. Bardach, *supra*, note 25, with S. Bailey and E. Mosher, ESEA: The Office of Education Administers a Law 207 (1968). Courts may be especially effective in the consideration of such problems. By judicious expansions and manipulations of the party structure and by clarifying the fact that certain options are unlawful, the parties may be induced to cooperate and devise workable methods for assembling the necessary consensus to achieve goals at the implementation stage.

27. H. Kalodner and J. Fishman, The Limits of Justice (1978). See also F. Wirt and M. Kirst, The Political Web of American Schools (1972), Kirp, "School Desegregation and the Limits of Legalism," 47 Public Interest 101 Spring (1977). But see U.S. Commission on Civil Rights, Fulfilling the Letter and Spirit of the Law (August, 1976), hereinafter "Letter and Spirit," and the related Civil Rights Commission Staff report entitled "Reviewing a Decade of School Desegregation, 1966–75: Report of a National Survey of School Superintendents" (1977), hereinafter "Superintendents' Survey." On the basis of 29 case studies, and a survey of 1,300 school districts, and other data, the commission concluded that major desegregation had been accomplished nationwide with minimal disruption of the education process. See, e.g., "Letter and Spirit" at 74, table 2.3. (Note, especially, columns headed "Community Disruption" and "Overall Progress"; and Superintendents' Survey, at 3.) Focusing on court-ordered desegregation, it was found that courts tended to intervene in larger districts having higher levels of segregation "where desegregation was most difficult to achieve," (*Id.* at 84), but that the court actions had "great effect" (*Id.* at 6).

28. Some commentators have argued that judges in public law litigation

gradually tend to escalate their use of remedial devices, beginning with ones that least preempt the discretion of public officials and, if resistance is experienced, progressing to more coercive methods as they are needed to overcome implementation. See, e.g., Goldstein, "A *Swann* Song for Remedies: Equitable Relief in the Burger Court," 13 Harv. C.R-C.L.L. Rev. 1, 46 (1978); Note, "Implementation Problems in Institutional Reform Litigation," 91 Harv. L. Rev. 428 (1977).

29. See, e.g., Smith, Downs, and Lachman, Achieving Effective Desegregation (1973).

30. See, Kirp, Buss, and Kuriloff, "Legal Reform of Special Education: Empirical Studies and Procedural Proposals," 62 Cal. L. Rev. 40 (1974); Rebell, "Implementation of Court Decrees in Special Education Cases: The Problems and the Potential," 10 J. Law & Ed. 335 (1981).

31. See, e.g., Wyatt v. Stickney, 344 F. Supp. 373, 344 F. Supp. 387 (M.D. Ala. 1972), *aff'd sub nom.* Wyatt v. Aderholt, 503 F. 2d 1305 (5th Cir. 1974); see also Note, "The *Wyatt* Case: Implementation of a Judicial Decree Ordering Institutional Change," 84 Yale L.J. 1338 (1975). In Wyatt, as in the cases in our sample, defendants actively participated in the decree formulation, apparently agreeing with 90% of the detailed standards set forth in the decree. 84 Yale L.J. at 1367. Similar results apparently obtained in improving conditions at Willowbrook State Hospital under the decree in New York State Association for Retarded Children v. Rockefeller, 357 F. Supp. 752 (E.D.N.Y. 1973), 393 F. Supp. 715 (E.D.N.Y. 1975). Compare in this regard Rhem v. Malcolm, 371 F. Supp. 594, 377 F. Supp. 995 (S.D.N.Y. 1974), *aff'd and remanded,* 507 F. 2d 333 (2d Cir. 1974), *on remand,* 389 F. Supp. 964, *amended,* 396 F. Supp. 1195 (S.D.N.Y. 1975), *aff'd* 527 F. 2d 1041 (2d Cir. 1975), 432 F. Supp. 769 (S.D.N.Y. 1977), a case involving extensive reform of procedures at the Manhattan House of Detention. Here, as in the desegregation cases, defendants resisted the court's involvement and the legitimacy of its imposing its judgment on questions of prison security. Compliance in this situation has apparently been minimal. See Note, "Section 1983 and Federalism," 90 Harv. L. Rev. 1133, 1231–37 (1977). Compliance apparently has been better, however, in other prisons cases where security issues may have been less pressing. See Comment, "Confronting the Conditions of Confinements: An Expanded Role for Courts in Prison Reform," 12 Harv. C.R.-C.L.L.Rev. 367, 389–92 (1977), cf. Robbins and Buser, "Punitive Conditions of Prison Confinement: An Analysis of *Pugh* v. *Locke* and Federal Court Supervision of State Penal Administration Under the Eighth Amendment," 29 Stan. L. Rev. 893 (1977).

32. This term was first suggested to us (but was used in somewhat different fashion) by Tribe, "Structural Due Process," 10 Harv. C.R.-C.L.L. Rev. 269 (1975).

33. Note that in the recent litigation concerning conditions for mentally retarded inmates at Pennhurst State Hospital, defendant state and local public officials strongly objected to the courts' mandating a policy of "deinstitutionalization," but apparently were prepared to accept the more "conservative" alternative of the court undertaking ongoing supervision of conditions in the institution, an involvement which was considered radical in *Wyatt* and similar cases only a few years later. Halderman v. Pennhurst State School and

Hospital, 612 F. 2d 131 (3d Cir. 1979) *rev'd and remanded,* 101 S.Ct. 1531 (1981).

34. "Put most simply, when the stakes are high, conflict is likely to be most intense and the loser's will to resist likely to be at its strongest." P. Schiengold, The Politics of Rights 218–19 (1974). Cf. van Meter and van Horn, "Policy Implementation Process," 6 Administration and Society 445, 462 (1975) (successful implementation of public policy is a function of the degree of change, the policy required and the amount of consensus around the policy objectives).

35. By way of contrast, certain moral flux issues (such as many First Amendment or maternity leave issues) may seem controversial in the minds of school administrators, faculty, or students, but these matters do not raise major passions in the public arena. A school administration which felt strongly disgruntled with a court's stance on such issues would not be in a position, even if personally so inclined, to resist blatantly or subvert judicial orders because it would not receive deep-rooted support from a large segment of the general public to do so.

36. See, e.g., D. Kirby, T. Harris, R. Crain, and C. Rossell, Political Strategies in Northern School Desegregation (1973). Forceful administrative action, as in the early days of the implementation of Title VI of the 1964 Civil Rights Act, can be highly effective (see G. Orfield, The Reconstruction of Southern Education [1969]; H. Rodgers and C. Bullock, From Coercion to Compliance [1976]), but most commentators have agreed that, even here, success depended in large part on the collaborative relationship that developed between HEW's efforts and the courts. See, e.g., J. H. Wilkinson, From *Brown* to *Bakke* 107 (1979); Note, "The Courts, HEW and Southern School Desegregation," 77 Yale L.J. 321 (1976).

37. Our analysis also shows the inappropriateness of making institutional comparisons using simple dichotomies between the judicial and legislative roles. There are important and often constructive interrelationships that occur between court decisions and actions by the other branches. For example, the Colorado case studies showed how the Supreme Court's *Lau* decision (which did not, in itself, involve intrusive court-ordered remedies) created an aura of legal legitimacy for bilingual education in a manner that facilitated curriculum reform through the "mutual adjustment" process of the Colorado legislature. In general, successful court intervention appears to be organically related to contemporary social, political, and scientific trends. For example, the federal district court in New York City may have been fatally overburdened if it had attempted major reforms in the supervisory selection process before the advent of school decentralization. But we believe it was more than coincidental, historically speaking, that the case was not filed until decentralization had created the mechanisms that ultimately made the *Chance* remedy judicially manageable.

38. For a discussion of these trends, see generally Symposium on "The End of Consensus," Daedalus, Summer 1980; J. Lieberman, The Litigious Society (1981); C. Lasch, Haven in a Heartless World (1977); R. Nisbet, The Twilight of Authority (1975); A. Ahlstrom, "National Traumas and Changing Religious Values," Daedalus, Winter 1978; R. Bellah, The Broken Covenant: American Civil Religion (1975). According to the latest Gallup poll findings, the percentage of people stating that religion is "very important" in their lives declined between 1952 and 1978 from 75% to 53% (R. Gallup and D. Poling, The Search for America's Faith [1980], Appendix J).

39. "Law varies inversely with other social control." D. Black, The Behavior of Law 6 (1976).

40. For example, Congress has left for judicial determination the issue as to whether a handicapped person is receiving a "free appropriate public education." Education of the Handicapped Act, 20 U.S.C. §1401 et seq. See Rowley v. Ambach, 632 F. 2d 945 (2d Cir. 1980), *cert. granted,* 50 U.S.L.W. 3334 (Nov. 3, 1981), Battle v. Pennsylvania, 629 F. 2d 269 (3d Cir. 1980).

41. See McCloskey, The American Supreme Court (1960). Wirt and Kirst concluded in their study of southern school desegregation that there was almost total resistance in the deep South during the first decade after the Supreme Court's *Brown* decree. But twenty years later, attitudes and desegregation patterns had changed dramatically. The process of change was long and bitter, but without the Court's principled stance, "little would have changed in the South." Wirt and Kirst, *supra* note 27, at 201. They also cited relevant surveys of public attitudes toward the Court and concluded that over the long run the Court's moral authority was not damaged by its involvement. See also Schiengold, *supra* note 34, at 7, 143. For a detailed analysis of the Court's desegregation activities during this period, see Wilkinson, *supra* note 36, ch. 5. An appropriate symbol of these attitudinal changes was the 1979 farewell address of George Wallace as governor of Alabama in which he stated that he no longer believed, as in his first inaugural address, in "segregation today, segregation tomorrow, segregation forever." "It is good that it's been changed. It's good that the civil rights bill has passed. It hasn't been the evil that we thought in attacking property rights. That's what we were against it for" (*New York Times,* January 7, 1979, p. 26).

Orfield, in discussing the major busing cases outside of the South, has noted that " . . . in the seventies the courts were attempting to change the practices of the majority. The urban segregation cases polarized public opinion and generated sustained criticism of the court." G. Orfield, Must We Bus 12 (1978).

42. See I. Jenkins, Social Order and the Limits of Law (1980). The courts themselves are not unaffected by the problem created by the demise of traditional religious and other value-creating institutions. To some extent, the law has, to use Max Weber's terminology, "lost its metaphysical dignity." M. Weber, On Law and Economy 298 (Rheinstein ed. 1954). As society increasingly looks to the courts to provide anchors of principle in a churning sea of disintegrating traditional values, the courts themselves, especially when articulating confrontational principles, must "live off the capital of the principle" amassed by previous generations in order to cope with this situation. See also R. Unger, Law in Modern Society 298 (1977).

## Appendix B

1. Also, the main issues in these cases are usually First Amendment freedom of religion issues that are not really germane to educational policy.

2. All federal district court opinions are public information. However, judges do not always submit all of their opinions for publication. In the *Federal Supplement,* the West Publishing Company publishes only those opinions submitted to it by the courts. There are specialty reporting services, however, which routinely screen federal court records and select for publica-

tion opinions of interest to their subscribers, regardless of whether the judge
has specifically forwarded them for publication. The LEXIS computer bank is
fed opinions from both of these sources. Almost all of the opinions cited to us
by LEXIS were printed in *Federal Supplement,* although there were a few
opinions published only in *Employment Practices Decisions.*

3. Also included were words derived from the same roots, e.g., "educational," "policies," "injunction."

4. Compared to this procedure, conventional legal research tools are very
inflexible. They are based on standard typologies of legal issues and force the
researcher to choose from the given categories in this scheme. Thus, the
material retrieved in this way is dependent on prior judgments made by
other lawyers—the ones who indexed the opinions. Our research objectives
were particularly unsuitable to conventional systems because our universe was
defined by a combination of structural (systemwide injunctions) and subject
matter (public school policy disputes) criteria. LEXIS enabled us to program
both kinds of variables into our initial search request.

5. This separate screening is described more fully below where note 6 is
cited.

6. Vols. 307–425.

7. There was some overlap in these categories. All 59 of the pre-1977
LEXIS cases also had opinions published in *Federal Supplement* (one 1977 case
did not): 51 of these opinions were digested under "Schools and School Districts."

8. Two exceptions should be noted: (a) Four of the "School Finance" cases
alleged unlawful disparities in the intradistrict allocation of funds. However,
only one was digested by West under the heading "Schools and School Districts." Three out of the four were identified by LEXIS. (b) There is a disparity of 51%(LEXIS) versus 42%(*F. Supp.*) in the student speech/conduct category. This difference can be traced to a greater proportion of grooming cases
in the *Federal Supplement* sample. Since the LEXIS sample already included
eight grooming cases, no problem of underpresentation was evidenced by
these numbers.

9. 1978 Annual Report of the Director 58 (Administrative Office of the
United States Courts).

10. The categories are: "Actions under statutes/civil rights" and "Actions
under statutes/other." Our statement is based on the procedures set forth in
"Manual of Instructions, Civil Docket Package and Civil Cover Sheet Form
J544" (Administrative Office of the United States Courts, undated) and on
the federal court clerks' classification entries for the 65 cases in our sample (as
found on the forms #106A we obtained from the courts).

11. An alternative approach would be to screen a random sample of the
100,000 cases; but it would still be necessary to review approximately 10,000
cases to come up with a workable sample. For example, if the larger universe
was 650 cases, and the goal was to identify 65 of them for further study, one
would have to screen one-tenth of the pool (i.e., 10,000 out of 100,000 cases)
in order to find one-tenth of the universe (i.e., 65 out of 650 cases). Even at
that, the cases identified would not necessarily have written opinions (published or unpublished) in the record to reveal much about the basis of the
court's decision. Still more cases would have to be screened to find ones with
records suitable for substantial analysis.

12. And which, for the very reason that they are unpublished, are of less significant precedental value.

13. Cf. McCloskey, "Survey Research in Political Science," in C. Glock, ed., Survey Research in the Social Sciences, 68–69 (1967) (attempts to reduce systematic bias).

14. As we have mentioned, we borrowed the term "caselet" from Professor Chayes, whose use of a questionnaire in working up a file of small case studies influenced the early stages of development of the EPAC caselet questionnaire.

15. This time is exclusive of correspondence with courts and attorneys to obtain necessary documents and of other necessary administrative duties, and training and revision time.

16. Under arrangements worked out through the Administrative Office of the United States Courts, most of the District Court clerks graciously fulfilled our requests for substantial amounts of photocopying, both in initial requests and in follow-up orders concerning additional documents.

17. Question 11.c read as follows:
    c. Administration of order
        i. Did court retain jurisdiction?
           For how long?
        ii. Was defendant required to file reports periodically?
           With plaintiff
           With court
           With master
        iii. Investigative/discovery authority granted to:
           Plaintiff
           Master
           Other
        iv. Degree of compliance
           a) Complete
           b) Partial but substantial
           c) Token
           d) None
           e) Other
           f) If answer b–e above, to what extent was less than full compliance a result of bad faith by defendant?
        v. Were contempt motions brought?
           Disposition?
        vi. Sanctions for violations of order
        vii. Was decree modified?
           a) Modifications were
               i. Minor
               ii. Substantial
               iii. Very substantial
           b) Were modifications because of practical difficulties for good faith implementation? Other reasons?
        viii. Did the court attempt to enlist any non-parties in administration of the decree?"

18. See ch. 5, pp. 65–66.

19. See *id.*, p. 65.

20. See ch. 4, note 1 p. 255, and note 18 p. 257.

21. The test referred to here is that of computing the variance, taking the square root of the variance to obtain the standard error, and then multiplying the standard error by the constant, 1.96, to assure a confidence level of 95%. This estimation rule cannot be applied to observations of our sample without important qualifications—namely, that the sample we are studying was not drawn strictly at random, and that the population from which the sample was drawn did not consist of homogenous, independent units (since earlier court decisions affect later court decisions). Thus, because of the limited applicability of this formal validation technique, we adopted the cautious approach of using it solely for the purpose of eliminating some comparisons that might otherwise have been made. We have not cited this estimation rule as affirmative proof of the significance of any comparison that would not be seen as having those implications already in a common-sense evaluation.

# Index